Climate Change, Economic Channels, and Historical Junctures

Sherif Khalifa

Climate Change, Economic Channels, and Historical Junctures

How Climate Change Shaped Human History

palgrave macmillan

Sherif Khalifa
Department of Economics
California State University, Fullerton
Fullerton, CA, USA

ISBN 978-3-031-91866-7 ISBN 978-3-031-91867-4 (eBook)
https://doi.org/10.1007/978-3-031-91867-4

This Palgrave Macmillan imprint is published by the registered company Springer Nature Switzerland AG.
The registered company address is: Gewerbestrasse 11, 6330 Cham, Switzerland

To Ibn Khaldun
The first to point our attention to the clear, but not so acknowledged, connection between the physical setting and the social outcomes. He is widely considered by many to be one of the greatest social scientists of all times and the true father of historiography and sociology.

ACKNOWLEDGMENTS

The development of the first draft of this book took place during a sabbatical leave from California State University at Fullerton. I spent that year as a visiting professor in another university in Istanbul, a choice that seemed pertinent to the content of this manuscript in many aspects. Istanbul has a unique geographic location between the East and the West; it straddles between Europe and Asia through a corridor or waterway that links two seas with important trade implications. The city is also located along fault lines that cause recurrent seismic shocks with an expected big earthquake on the horizon. The city has a long history, which is quite unique. This is considering it enjoyed the status of being the center of the universe for some empires, including the Byzantine and Ottoman, and the heart of belief systems, including Christianity and Islam. The environment of this city, including its location, climate, and topography, seems to contribute to its destiny over time and will probably continue to play a role in shaping its future as well. Thus, this city seems like a microcosm of the entire planet in how the environmental and natural factors can play such a crucial role in the fate of humanity.

I would like to take this opportunity to thank those who made this contribution possible. I start by thanking the university that hosted me during this year and allowed me to complete writing this book, the Turkish German University in Istanbul. I thank the Department of Economics and its members for welcoming me to their department, inviting me to such a friendly and collegial environment, providing me with the much-needed calm atmosphere that was conducive to producing such work, and allowing me access to the resources needed to accomplish this task. In particular, I would like to acknowledge Dr. Aykut Kibritçioğlu, the former Department Chair; Dr. Erdem Kılıç, the current Department Chair; and other members of the Department including Dr. Levent Yilmaz, Dr. Elif Nuroğlu, Dr. Semih Emre Çekin, Dr. Hamza Polattimur, and Dr. Guido Neidhofer. I would like to extend my deepest gratitude to each and every one of them.

Besides the accommodations afforded me by Turkish German University, I was also fortunate enough to spend my time working on this manuscript in an apartment overlooking the stunning Bosphorus Strait. This was not only a breathtaking scene that I was fortunate enough to enjoy every day during that year, and a source of inspiration for increasing productivity, but it was also a constant reminder of where I was and how it related to what I was working on. In this regard, I extend my thanks to Mrs. Pinar Kollu Ersin for allowing me and my family to stay at her late father's apartment during that year. Upon my return to California, I was also immediately reminded of the effect of climate change in our lives especially with the wildfires that surround us in the windy season when the vegetation is dry due to the long drought that we have been enduring in this part of the world.

At the end, I also thank my wife, Beatriz Suarez, and my son, Yusef Khalifa, for their continual support, patience, and understanding, without which I would not have been able to complete this work on time. I am also grateful to my late mother, Nabila Ali, and my father, Hussein Khalifa. Growing up, both have always instilled in us an aspiration to become the best that we can be.

Finally, this work is also a message I am sending my son over time that will hopefully reach him when he is old enough to be able to read and comprehend its content. His generation will be the one who will have to deal with the consequences of climate change, will have to decide on how to deal with it, and will have to take a stance on how seriously to address it.

Competing Interests The author has no competing interests to declare that are relevant to the content of this manuscript.

Contents

About the Author

Sherif Khalifa is Professor of Economics at California State University, Fullerton. He attained his Bachelor of Arts in Economics from the American University in Cairo in 1995. Afterward, the author joined the Egyptian Ministry of Foreign Affairs as a diplomat. He continued to serve in the diplomatic corps for about a decade, during which he traveled to many countries, lived in many others, and attended different international platforms where climate change was always an issue of discussion. During that period, the author earned a scholarship from the Government of the United Kingdom to earn a Master of Science in Economics from the University of Warwick in 1999. The author also earned a fellowship from Johns Hopkins University to join the PhD Program in Economics in 2001. The author earned his doctorate degree in 2006 and was subsequently offered a faculty position at California State University, Fullerton. The author has lots of academic publications and opinion articles in the fields of Development Economics, International Economics, Political Economy, and others. The author completed his first book entitled *Egypt's Lost Spring: Causes and Consequences* that was published by Bloomsbury in 2015. The author also has his second book entitled *Geography and the Wealth of Nations* that was published by Bloomsbury in 2022.

CHAPTER 1

Introduction: Constant Companions

Climate change is a word that is becoming ubiquitous in our contemporary life. We hear it in the media outlets, and we see it in the headlines of major news avenues. It is repeatedly mentioned by leaders, government officials, state dignitaries, spokes personnel, representatives of international organizations, public figures, and celebrities. The repercussions of climate change turned into an issue that is becoming an integral component of the agendas of political parties, the programs of politicians, and the core missions of international agencies and global forums. Curbing climate change became a component of the policies adopted by some countries, while activists around the world continue to pressure their governments for more action. Peaceful protests, or riots sometimes, erupt at every corner to save the planet from the consequences of climate change. It is becoming part of the continuous intense political debate between those who believe it is an existential threat to our planet and those concerned about the consequences of combatting it on the economy. It is also becoming an item that the public is coming to care about and a topic that guides their voting patterns, as seen in opinion polls prior to many elections.

Climate can be defined as the long-term weather pattern in an area, the state of the components of the climate system, and the average value of meteorological variables over a time spanning from months to millions of years. Some of the variables that are commonly considered are

S. Khalifa, *Climate Change, Economic Channels, and Historical Junctures*, https://doi.org/10.1007/978-3-031-91867-4_1

temperature, humidity, atmospheric pressure, wind, frost, and precipitation. The climate of any location is affected by its latitude, longitude, altitude, terrain, land use, and nearby water bodies and their currents.

In this context, climate change is long-term alterations in weather patterns. Such shifts can be natural, due to changes in earth's orbital cycles, changes in solar activity, changes in ocean circulation, large volcanic eruptions, or others. In the last couple of centuries, though, human activities have been the main cause of climate change primarily due to the burning of fossil fuels like coal, oil, and natural gas. Burning fossil fuels generate greenhouse gas emissions that act like a blanket wrapped around the Earth. This traps the sun's heat and accordingly increases global temperatures. The main greenhouse gas that is causing climate change is carbon dioxide. This spreads due to the use of gasoline for driving cars, coal for heating, industrial activities, clearing land for farming, large-scale agriculture, cutting down forests, and others. This makes it clear that human activity is behind the current episode of climate change.

There is abundance of scientific evidence for climate change that can be seen in the increase in average global surface temperature, the increase in sea levels, the decrease in ice sheets of Greenland and the poles, the retreat of glaciers around the world, the decrease in snow cover in the Northern Hemisphere, the increased frequency and severity of extreme weather events, and others. In this context, the Intergovernmental Panel on Climate Change states,[1] "Ice cores drawn from Greenland, Antarctica, and tropical mountain glaciers show that Earth's climate responds to changes in greenhouse gas levels. Ancient evidence can also be found in tree rings, ocean sediments, coral reefs, and layers of sedimentary rocks. This ancient, or paleoclimate, evidence reveals that current warming is occurring roughly 10 times faster than the average rate of warming after an ice age. Carbon dioxide from human activities is increasing about 250 times faster than it did from natural sources after the last Ice Age."

This conclusion is derived from a large body of scientific work that shows the effect of climate change on global temperatures, ice sheets, glaciers, snow covers, sea levels, and others. For the effect on temperatures, some scientists find that[2] "anthropogenic global warming is still on a steady course, with recent years tracking near the expectation from the linear 50-year rate." For the effect on ice sheets, scientists show that[3] "Greenland ice imbalance with the recent (2000–2019) climate commits at least 274 ± 68 mm SLR from $59 \pm 15 \times 103$ km2 ice retreat, equivalent to $3.3 \pm 0.9\%$ volume loss." For changes in sea levels, studies show that the rising rate[4] "is accelerating at 0.084 ± 0.025 mm/y2, which agrees well with climate model projections. If sea level continues to change at this rate and acceleration, sea-level rise by 2100 (~65 cm) will be more than double the amount if the rate was constant at 3 mm/y." Other scientific work finds that human-caused warming caused declines in Northern Hemisphere snowpack over the 1981–2020 period and emphasize that[5] "human-forced snow losses and their water consequences are attributable—even absent their clear detection in individual snow products—and will accelerate and homogenize with near-term warming, posing risks to water resources in the absence of substantial climate mitigation." All this evidence points to the fact that we are living in another episode of climate fluctuations.

1 Hysterics or Hoax

The opinions on the consequences of climate change, however, usually swing between two points of view. The first is a hysteria of an impending doom or end of the world scenario, a climate apocalypse, or a climate change endgame. This implies that the current trend of climate change will eventually lead to the end of humanity, if not mitigated in time. There is another dismissive approach that perceives these claims about the consequences of climate change as a hoax. This implies that the evidence for climate change is not conclusive enough to raise the alarm. There are also so many opinions between these two extremes.

Climate change in the former doomsday scenario is an existential threat. Some scholars argue that there are tangible causes for panic, and[6] "there are ample reasons to suspect that climate change could result in a global catastrophe." This view is based on a few factors. First, there are warnings from human history. Climate change has played a role in cases of mass extinction, the collapse of complex societies, the spread of deadly diseases, and other critical junctures in human history. This is of concern since the current fluctuations in climate are occurring at an unprecedented speed surpassing thresholds that contributed to previous cases of societal collapse and extinction of species. Second, climate change could increase the likelihood of other catastrophic risks, such as international conflict, infectious diseases, or natural disasters. Third, climate change could exacerbate existing vulnerabilities and cause indirect stress in the form of economic damage, loss of land, water shortage, and food insecurity that coalesce into widespread failures. Finally, climate change could irrevocably impair our ability to recover from other forms of catastrophes.

Some scholars also address the threat of climate change by arguing that[7] "[b]ecause civilization cannot exist in unlivable or uninhabitable places, all of the above warnings can be understood as asserting the potential for anthropogenic climate change to cause civilization collapse (or 'climate collapse') to a greater or lesser extent." Then, the study proposes some mechanisms causing such collapse which include direct effects, feedback effects, and exogenous shock vulnerability. The first implies that compounding climate effects could undermine agriculture, water availability, and other essential bases of civilization. Socio-climate feedback implies that adverse effects of climate change on food supply may cause political conflict and warfare that undermine stability, spread destabilization, and hasten collapse. Finally, the vulnerability channel suggests that climate change could weaken our capacity for adaptation leaving societies susceptible to collapse triggered by other shocks in the form of wars or pandemics.

The advocates of this approach turn our attention to dramatic events that are caused by climate change including higher likelihood of conflicts, higher incidence of natural disasters, higher prevalence of diseases, and others. Some of these studies attribute a few of the latest conflicts to the current changes in climate. For instance, climate change was accused of inciting some episodes of the Arab Spring. This was a series of anti-government demonstrations and popular uprisings that spread across much of the Arab world in the early 2010s. In this context, some scholars argue,[8] "A proximate factor behind the unrest was a spike in global food crises, which in turn was due in part to the extreme weather throughout the globe over the past year." Even though the[9] "Arab Spring would likely have come one way or another, but the context in which it did is not inconsequential. Global warming may not have caused the Arab Spring, but it may have made it come earlier." This implies that climate change is not the sole cause for such an outcome, but it likely facilitated its occurrence earlier than it would have otherwise.

A drastic case in the Arab Spring was the Syrian uprising that led to more than a decade of suffering, hundreds of thousands of casualties, millions of migrants, and unspeakable destruction in that country. Some argue that this occurred as the country suffered an unprecedented severe drought that lasted from 2006 to 2010 CE. That severe[10] "multiyear drought beginning in the mid-2000s, combined with inefficient and often unmodernized irrigation systems and water abstractions by other parties in the eastern Mediterranean, including especially Syria, contributed to the displacement of large populations from rural to urban centers, food insecurity for more than a million people, and increased unemployment—with subsequent effects on political stability." To put this into perspective, some point our attention to the observation that there has been[11] "a long-term warming trend in the Eastern Mediterranean, adding to the draw-down of soil moisture. No natural cause is apparent for these trends, whereas the observed drying and warming are consistent with model studies of the response to increases in greenhouse gases."

Besides its potential impact on conflict, other studies focus on the effect of climatic fluctuations on the increased frequency of natural disasters. The United Nations Environment Programme asserts that[12] "[c]limate change is affecting the hydrological cycle and increasing the frequency and intensity of storms. Over 90 per cent of 'natural' disasters are weather-water-related, including drought and aridification, wildfires, pollution and floods. They lead to death, injury, loss of livelihoods and displacement and place a huge burden on societies, economies and the environment." The United Nations also explains that climate change and extreme weather events have caused a surge in natural disasters over the past 50 years disproportionately impacting poorer countries. According to the World Meteorological Organization and the United Nations Office for Disaster Risk Reduction,[13] "from 1970 to 2019, these natural hazards accounted for 50 per cent of all disasters, 45 per cent of all reported deaths and 74 per cent of all reported economic losses."

Others argue that climate change has contributed to the spread of diseases worldwide and its subsequent effects on lives, livelihoods, communities, and economies. For instance, the World Health Organization postulates that[14]

> [c]limate change is impacting health in a myriad of ways, including by leading to death and illness from increasingly frequent extreme weather events, such as heatwaves, storms and floods, the disruption of food systems, increases in zoonoses and food-, water- and vector-borne diseases, and mental health issues. Furthermore, climate change is undermining many of the social determinants for good health, such as livelihoods, equality and access to health care and social support structures. These climate-sensitive health risks are disproportionately felt by the most vulnerable and disadvantaged, including women, children, ethnic minorities, poor communities, migrants or displaced persons, older populations, and those with underlying health conditions.

Their prediction is that[15] "between 2030 and 2050, climate change is expected to cause approximately 250,000 additional deaths per year, from undernutrition, malaria, diarrhea and heat stress alone." Some scientists even claim that[16] "58% (that is, 218 out of 375) of infectious diseases confronted by humanity worldwide have been at some point aggravated by climatic hazards."

On the other hand, others claim that these arguments are speculative at best. Some even go as far as to decry these claims about climate change as a hoax. This view argues that the warnings about potential mass extinction are exaggerated. According to some who adopt a more sober approach within this camp, the risks should not be understated or overstated but[17] "such scenarios should be studied, and society should prioritize avoiding catastrophic outcomes. However, history also shows risks in overemphasizing the likelihood of calamity." The rationale behind that advice is a deep concern that the focus on apocalyptic futures can be used as a pretext to support despotism, to deprive people of their hard-earned rights and guaranteed freedoms, and to lead to potential recklessness in policy making. This implies that authorities could use these concerns about climate change to impose draconian measures that could reinforce their absolute control, could impose restrictions that constrain individuals and entities by limiting their choices, and could pressure authorities to adopt and execute policies that may have dire economic consequences.

In addition to these concerns, some argue that climate catastrophism may be contributing to a mental health crisis among the youth caused by anxiety about the possible consequences of climate change. In a global survey of 10,000 children and young people,[18] more "than 45% of respondents said their feelings about climate change negatively affected their daily life and functioning, and many reported a high number of negative thoughts about climate change (eg, 75% said that they think the future is frightening and 83% said that they think people have failed to take care of the planet)." This condition is referred to as eco-anxiety which[19] "suggest[s] that climate change, climate anxiety, and inadequate government response are all chronic stressors that could threaten the mental health and wellbeing of children and young people around the world."

Some in this camp also argue that the effect of climate change on conflict is overstated. In their view, climate change does not trigger conflict, but only intensifies existing political, economic, social, and cultural pressures that could lead to conflict. In this context, some scholars attempt to refute the claim that climate change, in the form of a severe drought, contributed to the Syrian uprising. Their study[20] "shows that there is no clear and reliable evidence that anthropogenic climate change was a factor in Syria's pre-civil war drought; that this drought did not cause anywhere near the scale of migration that is often alleged; and that there exists no solid evidence that drought migration pressures in Syria contributed to civil war onset."

In a more confrontational approach, some political movements see this concern about climate change, and the actions required to curb its repercussions, as serious threats to the economy. In their opinion, any steps taken to check climate change can limit the ability of companies and firms to produce. The cut in production could, in turn, lead to attempts to cut down costs by laying off workers causing high levels of unemployment with all its detrimental effects on individuals and households. These outcomes could adversely affect efforts to achieve higher economic prosperity and attempts to alleviate poverty. However, some politicians attempt to eschew being accused of not caring enough about the environment by casting doubt on the authenticity of the evidence that warns about the dire consequences of the current direction toward which our planet is heading. Thus, they claim that warnings about the effects of climate change are a hoax that is not corroborated by proper scientific evidence.

2 A Humble Contribution

This book is a humble contribution to this controversial issue. The book specifically aims to highlight the consequences of climate change in human history. To achieve this objective, the book covers the effect of climate change on such historical events such as human evolution, human dispersal from the cradle of humanity, human settlement with the transition to agriculture, and the collapse of complex societies. The argument is that if we comprehend the influence climatic fluctuations had on the life of our species, we might be able to ascertain its effect on our future as well. This is especially pertinent if the current trend of climate change proceeds unchecked.

This book argues that climate change and our species have been constant companions from the outset until the current moment. This starts with the evolution of hominins to anatomically modern humans, continues with the dispersal of humans to populate the entire world, and the eventual drastic change in our lifestyle from wanderers who lived on hunting and gathering to settlers who adopted agriculture. Settlements allowed for the emergence of complex societies that developed eventually to great civilizations with remarkable accomplishments that stood the test of time. Some of these civilizations could not, however, handle drastic changes in their natural surroundings. They collapsed and were delegated to oblivion. All these historical junctures coincided with episodes of climate change as shown by scholarly studies that attempt to reconstruct the climate around the time of these events.

The core argument of this book is that the connection between climate change and these historical junctures is an economic transmission channel. The book, thus, attempts to identify the economic channel between climatic fluctuations and each one of these historical events. To be able to tell that narrative, we must first recount the human story, the concomitant climate change event, and the mechanism that led from one to the other. In this context, this book makes various contributions. First, the book narrates each historical event in sufficient detail not only to tell the story but also to highlight its significance in human history. Second, the book refers to studies that attempt to reconstruct climatic conditions around the time that the event occurred to show that climate change was not a coincidence but also a contributor to that historical outcome. Third, the book argues that the mechanism through which climate change led to these historical junctures is an economic channel in nature. Changes in climate alter the resource base of the surrounding area and the modes of production that societies depend on. This creates certain stresses that need to be addressed by these societies. If these societies cannot handle these challenges, they break down, crumble, and wither away.

In this context, scholars have taken advantage of the scientific advances that allow for the recreation of climatic conditions long time ago. Scientists examine samples from oceans, seas, lakes, soils, fauna, and flora in a particular area to recreate its climate. By reconstructing the climate, it is possible to see scientific evidence of climate change that could have contributed to the eventual outcome that we are focusing on. By studying the economic structure of that part of the world, arguments can be forwarded as to how the climatic event disturbed the balance of that economic system, challenged the members of that community, and led eventually to that specific historical outcome.

There are many ways of recreating climates of the past. On the one hand, climatologists can focus on the interaction between the ocean and the atmosphere, by conducting marine oxygen isotope analysis. Estimating the ratio of different oxygen isotopes in marine sediments can disclose information about past ocean temperatures, ice volume, and evaporation trends. Scholars also examine records of ocean dust. Dust plumes from continents are the outcome of strong seasonality of precipitation and the winds that carry the dust to the ocean. Aeolian[21] dust accumulations found in ocean sediment cores, thus, offer a record of long-term change in seasonality and wind patterns.

Besides oceans, examination of lake sediments is also used in these types of studies. Lakes are considered habitats for environmentally sensitive organisms. Studying these organisms can yield a precise history of lake depth, salinity, and other factors that are strongly influenced by climatic fluctuations. Lacustrine sediments can also record climatic changes that occurred in proximity to the lake.

Scholars also use stable isotope analysis of ancient soils. Buried soils, or paleosols, preserve organic and carbonate deposits that carry a stable-isotopic signal of past vegetation. These paleosols are soils formed long ago that have no connection with the characteristics of present-day climate or vegetation. Thus, the analysis of these ancient soils can offer valuable information about past climates. Scholars also examine sedimentary facies. Sedimentation commonly occurs in areas where the sediment lies undisturbed for a long time. Certain types of sedimentary deposits are indicative of specific environmental conditions.

Faunal analysis identifies the type of animal remains. The abundance of different animal species allows for a general characterization of the habitat, under the assumption that certain taxonomic groups are associated with specific habitats in the past as in the present. Scholars also conduct analyses of fossil pollen sequences to interpret past climates. This is because they are from floral varieties or plants related to current species, for which we know their climate conditions. There are other methods as well that allow us to have a better estimate of climatic conditions at a point in time.

This book refers to historical, archaeological, and anthropological work that shows the footprints of humans at a specific time and location. This information is combined with reconstructions of climate during the time and within the location where a historical event occurred. This combination confirms if the climate event is coincident with the historical juncture in question. Afterward, the economic channel of transmission is discussed to explain the connection between the climatic event and the historical outcome.

Discussing the contribution of climate change in the context of historical developments is not the same as inferring causality. The discussion in this book is not intended to argue that climate change single-handedly caused these events, as much as it aims to highlight its contribution, among other factors, to the development of that outcome. There is no determinism in studying the history of our species. Historians cannot claim, with certainty, that a certain factor caused an outcome to occur. They, however, can pinpoint the confluence of factors that likely contributed to the emanating situation at the time. Whether that outcome would have occurred without such factor manifesting itself or not is almost impossible to know. However, if we observe that such a factor occurs enough times before certain historical outcomes, we can safely conclude that it cannot be a mere coincidence but rather an association that is worthy of our attention. To achieve its objective, the book is divided into several chapters; each is dedicated to a historical event that coincides with an episode of climate change.

The second chapter, entitled "Nature and the History of Nations," discusses the necessity of the study of human history. The chapter attempts to address a few questions that we face whenever we try to make sense of the story of mankind. These questions focus on the following: What are the most prominent explanations for critical historical junctures? What stimulates societies to adopt one change or to adapt to another? Whether history is written by individuals who act as heroic legends or by ordinary men and women? How does the relationship between the leaders and those they lead influence historical outcomes? How does the strength of social solidarity affect historical outcomes? What is the contribution of the natural surrounding to human history? Do historical events exhibit a certain predictable pattern? Is there an end to history where a final chapter can be agreed upon? Then, we conclude with the core argument of the book that combines these ideas. The argument is that climate change acts as a challenge that stimulates societies to react, that the reaction is taken by members of the society along with its leaders, that the outcome of that reaction depends on the relationship between these leaders and the ones they are leading, and that these recurrent climatic shocks can offer a pattern in history that shows periodic encounters between humans and these fluctuations. Whether the current anthropogenic climate change episode can be considered an end of history scenario is another issue considered as well.

The third chapter, entitled "Environment and Evolution," discusses the effect of climate change on human evolution. The chapter starts with an overview of the process of evolution of hominins and the differences between each genus in the human lineage. The chapter also discusses how certain anatomical traits were selected purely for the survival of the species, how natural selection can explain the way humans adapt to their environment, and how this process considers alterations to the environment that include climate change. The chapter also offers an exposition to the different hypotheses on the association between climate change and human evolution. These include a discussion of the Habitat-Specific hypotheses and the Variability Selection hypotheses. The chapter concludes with an illustration of some scholarly studies that attempt to provide evidence on the coincidence of climate variability, in terms of high amplitude and high frequency, with events of human evolution in the Pliocene and the Pleistocene.

The fourth chapter, entitled "Disturbance and Dispersal," discusses the effect of climate change on the dispersal of humans from their cradle in Africa to populate the entire world. The chapter starts with a discussion of the models of origin including the multiregional model, the African origin model, and the African multiregional model. The chapter also discusses the potential routes that humans took to migrate from the origin, and the different dispersal views including the Single Late Dispersal and the Multiple Early Onset Dispersals hypotheses. The chapter covers the climatic factors that caused humans to leave their initial habitat. This includes an overview of scholarly studies on the association between climate change and dispersal episodes in the cradle in East Africa, and how climate change opened corridors for humans to cross to other parts of the world. The chapter also includes a synopsis on the dispersal of humans from Africa to Eurasia and the Americas.

The fifth chapter, entitled "Turbulence and Transition," discusses the effect of climate change on the transition from hunting-gathering to agriculture and the subsequent settlement of human societies. The chapter starts with an overview of human life during the hunter-gatherer times. Then, it discusses the transition to agriculture and the far-reaching ramifications of such a consequential change in lifestyle. The chapter then clarifies the factors behind such transition and the potential contribution of climate. Different hypotheses on the association between climate change and the transition to farming are covered including the Oasis Theory, the Hilly Flanks Theory, and others. The chapter, then, discusses the scholarly work that provides evidence on the association between climate change and the adoption of agriculture in certain areas. Then, the chapter highlights the scholarly studies on the effect of climatic fluctuations on the diffusion of agriculture from the adoption core areas to other parts of the world.

The sixth chapter, entitled "The Last Straw," discusses the connection between climate change and societal collapse. The chapter starts with a discussion on how climate change contributed to the dawn of civilizations which was a consequence of human settlement. This is followed by a discussion on how climate change posed a threat to these civilizations as well. Some societies had to either withstand climate shocks or wither away from the books of history. Then, the chapter focuses on the contribution and culpability of climate change to societal collapse, and the channels through which climate fluctuations can lead to this outcome. These channels include conflict, famine, disasters, and disease. The chapter, then, elaborates on how climate change can instigate conflict and provides an overview of studies that show the association between them. The chapter also discusses how climate change can damage the carrying capacity of a society and its ability to feed itself, how climate change can increase the frequency of natural disasters that could hit these societies hard, and how climate change can cause the spread of some diseases. Each of these outcomes of climate change, or a combination of them, can in turn lead to societal collapse.

The seventh chapter, entitled "4200 Years Before Present," discusses the climate anomaly called the 4.2 ka event. The chapter starts with a description of this climatic event and how it affected civilizations that developed along river valleys. The stories of some of these societies are narrated including their greatest achievements, their contributions to human history, and their final collapse. The chapter also overviews the scientific studies that provide evidence for the association between climate change during that era and the ensuing collapse. These include the stories of the first empire in human history that thrived between the Tigris and Euphrates, called the Akkadian empire. The chapter tells the story of the rise of this empire, its monumental accomplishments, the weakness that lurked within, and the final collapse. The chapter also covers the studies that recreate the climate at the time on the Tigris-Euphrates basin, and in the surrounding areas, to show the coincidence of such changes and the eventual collapse. This, in addition to the story of the Old Kingdom in Egypt, its great achievements that are exemplified by the building of the great pyramids, the weaknesses of the kingdom, and the prolonged period of drought that brought about its ultimate collapse. Then, the chapter concludes with scholarly studies that provide evidence from the source of the Nile, from its valley, and from its sink in the Nile Delta, to present climate change records at the time of the final breakdown. The chapter also includes the story of the Liangzhu culture in ancient China on the Yangtze delta from its emergence to its demise. This is followed by the story of the Indus Valley Civilization, called the Harappan, which was the first in India. The chapter overviews the achievements of this civilization in terms of the development of its great cities, its agricultural system, and other innumerable accomplishments. The chapter also covers the abandonment of these cities due to climate stress, and the scholarly evidence for this association from the sea, the lakes, and the Himalayas.

The eighth chapter, entitled "The Late Bronze Age Crisis," discusses the 3.2 ka event and how it affected civilizations around the Mediterranean basin 3200 years ago. The chapter discusses the causes of the Late Bronze Age collapse and narrates the stories of some of the civilizations that suffered this lamentable fate. These include a discussion of the story of the Minoan civilization in the island of Crete, which was the forerunner of the Greek civilization and the cradle of European culture. The chapter talks about the rise of this society, its contributions to humanity, its collapse, and some evidence of the climatic causes of such a destiny. The chapter also covers the story of the so-called palace economy, also known as the Mycenaean, in the Peloponnese of Greece. The greatest achievements of such an economy are highlighted, in addition to the studies that provide evidence for the contribution of climate change to its final demise. This is followed by the story of another victim of climate change in Anatolia, the Hittite Civilization. The chapter recounts the story of the Hittites from the onset and the culpability of climate change to their dramatic end. The story of Canaan in the Levant is also narrated in this chapter, and its final collapse is discussed in the framework of scientific evidence that show the coincidence of this episode with climate change. The chapter, then, concludes with a discussion of how climate change dealt a last blow to Babylon.

The ninth chapter, entitled "Climate and Collapse Before Columbus," focuses on societal collapse events that coincided with climate change in the Americas before the arrival of Christopher Columbus. This starts with the collapse of the Tiwanaku in the Andes. The chapter describes the way of life in the Tiwanaku empire, and its sphere of influence, and the drought that brought about the end of such a civilization. The chapter also covers the effects of climate change in Mesoamerica, especially that of the Maya civilization. The history of the Mayas, their story lurking in the ruins they left behind, their final collapse, and the scholarly evidence on the potential impact of climate change are discussed in detail. The chapter also covers the fatal effect of climatic fluctuations on the Puebloan culture in North America, with some scholarly evidence on the subject. This is followed by the story of the climate shock to the society in the Easter Island in the Southeast Pacific and the Cahokia culture in North America.

The tenth chapter, entitled "Climate Change in the Common Era," focuses on climate change–induced societal collapse that occurred in the Common Era. The chapter starts with the story of the emergence and collapse of the Western and Eastern Roman empires. This covers the story of the Western Roman Empire, its greatest achievements, its rise to the pinnacle of world dominance, and the challenges it faced. This is followed by the decline and fall of the empire and the supporting evidence that show the contribution of climate change to closing this remarkable era in human history. The discussion also highlights the debilitating effect of climate change on the Eastern Roman Empire. The chapter, then, moves to the story of the Khmer Empire centered around the city of Angkor and beyond. A discussion of the hydraulic achievements of such a civilization, and how climate deterioration affected that elaborate system leading to its collapse, is included. The chapter concludes with the stories of several Chinese dynasties such as the Han, the Tang, the Song, the Yuan, and the Ming dynasties. Then, the chapter closes with a discussion of some studies that analyze the statistical association between climate disturbance and dynastic collapse in China.

The eleventh chapter, entitled "One Little Climate Anomaly," discusses the Little Ice Age and its consequences. The chapter starts with a description of such a climate anomaly and the causes of the Little Ice Age. These factors include changes in the orbital cycles of the planet, in solar activity, in volcanic activity, in ocean circulation, and in the world population. This is followed by a discussion of the consequences of the Little Ice Age in terms of the challenges it posed to the status quo, which drastically changed our lives thereafter. These include challenges to the religious status quo as exemplified by the Thirty Years' War and the Eighty Years' War. Examples of challenges to the political status quo include the French Fronde, the French Revolution, the English Civil War, and the English Glorious Revolution. Challenges to the economic status quo were also discussed in terms of the transition from feudalism to capitalism. The chapter concludes with the challenges to the social status quo in terms of the persecution of minorities and changes to some cherished traits and revered values of some societies, in addition to its effects on art, literature, and other cultural aspects.

The twelfth and final chapter, entitled "Perturbations and Pestilence," discusses the effect of climate change on the spread of diseases including plagues. The chapter starts by discussing how climate change can cause the spread of diseases through its effect on the lifecycles of pathogens, vectors, and hosts. Then, the chapter narrates the stories of the climate-induced pandemics that occurred in human history. These include the Antonine Plague, the Cyprian Plague, the Justinian Plague, the Black Death, the Third Plague, and the Spanish Flu. The chapter discusses the events that occurred during the times of the spread of the disease and the scholarly evidence on the effect of climate change on that spread.

By elaborating on these issues, the book aspires to show how climate change has been a constant companion to our species from the outset until the current moment. This is an attempt to put the current discussion on the effects of the present episode of climate change in perspective. Climate change is not a newcomer in human history. We owe so many changes that humans experienced to prior episodes of climate change. This current episode is but one of a series of climatic events that occurred over a long time. By knowing the challenges that humans had to address when they faced these fluctuations, and how they reacted to them, we can shed some light on what to expect nowadays with this current episode of climate change. The argument is that if these changes caused drastic political, economic, social, and cultural consequences in the past, then another climatic event could lead to similar outcomes. The knowledge we acquire from these historical experiences allows us to be well prepared for the future with a plan on the best way to come out of this predicament with the least number of bruises. This is to heed the warning of one philosopher who asserted that those who do not learn from history are condemned to repeat its mistakes.

On a final note, this book can be considered as a continuation of a former book of mine entitled *Geography and the Wealth of Nations*. That earlier book focuses on the effect of geographic factors on the determinants of economic outcomes that have been identified by economists and social scientists. These geographic factors include climate, location, topography, the abundance of natural endowment, and the incidence of natural disasters. In other words, that earlier book focuses on the geographic origins of the factors that determine economic success. These factors include the institutional framework, the cultural paradigms, the historical background, the demographic composition, the integration into the world economy, and others. In other words, the book examines how these geographic features, such as climate and otherwise, influence those other factors that affect economic outcomes. In simpler terms, it discusses the indirect effect of geographic and natural features on economic performance.

This book, in our hands, expands on that discussion by focusing on the effect of one geographic factor, climate change, on historical outcomes. Thus, this book expands on the previous one in two dimensions. First, it argues that if our environmental characteristics have an influence on the factors that determine economic outcomes, then the change in that natural setting will also have a profound effect not only on economic outcomes but also on historical ones. The second is that the channel of transmission between climate change and historical outcomes must be an economic transmission mechanism. The discussion of this economic channel between climate change and historical junctures is the core contribution of this book.

Notes

1. https://www.ipcc.ch/report/ar6/wg1/downloads/report/IPCC_AR6_WGI_Chapter02.pdf
2. B. H. Samset, C. Zhou, J. S. Fuglestvedt, M. T. Lund, J. Marotzke, and M. D. Zelinka. "Steady Global Surface Warming from 1973 to 2022 but Increased Warming Rate after 1990." Nature Communications: Earth & Environment, 4, 400, 2023.
3. Jason E. Box, Alun Hubbard, David B. Bahr, William T. Colgan, Xavier Fettweis, Kenneth D. Mankoff, Adrien Wehrlé, Brice Noël, Michiel R. van den Broeke, Bert Wouters, Anders A. Bjørk, and Robert S. Fausto. "Greenland Ice Sheet Climate Disequilibrium and Committed Sea-level Rise." Nature, Climate Change, 12: 808–813, 2022.
4. R. S. Nerem, B. D. Beckley, J. T. Fasullo, B. D. Hamlington, D. Masters, and G. T. Mitchum. "Climate-Change–Driven Accelerated Sea-Level Rise Detected in the Altimeter Era." PNAS, 115, 9: 2022–2025, 2018.
5. Alexander R. Gottlieb and Justin S. Mankin. "Evidence of Human Influence on Northern Hemisphere Snow Loss." Nature, 625: 293–300, 2024.
6. Luke Kemp, Chi Xu, Joanna Depledge, Kristie L. Ebi, Goodwin Gibbins, Timothy A. Kohler, Johan Rockstrom, Marten Scheffer, Hans Joachim Schellnhuber, Will Steffen, and Timothy M. Lenton. "Climate Endgame:

Exploring Catastrophic Climate Change Scenarios." PNAS, 119, 34, e210814611, 2022.
7. Daniel Steel, C. Tyler DesRoches, and Kian Mintz-Woo. "Climate Change and the Threat to Civilization." PNAS, 119, 42, e221052511, 2022.
8. Sarah Johnstone and Jeffrey Mazo. "Global Warming and the Arab Spring." Survival, 53, 2: 11–17, 2011.
9. Ibid.
10. Peter Gleick. "Water, Drought, Climate Change, and Conflict in Syria." Weather, Climate, and Society, 6, 3: 331–340, 2014.
11. Colin P. Kelley, Shahrzad Mohtadi, Mark A. Cane, Richard Seager, and Yochanan Kushnir. "Climate Change in the Fertile Crescent and Implications of the Recent Syrian Drought." PNAS, 112, 11: 3241–3246, 2015.
12. https://www.unep.org/topics/fresh-water/disasters-and-climate-change/climate-change-and-water-related-disasters
13. https://news.un.org/en/story/2021/09/1098662
14. https://www.who.int/news-room/fact-sheets/detail/climate-change-and-health
15. Ibid.
16. Camilo Mora, Tristan McKenzie, Isabella M. Gaw, Jacqueline M. Dean, Hannah von Hammerstein, Tabatha A. Knudson, Renee O. Setter, Charlotte Z. Smith, Kira M. Webster, Jonathan A. Patz, and Erik C. Franklin. "Over Half of Known Human Pathogenic Diseases Can be Aggravated by Climate Change." Nature Climate Change, 12: 869–875, 2022.
17. Matthew G. Burgess, Roger Pielke Jr., and Justin Ritchie. "Catastrophic Climate Risks Should be Neither Understated nor Overstated." PNAS, 119, 42, e221434711, 2022.
18. Caroline Hickman, Elizabeth Marks, Panu Pihkala, Susan Clayton, R Eric Lewandowski, Elouise E Mayall, Britt Wray, Catriona Mellor, and Lise van Susteren. "Climate Anxiety in Children and Young People and their Beliefs about Government Responses to Climate Change: A Global Survey." The Lancet Planetary Health, 5, 12: e863–e873, 2021.
19. Ibid.
20. Jan Selby, Omar S. Dahi, Christiane Fröhlich, and Mike Hulme. "Climate Change and the Syrian Civil War Revisited." Political Geography, 60: 232–244, 2017.
21. Arising from the action of wind.

CHAPTER 2

Nature and the History of Nations

1 While the Time Clock Is Ticking

While the time clock is ticking, and the pendulum is swinging from one side to another, we stare at the clock hand intensely watching time passing by. We call the time that passed days of yore, bygones, past times, or in a more formal manner history. History is the systemic study of the story of humanity and the detailed documentation of human deeds over time. Between its bounds, history books enfold the life of humanity from time immemorial till the present moment. History narrates our tale and recounts our incessant interaction with our surrounding environment and with each other. As Leo Tolstoy wrote in his masterpiece *War and Peace*,[1] "History is the life of nations and of humanity."

This chronological account of previous events and erstwhile stories is cherished by humans, in as much as people enshrine their personal memories. For without our past, we cannot fathom how we arrived at the current point in time nor how we can proceed forward. As such, history guides us in our ceaseless effort to make sense of our existence, to discern why we arrived at this destination and not to another, to instruct us on how to navigate our lives in this instant, to avoid committing the same mistakes of times past, and to chart a way for our future.

If anything, this implies that we cannot treat history as anecdotal stories, chronological records, memory recollections, reminiscent testimonies, or nostalgic statements. Humans acknowledged long time ago the

S. Khalifa, *Climate Change, Economic Channels, and Historical Junctures*, https://doi.org/10.1007/978-3-031-91867-4_2

need to comprehend the scenario, the plot, and the story line of the history that humanity is continuously writing. This reckoning comes with a desire to explore the historical dynamics, to discover the driving forces behind the historical junctures, to identify the factors leading to historical turning points, to highlight the determinants of historical sagas, and to comprehend the causes of historical twists and turns. Leo Tolstoy also reminds us that[2] "[m]an's mind cannot grasp the causes of events in their completeness, but the desire to find those causes is implanted in man's soul."

In this context, some historians choose to focus on specific occurrences or certain episodes while ignoring the bigger picture. This should come as no surprise since the burden of sorting out the entire story line of human history, and unraveling the plot that lies within, seems such a formidable undertaking. These historians contend that there are lots of historical details that call for meticulous attention and fastidious scrutiny. These particulars entail a scrupulous analytical approach that concentrates on these specifics across time and space. Thus, the analysis of a historical event involves a combination of efforts that may include a description of the circumstances that led to such an outcome, an examination of the context within which it occurred, an identification of the principal characters and their characteristics, a study of the contribution of each party involved, and a determination of the forces in action. This approach allows some historians to focus on these details without being lost in the wilderness of the bigger picture.

In an apt reprimand, though, historian Hugh Kearney scolds these historians for such timidity in approaching the study of history without having the boldness to look at the full sweeping picture.[3] In his opinion, these historians became[4] "creatures so blinded by the minutiae of their own special studies that they fail to observe the laws of civilisation explained by a master-historian. Their attitude would indeed be that of a plumber, who thought he has sufficient technical skill to install pipes in a building, lacks the imagination to stand back and appreciate the architectural beauty of the same building." Thus, it is a worthwhile pursuit to attempt to appreciate the beauty of the historical building no matter how daunting the endeavor may be.

Considering these admonitions, some historians opt to study our history in its entirety rather than that of one entity or one point in time. In this view, the study of history becomes like an impressionist painting. Impressionists use broken brush strokes of color to display sweeping visual effects. They were able to do so by recreating a sensation in our eyes to view a subject without delineating its details. Those impressionist paintings proffer an impression when seen from afar, but in proximity a spectator can be lost in minutiae. Nonetheless, these details are essential to produce the intended final effect or impression. The same applies to the study of history. It is essential to paint each brush stroke, or dissect each incident in history, to be able to step back and enjoy the bigger picture from all these combined specifics.

Thus, there has been a continuous effort by these historians to ascertain the laws of motion in our study of history, to deconstruct the complexity in historical occurrences, and to find the thread that ties the entire story together. The comforting notion that we can identify the causes behind historical outcomes allows us to explain why events occur to begin with, to project whether certain events will ensue others, and to make sense of it all. This can also assuage our dreaded fear that human history is but a series of haphazard events, coincidental occurrences, and inadvertent activities by some who happen to be accidentally in a specific place at a particular time. To avoid conceding to such disheartening conclusions, humans study history as a quest for purpose and as an expedition for meaning. In the words of Hugh Kearney, these pursuits are intended to bring intelligibility to the history of humanity.

Such scholars and historians attempt to offer an assortment of explanations, wherefores, and interpretations of our past actions. This is driven by a desire to provide humanity with a coherent and logical articulation of what caused societies to espouse some actions and not others. We can arrive at these conclusions by selecting those elements that seem to crop out of the pages of history books. The simple surmise is that if some of those elements frequently occur before a historical episode, it must be the case that the latter occurrence cannot likely transpire without that factor manifesting itself first. In a more cautious tone, we can speculate that the historical event is more likely to occur once that identified element takes place. As such, historians can claim to identify the factors that may, in most likelihood, lead to certain historical outcomes. This can be achieved by providing anecdotal evidence showing how these factors produced similar outcomes in the past. This can also be accomplished by showing that incidents that followed a certain incidence did not occur by accident but rather is an indication of either gentle association in some cases or even draconian causality in others. In this context, claiming wisdom in retrospect seems pertinent.

As such, some argue that history is to be treated as a science that has universal laws which apply in any location and at each point in time. This has a particular appeal to the advocates of this approach. Scientific explanations can be hard to unveil in general. But as soon as we arrive at them, they provide both the potential for generalization and the power of prediction. Furthermore, formulating historical interconnections in concrete terms can be quite entrancing, especially if it is elegantly articulated with the precision of a mathematical formula. A mathematical function offers clarity by transforming unclear associations into concrete relationships and by affording credence to the act of prognosis. In this context, historical systems can be treated as those of the natural sciences where one thing leads to another in calculable, determinable, and quantifiable ways.

For others, human conduct cannot be seen as a mechanical kneejerk reaction to another action. Humans are such complicated creatures that any study of societal transformations must consider two obstacles. The first is that individual choices of involved agents can only be understood taking into consideration their innate intricacies and inherent complexities. The second is that collective decisions of societies can only be understood taking into consideration a labyrinth of elaborate ties and involved connections between its complicated individual members. Both act as a Gordian knot waiting for someone to untie. According to the advocates of this view, history is not composed of sensible and sober actions that accomplish their contemplated deliberate intentions. Instead, it is full of unintended consequences of senseless deeds, impulsive actions, and impetuous exploits. Along these lines, Philosopher Arthur Danto argues that[5]

> though the phenomena with which history deals could conceivably be explained in a "scientific" manner, it is not the office of history to provide such explanations, nor does its lack of explanations in any way diminish either the effectiveness or importance of history. So, if my conclusions here suggest that history is not a science, and could not be one, they also suggest that it ought not to be one, but that it is a special and irreducible activity of the human spirit, with a function and justification of its own.

Between the proponents of precision and those on the other end of the spectrum, some historians chose another position by substituting high probabilities for invariable laws. In other words, a historical event can be explained by showing that, under certain conditions, the outcome was what usually or almost always occurs. This approach shows that generalizations in history have a high degree of probability without the certainty that some have attempted to arrive at, but in vain.

Whether the analysis of historical systems can be reduced to a concrete formula as proposed by some, or whether this approach can be dismissed as futile, or anywhere in between, the conversation is worthy of another visit. This chapter addresses a few questions we encounter whenever we try to make sense of the story of our species. These questions focus on what are the most prominent explanations for the critical historical junctures. What induces societies to adopt a change or adapt to another? Whether history is written by individuals who act as heroic legends or by common folks? Whether history is written by humans only without consideration of their surroundings? Do historical events exhibit a certain predictable pattern? Is there an end to history where a final chapter can be agreed upon?

By analogy, we are trying to look at history as a vehicle. In the context of our discussion, we want to know who the driver of such a vehicle is. What are the factors that cause the driver to steer the vehicle in that direction and not the other? Is there a pattern to the journey taken by such a vehicle? And is there a destination at the end of such a journey? These questions, and some of the proposed answers, will pave the way for the humble contribution of this book, which is discussed in detail at the end of this chapter.

2 The Hero of History

When studying history, the first question that comes to the fore is who is behind these historical events that we are trying hard to comprehend. In other words, can these historical occurrences be attributed to the will and actions of one, or to the determination and conduct of many. To answer that question, some scholars assert that history is but an assortment of stories of eminent personalities. In their opinion, these illustrious notables are the agents of crucial change, the champions of critical breakthroughs, and the pioneers of societal transformations. This emphasis on human agency is supported, in the view of these advocates, by the observation that certain individuals were able to change the trajectory of humanity. Examples include national heroes who led their nations to times of greatness, profound thinkers who changed our perception of life, inventors who altered our daily lives altogether, spiritual leaders who escorted societies to an alternate mindset, tyrants who led their nations to ruin, fanatics who drove scores into wars, bigots who chaperoned herds to commit atrocities, and many others. The stories of these individuals are put forth as evidence of how human agency instigated change despite inauspicious circumstances in some cases.

According to the proponents of this opinion, chapters in history books ought to be flooded with stories of those larger-than-life heroes, champions, icons, paragons, and protagonists. In their viewpoint, today's world came to be what it is because of the vision, sagacity, daring, audacity, fortitude, and determination of great conquerors such as Alexander the Great, Julius Caesar, Charlemagne, Napoleon Bonaparte, Genghis Khan, Tamerlane, Attila the Hun, and Cyrus the Great, only to name a few. Spiritual transformations were not possible without those revered by many around the world including Abraham, Moses, Jesus, Mohamed, Buddha, Confucius, Zoroaster, Zhuang Zhou, Martin Luther, and others. Intellectual insights that transformed our way of thinking were not likely to occur without Thucydides, Plato, Aristotle, Socrates, Plutarch, Avicenna and Averroes, Niccolo Machiavelli, Thomas Hobbes, Baruch Spinoza, John Locke, David Hume, Adam Smith, Alexis de Tocqueville, Jean-Jacques Rousseau, Edmund Burke, Emmanuel Kant, Friedrich Hegel, John Stuart Mill, Karl Marx, Friedrich Nietzsche, Martin Heidegger, and many others. Discoverers and adventurous explorers who are claimed by some to have widened our horizons include Ibn Battuta, Marco Polo, Zheng He, Christopher Columbus, Vasco Da Gama, Amerigo Vespucci, Hernan de Soto, Ferdinand Magellan, Sir Francis Drake, Sir Walter Raleigh, James Cook, and many more.

Biographies of such influential figures and many others have become an indispensable component of history writing. Lots of historical books are awash with the names of these heroes, the acts of heroism they undertook, and the dates in which these actions occurred. For some, history is but a compilation of such stories. These prominent names include the good, the bad, and the ugly. The common attributes of these immortals are argued to be traits that are uncommon with ordinary people. They supposedly possess personal qualities and characteristics that others do not. Simon Sebag Montefiore in his *Titans of History: The Giants Who Made Our World* asserts:[6]

> The political and artistic genius of even the most admirable of these characters requires ambition, insensitivity, egocentricity, ruthlessness, even madness, as much as it demands decency, skills, empathy, and heroism.

> 'Reasonable people,' said George Bernard Shaw, 'adapt themselves to the world. Unreasonable people adapt the world to themselves. Therefore, change is only possible through unreasonable people.' Greatness needs courage (above all) and willpower, charisma, intelligence, and creativity, but it also demands characteristics that we often associate with the least admirable people: reckless risk-taking, brutal determination, sexual thrill-seeking, brazen showmanship, obsession close to fixation and something approaching insanity.

No matter what their contribution is, our tendency to idolize our heroes, and to put them on a pedestal, comes from a desire to attribute herculean deeds to mere mortals. This seems to be essential for some to feel the hope that we are capable of such affairs, to offer examples of heroism to emulate, to distinguish our heroes from those of others, and to find a simple explanation for turning points that are otherwise hard to comprehend.

There are plenty who seem to concur with this world view. For instance, philosopher Sidney Hook declares that[7] "[h]istory is written so as to leave no doubt that it was either the work of heroes, predecessors of the leader, or the work of villains, prototypes of the leader's enemies." He also asserts that we[8] "cannot write history without recognizing that at least some individuals, at some critical moments, play a decisive role in redirecting the historical wave." Along the same vein, philosopher William James emphasizes that the[9] "mutations of societies from generation to generation are in the main due directly or indirectly to the acts or examples of individuals whose genius was so adapted to the receptivities of the moment, or whose accidental position of authority was so critical that they became ferments, initiators of movements, settlers of precedent or fashion, centers of corruption, or destroyers of other persons whose gifts, had they had free play, would have led society in another direction." Historian and philosopher Thomas Carlyle also celebrates the contributions of heroes in history by stating:[10]

> For as I take it, Universal History, the history of what man has accomplished in this world, is at bottom the History of the Great Men who have worked here. They were the leaders of men, these great ones; the modelers, patterns, and in wide sense creators, of whatsoever the general mass of men contrived to do or to attain; all things that we see standing accomplished in the world are properly the outer material result, the practical realization and embodiment, of Thoughts that welt in the Great Men sent into the world:

> the soul of the whole world's history, it may justly be considered, were the history of these.

However, there is another point of view that begs to differ. According to these, individuals who happen to be at the helm during some historical developments were there by chance at a time when these transformations would have occurred with or without them. The real actors are the ordinary people, the unremarkable public, the common folks, and the simple masses. The individual hero, in this case, is either an instrument in times of social churning or merely a bystander spectator of historical commotion. In the former, these prominent ones merely contribute to the developing event by virtue of their position, which permits them at the time to participate in the emanating situation but not to steer it in another direction. In the latter, these distinguished characters solely observe the evolving event without exerting much influence on its final outcome.

To clarify this idea, some argue that[11] "the great men were thrown up by 'chance' in the processes of natural variation while the social environment served as a selective agency in providing them with the opportunities to get their work done." Thus,[12] "social needs 'work themselves out' through the movements of the masses whose individual components, seen from a distance, could not be distinguished from each other. To them only the masses or classes were heroes." In a similar vein, Leo Tolstoy argues that we should discard our obsession with heroes and our fixation on how they influence outcomes. He suggests that we focus instead on the forces that lead the crowd to go in that direction and not the other:[13]

> To study the laws of history we must completely change the subject of our observation, must leave aside kings, ministers, and generals, and study the common, infinitesimally small elements by which the masses are moved. No one can say in how far it is possible for man to advance in this way toward an understanding of the laws of history; but it is evident that only along that path does the possibility of discovering the laws of history lie.

Given these considerations, a new wave of historians decided to write an alternative story of the crowd. In this context, ordinary people go about their daily lives taking decisions to enable themselves to survive the hardships of life, to make ends meet, to shelter their loved ones, to fight the injustices they are subjected to, to stand up for what they believe in, to alter their conditions, to improve their livelihood, and to even thrive if possible. These decisions are taken given their innate personalities, their surrounding circumstances, the challenges they encounter, and a whole set of constraints that are imposed upon them. According to this view, it is the motion created by these masses that stirs the whirlpool of history. As such, historical developments are only the outcome of collective decisions made by the multitudes, given the set of circumstances and constraints that surround them.

In this context, historian Chris Harman introduces his sweeping historical account by stating,[14] "Since the time of the first Pharaohs (5,000 years ago) rulers have presented history as being a list of 'achievements' by themselves and their forebears. Such 'Great Men' are supposed to have built cities and monuments, to have brought prosperity, to have been responsible for great works or military victories-and, conversely, 'Evil Men' are supposed to be responsible for everything bad in the world." However, he argues that there is[15] "another way of looking at history" where humans make choices, within a greater struggle, whose outcome will lead to developments that sometimes we attribute to the will of one. The choices taken by people are an upshot of the position of each person within societal structures at the outset of the dramatic turn of events such that[16]

> [t]he sequence of these great struggles provides the skeleton round which the rest of history grows. This approach does not deny the role of individuals or the ideas they propagate. What it does is to insist that the individual or idea can only play a certain role because of the preceding material development of society, of the way people make their livelihoods, and of the structure of classes and states.

Similarly, historian Neil Faulkner asserts that historical processes come about through the collective decisions and aggregated actions of people, living within the confines of the economic, political, cultural, institutional, and social structures of their times. Accordingly, history is[17] "continually created and recreated by conscious, collective human action." These actions[18]

> are framed by the economic, social, and political structures of their age. But, subject to these constraints—indeed, because of them—humans face a succession of choices. Sometimes, they choose not to act, but to acquiesce. Then they remain history's victims, in thrall to the decisions of others, their

> rulers, the self-appointed arbiters of human destiny. Other times, far too rarely perhaps, they choose to organise and fight. When enough make this choice, they become a mass movement and an historical force. And then the earth shakes.

Given these contrasting views, it seems reasonable not to advocate one nor to decry the other. History can neither be written by leaders without the participation of those they lead, nor can it be composed by the commons with their commanders standing as a passive observer. History is continuously written by an incessant feedback loop between the decisions taken by the individuals in a community and the initiatives of those who happen to be at the helm at that place and time.

3 The Stimulus of History

Besides the identity of the driver of the vehicle of history, historians also wonder about the factors that cause the driver, whether a hero or the crowd, to steer the wagon to one direction and not the other. In other words, we need to know what stimulates societies to suddenly decide to adopt a change in course. Nothing seems more pertinent than the notion proposed by historian Arnold Toynbee on how a challenge acts as a societal stimulus. In his exhaustive study of human history, Toynbee discusses the genesis and growth of civilizations as a process through which a society is first faced with a challenge. The ability and the process through which societies deal with that challenge plays a critical role in how civilizations come to be and continue to exist. Thus, a society[19] "is confronted in the course of its life by a succession of problems and that 'the presentation of each problem is a challenge to undergo an ordeal.'" This challenge creates a call to action or a stimulus for some societies. Thus, civilizations cannot grow to become what they were without these stimulating challenges since[20] "ease is inimical to civilization." Toynbee elaborates on how these stimulants evoke a societal action with its momentum or what he refers to as *élan*:[21]

> Civilizations, it would seem, grow through an *élan* which carries them from challenge through response to further challenge, and this growth has both outward and inward aspects. In the Macrocosm growth reveals itself as a progressive mastery over the external environment; in the Microcosm as a

> progressive self-determination or self-articulation. In either of these manifestations, we have a possible criterion of the progress of the *élan* itself.

Thus, Toynbee posits that societies face two types of challenges. The external comes from other societies or the surrounding natural environment, while the internal comes from within. The former is concerned with threats from others or natural challenges of some sort. The latter is concerned with the inner strength of a society best exemplified by the closer ties between the elite and the commons or the leaders and those they lead. Comparing between these challenges to determine which one the society needs to overcome, we must[22] "reckon less and less with challenges delivered by external forces and demanding responses on an outer battlefield, and more and more with challenges that are presented by itself to itself in an inner arena." In this case, Toynbee is not undermining the external challenges compared to the internal ones, as much as asserting that addressing the latter is imperative to be able to deal with the former.

In doing so, deliberately or not, Toynbee associates the stimulus of societal change with our earlier discussion on whose hands are on the driving wheel. As much as the study of history assists us in acknowledging that challenges stimulate societies to react, their reaction will determine the outcome depending on how creative the leaders choose to be and how harmonious they can work with those they are leading to overcome such an ordeal. Toynbee, thus, argues that the interaction between the leaders and the ones they lead is critical and that the creativity in the leading echelon is not enough in dealing with a challenge without the ability to work with the others to carry out their vision. This is since[23] "[g]rowth is the work of creative personalities and creative minorities; they cannot go on moving forward themselves unless they can contrive to carry their fellows with them in their advance; and the uncreative rank and file of mankind, which is always the overwhelming majority, cannot be transfigured *en masse* and raised to the stature of their leaders in the twinkling of an eye." Otherwise, the lack of harmony can cause societies to breakdown since this[24] "secession of the led from the leaders may be regarded as a loss of harmony between the parts which makes up the whole *ensemble* of the society. In any whole consisting of parts, a loss of harmony between the parts is paid for by the whole in a corresponding loss of self-determination. This loss of self-determination is the ultimate criterion of breakdown."

In a fitting criticism, however, Hugh Kearney warns that while we can conceive of individuals deliberately and consciously reacting to a challenge, an entire society is incapable of such purposeful action. He admonishes Toynbee's view as[25] "[i]t conveys the impression that a particular society is possessed of a will of its own and a freedom of choice in a particular situation. Challenge and response may be valid in the life of each individual, but it is excessive simplification when applied to the life of a society or an institution." This admonition notwithstanding, the proposition that a challenge stimulates a society to a reaction, whose outcome depends on the nature of connections between the leaders and those they lead, seems to be a sensible and plausible description of what induces societal transformations. This also ties this discussion to our previous conclusion that historical developments occur through a continuous feedback loop between the actions of the leaders and the reactions of those they lead.

4 The Cycles of History

Yet another question that poses itself when we study human history is whether historical events follow a recurrent pattern and adhere to a trend that repeats itself. In other words, historians wonder whether societal changes follow a cyclical pattern where one thing leads to another and then the cycle replicates itself. The answer to such a question is critical for historical analysis. This is because if we identify a pattern to historical developments, then we can determine not only what causes this trend or the other but also predict what comes next when we are at that point on a trend or another.

To answer this question, a new field of historical analysis took stock of the advances in the field of dynamics. In general, dynamics is concerned with the laws of motion of bodies under the action of forces which stimulate change within a system. Some scholars apply this dynamical systems' approach to social sciences in general and to the study of historical dynamics in particular. This framework can be used to explain historical cycles such as the emergence and fall of states and empires, population booms and busts, economic cyclical patterns, the spread and disappearance of cultural waves and social trends, and others.

No better example to apply this approach than the identification of the forces behind the expansion and contraction of states. Historians in this field endeavor to find a template model that puts forth the factors that cause states to grow and expand and those that lead these same states to wither and wane. In this context, the process of expansion carries with it the seeds that may cause the same entity to eventually diminish and dwindle. In the same vein, the contraction phase also carries within its fold the promise of another wave of expansion. Thus, each expansion is followed by a potential contraction. The latter can also be succeeded by the former, and so on and so forth. This produces cycles of expansion and contraction that can repeat itself. Thus, these templates allow us to visualize these historical changes diagrammatically and to compress the system into a more concrete model. This step, in turn, allows us to determine where a society is on the curve and where it will end up subsequently. One of the pioneers of this field, Peter Turchin, follows the true father of sociology Ibn Khaldun in proposing that the existence or loss of *asabiya* or social solidarity is a critical factor that causes these types of cyclical patterns by stating:[26]

> Desert tribes with high asabiya conquer civilized people with low asabiya and establish a ruling dynasty (a state) over them. Under conditions of civilized life, however, asabiya inevitably declines. In approximately four generations, asabiya becomes so low that the state collapses as a result of factional conflict. This is the point at which the civilized area becomes vulnerable to another conquest by desert tribes.

In this framework, Ibn Khaldun formulates a theory for the expansion and the ensuing contraction of states. When a state in the civilization zone ends with low *asabiya* and internal strife, it also becomes susceptible to conquest from those in the desert. A coalition of desert tribes with high *asabiya* takes advantage of this weakness lurking within to conquer the civilization zone and establishes a new state there. The conquering generation and their offspring continue to preserve their desert ways and to treasure their group solidarity. As time passes by, however, wealth accumulation and a life of luxury lure their descendants away from their simple life. As generations succeed generations, the corrosive effects of indulgent life on solidarity begin to erode *asabiya*. At that point, the dynasty goes into decline and eventually another coalition arises to conquer them. Thus, the cycle repeats itself. In this context, *asabiya* is considered the linchpin upon which states emerge and grow. This is due to the contribution of social solidarity in holding the group tightly together. The loss of such a societal condition with time due to the adverse effects of affluence is also the first cause of state decline. According to these arguments, societies go through cycles of growth spurred by social solidarity and internal cohesion, followed by decline caused by decadence and fissures in the social fabric. This pattern repeats itself to create these cyclical dynamics.

Building upon the conjecture of Ibn Khaldun, Peter Turchin argues that solidarity between the components of a nation, and collective action, is a critical factor not only in keeping it together but also in its expansion. This is since[27] "[t]he ability of an empire to expand territory and to defend itself against external and internal enemies is determined largely by the characteristics of its imperial nation, especially its asabiya." He also adds that[28] "[i]n the pressure cooker of a metaethnic frontier, poorly integrated groups crumble and disappear, whereas groups based on strong cooperation thrive and expand."

Peter Turchin elaborates on how the dissipation of solidarity can lead to societal disintegration and the eventual decline of empires. According to his view, the tensions between the poor and the elite, and the frictions within the elite groups, are demonstrations of such loss of *asabiya*. In this context, it is the political stability and economic prosperity of the expansion phase that boost the population. As the numbers grow due to favorable conditions, overpopulation comes with its attendant evils. The abundance of workers lowers wages, while the high demand for land increases rents. This skews the income distribution in favor of the landlords. These disproportionate conditions, however, cause an increase in the numbers of the privileged who eventually start to feel the agony of over-crowdedness in their midst. The eventual deterioration in their living conditions causes a decline in the tax income for a state whose budget is already burdened by their increased demands for assistance. This does not allow the state to ensure security at a time where strife increases within the ranks of the elite, whose numbers start to decline as an outcome of the ensuing violence. As competition subsides, stability prevails once more allowing for another cycle to start. Thus, this view offers a generalized framework of identifying the reasons for the rise of societies and the factors for their eventual decline and fall. Along these lines, Peter Turchin clarifies these trends as follows:

> The very stability and internal peace that strong empires impose contain with them the seeds of future chaos. Stability and internal peace bring prosperity, and prosperity causes population increase. Demographic growth leads to overpopulation, overpopulation causes lower wages, higher land rents, and falling per capita incomes for the commoners. At first, low wages and high rents bring unparalleled wealth to the upper classes, but as their

> numbers and appetites grow, they also begin to suffer from falling incomes. Declining standards of life breed discontent and strife. The elite turn to the state for employment and additional income, and drive up its expenditures at the same time that the tax revenues decline because of the growing misery of the population. When the state's finances collapse, it loses control of the army and police. Freed from all restraints, strife among the elites escalates into civil war, while the discontent among the poor explodes into popular rebellion. The collapse of order brings in its wake the four horsemen—famine, war, pestilence and death. Population declines and wages increase, while rents decrease. As incomes of commoners recover, the fortunes of the upper classes hit bottom. Economic distress of the elites and lack of effective government feed the continuing internecine wars. However, civil war thins the ranks of the elites. Some die in factional fighting, others succumb to feud with neighbors, and many simply stop trying to maintain their aristocratic status and quietly slip into the ranks of commoners. Intra-elite competition subsides, allowing the restoration of order. Stability and internal peace bring prosperity, and another cycle begins.

Critics of such approach, however, often argue that the intricacies of social evolution cannot be reduced to definite diagrams, quantifiable formulas, or analyzable observations. For doing so, we overlook each society's unique characteristics and particular circumstances. It is appropriate to refer to philosopher Karl Popper who criticized vehemently the illusion of historical prophecy. In his arguments, a description of the whole of society is impossible because the list of characteristics making up such a depiction would be infinite, that individual actions and reactions cannot be predicted with certainty or accuracy, and that a social law may enable us to exclude the possibility of certain events but not to narrow down the list of possible outcomes to only one. Karl Popper declares that[29] "a statement asserting the existence of a trend at a certain time and place would be a singular historical statement and not a universal law."

Despite these valid criticisms, a pattern for societal progression can be a portrayal of what we expect to occur next given a set of circumstances and conditions and not just a law of motion that acts on its own without any input from the components of that society. In addition, this discussion also emphasizes social solidarity or the ties between members of a society. This complements our earlier discussion on the critical role of the ties between the leaders and those they lead in the ability of a society to react to challenges. In the context of our discussion, societies are faced with challenges that stimulate them to react. The outcome of their reaction will depend not only on the harmonious ties between the leaders and those they lead as we have established before, but also on the strength of social solidarity between the components of society.

5 The Climate of History

Another question that comes to mind when we study history is whether humans shape their destiny alone without any contribution from their natural surroundings. Historians came to concede that historical outcomes were not only determined by the interaction between people and their leaders, nor by the collective ties between people, as we have discussed before. Since humans do not live in a vacuum, their history is also determined by the interplay between humans and their environmental setting. Thus, the story of humanity cannot be complete without incorporating nature as a principal character. One of the core components of our nature is climate. Climate refers to the long-term patterns of weather or the general weather trends in an area. Climate is critical for the human story, especially in its influence on where humans can settle, the activities they can engage in for survival, the resources available at their disposal, their modes of production, their cultural practices and faith paradigms, their way of life, and the vision of the world that they hold dear.[30] The variation in our natural environment could also bring about challenges that we have to deal with, or adapt to, to ensure our survival. In this context, climate change refers to variations in the average weather patterns.

One of the earliest contributions on the effect of climate on humanity dates back to Ibn Khaldun in his opus magnum *Al Muqaddimah*, in which he proposes that climate influences a nation's culture.[31] Ibn Khaldun was the first to study the influence of the physical settings of a location on the non-physical characteristics of the society that occupies it. He attempted to explain the difference between societies, including their customs, in terms of their environmental habitat and climatic conditions. For instance, Ibn Khaldun observes that the area he studied is divided by an environmental frontier into two zones. In the north, there are territories where rainfall is plentiful for farming. This area, which he calls the civilization zone, contains towns, states, and empires. South of the civilization zone lies the desert inhabited by Bedouin tribes. In these areas, each tribe can depend only on itself for survival against both the harsh environment and the perils imposed by other tribes. Thus, these tribes are held together by a high level of *asabiya* because life in the desert eradicates any community that lacks solidarity. By contrast, no constant struggle occurs for survival within the civilization zone that would nurture a high level of *asabiya*. From our earlier discussion, *asabiya*, or the lack thereof, determines the destiny of these societies. Thus, Ibn Khaldun is arguing that climatic conditions can influence social outcomes by formulating the level of *asabiya* in each society.

His philosophy of history made him a predecessor of Charles-Louis de Secondat, known as Baron de Montesquieu.[32] The latter argues that different climates could lead to differences in character, temperament, and inclination.[33] These differences, in turn, could lead to distinct historical outcomes. For instance, Montesquieu claims that differences between the attributes of people in the tropics and temperate zones could be attributed to temperature since[34] "[y]ou will find in the climates of the north, peoples with few vices, many virtues, sincerity and truthfulness. Approach the south, you will think you are leaving morality itself, the passions become more vivacious and multiply crimes....The heat can be so excessive that the body is totally without force. The resignation passes to the spirit and leads people to be without curiosity, nor the desire for noble enterprise."

These prejudicial views on the climatic-induced differences in temperament led Montesquieu to even argue that those in favorable climates can dominate those who are not. This, in turn, offers a framework to explain some historical outcomes such as the subjugation of the inhabitants of warmer climates by others through the slave trade and colonial expansion. In a similar vein, economic historian David Landes states,[35] "It is no accident that slave labor has historically been associated with tropical and semitropical climes." He proposes that slavery can be explained by the fact that Europeans, who are not adapted to the discomfort of heat, were unable to work in plantations in the tropics. Thus, the plantation owners depended on slaves to do the work for them.

Some scholars also argue that climate influences the components of a civilization in terms of its institutional structures, its social systems, its cultural paradigms, and its ties with others. For instance, Ellsworth Huntington proposes that climate and civilization are connected because the[36] "nature of a nation's religious faith, its form of government, its social organization, its ease of intercourse with other nations, and various other conditions play a fundamental part in the distribution of civilization. Yet each is conditioned by the degree of energy possessed by a people. Energy, in turn, seems to depend upon climate, and thus climate becomes an essential element in determining the status of civilization."

These endeavors seem to point our attention to an obvious observation that the destiny of societies is shaped, to a certain extent, by the environmental surroundings, especially climate. Thus, differences in climatic conditions can drive these societies to distinct outcomes. That also implies that any change in the climatic setting pushes a society to change their ways to adapt to the new conditions. Either way, history telling cannot be complete without incorporating the contribution of the natural elements. To put this into the context of our earlier discussion, changes to our natural climatic conditions could pause a challenge to societies that call for action. The outcome of the reaction to that challenge will depend, as suggested earlier, on the ties between the leaders and those they lead in addition to social solidarity or *asabiya* between the people who comprise the units of that society.

6 The End of History

A final question that comes frequently to the fore is whether there is a deterministic end to our story. Within the framework of historical determinism, the claim of an end of history designates a concluding denouement of the story of humanity. In this context, not only has the past already been concluded, but the future is foreclosed to any further developments. Some notable thinkers of their time supported such a way of thinking about how history evolves.

For instance, Friedrich Hegel claimed that history was a process of development by esoteric forces that could be understood by anyone willing to look at it holistically. In essence, this[37] "formal determination is Spirit, which uses world history as its theater, its property, and the field of its actualization. Spirit does not toss itself about in the external play of chance occurrences; on the contrary, it is that which determines history absolutely, and it stands firm against the chance occurrences which it dominates and exploits for its own purpose." Sidney Hook explains this Hegelian determinism by stating,[38] "For Hegel every age gets the 'great men' it deserves, but what it deserves depends not on its responsible choice between alternatives but on a predetermined pattern laid up in heaven, existing out of time and yet in some mysterious way pervading events in time."

Hegel had a notable disciple in Karl Marx who adapted his dialectic away from the world of Spirit toward a more materialist conception of history. In the latter's argument, the underlying economic framework and social structure critically determine the unfolding of human history toward the final establishment of a Socialist society. Thus, there is a conclusion, culmination, and climactic consummation of the human experience when an existing economic system is substituted by another permanently. Karl Marx and Friedrich Engels in their *Communist Manifesto* predict that a capitalist society creates its own gravediggers for its ultimate burial which would be but a prelude to a proletarian transformation. Thus, in their view, history is heading toward an end where socialism replaces capitalism as an economic paradigm and a social structure.

Along the same vein, Bhaskar Sunkara in the *Socialist Manifesto* states that the rhetoric of the Socialists reeks of a certain foretelling of the future with certitude which[39] "seemed to mimic the messianic appeal of Christianity. Christians knew that Christ would come again in his glory to judge the living and the dead. Social Democrats knew that every moment drew them closer to salvation on Earth." The believers of such a predetermined fate[40] "had traditionally thought that revolution would occur in stages. The first would be 'bourgeois-democratic,' paving the way for peasant land reform and further urban industrialization and creating a capitalist republic with freedom of speech and assembly. The new situation would allow social democrats to patiently organize for a second, socialist revolution."

However, this view is not only espoused by those of Socialist tendencies. The dissolution of the self-proclaimed Socialist experience, the Soviet Union, brought the believers in free markets and liberal democracy into the fold of determinism by claiming that the end of history is a Socialist collapse rather than a proletariat renaissance. Due to the Western euphoria that accompanied the collapse of the Soviet Union, political scientist Francis Fukuyama declares,[41] "What we may be witnessing is not just the end of the Cold War, or the passing of a particular period of postwar history, but the end of history as such: that is, the end point of mankind's ideological evolution and the universalization of Western liberal democracy as the final form of human government." In another contribution, Fukuyama reiterates that[42] "liberal democracy may constitute the 'end point of mankind's ideological evolution' and the 'final form of human government,' and as such constituted the 'end of history.'"

According to this view, liberal democracy and free market capitalism have proven to be fundamentally superior systems compared to the alternative and that there can be no progression from them to any other. These political and economic systems are intertwined in the sense that as much as capitalism can lead to a society of different classes with contrasting economic interests, a democratic system of governance can provide each with a voice in the political arena where policies with economic implications are determined. In this context, Fukuyama does not claim that events will cease to occur in the future, but rather that what will happen is that democracy as a system of governance, and capitalism as an economic structure, will prevail in the long term.

As such, advocates of an end to history tend to predict an outcome that is consistent with their predispositions, that appeals to their followers, that encourages their rank and file to believe that their efforts will not be in vain, and that closes the door on any despair if their struggle seems to take a wrong turn. However, others criticize such a deterministic conclusion to the human story as it undermines the ability of humans to change outcomes and to continue shaping their story as long as our species continues to exist.

Whether history has an end, or it continues from one end to another so long as humans are here on earth, will continue to be a topic of fierce debate. The controversy will continue to be between those who believe that humanity is heading to a terminal destination as a declaration of victory over those who are on the opposite side, against those who believe that history is an endless sequence of events like a train pushing forward without any final station. In the context of our earlier discussion, challenges that societies face could be sufficiently drastic to cause what seems an implausible outcome to be the only one likely to occur. Thus, challenges in the form of extreme climate change are considered by some to be an existential threat to humanity or an endgame.[43] If climate change is a challenge that creates these cyclical patterns, where a climate shock is followed by a societal reaction, then shocks that are sufficiently forceful to render any reaction futile could bring about an end to that story.

7 The Study of History

It was once said that it is more important to read history than to write it. In doing so, we need to know what happened even if the findings disturb our biased sentiments or contrast with our preconceptions. Thus, we should not offer a sanitary version to soothe our sensitivities. Nor should we fit historical events into our view of how things should work, by offering examples that support the arguments we advance just to prove we are correct to begin with. This is quite pertinent within the scope of this book.

The purpose of this book is to explore the contribution of climate change in human history. Our previous discussion establishes that societies are exposed to shocks that challenge their usual existence. These challenges stimulate these societies to react. The outcome of that reaction will depend on the creativity of the leaders, their harmonious connections with the ones they lead, and the solidarity between the components of such society. Thus, overcoming internal challenges can assist in addressing external ones. If these shocks come periodically, this brings about a recurrent pattern where a challenge is followed by a change. If there is an end to such a story, then that will depend on whether the challenge is so severe to hand a final blow to humanity. This shock could be a natural one in the form of climate change.

Thus, the core argument of this book is that any shock to the natural processes can bring about dramatic changes in the trajectory of human societies that are exposed to it, any disruption to the way humans interact with their surrounding environment can produce material transformations to these communities, and any interruption to the typical natural trends can lead to substantial deviations in humanity's continuous adventure. These disturbances to our natural environment may include climatic fluctuations.

Climate shocks pose considerable challenges to societies as they change our surrounding habitat in such a way that we cannot carry on as usual. To be specific, fluctuations in climate cause a drastic change in how societies can function in a new environment, endure the newly created hardship, and withstand these unfamiliar conditions. This is because climate change can alter the surrounding environment in such a way that makes it harder for humans to subsist by pursuing the same ways that allowed them to persevere till then. This implies that members of that society must either adapt to these challenges by introducing new ways of living, migrate to a new land where these challenges are not encountered, or perish altogether due to the inability to handle them.

To address this type of challenge, creativity by the leaders of such a society is needed to find a way out of this predicament. These climate challenges also entail a concerted reaction by both the affected crowd and their leadership, combining both the role of the common people and their heroes in episodes of drastic social change. It also demands collective fortitude and social tenacity to overcome them, consistently with the indispensability of *asabiya* that we discussed earlier. The destiny of that society to weather this challenge or to wither away will be determined by this consequential choice. This choice will depend on the ingenuity of the leadership, their close connection to their people, and the strength of social ties between the components of that community.

This discussion also permits a recurrent pattern that admits a connection between climatic shocks and historical outcomes, which allows for an explanation of historical occurrences as consequences and not as coincidences. This pattern is one where climate shocks have drastic consequences on societies that are exposed to them. Every time these shocks occur, these outcomes are likely to follow in the future as they did in the past. This does not indicate a deterministic pattern, where the cause is followed by an effect with certitude, as much as it associates these changes with the subsequent outcomes potentially where the cause is likely and credibly succeeded by the effect. The end of history could be lurking behind the man-made climate change that we are witnessing nowadays. This could be the case if climate deteriorated to the point of no return where no future action could repair the damage already done.

In this context, the book illustrates how climate change led to substantial changes in human history. These transformations include the process of evolution of our species to anatomically modern humans, human dispersal from the cradle of humanity, the peopling of our world over time, the transition to sedentary life and farming, the collapse of complex societies, the demise of civilizations, the decline of kingdoms and empires, the outbreak of conflicts, the adoption of new cultural traits and norms, the spread of infectious diseases and plagues, and other critical historical junctures. Thus, climate has been a constant companion in the journey of humanity from the outset.

The other contribution of this book is its focus on the economic channel between climate change and these historical outcomes. From the outset, hominins faced the various challenges to survival and threats of extinction by natural selection. The adaptive traits favored in the evolutionary process ensured the survival of the hominins in a challenging and changing habitat due to environmental variability. Then, humans had to deal with other climatic challenges to their initial habitat with dispersal from the cradle of humanity to eventually populate the entire world. Afterward, humans had to adjust to the fluctuations in climate by changing their way of life from a nomadic to a sedentary one that adopts agriculture. After humans settled and established complex societies and great civilizations, their ability to deal with climate change determined their continuity or collapse. This is especially the case as climate change contributed to conflict, famine, pestilence, catastrophes, or a combination of all these factors that threatened the existence of these societies. In all these cases, the determination of our species to survive was the incentive to act in the face of changing climatic conditions. Economics, in its basic form, is about creating and expanding the means through which we can ensure our sustenance. Therefore, we cannot discuss the effect of climate change on humanity without putting the spotlight on these economic incentives. Thus, climate, economics, and our species became constant companions in this epic adventure.

This is particularly important nowadays given the abundant natural challenges that humanity faces in terms of the changes to our surrounding environment that manifests itself in climate change, worsening natural disasters, loss of biodiversity, deforestation, desertification, and others. The knowledge of how climate change affected our past can guide us in finding out how it might affect our present and what may lay ahead in our future as well. This narrative also allows us to learn from some of our ancestors, who weathered the storm they encountered, how to handle these challenges. In other cases, it serves as a warning about the lamentable fate of those other ancestors who did not deal with these existential threats in the manner that would be most suitable for them to ride out the storm.

Notes

1. Leo Tolstoy. War and Peace. Bookbyte Digital Edition (P. 1429).
2. Ibid. (P. 1186).
3. Hugh Kearney. "Arnold Toynbee; Challenge and Response." University Review, 1, 4: 33–41, 1955.
4. Ibid.
5. Arthur Danto. "On Explanations in History." Philosophy of Science, 23, 1: 15–30, 2022.
6. Simon Sebag Montefiore. Titans of History: The Giants Who Made Our World. Vintage Books, 2017. (P. 19).
7. Sidney Hook. The Hero in History: A Study in Limitation and Possibility. Beacon Press, 1967. (P. 10).
8. Ibid. (P. 12).
9. William James. "Great Men and their Environment." In Selected Papers on Philosophy, Everyman Edition. (P. 174).
10. Thomas Carlyle. On Heroes and Hero Worship and the Heroic in History. Yale University Press, 2013.

11. Sidney Hook. The Hero in History: A Study in Limitation and Possibility. Beacon Press, 1967. (P. 15).
12. Ibid. (P. 60).
13. Leo Tolstoy. War and Peace. Bookbyte Digital Edition (P. 989).
14. Chris Harmann. A People's History of the World: From the Stone Age to the New Millennium. Verso, 2008. (P. ii).
15. Ibid. (P. iii).
16. Ibid. (P. iv).
17. Neil Faulkner. A Radical History of the World. Pluto Press, 2018. (P. ix).
18. Neil Faulkner. A Marxist History of the World: From Neanderthals to Neoliberals. Pluto Press, 2013 (P. 296).
19. Arnold Toynbee. A Study of History. Oxford University Press, 1946. (PP. 61–62).
20. Ibid. (P. 88).
21. Ibid. (P. 189).
22. Ibid. (P. 208).
23. Ibid. (P. 276).
24. Ibid. (P. 279).
25. Hugh Kearney. "Arnold Toynbee; Challenge and Response." University Review, 1, 4: 33–41, 1955.
26. Peter Turchin. Historical Dynamics: Why State Rise and Fall. Princeton University Press, 2003. (P. 40).
27. Peter Turchin. War and Peace and War: The Rise and Fall of Empires. Plume, 2007. (P. 6).
28. Ibid. (P. 6).
29. Karl Popper. The Poverty of Historicism. Beacon Press, 1957. (P. 115).
30. Sherif Khalifa. Geography and the Wealth of Nations. Bloomsbury, 2022.
31. Ibn Khaldun. Al Muqqadimah: Prolegomena. Jiahu Books, 2014.
32. Warren Gates. "The Spread of Ibn Khaldun's Ideas on Climate and Culture." Journal of the History of Ideas, 28, 3: 415–422, 1967.
33. Charles de Montesquieu. The Spirit of the Laws. Cambridge University Press, 1989.
34. Elizabeth Van Voorhees, Sarah Wilson, Patrick Calhoun, Eric Elbogen, Jean Beckham, and Nathan Kimbrel. "Sociocultural Discourse in Science: Flawed Assumptions and Bias in the CLASH Model." Behavioral and Brain Sciences, 40, e100, 2017.
35. David Landes. The Wealth and Poverty of Nations: Why Some Are So Rich and Some So Poor. W.W. Norton and Company, 1999. (P. 7).
36. Ellsworth, Huntington. Civilization and Climate. HardPress Publishing, 2013. (P. 207).
37. Georg Wilhelm Friedrich Hegel. Introduction to the Philosophy of History. Hackett Publishing Company, 1988. (P. 58).

38. Sidney Hook. The Hero in History: A Study in Limitation and Possibility. Beacon Press, 1967. (PP. 61–62).
39. Bhaskar Sunkara. The Socialist Manifesto. Basic Books, New York, 2020. (P. 61).
40. Ibid. (P. 87).
41. Francis Fukuyama. "The End of History." The National Interest, 16: 3–18, 1989.
42. Francis Fukuyama. The End of History and the Last Man. Avon Books, 1992. (P. xi).
43. Luke Kemp, Joanna Depledge, Kristie L. Ebi, Goodwin Gibbins, Timothy A. Kohler, Johan Rockström, Marten Scheffer, Hans Joachim Schellnhuber, Will Steffen, and Timothy M. Lenton. "Climate Endgame: Exploring Catastrophic Climate Change Scenarios." PNAS, 119, 34, e2108146119, 2022.

CHAPTER 3

Environment and Evolution

1 In the Beginning There Was a Hominin

To study our history, we have no alternative but to go back to the very beginnings of the human journey. Going back that far, we encounter our ancestors, from the onset, going through a continuous odyssey of change. The process of transformation changed our ancestors from what they were to what we are now. This was an evolutionary adventure which is typically defined as an experience through which existing living organisms can trace their origin to other preexisting ones. The differences between the former and the latter can be attributed to anatomical alterations and genetic mutations over successive generations.[1] In this context, human evolution is a scenario by which current human beings developed from primates that are now extinct. This is considered the process that led to the emergence of anatomically modern humans as a distinct species of the hominin family almost 200,000 years ago.[2] Some scholars consider this a course which led gradually to anatomical changes to facial features, cranial capacity, cognitive capabilities, skeleton shape, limb structure, differences between sexes, and others. These transformations were essential in an environmental context, as they favored advantageous features that allowed our ancestors to survive in their habitats, endure in certain environments, and adjust to new ones.

These changes include the gradual development of traits such as bipedalism which is a form of terrestrial locomotion by means of the two rear

S. Khalifa, *Climate Change, Economic Channels, and Historical Junctures*, https://doi.org/10.1007/978-3-031-91867-4_3

limbs.[3] Bipedal hominins evolved from a knuckle-walking ancestor.[4] Knuckle-walking is a form of quadrupedal locomotion in which the fore-limbs are used in a posture that allows body weight to press down on the knuckles. Bipedalism was favored because it freed the hands to grab and carry food, enabled long-distance hunting and foraging, provided an enhanced field of vision, saved energy during locomotion, helped avoid hyperthermia by decreasing the surface area exposed to direct sun,[5] and allowed hominins to stand up to fight in a hostile environment.[6] In this context, bipedal walking is[7] "associated with reduced energy costs and increased endurance. We suggest that relaxing these constraints provided bipedal hominins important benefits associated with long distance foraging and mobility." Thus, bipedalism[8] "in early, ape-like hominins could indeed have been less costly than quadrupedal knucklewalking," and that[9] "hominin walking was less costly than that of other apes. This supports the hypothesis that locomotor energy economy was an important evolutionary pressure on hominin bipedalism."

Another trait that was favored in this process is dexterity or enhanced ability in performing tasks with hands.[10] Dexterity was essential in evolution since it allowed hominins to create and wield tools for killing large animals for consumption.[11] Shorter fingers and longer opposable thumbs produced a hand assembly that is better at grasping. Without such a precise grip, tool making technology could not have emerged.[12] This also allowed hominins to increase their engagement in other creative activities eventually.

Another favored trait is encephalization or increased brain to body proportion. Encephalization was favored due to the need for solving social problems as human communities became more complex.[13] It is also tied to sociality or the tendency to associate in social groups.[14] This evolutionary aspect is also connected to improved diet, where enhanced levels of knowledge and coordination were essential to exploit the suite of foods humans started to consume.[15]

Decreased sexual dimorphism, which is the existence of differences in physical form between individuals of opposite sex in the same species, was another favored trait.[16] In other words, it is the condition where sexes of the same species have dissimilar features including those not directly related to reproduction. Decreased sexual dimorphism led to lessened male competition for mates. Anthropologist Clark Spencer Larsen proposes that these changes opened a window onto the evolution of human social behavior and cooperation as[17] "[m]onomorphic species of living primates (those taxa exhibiting low levels of sexual dimorphism) tend to express minimal male–male competition, whereas dimorphic species tend to express relatively high levels of competition." Accordingly, this evolutionary trait led to a social structure characterized by cooperating and noncompeting kin groups.

Another favored trait is lengthened ontogeny. Ontogeny refers to the development of an organism over its lifespan or the process through which an organism goes through all developmental stages over its lifetime.[18] Lengthened Ontogeny was essential for the evolution of human intimacy and social cooperation. This is since[19] "(i) human infants' initial skills of shared intentionality are mostly adapted for interaction not with peers but with adults; (ii) infants' engaging with adults in acts of shared intentionality is inherently pleasurable for both parties and so, presumably, serves to enhance their relationship; and (iii) older children begin to develop further skills and motivations for engaging in acts of shared intentionality with peers."

Another activity that contributed to the evolutionary process is hybridization and admixture with other ancient human lineages in the evolution of our species.[20] Hybridization creates new variations and combinations which could boost resilience, especially useful when facing changing or challenging environmental conditions. Thus, hybridization may have provided ancient humans with genetic and anatomical features which afforded them critical advantages that[21] "helped shape our physically diverse and evolutionarily resilient species."

This implies that evolution favored traits that allowed humans to survive in an environment that is ever changing by providing our ancestors with the tools to walk for long distance to be able to find food, to have a long vision to see far in search for food or foes, to grab and carry food, to improve their diet for consumption, to fight adversaries in a never ending competition for survival, to tackle complex social circumstances, to benefit from a more cooperative environment with strong social ties, and to engage in creating and wielding tools. All these transformations and others allowed our ancestors not only to survive in their environment and adapt to an ever changing one, but also to become the more evolved species that have started to leave an indelible mark on their planet.

2 Our Line of Lineage

These findings, and others, were arrived at through evidence extracted from fossils found and studied by scientists and scholars from different fields. According to their findings, we are now the only living members of what many scientists refer to as the human tribe, or hominins. There is plentiful testimony in fossils to indicate that we were preceded for millions of years by other hominins. The oldest known fossil belonging to the human lineage existed around 6–7 million years ago.[22] During that extended time, there were appearances followed by extinctions of multiple members of the human lineage. Thus, our ancestors evolved from one hominin species to another with different anatomical and behavioral characteristics leading to modern humans. In this context, the fossil evidence[23]

> suggests four main stages in hominin evolution: (i) the appearance of the earliest (proto) hominins attributed to the genera Sahelanthropus, Orrorin and Ardipithecus between 4 and 7 Ma, (ii) the appearance of the Australopithecus genus around 4 Ma and the appearance of the robust Paranthropus genus around 2.7 Ma, (iii) the appearance of the genus Homo around the Plio-Pleistocene boundary between 1.8 and 2.5 Ma, and (iv) the appearance of H. heidelbergensis at 800 ka and anatomically modern humans around 200 ka.

The earliest known genus of the human tribe, *Ardipithecus*, lived during the Late Miocene and Early Pliocene epochs.[24] Whether this genus is a hominin or not is an issue of some debate.[25] Within this debate, some scholars argue that the[26] "Ardipithecus ramidus, recovered in ecologically and temporally resolved contexts in Ethiopia's Afar Rift, now illuminates earlier hominid paleobiology and aspects of extant African ape evolution." Others caution about the difficulties in substantiating the claims that *Ardipithecus* is an early member of the hominin clade.[27] The main features of *Ardipithecus* include a small skull.[28] There is other evidence indicative of terrestrial bipedality and upright walking.[29] Dental evidence shows blunt canines[30] and human-like canine sexual dimorphism.[31] This species consumed a predominantly plant-based diet, and its ecological habitat appears to have been largely woodland.[32] This genus combined[33]

> arboreal palmigrade clambering and careful climbing with a form of terrestrial bipedality more primitive than that of Australopithecus. Ar. ramidus had a reduced canine/premolar complex and a little-derived cranial

> morphology and consumed a predominantly C3 plant–based diet (plants using the C3 photosynthetic pathway). Its ecological habitat appears to have been largely woodland-focused. Ar. ramidus lacks any characters typical of suspension, vertical climbing, or knuckle-walking.

According to some, the *Ardipithecus* are the likely ancestors of the *Australopithecus.*[34] The fossils of *Australopithecus* show a genus of early hominins that existed in Africa during the Pliocene and Early Pleistocene. They may have been the first primates to be able to walk upright. Evidence from fossils show a spine with curvatures allowing standing posture and a broad pelvis as leverage for propulsion and balance over the two lower limbs.[35] Compared to modern humans, the *Australopithecus* had a smaller cranial capacity,[36] smaller canine size dimorphism,[37] and a similar skeletal size dimorphism.[38] Analysis of dental microwear and enamel of *Australopithecus* show herbivorous dietary components which include fruits, vegetables, leaves, and tuber.[39] They also lived in a range of heterogeneous environments compared to their predecessors since they were[40] "able to accommodate to periods of directional cooling, climate stability, and high variability."

This was followed by the appearance of the genus *Homo* which includes several extinct species besides the extant Homo sapiens. Scholars discovered the remains of an early hominin species called *Homo habilis* that lived between 2.5 and 1.5 million years ago in Africa in the Early Pleistocene.[41] *Homo habilis* means the handy man. Other anatomical characteristics have been found in *Homo habilis* that differed from those of their ancestors. Those features include long legs which may imply long distance terrestrial travel.[42] However, the *Homo habilis* continued to engage in frequent arboreal activities,[43] since they had proportionally long arms adapted for climbing and swinging. Their features also include an increased cranial capacity with larger brain than their predecessors.[44] The *Homo habilis* are known for making stone tools, known as the Oldowan stone-tool industry, used in butchering since they consumed large quantities of meat from scavenging.[45] Analysis of dental microwear points to an increasingly omnivorous diet.[46] They did not specialize on consuming very hard foods but[47] "ate, at least occasionally, more brittle or tough items than other fossil hominins studied."

This species was followed by *Homo erectus*, which lived almost 2 million years ago in Africa, Asia, and Europe. *Homo erectus* means the upright man because these early hominins walked straight and had a lithe frame resembling later humans. *Homo erectus* had about the same limb configurations as modern humans, implying human-like locomotion.[48] They also featured a larger cranial capacity than that of their forebears,[49] a flatter skull compared to earlier hominins,[50] a projecting nose,[51] and a dentition that indicates they ate more brittle foods that were cooked using fire.[52] *Homo erectus* lived in bands and practiced foraging in coordinated groups.[53] They created tools to help in hunting and are associated with the Acheulian stone-tool industry which developed from the more primitive Oldowan technology.[54] *Homo erectus* moved out of Africa approximately 1.9 million years ago.[55] Thus, this period includes the first hominin exodus out of Africa into Eurasia. This is since the emergence of *Home erectus*[56]

> represents a fundamental turning point in hominin evolution. The dramatic increase in brain size was also accompanied by changes in life history (shortened inter-birth intervals, delayed development), pelvic morphology, body size and dimorphism, shoulder morphology allowing throwing of projectiles, adaptation to long-distance running, ecological flexibility and social behaviour. Some of these changes are consistent with a change in strategy towards flexibility and the ability to colonize novel environments.

Fossils also show another member of our lineage, *Homo neanderthalensis*, who inhabited Eurasia between 250,000 and 200,000 years before present. The Neanderthals lived before and during the last glaciation of the Pleistocene in some of the most unforgiving environments ever inhabited by hominins. Their survival during tens of thousands of years in these harsh climates is a testament to their resilience. Neanderthals started disappearing at different times in different parts of the world but had a significant temporal overlap with anatomically modern humans of about 2600–5400 years.[57] They developed an improved way of life that was based on hunting and local plant collection,[58] fire-making technology,[59] fiber technology,[60] cloth-making technology,[61] healthcare technology,[62] seafaring technology,[63] bone tool technology,[64] and stone tool technology known as the Levallois technique of stone knapping.[65]

Homo heidelbergensis is another extinct species of the homo family that is identified in both Africa and western Eurasia around the Middle Pleistocene.[66] They are commonly seen to have developed from *Homo erectus* and to have paved the way for *Homo sapiens*. However, this is the subject of much debate.[67] They are considered, though, as a distinct species with higher brain capacity than their ancestors. Thus, they were more inventive with sophisticated tools used for hunting strategies involving larger prey animals.[68] This also indicates a potential presence of a higher level of sophistication and social cooperation.

The *Denisovans* are another extinct species who lived nearly 200,000 years ago.[69] They may have been widespread in Asia, especially in Siberia,[70] Southeast Asia,[71] and the Tibetan Plateau.[72] They overlapped with the ancestors of modern-day humans, and there is genetic evidence of their hybridization with modern human populations in Southeast Asia and Oceania.[73] Their complete morphology remains unknown. However, some studies find that[74] "Denisovans likely shared with Neanderthals traits such as an elongated face and a wide pelvis. We also identify Denisovan-derived changes, such as an increased dental arch and lateral cranial expansion."

Homo sapiens, which is Latin for wise man, are the species to which all modern humans belong. *Homo sapiens* is one of several species grouped into the genus *Homo*, but it is the only one that is not extinct. Scholars argue that the features that characterize *Homo sapiens* include[75] "neurocranial globularity, a supraorbital torus divided and central and lateral portions, face retreated below the forepart of the brain, a bony chin even in infants, a gracile tympanic bone, the absence of the iliac pillar, and a short and thickened superior pubic ramus." Characterized by their high intelligence compared to their predecessors, this species has advanced cognitive abilities to thrive and adapt in varied environments, has lots of curiosity to understand surroundings and influence phenomena, and has the desire to develop highly complex tools and to form sophisticated social structures. They also constructed their own shelters eventually forming settlements that evolved into great civilizations. Some scholars show that genetic evolution contributed to a healthier longevity for modern humans, which was a factor for the development of creativity:[76]

> Living longer, healthier lives may have promoted and valorized the extended periods of juvenile and adolescent learning that allow the accumulation of knowledge that is such a remarkable feature of behaviorally modern humans, and that is such an important factor in the economic success and complex social structures and relationships of Homo sapiens. It may also have encouraged cooperation among individuals to promote the success of their children, grandchildren, and others in their extended communities, enabling the technological innovativeness, behavioral flexibility, and exploratory

disposition needed to allow Homo sapiens to spread throughout the world more successfully than other human lineages.

3 No Escape from Our Surrounding

Going back that far, it is natural to surmise that species evolve due to changes in their surrounding environment. If the context in which we live is static, we can continue to survive with the current devices we are endowed with. Thus, there will be no need for adaptation. If the surrounding environment is constantly changing, however, adaptation becomes essential for survival. One of the most important components of our natural environment is climate. Climate has been a constant companion to humanity in its long journey. It does not only determine long-term patterns of weather conditions that humans have to live with, but also the habitat in which we live in and the faunal and floral varieties upon which humans can depend on for survival. Thus, fluctuations in climate can create new conditions to which humans have to adapt to, escape from, or perish altogether. Notable hominin speciation, extinction, and other evolutionary events appear to be associated with changes in climate in the past 5 million years. In this context, human history from the outset is tightly connected with changes in climate such that[77]

> [c]limate change influenced and, in several periods, helped create the pressures for the natural selection that led to the emergence of humans. The cooling and drying that shrank the rain forests of Africa created an advantage for individuals who could eat a wide array of food in more broken forests. In turn, living in and near the savannas created advantages for individuals better able to move long distances in search of prey and for individuals better able to communicate and work together. Cooling in African habitats was a major force that helped lead to the emergence of australopiths and to the later rise of *Homo erectus*. The pattern of glacial and interglacial oscillations affected *Homo erectus* and the species that emerged from *Homo erectus*, including *Homo sapiens* and our closest human relatives.

The association between climate change and hominin evolution has generated numerous hypotheses. These include ideas that depend on the concept of adaptability or the flexibility of a population in the face of the surrounding conditions. This can enhance the ability of the members of that population to endure variations in their environment, to survive in novel conditions, to disperse to new habitats, or to respond in new ways to their changing surroundings.

Scientists posit that the primary mechanism by which organisms adapt to their environment is natural selection, which is the process by which new adaptive tools evolve. The adaptation of an organism to its environment occurs by recreating changes in its genotype or genetic constitution. Those variations in the genotype, through mutation and recombination, increase an organism's chances of continuation and procreation. Mutation refers to changes in the genetic sequence which cause diversity within organisms. Recombination is the exchange of genetic elements between different organisms leading to combinations of traits in offsprings that differ from those found in either parent. These genetic variations are maintained and multiplied from one generation to another at the expense of less advantageous ones. Thus, an organism's environment selects the traits that proliferate across a population and persist over time. Organisms that are more adapted to their environment are more likely to subsist and pass on the genes that contributed to their success. In the words of paleoanthropologist Ian Tattersall,[78]

> natural selection is simply the preferential survival and reproduction of individuals that are better "adapted" to their environments than their fellows, in features inherited from their parents. And it is pretty much a mathematical consequence of the fact that, in all species, each generation produces more offspring than survive to reproduce. The idea here is that, over enough time, those with more advantageous inherited characteristics will have greater reproductive success, and therefore will nudge the population in the direction of better adaptation. In this way, members of the lineage will change in average appearance and ultimately evolve into a new species.

In another contribution, Ian Tattersall clarifies further the process through which natural selection transforms species over time by stating that[79]

> in any variable population some individuals are inevitably better endowed than others in hereditary traits that enhance their survival and reproduction; and because those better adapted ("fitter") individuals will survive and reproduce more successfully than the rest, their descendants and their favorable traits will inevitably multiply in the population with the passage of time and the generations, even as inferior adaptations disappear. Repeated over enough generations, this blind natural process of selection of fitter individuals

> will slowly and inevitably transform each species/lineage, with only time and circumstance limiting the amount of accumulated change possible.

Shifts in climatic conditions can, thus, offer opportunities for natural selection. In this context, there are two approaches to viewing the association between the environment and this evolutionary process. The first argues that evolution occurs due to a change in climatic conditions. This implies that climate change can lead to novel conditions that necessitate a way to adapt to them. The second argues that it is not the change in climate, but rather the variability in climate change, that leads to such situations where adaptability becomes essential for sustenance. The former is referred to as the Habitat-Specific hypotheses, and the latter as the Variability Selection hypotheses. Each deserves to be discussed in detail in the coming sections.

4 Habitat-Specific Hypotheses

Some views on this issue can be considered under the Habitat-Specific hypotheses. Each of these scenarios point to a particular type of habitat with climatic conditions in which hominins were assumed to live and then sets forth the causes certain adaptations emerge to satisfy the specific demands of that setting. Other scenarios identify a specific direction of climate change, like the onset of new climatic conditions. This leads to adaptations needed to satisfy the demands of the new setting. In either case, natural selection improves the adaptive opportunities as a way of addressing the challenges posed by a particular habitat or those imposed by an altering trend from one habitat to another. In other words, the prevailing view of the Habitat-Specific hypotheses is that adaptations evolve in reaction to problems posed by a specific environmental situation or by consistent trends from one environmental condition to another.

In this context, some studies advocate a Woodland-Forest hypothesis based on the observation that early hominins lived in wooded environments, engaged in arboreal activity, and were adapted to closed habitats. To provide evidence that hominins lived in such a habitat, paleontologists Richard Rayner and Ann Cadman examine sediments in Makapansgat in South Africa, where remains of *Australopithecus africanus* were found.[80] The authors show that the palynological[81] evidence suggests that the preferred habitat of this species was "forest or forest margin." In a related paper, Richard Rayner and other scholars conclude that a reconstruction of the Makapansgat valley when it was occupied by *Australopithecus africanus* indicates conditions that supported patches of[82] "subtropical forest and thick bush."

Life in these closed habitats was followed by another where hominins inhabited a more open environment. This is known as the Savanna hypothesis which posits that life in the open savanna was the context that triggered the emergence of fundamental human traits that allowed them to live in that type of environment.[83] According to this hypothesis, hominins left the arboreal lifestyle in the forests that had previously been their natural habitat for millions of years and adapted to a new one in the savannas. This adaptation to drier, more arid, and open environments was the background for hominin evolution turnover events, especially the transition to *Homo*. In a synthesis of the various theories on human evolution, some scholars point out that the Savanna hypothesis suggests that[84]

> hominins were forced to descend from the trees and adapted to life on the savannah facilitated by walking erect on two feet. This theory was refined as the aridity hypothesis, which suggested that the long-term trend towards increased aridity and the expansion of the savannah was a major driver of hominin evolution. A key addition to this theory was the suggestion that during periods when aridification accelerated, owing to thresholds in the global climate system, then thresholds in evolution were reached and major hominin speciation events occurred.

In this context, some studies examine whether the evolutionary transition from *Australopithecus* to *Homo* in Africa was associated with the spread of open and arid environments during the Pliocene–Pleistocene. For instance, anthropologist Kaye Reed compares mammal fossil assemblages from East and South Africa with multiple extant mammalian communities from different habitats.[85] The author, then, derives the vegetative habitat of these fossil assemblages based on each species' current favorite ecological conditions. These reconstructions show that the *Australopithecus* existed in wooded and amply watered areas, while *Homo* was the first hominid to exist in areas of extremely arid and open landscapes.

In another study, Kaye Reed and other scholars examine 2.84–2.58-million-year-old vertebrate fossil and hominin-bearing sediments in the Ledi-Geraru area of Afar in Ethiopia.[86] This is an area where the earliest record of the genus *Homo* was found.[87] The authors find that these fossils show a faunal turnover indicative of more open and arid habitats than those reconstructed for earlier periods. In yet another article, Kaye Reed and other scholars use mammalian fauna, from Ledi-Geraru and the Turkana Basin, to construct a record of climate change in the late Pliocene.[88] The authors conclude that their data "indicates a trend towards more open, arid, and seasonal environments in the LAV (Lower Awash Valley) and Turkana Basin."

In a similar vein, paleoclimatologist Peter deMenocal attempts to define climate change in Africa in the last 5 million years using sediments off the subtropical African coast.[89] The study shows that African climate became cooler and drier about 2.8 million years ago. This led to the expansion of arid-adapted flora and fauna, since a pollen record indicates that[90] "humid taxa were replaced by arid-adapted taxa between 3.2 and 2.6 million years ago." In a related paper, Peter deMenocal finds that the paleoclimatic records from marine sediment sequences show that shifts toward increasingly drier conditions were accompanied by some changes in African faunal assemblages.[91] These long-term trends[92] "toward increased abundances of arid-adapted taxa during the Pliocene-Pleistocene are evident, with indications for faunal changes between 2.9 and 2.4 Ma (the age range encompassing major faunal transitions) and after 1.8 Ma."

Despite this evidence, the Savanna hypothesis has been challenged by other scholars since data collected from some hominid sites suggest that the shift to open landscapes and grass-dominated environments happened later than previously thought. Some of this evidence is provided by geologist Thure Cerling who uses a stable carbon isotopic composition of paleosol, or buried soil, carbonates from fossil localities in East Africa to conclude that[93] "there is no evidence for a relatively pure C_4 grassland until about 1 Ma. These results suggest that the Serengeti-type grassland may be a relatively recent phenomena in East Africa." In another study, Thure Cerling, Nancy Sikes, and other scholars examine stable carbon isotopic composition from paleosol carbonates at Fort Ternan in western Kenya and show that their evidence[94] "demonstrates a woodland or forest setting rather than a wooded grassland habitat for Fort Ternan." In the same vein, Nancy Sikes examines stable isotopic composition of paleosol carbonates collected from trenches excavated at the Olduvai Gorge in Tanzania to show that[95] "Plio-Pleistocene hominids in East Africa may have preferred relatively closed woodland habitats that may have offered food, shade, and predator and sleeping refuge." This evidence shows that the transition from a closed to an open environment occurred later than previously concluded and accordingly cannot be attributed the contribution it was assumed in the evolutionary process.

Despite the views that advocate the idea that the evolutionary events occurred due to a change in human habitat from woodland forest to open landscapes, other scholars argue that our ancestors adapted to diverse habitats and that the course of human evolution[96] "should be considered within the context of a heterogeneous mosaic of environments rather than an abrupt replacement of rain forests by grassland and wood-land biomes."

There is also a debate about whether evolutionary events occur due to sudden shifts in the environment or due to a continuous process of change. In this context, the first view is the Turnover Pulse hypothesis. The essence of this hypothesis is that bursts of biotic change,[97] or turnover, were prompted by fundamental shifts in climate. This hypothesis was formulated by paleontologist Elisabeth Vrba, who proposes that sudden directional changes in habitat induce an array of evolutionary consequences and high turnover of new species in a brief period.[98] An alternative to this view is the Red Queen hypothesis, formulated by evolutionary biologist Leigh Van Valen, which proposes that extinction occurs in a constant turnover instead of pulses.[99] According to this opinion, species must constantly adapt to survive against ever-evolving opposing species. Thus, the Red Queen hypothesis suggests that[100] "continued adaptation is needed in order for a species to maintain its relative fitness among co-evolving systems and that biotic interactions, rather than climate, are driving evolutionary forces."

Some studies, however, challenge this entire turnover approach. For instance, testing the underlying premise of the turnover hypothesis using faunal records from South Africa shows that[101] "climate change drives faunal turnover in the form of migration and extinction, but the role of climate as a driver of speciation remains uncertain." Some scholars also examine a sample of fossils from localities in the Turkana Basin of Kenya and Ethiopia and show that[102] "late Pliocene evolution in East Africa was affected by the cumulative ecological consequences of cooler, drier, and more variable climatic conditions rather than by a sudden change toward open habitats."

5 Variability Selection Hypotheses

Another view on the association between climate and evolution argues that important adaptive alterations arise in response to environmental variability rather than climate change. Thus, organisms are adapted not to the variation per se but to the pattern of variation. In this context, the Variability hypotheses can be divided into short-term or seasonal variations and long-term or variability selection.

The short-term seasonality hypothesis pays special attention to variations experienced by an organism over the span of its lifetime, especially seasonal fluctuations or changes from one year to another. This approach places emphasis on variations in the lifetime adaptive setting of an organism or how a living organism adjusts to alternative environments during its life cycle. This is because these fluctuations have a significant effect on the lives of these organisms. For instance, short-term variations in climate could lead to critical shifts within each year in the abundance of vital supplies and the availability of essential resources. These types of shifts demand adaptations that ensure the survival of the species.

The long-term perspective is often referred to as the Variability Selection hypothesis. This highlights the significance of changes in climatic variability, in terms of amplitudes and durations of departures from the mean climatic state, on evolution. Thus, this hypothesis focuses on two aspects of climate change. The first is the extent of deviation from the average climatic conditions, or amplitude. The second is the recurrence of such patterns over time, or frequency. According to this view, these environmental variations are accentuated over time. During those periods when climate variability changed drastically, events of speciation, adaptation, and extinction occur.

Accordingly, this is the first hypothesis to invoke the idea that amplified environmental dynamics can potentially lead to an enhancement in the adaptive versatility of hominins and how they interact with their surroundings. Climate variability could result in resource uncertainty and other disruptions to the environmental setup that is pertinent to the survival of living organisms. Adaptation in this context enables the organism to call upon an enlarged variety of options, allows it to alter its resource base, induces it to diversify its social behavior, and permits it to buffer the impacts of unpredictable situations or novel environmental conditions. This process of adaptive evolution enhances an organism's capacity to thrive in novel conditions, including ones never previously encountered, and to out-compete others that only succeed in a narrower array of survival conditions. Thus,[103] "human environmental adaptations are closely associated with strong, complex variability in the settings inhabited by early hominins. Evolutionary processes favored any response that could enhance survival in a changing world."

In other terms, a lineage of an organism may face substantial disparities in their environment over time. Thus, different generations of the same lineage may experience stark inconsistencies in their adaptive setting. This shapes a selective environment which ultimately favors genes that provide tools of adaptive versatility. Thus,[104] "individuals of a lineage living at different times experience different adaptive conditions. Over a span of recurrent extremes, some gene combinations and complex behaviors may be favored that enable resilient and novel responses to new conditions." In other words, individuals of a lineage[105] "experience maximally different adaptive conditions at widely different times. As a result, certain genetic combinations and developmental patterns are favored that build mechanisms designed for complex response to novel or unpredictable environmental information." This implies that[106] "[e]arly bipedality, stone transport, diversification of artifact contexts, encephalization, and enhanced cognitive and social functioning all may reflect adaptations to environmental novelty and highly varying selective contexts."

An offshoot of this view is the Pulsed Climate Variability hypothesis which suggests that the long-term drying trend in East Africa was interrupted by episodes of short alternating periods of extreme humidity and aridity which may have driven hominin speciation. This hypothesis emphasizes[107] "the role of short periods of extreme climate variability specific to East Africa in driving hominin evolution."

6 Thus, Spoke the Fossils

Increased research efforts using reliable proxies for paleoclimatic[108] conditions have provided a growing body of data with which to test such hypotheses. These studies attempt to recreate the climate in ancient times. Then, they determine whether incidents of climate change coincide with major events in evolution, especially periods of appearance and disappearance of hominin lineages. Many of these studies provide support for the Variability Selection hypothesis by showing that major evolutionary events coincided with periods of high-amplitude and high-frequency climate variability. Amplitude and frequency are both characteristics of waves.

While amplitude is the distance between the wave's lowest point and highest displacement, the frequency is the number of waves that pass a specific point in a period of time.

6.1 *High Amplitude*

Some studies provide evidence for the coincidence between periods of high climate variability and approximate dates of the appearance and disappearance of human lineages. In this context, scholars focus on studying the past 5 million years which is the period where major evolutionary events occurred. For instance, Richard Potts and Tyler Faith attempt to define the time boundaries of periods of climate variability and test the hominin evolutionary response to repeated transitions between low and high variability.[109] Using deep-sea evidence, sapropels,[110] stratigraphic observations,[111] and paleoclimatic records from different sources, the authors show a significant association between first and last appearance datums of major hominin lineages and intervals of prolonged high climate variability. This is since[112] "the novel suites of behavior signaled by the onset and spread of the Oldowan, Acheulean, Middle Stone Age, and Late Stone Age in East Africa corresponded with long duration phases of high environmental variability, as did the first appearances of each of the three genera Australopithecus (Australopithecus anamensis), Paranthropus (P. aethiopicus), and early Homo." This is attributed to the association between climate variability and resource instability which provided a test of adaptability and survival strategies such that the[113] "most prolonged eras of magnified environmental variability may have offered the most likely opportunities for novel strategies of adaptive versatility and cultural buffering to take hold and proliferate."

Other studies provide evidence for the coincidence between periods of high climate variability and hominin species turnovers and dispersal out of Africa. For instance, some scholars analyze organic geochemical indicators of climate from West Turkana of Kenya that spans the period from 1.9 to 1.4 million years before present.[114] An interval of particularly high-amplitude hydrologic variation at around 1.7 million years ago is observed to overlap with multiple hominin species turnovers, the appearance of new stone tool technology, and hominin dispersal out of Africa. This evidence supports the notion that these hydrological changes played a critical role in hominin evolution by altering vegetation structure, habitats, and resource supply. In addition, changes in hydrological features such as large lakes can act as physical barriers in some cases or as an alley allowing population mixing in others. These could also drive evolutionary changes. The authors conclude that the[115] "~1.8-1.7 Ma interval coincides with multiple shifts in the hominin fossil record in the Turkana Basin and the H. erectus dispersal out of Africa. We suggest that the rapid, extreme climate shifts may have driven these changes in fossil hominins towards enhanced adaptability." Thus, the analysis[116] "lends support to the variability selection hypothesis, which is consistent with the relationship between hominin evolution and regional climate offered by our observations of paleohydrology in the Turkana Basin."

Some studies show a coincidence between high climate variability and the first evidence of *Homo sapiens.* Focusing on the last one million years which is the period of Homo evolution, Richard Potts, Peter deMenocal, and other scholars attempt to identify the potential connections between the anatomical and behavioral developments in Homo and the changes in climatic conditions that may have affected East Africa.[117] To quantify environmental variation, the authors examine a sediment core spanning the last one million years that was extracted from the Koora Basin which is adjacent to the archaeological site of Olorgesailie in the Kenya Rift. The study provides evidence for an increase in environmental variability throughout the mid-to-late Pleistocene, with a particularly high-amplitude environmental variability interval occurring from about 275,000 to 180,000 years ago. This event coincides with evidence for the first *Homo sapien* fossils in East Africa when the landscape and resource base became less dependable due to these unstable conditions. Thus, their evidence demonstrates that[118] "major evolutionary events, including the first evidence of traits associated with H. sapiens in eastern Africa, occur in the context of large landscape and resource fluctuations. The progressive increase in variance could indicate that hominins and other species experienced an increasingly unstable resource base over the last 1 Myr, culminating in the selection of generalist morphologies and traits of plasticity."[119]

6.2 *High Frequency*

It is not only the amplitude of climate variability that matters, but scholars also focus on frequency which refers in this context to the time scale. In our context, some studies compare the effects of different time scales, secular or orbital, in assessing the association between environmental variability and hominin evolution. Secular climate variability refers to long-term climate trends or changes that occur slowly over a long period of time spanning millions of years. Secular variations are, thus, of low frequency. On the other hand, orbital-scale climate variability is a cyclical pattern of climate change, caused by changes in the orbit of the Earth, which happens on a shorter time scale from tens of thousands to hundreds of thousands of years. These variations are of high frequency. In this context, there is evidence in favor of a significant effect of high frequency changes on the evolutionary journey of humanity.

For instance, some scholars compile a composite history of African environmental variability spanning the Pliocene-Pleistocene epoch to estimate its association with faunal speciation and extinction from East Africa.[120] Their findings[121] "do not eliminate the possibility that higher-frequency variability (e.g., eccentricity- or precession scale), which is clearly evident in our composite record in the 20-ky bin analysis, drove faunal turnover events during the Plio-Pleistocene.[122] Indeed, empirical data compilations suggest that some aspects of variability selection could play out on these shorter timescales."

Other scholars present evidence of vegetation alteration in the late Pliocene derived from a drill core from the Chemeron Formation located in the Baringo Basin of the Kenya Rift Valley.[123] Their data show a secular change where vegetation in that area turned to grasslands, as part of a larger-scale drying trend in East Africa. Besides this long-term trend, orbital-scale variations in precipitation also caused significant changes in vegetation during the late Pliocene. By comparing the two types of changes, orbitally driven solar insolation changes were found to have a larger effect. This is because these variations led to changes in resource supply which necessitated a change in foraging strategies as evidenced by the hominin fossils. Therefore, the[124] "shift in mean vegetation at ~3.04 Ma, and the persistently high environmental variability throughout our record, suggest that high frequency, high-amplitude changes in vegetation could have been the environmental stressor that drove hominin evolutionary transitions."

6.3 Amplifier Lakes

The East African Rift system was home to large numbers of "amplifier lakes" that formed briefly during short intervals of high precipitation and then evaporated quickly. Lacustrine sediments show that water availability fluctuated dramatically as can be seen in shifts from deep freshwater lakes to shallow lakes to completely desiccated ones. Fast changes in freshwater availability may have exerted severe environmental stress on humans and entailed high levels of adaptability from those living in the area. These basins, when extremely dry or filled, also form important barriers for mobility and mixing of populations. These findings led some to develop an evolutionary hypothesis based on the amplifier lakes dynamics. Some of these scholars propose that the record of these ephemeral lakes could be a proxy for the paleoclimate conditions experienced by early hominins.[125] The proposed model[126]

> of amplifier lakes serving as natural barriers, aggravated by cultural differences between highly mobile organisms such as humans living on both sides of the barrier might have contributed to habitat fragmentation, to reducing migration, expansion and dispersals of animals including humans and therefore increase biodiversity in the surroundings of the rift valley. The East African amplifier lakes are therefore a keystone in this scenario and may help explain why East Africa eventually became the place where early humans evolved.

To provide evidence for this hypothesis, the climate of East Africa is examined using paleoclimate records from fluviolacustrine sediments collected from ten exposed lake basins in the Ethiopian, Kenyan, and Tanzanian Rifts.[127] The study finds that the climate of East Africa experienced a long-term drying trend punctuated by episodes of short alternating periods of extreme wetness and dryness. The authors pinpoint these periods of extreme climate variability at 2.7–2.5, 1.9–1.7, and 1.1–0.9 million years before present which[128] "may have provided a catalyst for evolutionary change and driven key speciation and dispersal events amongst mammals and hominins in East Africa." In this context, ephemeral lakes[129] "expanding and contracting on precessional timescales, would have evoked the widespread, regional-scale, rapid, and extreme environmental variability, required by the Variability Selection Hypothesis of human evolution."

In a related paper, the climate history of East Africa is examined from lake sediments in ten Ethiopian, Kenyan, and Tanzanian rift basins.[130] The data suggest that there were three humid periods during 2.7–2.5, 1.9–1.7, and 1.1–0.9 million years before present, within the longer-term aridification trend of East Africa. These humid periods could have had important implications on hominin speciation since the origin of the genus *Homo* coincides with that time frame. If these lakes[131] "are ephemeral features of the landscape forced by precession, that strongly supports the Variability Hypothesis of human evolution, because the environment inside the East African Rift Valley would have varied rapidly between sustained humid and arid periods, providing the stress required to initiate speciation."

6.4 Conclusion

Despite the sheer evidence supporting the association between environmental variability and evolution, there is one study that focuses on its influence on mammalian macroevolution in Africa.[132] The study develops a composite history of environmental variability spanning the last 5.3 million years, relying on terrestrial records from 17 African locations. The authors find a long-term trend of increasing variability starting from 3.75 million years before present. Analyzing a fossil dataset for eastern African mammals, the authors do not find a statistically significant association between environmental variability and estimated speciation or extinction. These findings[133] "do not currently support hypotheses linking EV (environmental variability) with macroevolutionary aspects of faunal turnover in the African fossil record." Despite this conclusion, the authors also add that these findings[134] "do not eliminate the possibility that higher-frequency variability (e.g., eccentricity- or precession-scale), which is clearly evident in our composite record in the 20-ky bin analysis, drove faunal turnover events during the Plio-Pleistocene." They also do not dismiss the possibility that heightened environmental variability might have microevolutionary implications and recommend more rigorous testing using better fossil records. Thus, this study cannot be used to dismiss completely the Variability Selection hypothesis. It only calls for a more scrupulous approach to testing the evolutionary impact of environmental variability.

Notes

1. Nick Patterson, Daniel Richter, Sante Gnerre, Eric Lander, and David Reich. "Genetic Evidence for Complex Speciation of Humans and Chimpanzees." Nature, 441, 7097: 1103–1108, 2006.
2. Céline M. Vida, Christine S. Lane, Asfawossen Asrat, Dan N. Barfod, Darren F. Mark, Emma L. Tomlinson, Amdemichael Zafu Tadesse, Gezahegn Yirgu, Alan Deino, William Hutchison, Aurélien Mounier, and

Clive Oppenheimer. "Age of the Oldest Known Homo Sapiens from Eastern Africa." Nature, 601, 7894: 579–583, 2022.

3. W. E. H. Harcourt-Smith and L. C. Aiello. "Fossils, Feet and the Evolution of Human Bipedal Locomotion." Journal of Anatomy, 204: 403–416, 2004. William H. E. Harcourt-Smith. "The First Hominins and the Origins of Bipedalism." Evolution Education and Outreach, 3: 333–340, 2010.
4. Brian Richmond and David Strait. "Evidence that Humans Evolved from a Knuckle-walking Ancestor." Nature, 404: 382–385, 2000.
5. Tamas David-Barrett and Robin I.M. Dunbar. "Bipedality and Hair Loss in Human Evolution Revisited: The Impact of Altitude and Activity Scheduling." Journal of Human Evolution, 94: 72–82, 2016.
6. David Carrier. "The Advantage of Standing Up to Fight and the Evolution of Habitual Bipedalism in Hominins." PLOS One, 6, 5: e19630, 2011.
7. David Raichlen and Herman Pontzer. "Energetic and Endurance Constraints on Great Ape Quadrupedalism and the Benefits of Hominin Bipedalism." Evolutionary Anthropology, 30, 4: 253–261, 2021.
8. Michael Sockol, David Raichlen, and Herman Pontzer. "Chimpanzee Locomotor Energetics and the Origin of Human Bipedalism." PNAS, 104, 30: 12265–12269, 2007.
9. Herman Pontzer, David Raichlen, and Michael Sockol. "The Metabolic Cost of Walking in Humans, Chimpanzees, and Early Hominins." Journal of Human Evolution, 56, 1: 43–54, 2009.
10. Fotios Alexandros Karakostis, Daniel Haeufle, Ioanna Anastopoulou, Konstantinos Moraitis, Gerhard Hotz, Vangelis Tourloukis, and Katerina Harvati. "Biomechanics of the Human Thumb and the Evolution of Dexterity." Current Biology, 31, 6: 1317–1325, 2021.
11. Fotios Alexandros Karakostis, Daniel Haeufle, Ioanna Anastopoulou, Konstantinos Moraitis, Gerhard Hotz, Vangelis Tourloukis, and Katerina Harvati. "Biomechanics of the Human Thumb and the Evolution of Dexterity." Current Biology 31: 1317–1325, 2021.
12. Matthew M Skinner, Nicholas B Stephens, Zewdi J Tsegai, Alexandra C Foote, N Huynh Nguyen, Thomas Gross, Dieter H Pahr, Jean-Jacques Hublin, and Tracy L Kivell. "Human Evolution. Human-like Hand Use in Australopithecus Africanus." Science, 347, 6220: 395–399, 2015. Tracy L Kivell, Job M Kibii, Steven E Churchill, Peter Schmid, and Lee R Berger. "Australopithecus Sediba Hand Demonstrates Mosaic Evolution of Locomotor and Manipulative Abilities." Science, 333, 6048: 1411–1417, 2011.
13. Markus Bastir, Antonio Rosas, Philipp Gunz, Angel Peña-Melian, Giorgio Manzi, Katerina Harvati, Robert Kruszynski, Chris Stringer, and Jean-

Jacques Hublin. "Evolution of the Base of the Brain in Highly Encephalized Human Species." Nature Communications, 2, 588, 2011.

14. Susanne Shultz and Robin Dunbar. "Encephalization is not a Universal Macroevolutionary Phenomenon in Mammals but is Associated with Sociality." PNAS, 107, 50: 21582–21586, 2010. Robin Dunbar. "Neocortex Size as a Constraint on Group Size in Primates." Journal of Human Evolution, 22, 6: 469–493, 1992.
15. Roberto Carlos Burini and William R. Leonard. "The Evolutionary Roles of Nutrition Selection and Dietary Quality in the Human Brain Size and Encephalization." Nutrire, 43, 19, 2018. Jennifer Fish and Charles Lockwood. "Dietary Constraints on Encephalization in Primates." American Journal of Physical Anthropology, 120, 2: 171–181, 2003.
16. George Armelagos and Dennis Van Gerven. "Sexual Dimorphism and Human Evolution: An Overview." Journal of Human Evolution, 9, 5: 437–446, 1980.
17. Clark Spencer Larsen. "Equality for the Sexes in Human Evolution? Early Hominid Sexual Dimorphism and Implications for Mating Systems and Social Behavior." PNAS, 100, 16: 9103–9104, 2003.
18. Christoph P. E. Zollikofer, Thibault Bienvenu, Yonas Beyene, Gen Suwa, Berhane Asfaw, Tim D. White, and Marcia S. Ponce de Leon. "Endocranial Ontogeny and Evolution in Early Homo Sapiens: The Evidence from Herto, Ethiopia." PNAS, 119, 32, e2123553119, 2022. Naoki Morimoto, Masato Nakatsukasa, Marcia S. Ponce de León, and Christoph P. E. Zollikofer. "Femoral Ontogeny in Humans and Great Apes and its Implications for their Last Common Ancestor." Nature, Scientific Reports, 8, 1930, 2018.
19. Michael Tomasello and Ivan Gonzalez-Cabrera. "The Role of Ontogeny in the Evolution of Human Cooperation." Human Nature, 28, 3: 274–288, 2017.
20. Rebecca Rogers Ackermann, Alex Mackay, and Michael L. Arnold. "The Hybrid Origin of "Modern" Humans." Evolutionary Biology, 43: 1–11, 2016. Rebecca R. Ackermann, Michael L. Arnold, Marcella D. Baiz, James A. Cahill, Liliana Cortés-Ortiz, Ben J. Evans, B. Rosemary Grant, Peter R. Grant, Benedikt Hallgrimsson, Robyn A. Humphreys, Clifford J. Jolly, Joanna Malukiewicz, Christopher J. Percival, Terrence B. Ritzman, Christian Roos, Charles C. Roseman, Lauren Schroeder, Fred H. Smith, Kerryn A. Warren, Robert K. Wayne, and Dietmar Zinner. "Hybridization in Human Evolution: Insights from Other Organisms." Evolutionary Anthropology, 28, 4: 189–209, 2019. Rebecca Rogers Ackermann, Jeffrey Rogers, and James M Cheverud. "Identifying the Morphological Signatures of Hybridization in Primate and Human Evolution." Journal of Human Evolution, 51, 6: 632–645, 2006.

21. K. Harvati and Rebecca Ackermann. "Merging Morphological and Genetic Evidence to Assess Hybridization in Western Eurasian Late Pleistocene Hominins." Nature Ecology and Evolution, 6: 1573–1585, 2022.
22. Michel Brunet, Franck Guy, David Pilbeam, Hassane Taisso Mackaye, Andossa Likius, Djimdoumalbaye Ahounta, Alain Beauvilain, Cécile Blondel, Hervé Bocherens, Jean-Renaud Boisserie, Louis De Bonis, Yves Coppens, Jean Dejax, Christiane Denys, Philippe Duringer, Véra Eisenmann, Gongdibé Fanone, Pierre Fronty, Denis Geraads, Thomas Lehmann, Fabrice Lihoreau, Antoine Louchart, Adoum Mahamat, Gildas Merceron, and Christoph Zollikofer. "A New Hominid from the Upper Miocene of Chad, Central Africa." Nature, 418: 145–151, 2002. Michel Brunet, Franck Guy, David Pilbeam, Daniel E. Lieberman, Andossa Likius, Hassane T. Mackaye, Marcia S. Ponce de León, Christoph P. E. Zollikofer, and Patrick Vignaud. "New Material of the Earliest Hominid from the Upper Miocene of Chad." Nature, 434: 752–755, 2005.
23. Mark Maslin, Susanne Schultz, and Martin Trauth. "A Synthesis of the Theories and Concepts of Early Human Evolution." Philosophical Transactions Royal Society B, 370, 1663: 20140064, 2015.
24. Owen Lovejoy. "Reexamining Human Origins in Light of Ardipithecus Ramidus." Science, 326, 5949: 74–74e8, 2009. Owen Lovejoy, Gen Suwa, Scott W Simpson, Jay H Matternes, and Tim D White. "The Great Divides: Ardipithecus Ramidus Reveals the Postcrania of Our Last Common Ancestors with African Apes." Science, 326, 5949: 100–106, 2009.
25. Tim D. White, C. Owen Lovejoy, Berhane Asfaw, Joshua P. Carlson, and Gen Suwa. "Neither Chimpanzee nor Human, Ardipithecus Reveals the Surprising Ancestry of Both." PNAS, 112, 16: 4877–4884, 2015.
26. Tim D White, Berhane Asfaw, Yonas Beyene, Yohannes Haile-Selassie, C Owen Lovejoy, Gen Suwa, and Giday Wolde Gabriel. "Ardipithecus Ramidus and the Paleobiology of Early Hominids." Science, 326, 5949: 75–86, 2009.
27. Bernard Wood and Terry Harrison. "The Evolutionary Context of the First Hominins." Nature, 470: 347–352, 2011.
28. Gen Suwa, Berhane Asfaw, Reiko T Kono, Daisuke Kubo, C Owen Lovejoy, and Tim D White. "The Ardipithecus Ramidus Skull and its Implications for Hominid Origins." Science, 326, 68e1–68e7, 2009.
29. C. Owen Lovejoy, Gen Suwa, Linda Spurlock, Berhane Asfaw, and Tim D White. "The Pelvis and Femur of Ardipithecus Ramidus: the Emergence of Upright Walking." Science, 326, 71e1–71e6, 2009. C Owen Lovejoy, Bruce Latimer, Gen Suwa, Berhane Asfaw, and Tim D White. "Combining

Prehension and Propulsion: The Foot of Ardipithecus Ramidus." Science, 326, 72e1–72e8, 2009.
30. Gen Suwa, Reiko T Kono, Scott W Simpson, Berhane Asfaw, C Owen Lovejoy, and Tim D White. "Paleobiological Implications of the Ardipithecus Ramidus Dentition." Science, 326: 94–99, 2009. Yohannes Haile-Selassie, Gen Suwa, and Tim D White. "Late Miocene Teeth from Middle Awash, Ethiopia, and Early Hominid Dental Evolution." Science, 303, 5663: 1503–1505, 2004.
31. Gen Suwa, Tomohiko Sasaki, Sileshi Semaw, Michael J Rogers, Scott W Simpson, Yutaka Kunimatsu, Masato Nakatsukasa, Reiko T Kono, Yingqi Zhang, Yonas Beyene, Berhane Asfaw, and Tim D White. "Canine Sexual Dimorphism in Ardipithecus Ramidus was Nearly Human-like." PNAS, 118, 49: e2116630118, 2021.
32. Tim D White, Berhane Asfaw, Yonas Beyene, Yohannes Haile-Selassie, C Owen Lovejoy, Gen Suwa, and Giday Wolde Gabriel. "Ardipithecus Ramidus and the Paleobiology of Early Hominids." Science, 326, 5949: 75–86, 2009. Tim D White, Stanley H Ambrose, Gen Suwa, Denise F Su, David DeGusta, Raymond L Bernor, Jean-Renaud Boisserie, Michel Brunet, Eric Delson, Stephen Frost, Nuria Garcia, Ioannis X Giaourtsakis, Yohannes Haile-Selassie, F Clark Howell, Thomas Lehmann, Andossa Likius, Cesur Pehlevan, Haruo Saegusa, Gina Semprebon, Mark Teaford, and Elisabeth Vrba. "Macrovertebrate Paleontology and the Pliocene Habitat of Ardipithecus Ramidus." Science, 326, 5949: 87–93, 2009. Giday Wolde Gabriel, Stanley H Ambrose, Doris Barboni, Raymonde Bonnefille, Laurent Bremond, Brian Currie, David DeGusta, William K Hart, Alison M Murray, Paul R Renne, M C Jolly-Saad, Kathlyn M Stewart, and Tim D White. "The Geological, Isotopic, Botanical, Invertebrate, and Lower Vertebrate Surroundings of Ardipithecus Ramidus." Science, 326, 5949: 65e1–5, 2009.
33. Tim D White, Berhane Asfaw, Yonas Beyene, Yohannes Haile-Selassie, C Owen Lovejoy, Gen Suwa, and Giday Wolde Gabriel. "Ardipithecus Ramidus and the Paleobiology of Early Hominids." Science, 326, 5949: 75–86, 2009.
34. Tim D White, Giday WoldeGabriel, Berhane Asfaw, Stan Ambrose, Yonas Beyene, Raymond L Bernor, Jean-Renaud Boisserie, Brian Currie, Henry Gilbert, Yohannes Haile-Selassie, William K Hart, Leslea J Hlusko, F Clark Howell, Reiko T Kono, Thomas Lehmann, Antoine Louchart, C Owen Lovejoy, Paul R Renne, Haruo Saegusa, Elisabeth S Vrba, Hank Wesselman, and Gen Suwa. "Asa Issie, Aramis and the Origin of Australopithecus." Nature, 440, 7086: 883–889, 2006.
35. Carol V Ward, William H Kimbel, and Donald C Johanson. "Complete Fourth Metatarsal and Arches in the Foot of Australopithecus Afarensis."

Science, 331, 6018: 750–753, 2011. Carol Ward. "Interpreting the Posture and Locomotion of Australopithecus Afarensis: Where Do We Stand?" American Journal of Physical Anthropology, 35:185–215, 2002.
36. Phillip Tobias. "The Brain of Homo Habilis: A New Level of Organization in Cerebral Evolution." Journal of Human Evolution, 16, 7–8: 741–761, 1987.
37. T D White, G Suwa, S Simpson, B Asfaw. "Jaws and Teeth of Australopithecus Afarensis from Maka, Middle Awash, Ethiopia." American Journal of Physical Anthropology, 111, 1: 45–68, 2000. Charles Lockwood. "Sexual Dimorphism in the Face of Australopithecus Africanus." American Journal of Physical Anthropology, 108, 97–127, 1999. Charles A. Lockwood, Brian G. Richmond, William L. Jungers, William Kimbel. "Randomization Procedures and Sexual Dimorphism in Australopithecus Afarensis." Journal of Human Evolution, 31, 6: 537–548, 1996.
38. Philip L. Reno, Richard S. Meindl, Melanie A. McCollum, and C. Owen Lovejoy. "Sexual Dimorphism in Australopithecus Afarensis was Similar to that of Modern Humans." PNAS, 100, 16: 9404–9409, 2003.
39. Laura Monica Martinez, Ferran Estebaranz-Sanchez, Jordi Galbany, Alejandro Perez-Perez. "Testing Dietary Hypotheses of East African Hominines Using Buccal Dental Microwear Data." PLoS ONE, 11, 11: e0165447.
40. R. Bonnefille, R. Potts, F. Chalie′, D. Jolly, and O. Peyron. "High-Resolution Vegetation and Climate Change Associated with Pliocene Australopithecus Afarensis." PNAS, 101, 33: 12125–12129, 2004.
41. Donald C. Johanson, Fidelis T. Masao, Gerald G. Eck, Tim D. White, Robert C. Walter, William H. Kimbel, Berhane Asfaw, Paul Manega, Prosper Ndessokia, and Gen Suwa. "New Partial Skeleton of Homo Habilis from Olduvai Gorge, Tanzania." Nature, 327: 205–209, 1987.
42. Martin Haeusler and Henry McHenry. "Body Proportions of Homo Habilis." Journal of Human Evolution, 46, 4: 433–465, 2004.
43. Christopher Ruff. "Relative Limb Strength and Locomotion in Homo Habilis." American Journal of Physical Anthropology, 138, 1: 90–100, 2009.
44. Phillip Tobias. "The Brain of Homo Habilis: A New Level of Organization in Cerebral Evolution." Journal of Human Evolution, 16, 7–8: 741–761, 1987. Fred Spoor, Philipp Gunz, Simon Neubauer, Stefanie Stelzer, Nadia Scott, Amandus Kwekason, and M. Christopher Dean. "Reconstructed Homo Habilis Type OH 7 Suggests Deep-rooted Species Diversity in Early Homo." Nature, 519: 83–86, 2015.
45. Phillip Tobias. "Homo Habilis and Homo Erectus: From the Oldowan Men to the Achuelian Practitioners." Anthropologie, 18, 2/3: 115–119,

1980. Phillip Tobias. "Australopithecus, Homo Habilis, Tool-Using and Toolmaking." The South African Archaeological Bulletin, 20, 80: 167–192, 1965.
46. Peter Ungar. "Dental Evidence for the Reconstruction of Diet in African Early Homo." Current Anthropology, 53: S318–S329, 2012.
47. Peter Ungar, Frederick Grine, Mark Teaford, and Sireen Zaatari. "Dental Microwear and Diets of African Early Homo". Journal of Human Evolution, 50, 1: 78–95, 2006.
48. Christopher Ruff. "Femoral/Humeral Strength in Early African Homo Erectus." Journal of Human Evolution, 54, 3: 383–390, 2008.
49. Philip Rightmire. "Homo Erectus and Middle Pleistocene Hominins: Brain Size, Skull Form, and Species Recognition." Journal of Human Evolution, 65, 3: 223–252, 2013.
50. Hisao Baba, Fachroel Aziz, Yousuke Kaifu, Gen Suwa, Reiko Kono, and Teuku Jacob. "Homo Erectus Calvarium from the Pleistocene of Java." Science, 299, 5611: 1384–1388, 2003.
51. Robert G. Franciscus and Erik Trinkaus. "Nasal Morphology and the Emergence of Homo Erectus." American Journal of Biological Anthropology, 75, 4: 517–527, 1988.
52. Irit Zohar, Nira Alperson-Afil, Naama Goren-Inbar, Marion Prévost, Thomas Tütken, Guy Sisma-Ventura, Israel Hershkovitz, and Jens Najorka. "Evidence for the Cooking of Fish 780,000 Years Ago at Gesher Benot Ya'aqov, Israel." Nature Ecology & Evolution, 6: 2016–2028, 2022.
53. Kevin G. Hatala, Neil T. Roach, Kelly R. Ostrofsky, Roshna E. Wunderlich, Heather L. Dingwall, Brian A. Villmoare, David J. Green, John W. K. Harris, David R. Braun, and Brian G. Richmond. "Footprints Reveal Direct Evidence of Group Behavior and Locomotion in Homo Erectus." Nature, Scientific Reports, 6, 28766, 2016.
54. Sileshi Semaw, Michael J. Rogers, Scott W. Simpson, Naomi E. Levin, Jay Quade, Nelia Dunbar, William C. McIntosh, Isabel Cáceres, Gary E. Stinchcomb, Ralph L. Holloway, Francis H. Brown, Robert F. Butler, Dietrich Stout, and Melanie Everett. "Co-occurrence of Acheulian and Oldowan Artifacts with Homo Erectus Cranial Fossils from Gona, Afar, Ethiopia." Science Advances, 6, eaaw469, 2020.
55. Carotenuto F, Tsikaridze N, Rook L, Lordkipanidze D, Longo L, Condemi S, and Raia P. "Venturing Out Safely: The Biogeography of Homo Erectus Dispersal Out of Africa". Journal of Human Evolution, 95: 1–12, 2016.
56. Mark Maslin, Susanne Schultz, and Martin Trauth. "A Synthesis of the Theories and Concepts of Early Human Evolution." Philosophical Transactions Royal Society B, 370, 1663: 20140064, 2015.

57. Tom Higham, Katerina Douka, Rachel Wood, Christopher Bronk Ramsey, Fiona Brock, Laura Basell, Marta Camps, Alvaro Arrizabalaga, Javier Baena, Cecillio Barroso-Ruiz, Christopher Bergman, Coralie Boitard, Paolo Boscato, Miguel Caparros, Nicholas J. Conard, Christelle Draily, Alain Froment, Bertila Galvan, Paolo Gambassini, Alejandro Garcia-Moreno, Stefano Grimaldi, Paul Haesaerts, Brigitte Holt, Maria-Jose Iriarte-Chiapusso, Arthur Jelinek, Jesus F. Jorda Pardo, Jose´-Manuel Maillo-Fernandez, Anat Marom, Julia Maroto, Mario Menendez, Laure Metz, Eugene Morin, Adriana Moroni, Fabio Negrino, Eleni Panagopoulou, Marco Peresani, Stephane Pirson, Marco de la Rasilla, Julien Riel-Salvatore, Annamaria Ronchitelli, David Santamaria, Patrick Semal, Ludovic Slimak, Joaquim Soler, Narcis Soler, Aritza Villaluenga, Ron Pinhasi, and Roger Jacobi. "The Timing and Spatiotemporal Patterning of Neanderthal Disappearance." Nature, 512: 306–309, 2014.
58. Laura Niven, Teresa E Steele, William Rendu, Jean-Baptiste Mallye, Shannon P McPherron, Marie Soressi, Jacques Jaubert, and Jean-Jacques Hublin. "Neandertal Mobility and Large-game Hunting: the Exploitation of Reindeer during the Quina Mousterian at Chez-Pinaud Jonzac (Charente-Maritime, France)." Journal of Human Evolution, 63, 4: 624–635, 2012.
59. A. C. Sorensen, E. Claud, and M. Soressi. "Neandertal Fire-making Technology Inferred from Microwear Analysis." Nature, Scientfic Reports, 8, 1, 10065, 2018.
60. B. L. Hardy, M.-H. Moncel, C. Kerfant, M. Lebon, L. Bellot-Gurlet, and N. Mélard. "Direct Evidence of Neanderthal Fibre Technology and its Cognitive and Behavioral Implications." Nature, Scientific Reports, 10: 4889, 2020.
61. Nathan Wales. "Modeling Neanderthal Clothing using Ethnographic Analogues." Journal of Human Evolution, 63, 6: 781–795, 2012.
62. Penny Spikins, Andy Needham, Barry Wright, Calvin Dytham, Maurizio Gatta, Gail Hitchens. "Living to Fight Another Day: The Ecological and Evolutionary Significance of Neanderthal Healthcare." Quaternary Science Reviews, 217: 98–118, 2019.
63. George Ferentinos, Maria Gkioni, Maria Geraga, and George Papatheodorou. "Early Seafaring Activity in the Southern Ionian Islands, Mediterranean Sea". Journal of Archaeological Science, 39, 7: 2167–2176, 2012.
64. Marie Soressi, Shannon P McPherron, Michel Lenoir, Tamara Dogandžić, Paul Goldberg, Zenobia Jacobs, Yolaine Maigrot, Naomi L Martisius, Christopher E Miller, William Rendu, Michael Richards, Matthew M Skinner, Teresa E Steele, Sahra Talamo, and Jean-Pierre Texier. "Neandertals Made the first Specialized Bone Tools in Europe." PNAS,

110, 35: 14186–14190, 2013. Naomi L Martisius, Frido Welker, Tamara Dogandžić, Mark N Grote, William Rendu, Virginie Sinet-Mathiot, Arndt Wilcke, Shannon J P McPherron, Marie Soressi, and Teresa E Steele. "Non-destructive ZooMS Identification Reveals Strategic Bone Tool Raw Material Selection by Neandertals." Nature, Scientific Reports, 10, 1, 7746, 2020.
65. James Blinkhorn, Clément Zanolli, Tim Compton, Huw S. Groucutt, Eleanor M. L. Scerri, Lucile Crété, Chris Stringer, Michael D. Petraglia, and Simon Blockley. "Nubian Levallois Technology Associated with Southernmost Neanderthals." Nature, Scientific Reports, 11: 2869, 2021.
66. Laura T. Buck and Chris B. Stringer. "Homo Heidelbergensis." Current Biology, 24, 6: R214–R215, 2014.
67. Philip Rightmire. "Homo in the Middle Pleistocene: Hypodigms, Variation, and Species Recognition." Evolutionary Anthropology, 17(1):8–21, 2008. Philip Rightmire. "Human Evolution in the Middle Pleistocene: The Role of Homo Heidelbergensis." Evolutionary Anthropology, 6, 6: 218–227, 1998.
68. Philip Rightmire. "The Human Cranium from Bodo, Ethiopia: Evidence for Speciation in the Middle Pleistocene?" Journal of Human Evolution, 31, 1:21–39, 1996. Phillip Rightmire. "Brain Size and Encephalization in Early to Mid-Pleistocene Homo." American Journal of Physical Anthropology, 124, 2: 109–123, 2004.
69. Samantha Brown, Diyendo Massilan, Maxim B. Kozlikin, Michael V. Shunkov, Anatoly P. Derevianko, Alexander Stoessel, Blair Jope-Street, Matthias Meyer, Janet Kelso, Svante Pääbo, Thomas Higham, and Katerina Douka. "The Earliest Denisovans and their Cultural Adaptation." Nature Ecology and Evolution, 6, 1: 28–35, 2021.
70. David Reich, Richard E. Green, Martin Kircher, Johannes Krause, Nick Patterson, Eric Y. Durand, Bence Viola, Adrian W. Briggs, Udo Stenzel, Philip L. F. Johnson, Tomislav Maricic, Jeffrey M. Good, Tomas Marques-Bonet, Can Alkan, Qiaomei Fu, Swapan Mallick, Heng Li, Matthias Meyer, Evan E. Eichler, Mark Stoneking, Michael Richards, Sahra Talamo, Michael V. Shunkov, Anatoli P. Derevianko, Jean-Jacques Hublin, Janet Kelso, Montgomery Slatkin, and Svante Pääbo. "Genetic History of an Archaic Hominin Group from Denisova Cave in Siberia." Nature, 468: 1053–1060, 2010.
71. Fabrice Demeter, Clément Zanolli, Kira E. Westaway, Renaud Joannes-Boyau, Philippe Duringer, Mike W. Morley, Frido Welker, Patrick L. Rüther, Matthew M. Skinner, Hugh McColl, Charleen Gaunitz, Lasse Vinner, Tyler E. Dunn, Jesper V. Olsen, Martin Sikora, Jean-Luc Ponche, Eric Suzzoni, Sébastien Frangeul, Quentin Boesch, Pierre-Olivier Antoine, Lei Pan, Song Xing, Jian-Xin Zhao, Richard M. Bailey,

Souliphane Boualaphane, Phonephanh Sichanthongtip, Daovee Sihanam, Elise Patole-Edoumba, Françoise Aubaile, Françoise Crozier, Nicolas Bourgon, Alexandra Zachwieja, Thonglith Luangkhoth, Viengkeo Souksavatdy, Thongsa Sayavongkhamdy, Enrico Cappellini, Anne-Marie Bacon, Jean-Jacques Hublin, Eske Willerslev, and Laura Shackelford. "A Middle Pleistocene Denisovan Molar from the Annamite Chain of Northern Laos." Nature Communications, 13, 557, 2022.

72. Fahu Chen, Frido Welker, Chuan-Chou Shen, Shara Bailey, Inga Bergmann, Simon Davis, Huan Xia, Hui Wang, Roman Fischer, Sarah Freidline, Tsai-Luen Yu, Matthew M. Skinner, Stefanie Stelzer, Guangrong Dong, Qiaomei Fu, Guanghui Dong, Jian Wang, Dongju Zhang, and Jean-Jacques Hublin. "A Late Middle Pleistocene Denisovan Mandible from the Tibetan Plateau." Nature, 569: 409–412, 2019.
73. David Reich, Nick Patterson, Martin Kircher, Frederick Delfin, Madhusudan R. Nandineni, Irina Pugach, Albert Min-Shan Ko, Ying-Chin Ko, Timothy A. Jinam, Maude E. Phipps, Naruya Saitou, Andreas Wollstein, Manfred Kayser, Svante Pääbo, and Mark Stoneking. "Denisova Admixture and the First Modern Human Dispersals into Southeast Asia and Oceania." The American Journal of Human Genetics, 89: 516–528, 2011.
74. David Gokhman, Nadav Mishol, Marc de Manuel, David de Juan, Jonathan Shuqrun, Eran Meshorer, Tomas Marques-Bonet, Yoel Rak, and Liran Carmel. "Reconstructing Denisovan Anatomy Using DNA Methylation Maps." Cell, 179: 180–192, 2019.
75. Huw S. Groucutt, Michael D. Petraglia, Geoff Bailey, Eleanor M.L. Scerri, Ash Parton, Laine Clark-Balzan, Richard P. Jennings, Laura Lewis, James Blinkhorn, Nick A. Drake, Paul S. Breeze, Robyn H. Inglis, Maud H. Devès, Matthew Meredith-Williams, Nicole Boivin, Mark G. Thomas, and Aylwyn Scally. "Rethinking the Dispersal of Homo Sapiens Out of Africa." Evolutionary Anthropology, 24, 4: 149–164, 2015.
76. I. Zwir, C. Del-Val, M. Hintsanen, K. M. Cloninger, R. Romero-Zaliz, A. Mesa, J. Arnedo, R. Salas, G. F. Poblete, E. Raitoharju, O. Raitakari, L. Keltikangas-Järvinen, G. A. de Erausquin, I. Tattersall, T. Lehtimäki, and C. R. Cloninger. "Evolution of Genetic Networks for Human Creativity." Molecular Psychiatry, 27: 354–376, 2022.
77. Benjamin Lieberman and Elizabeth Gordon. Climate Change in Human History: Prehistory to the Present. Bloomsbury, 2018. (P. 27).
78. Ian Tattersall. Masters of the Planet: The Search of Human Origins. Palgrave Macmillan, 2012. (P. 20).
79. Ian Tattersall. Understanding Human Evolution. Cambridge University Press, 2022. (P.33).

80. Richard Rayner and Ann Cadman. "Climatic Change and the Appearance of Australopithecus Africanus in the Makapansgat Sediments." Journal of Human Evolution, 18: 107–113, 1989.
81. Palynology is a scientific discipline concerned with the study of plant pollen, plant spores, and planktonic organisms.
82. RJ Rayner, BP Moon, and JC Masters. "The Makapansgat Australopithecine Environment." Journal of Human Evolution, 24: 219–231, 1993.
83. T. Jonathan Davies, Barnabas H. Daru, Bezeng S. Bezeng, Tristan Charles-Dominique, Gareth P. Hempson, Ronny M. Kabongo, Olivier Maurin, A. Muthama Muasya, Michelle van der Bank, and William J. Bond. "Savanna Tree Evolutionary Ages inform the Reconstruction of the Paleoenvironment of Our Hominin Ancestors" Nature, Scientific Reports, 10, 12430, 2020.
84. Mark Maslin, Susanne Schultz, and Martin Trauth. "A Synthesis of the Theories and Concepts of Early Human Evolution." Philosophical Transactions Royal Society B, 370, 1663: 20140064, 2015.
85. Kaye Reed. "Early Hominid Evolution and Ecological Change through the African Plio-Pleistocene." Journal of Human Evolution, 32: 289–322, 1997.
86. Erin N. DiMaggio, Christopher J. Campisano, John Rowan, Guillaume Dupont-Nivet, Alan L. Deino, Faysal Bibi, Margaret E. Lewis, Antoine Souron, Dominique Garello, Lars Werdelin, Kaye E. Reed, and J Ramón Arrowsmith. "Late Pliocene Fossiliferous Sedimentary Record and the Environmental Context of Early Homo from Afar, Ethiopia." Science, 347, 6228: 1355–1359, 2015.
87. Brian Villmoare, William H. Kimbel, Chalachew Seyoum, Christopher J. Campisano, Erin N. DiMaggio, John Rowan, David R. Braun, J Ramón Arrowsmith, and Kaye E. Reed. "Early Homo at 2.8 Ma from Ledi-Geraru, Afar, Ethiopia." Science, 347, 6228:1352–1355, 2015.
88. Joshua R. Robinson, John Rowan, Christopher J. Campisano1, Jonathan G. Wynn, and Kaye E. Reed. "Late Pliocene Environmental Change During the Transition from Australopithecus to Homo" Nature Ecology and Evolution, 1, 0159, 2017.
89. Peter deMenocal. "Plio-Plesitocene African Climate." Science, 270, 5233: 53–59, 1995.
90. Ibid.
91. Peter deMenocal. "African Climate Change and Faunal Evolution during the Pliocene-Pleistocene." Earth and Planetary Science Letters, 220: 3–24, 2004.
92. Ibid.

93. Thure Cerling. "Development of Grasslands and Savannas in East Africa During the Neogene." Palaeogeography, Palaeoclimatology, Palaeoecology (Global and Planetary Change Section), 97: 241–247, 1992.
94. T. E. Cerling, J. Quade, S. H. Ambrose, and N.E. Sikes. "Fossil Soils, Grasses, and Carbon Isotopes from Fort Ternan, Kenya: Grassland or Woodland?" Journol of Human Evolution, 21: 295–306, 1991.
95. Nancy Sikes. "Early Hominid Habitat Preference in East Africa: Paleosol Carbon Isotopic Evidence." Journal of Human Evolution, 27: 25–45, 1994.
96. John Kingston, Bruno Marino, and Andrew Hill. "Isotopic Evidence for Neogene Hominid Paleoenvironments in the Kenya Rift Valley." Science, 264, 5161: 955–959, 1994.
97. Changes relating to or resulting from living organisms.
98. Elizabeth Vrba. "Evolution, Species and Fossils: How Does Life Evolve? South African Journal of Science, 76:61–84, 1980. Elizabeth Vrba. "Environment and Evolution: Alternative Causes of the Temporal Distribution of Evolutionary Events." South African Journal of Science, 81:229–236, 1985. Elizabeth Vrba. "Climate, Heterochrony, and Human Evolution." Journal of Anthropological Research, 52, 1:1–28, 1996.
99. Leigh Van Valen. "A New Evolutionary Law." Evolutionary Theory, 1: 1–30, 1973.
100. Mark Maslin, Susanne Schultz, and Martin Trauth. "A Synthesis of the Theories and Concepts of Early Human Evolution." Philosophical Transactions Royal Society B, 370, 1663: 20140064, 2015.
101. Tyler Faith and Anna K. Behrensmeyer. "Climate Change and Faunal Turnover: Testing the Mechanics of the Turnover-Pulse Hypothesis with South African Fossil Data." Paleobiology, 39, 4: 609–627, 2013.
102. Anna K. Behrensmeyer, Nancy E. Todd, Richard Potts, and Geraldine E. McBrinn. "Late Pliocene Faunal Turnover in the Turkana Basin, Kenya and Ethiopia." Science, 278: 1589–1594, 1997.
103. Richard Potts. "Evolution and Environmental Change in Early Human Prehistory." Annual Review of Anthropology, 41:151–167, 2012.
104. Richard Potts. "Evolution and Climate Variability." Science, 273: 922–923, 1996.
105. Richard Potts. "Variability Selection in Hominid Evolution." Evolutionary Anthropology, 7, 3: 81–96, 1998.
106. Richard Potts. "Environmental Hypotheses of Hominin Evolution." Yearbook of Physical Anthropology, 41: 93–136, 1998.

107. Mark Maslin, Susanne Schultz, and Martin Trauth. "A Synthesis of the Theories and Concepts of Early Human Evolution." Philosophical Transactions Royal Society B, 370, 1663: 20140064, 2015.
108. Paleoclimatology is the scientific study of climates predating the invention of meteorological tools.
109. Richard Potts and Tyler Faith. "Alternating High and Low Climate Variability: The Context of Natural Selection and Speciation in Plio-Pleistocene Hominin Evolution." Journal of Human Evolution, 87: 5–20, 2015.
110. Sapropel describes dark-colored sediments that are rich in organic matter.
111. Stratigraphy is a branch of geology concerned with the study of rock layers.
112. Ibid.
113. Ibid.
114. R. L. Lupien, J.M. Russell, C. Feibel, C. Beck I. Castaneda, A. Deino, and A.S. Cohen. "A Leaf Wax Biomarker Record of Early Pleistocene Hydroclimate from West Turkana, Kenya." Quaternary Science Reviews 186: 225–235, 2018.
115. Ibid.
116. Ibid.
117. Rachel L. Lupien, James M. Russell, Avinash Subramanian, Rahab Kinyanjui, Emily J. Beverly, Kevin T. Uno, Peter de Menocal, Rene Dommain, and Richard Potts. "Eastern African Environmental Variation and its Role in the Evolution and Cultural Change of Homo over the Last 1 Million Years." Journal of Human Evolution, 157, 103028, 2021.
118. Ibid.
119. Plasticity is the process by which the ability of an organism to adjust to environmental changes evolves.
120. Andrew S. Cohen, Andrew Du, John Rowan, Chad L. Yost, Anne L. Billingsley, Christopher J. Campisano, Erik T. Brown, Alan L. Deino, Craig S. Feibel, Katharine Grant, John D. Kingston, Rachel L. Lupien, Veronica Muiruri, R. Bernhart Owen, Kaye E. Reed, James Russell, and Mona Stockhecke. "Plio-Pleistocene Environmental Variability in Africa and its Implications for Mammalian Evolution." PNAS, 119, 16, e2107393119, 2022.
121. Ibid.
122. The Plio-Pleistocene is an informal geological pseudo-period, which begins about 5 million years ago. It combines the time periods of the formally defined Pliocene and Pleistocene epochs.
123. Rachel L. Lupien, James M. Russell, Chad L. Yost, John D. Kingston, Alan L. Deino, Jon Logan, Anna Schuh, and Andrew S. Cohen. "Vegetation Change in the Baringo Basin, East Africa Across the Onset of

Northern Hemisphere Glaciation 3.3–2.6 Ma." Palaeogeography, Palaeoclimatology, Palaeoecology, 570, 109426, 2021.

124. Ibid.
125. Susanne Shultz and Mark Maslin. "Early Human Speciation, Brain Expansion and Dispersal Influenced by African Climate Pulses." PLoS ONE, 8, 10, e76750, 2013.
126. Martin H. Trauth, Mark A. Maslin, Alan L. Deino, Annett Junginger, Moses Lesoloyia, Eric O. Odada, Daniel O. Olago, Lydia A. Olaka, Manfred R. Strecker, and Ralph Tiedemann. "Human Evolution in a Variable Environment: The Amplifier Lakes of Eastern Africa." Quaternary Science Reviews, 29: 2981–2988, 2010.
127. Martin H. Trauth, Mark A. Maslin, Alan L. Deino, Manfred R. Strecker, Andreas G.N. Bergner, and Miriam Duhnforth. "High- and Low-latitude forcing of Plio-Pleistocene East African Climate and Human Evolution." Journal of Human Evolution, 53: 475–486, 2007.
128. Ibid.
129. Ibid.
130. Martin Trauth, Mark Maslin, Alan Deino, and Manfred Streker. "Late Cenozoic Moisture History of East Africa." Science, 309: 2051–2053, 2005.
131. Ibid.
132. Andrew S. Cohen, Andrew Du, John Rowan, Chad L. Yost, Anne L. Billingsley, Christopher J. Campisano, Erik T. Brown, Alan L. Deino, Craig S. Feibel, Katharine Grant, John D. Kingston, Rachel L. Lupien, Veronica Muiruri, R. Bernhart Owen, Kaye E. Reed, James Russell, and Mona Stockhecke. "Plio-Pleistocene Environmental Variability in Africa and its Implications for Mammalian Evolution." PNAS, 119, 16, e2107393119, 2022.
133. Ibid.
134. Ibid.

CHAPTER 4

Disturbance and Dispersal

1 Origin, Migration, and Range

The origin of modern humans and their migration from that cradle of humanity have been the topic of much debate. Attempts have been aimed at pinpointing the location of the cradle of humanity on the map, the timing of the dispersal from that cradle, the causes that induced humans to leave their initial habitat, and the routes taken from the origin to their subsequent destination. When we discuss the cradle of humanity, there are three hypotheses that prevail. The first is the multiregional model, the second is the one-region model, and the last one combines the features of both.

1.1 The Multiregional Model

According to the proponents of the multiregional model, there is no one time or place associated with the origin of modern humans.[1] This view asserts instead that anatomic and genetic evolutionary changes leading to modern day humans took place piecemeal across the Old World. Local differentiation led to the origination of regional populations which evolved over time to modern humans in different parts of the world. In this context, anatomically modern humans were the outcome of the coalescence

S. Khalifa, *Climate Change, Economic Channels, and Historical Junctures*, https://doi.org/10.1007/978-3-031-91867-4_4

of these changes because of gene flow between these populations. Gene flow is the movement of genes into or out of a population.

Contrary to some beliefs, the multiregional model does not claim that the appearance of modern humans was due to independent or parallel evolution in different parts of the Old World. In fact, this hypothesis is a multiple region model, not a multiple origin one. Thus, multiregional[2] "does not mean independent multiple origins, ancient divergence of modern populations, simultaneous appearance of adaptive characters in different regions, or parallel evolution." Instead, the underlying hypothesis is that[3] "a worldwide network of genetic exchanges, between evolving human populations that continually divide and reticulate, provides a frame of population inter-connections that allows both species-wide evolutionary change and local distinctions and differentiation."

However, some scholars did not find evidence supportive of this view in their assessment of the model's predictions. The model predicts that features characterizing the evolution of regional populations should be stable and consistently show higher incidence in those regions. Instead, the analysis of five current populations and a fossil sample of *Homo sapiens* indicate that[4] "these features do not support a multiregional origin, giving further support to the existing fossil, chronological and genetic evidence for a single African origin of all modern humans."

1.2 The African Origin Model

The out of Africa, or the African replacement, is a widely accepted model of the origin and early migration of our human ancestors.[5] Proponents of this model propose Africa as the probable continent of origin for *Homo sapiens* and that anatomically modern humans arose as a new species in Africa between 200,000 and 150,000 years ago. This was followed by a subsequent expansion out of Africa in the past 100,000 years when populations of this new species began propagating throughout the world replacing ancient species. In his overview of the models of human origins, anthropologist Christopher Stringer concludes that[6] "a recent African origin can be supported for H. sapiens, morphologically, behaviorally and genetically."

The African origin model posits that all modern non-African populations descended from *Homo sapiens* who left Africa. Thus, ancient populations in other areas of the world were replaced by the migrating populations with some hybridization between the two groups. Christopher Stringer explains that this model[7] "allows for a greater extent of hybridisation between the dispersing populations and the resident indigenous populations outside of Africa."

This view is an outcome of a synthesis of evidence from discovered fossils and the study of human nuclear and mitochondrial DNA. For instance, an attempt to compare the two contrasting views for the origin of modern humans using genetic data from current human populations and a Pleistocene fossil hominid confirms that both genetics and paleontology support an African origin for modern humans, rather than a long period of multiregional evolution accompanied by gene flow.[8] Other scholars examine fossil hominid crania from Herto, Middle Awash in Ethiopia, to provide evidence on the location, timing, and contextual circumstances of the emergence of *Homo sapiens*.[9] The study finds that the Herto hominids are morphologically intermediate between archaic African fossils and anatomically modern humans. Given their anatomy and antiquity, they represent the probable immediate ancestors of anatomically modern humans. This constitutes strong evidence for human emergence in Africa.

The Out of Africa hypothesis, or the idea of an African origin for modern humans, also owes its genesis and recognition to pioneering analyses and interpretations of mitochondrial DNA.[10] These studies examine the degree of variation in mitochondrial DNA of individuals from diverse populations. One interpretation of low levels of variation is that there was a genetic bottleneck in the past, as in the case of speciation, and little time afterward for subsequent variation to occur. The analysis shows that African samples of contemporary mitochondrial DNA have a higher degree of variability than samples from other populations. Since the degree of variability indicates the time elapsed since population members shared a common ancestor, this finding suggests a longer time span for the African sample compared to others. This, in turn, provides further evidence that Africa is the cradle of humanity.

The genetic evidence for an African origin for *Homo sapiens* is not confined to the mitochondrial analysis. Some scholars also present data from nuclear DNA suggestive of an African origin. In this context, polymorphism is the occurrence of two or more different morphs or forms in the population of a species. A haplotype is a group of genes within an organism that was inherited together from a single parent. Some geneticists find that most polymorphisms among the alpha- and beta-globin haplotypes are not found outside the African continent, and that this degree of genetic diversity in the African sample suggests it to be the most ancient[11] "making an African origin for man more likely than one in Eurasia."

1.3 The African Multiregional Model

Other scholars argue that some of the latest evidence moves us away from both the multiregional and the out of Africa models. This alternative view proposes an African metapopulation model, or an African multiregional one, of human origins.[12] According to this view, fossil data show that the physical features characterizing contemporary humans did not develop progressively in one location. Instead, they appeared across Africa in a mosaic-like fashion at different times and in various combinations. The evidence in this case suggests a fragmented continental-wide trend toward the modern human form. This also indicates that early *Homo sapiens* were strongly structured, or they[13] "comprised sets of interconnected subpopulations forming a metapopulation. A metapopulation model stresses the importance of structure and connectivity within evolutionary lineages as a continuous process of oscillating fission, fusion, gene flow and local extinction."

In this context, archaeologist Eleanor Scerri states,[14] "Independent lines of evidence suggests that humans evolved within a structured metapopulation living across much of the African continent at different points in time." Eleanor Scerri and other proponents of this view also conclude that[15] "our species originated and diversified within strongly subdivided (i.e., structured) populations, probably living across Africa, that were connected by sporadic gene flow." This can also be seen in the distribution of evidence of technological innovation. For instance, Eleanor Scerri and Manuel Will find that[16] "[i]nstead of a continent-wide, gradual accumulation of complex material culture, the record exhibits a predominantly asynchronous presence and duration of many innovations across different regions of Africa."

2 Out of the Cradle

If Africa was the cradle of humanity, obviously our ancestors eventually decided to leave and populate the rest of the world. The questions that arise in this case include the causes behind the decision to leave, the timing and frequency of that exodus, and the routes taken to the subsequent destination. One of the most intriguing questions pertaining to the exit of modern humans out of Africa is the passage that humans chose for their journey. The consensus view is that there are two possible routes, not mutually exclusive. The first is a Northern route through Egypt, the Sinai Peninsula, and the Levantine Corridor. The second is a Southern route through Ethiopia, Bab El Mandeb Strait, and the Arabian Peninsula. Different types of evidence point to one of these routes.

2.1 *Dispersal Passage*

Some fossil evidence indicates a Northern route was taken by our ancestors. Some of the earliest remains of anatomically modern humans outside of Africa, the Skhul and Qafzeh hominins, were found in the Levant and were dated at 120,000 and 100,000–90,000 years ago, respectively.[17] These fossils possibly indicate an early exit of modern humans traveling across the Sinai Peninsula to the Levant. Christopher Stringer and others postulate that[18] "it does appear that the oldest known symbolic burials are those of early modern humans at Skhul and Qafzeh. This supports the view that, despite the associated Middle Palaeolithic technology, elements of modern human behaviour were represented at Skhul and Qafzeh prior to 100 ka."

According to this view, environmental variations and demographic pressures during the Pleistocene drove human populations to disperse from their initial habitat in the East Africa Rift Valley toward more resource rich Eurasia.[19] To cross the inhospitable hyper arid zone of North Africa, humid corridors that were active for a short time, such as the Nile River Valley or the Sahara's lake-and-riverine-belts, have been exploited by humans. These temporary hydrologic features are obviously attributed to certain climatic conditions that prevailed only at the time. Once they arrived at the Mediterranean coastal areas, hominins were able to proceed toward Eurasia through the Levantine corridor.

In contrast, mitochondrial DNA studies have traditionally favored a Southern route across the Bab El Mandeb Strait at the mouth of the Red Sea. This is because some scholars provide genetic evidence that a particular mitochondrial haplogroup has been found at high frequency in both East Africa and South Asia.[20] This[21] "together with the virtual absence of haplogroup M in the Levant and its high frequency in the South-Arabian Peninsula, render M the first genetic indicator for the hypothesized exit route from Africa through eastern Africa/western India."

According to this view, complementary pathways for the dispersal out of Africa included the sea passages through Bab El Mandeb Strait and other sea arms.[22] These crossings were easily exploited during the Early Pleistocene because at the time they were less wide, shallower, and sometimes had discontinuous land bridges. Some scholars even show that[23] "crossing distances are much shorter during the Pleistocene than today with clear inter-visibility of the opposing shorelines, but that tidal currents were much stronger." These favorable crossing conditions have also been attributed to climatic factors that prevailed at the time since[24] "sea crossings would be easily accomplished during long periods of the glacial cycle."

2.2 *Dispersal Hypotheses*

A variety of dispersal models focus on the period between the first evidence of *Homo sapiens* in Africa around 200,000–150,000 years ago and the arrival of our species at the margins of the Old World between 50,000 and 40,000 years before present. These models propose alternative hypotheses on the time of dispersal, the frequency of dispersal, and the passage of dispersal. These views have largely fallen into two broad categories, emphasizing the time frames of Marine Isotope Stage[25] MIS5 (between 130,000 and 80,000 years ago) which is referred to as the Early Onset Dispersal Model, or post-MIS5 which is referred to as the Late Dispersal Model.

2.2.1 *Single Late Dispersal*

A single dispersal model states that anatomically modern humans migrated out of Africa to Eurasia as a single wave exiting via a single route around 60,000–50,000 years before present. The evidence for the single late dispersal comes from fossils found around the Indian Ocean Rim. Proponents of this model propose that the trail of stone tool assemblages from southern and eastern Africa and South Asia exhibit a high degree of similarity. This resemblance is presumed to provide evidence for demographic connections and dispersal along that passage.

Besides fossil evidence, there is also support for this hypothesis from genetics. In this context, dispersal out of Africa occurred initially through a single migrant group and continued in an iterative way as individuals dispersed into unoccupied areas and initiated new groups of founder individuals, who again expanded into other uninhabited areas. Some scholars argue that this serial founder process could lead to patterns of increasing genetic drift[26] and decreasing genetic diversity observed in groups as geographic distance from Africa increases.[27] In this context, geneticist Luca Cavalli-Sforza and other scholars argue that the[28] "increasing abundance of human genetic data has shown that the geographical patterns of worldwide genetic diversity are best explained by human expansion out of Africa. This expansion is modelled well by prolonged migration from a single origin in Africa with multiple subsequent serial founding events."

Along these lines, some scholars present a model based on a combination of genetic analysis and archaeological evidence from South Asia and East Africa.[29] The data support a coastal dispersal of modern humans from eastern Africa to southern Asia around 60,000–50,000 years ago showing that[30] "the archaeological and genetic evidence points to a single successful dispersal event, which took genetically and culturally modern populations fairly rapidly across southern and southeastern Asia into Australasia, and with only a secondary and later dispersal into Europe."

2.2.2 *Multiple Early Onset Dispersals*

This model proposes that successful dispersal out of Africa started much earlier, probably around 130,000–80,000 years ago. Proponents of this model assert that there was an initial dispersal through the Southern route to South Arabia then to Southeast Asia. This in addition to a second one using the Northern route, through the Levant, that led ultimately to peopling of the rest of Eurasia around 50,000 years ago. Thus, the[31] "first dispersals would have originated in Africa from where two different geographical routes were possible, one through Ethiopia/Arabia towards South Asia, and one through North Africa/Middle East towards Eurasia."

Along these lines, some scholars use estimates of climate and sea level changes over the past 125,000 years to simulate the dispersal of *Homo sapiens* consistently with archaeological and fossil data across the Arabian Peninsula and the Levant.[32] The simulation reproduces an early exodus of *Homo sapiens* out of Africa during MIS5 along the southern rim of Asia into southern China and subsequently into Australia during MIS3 and MIS4. The authors conclude,[33] "Consistent with the recently proposed early onset multiple dispersal model and supported by phenotype analyses of early human neurocranial geometries, we found evidence for multiple climate-mediated MIS 3–5 dispersal and mixing waves across the Africa/Asian nexus."

There is a plethora of studies that supports this dispersal version. For instance, archaeologists Michael Petraglia and Robin Dennell argue that environmental and archaeological evidence indicate that[34] "H. sapiens exited Africa much earlier than commonly thought and may have colonized much of southern Asia well before 60,000 years ago. Additionally, we cannot exclude the possibility that several dispersal events occurred, from both North and East Africa." Michael Petraglia and other scholars also conclude that based on fossil, genetic, and archaeological evidence,[35] "the expansion of H. sapiens out of Africa was a complex process, and not simply the consequence of a single, rapid coastal expansion at 60 ka ago. We argue that modern human expansion into Arabia is probably coincident with the ages of 130–70 ka for H. sapiens in the Levant, with populations reaching South Asia by 78 ka, and perhaps earlier."

In comparing the two views, it seems reasonable to conclude that the early onset multiple dispersals seem to be more consistent with the evidence than a single late dispersal. However, it also seems that the earlier dispersal was not as extensive and exhaustive as the latter one, as will be seen in the following discussion.

2.3 *Dispersal Journey*

Early migrations began about 2 million years with the exodus out of Africa by *Homo erectus*. This species left Africa via the Levantine Corridor and the Horn of Africa to Eurasia. There is evidence for *Homo erectus* in the Caucasus about 1.85–1.78 million years ago,[36] in southern Europe about 1.8 million years ago,[37] in central Europe,[38] in eastern Europe about 1.42 million years ago,[39] and in southwestern Europe approximately 1.2 million years before present.[40] *Homo erectus* also dispersed as far as Southeast Asia about 2.1 million years ago[41] and even Java about 1.8 million years ago.[42] Some studies show that[43] "H. erectus followed almost passively the large herbivore fauna during its dispersal." These results[44] "clearly point to the fact that predator avoidance may have conditioned its long-distance diffusion as it moved outside Africa."

This initial migration was followed by other archaic humans. For instance, *Neanderthals* spread across the Near East and Europe. Genomic data of fossils confirm that[45] "the first European modern humans mixed with Neanderthals and suggesting that such mixing could have been common." *Denisovans* also appear to have spread across Central Asia, Southeast Asia, and Oceania.[46]

Homo sapiens emerged in Africa as per our previous discussion. Based on the available fossils,[47] "H. sapiens appears to have originated from the coalescence of South and, possibly, East-African source populations." *Homo sapiens* expanded to other parts of Africa. This was followed by a migration out of Africa.

There were early migrations between 130,000 and 120,000 years ago that do not appear to have led to lasting colonization. There is some evidence that modern humans left Africa using two different routes: the first through the Sinai Peninsula and the Levant, and a second route through Bab-el-Mandeb Strait on the Red Sea crossing to the Arabian Peninsula.[48] The early dispersal was geographically restricted to the Levant, the Arabian Peninsula, and possibly parts of southern Asia. Some studies show[49] "that the modern humans who expanded into Eurasia 120,000 years ago lacked the functionally and structurally complex technology of recent hunter-gatherers. This technology, which includes, for example, mechanical projectiles, snares and traps, and sewn clothing, provides not only expanded dietary breadth and increased rates of foraging efficiency and success in places where plant and animal productivity is low, but protection from cold weather in places where winter temperatures are low." This was probably why this early dispersal was not as broad as the latter one.

The later dispersal, however, was wider in scope. This late dispersal took place about 75,000 years before present. This migration wave led to the lasting spread of modern humans throughout the world. Geneticist Luca Cavalli-Sforza and other scholars show that the[50] "[g]eographic distribution of contemporary haplotypes implies distinctive prehistoric human migrations: one to Oceania, one to Asia and subsequently to America, and a third one predominantly to Europe."

Homo sapiens migrated from East Africa roughly 75,000 years ago along the southern coast of Asia arriving at Oceania about 50,000 years ago. The early migrants crossed Bab-el-Mandeb strait or the Levant, to the Arabian Peninsula.[51] Their descendants spread along the coastal route of Arabia, Persia, and South Asia about 55,000 years ago. Some evidence show that[52] "Arabia was indeed the first staging post in the spread of modern humans around the world." Others show that the Persian plateau served as a hub for *Homo sapiens* after their dispersal out of Africa because it was[53] "suitable for human occupation and that it could sustain a larger population compared to other West Asian regions."

Afterward, humans dispersed deeper into Asia. Surveying the genetic history in Asia, using sequence data from humans who lived there as early as 45,000 years ago, show that[54] "comparing present-day Australasians and Asians show that they likely derived from a single dispersal out of Africa, rapidly differentiating into three main lineages: one that persists partially in South Asia, one that is primarily found today in Australasia, and one that is widely represented across Siberia, East Asia, and Southeast Asia." In this context, there is evidence for *Homo sapiens* in the northern parts of the Indian subcontinent about 74,000 years ago,[55] in Southeast Asia between 77,000 and 70,000 years ago,[56] in Sumatra between 73,000 and 63,000 years ago,[57] in Korea between 40,900 and 44,900 years ago,[58] and in the Japanese Archipelago about 38,000 years before present.[59]

Homo sapiens eventually colonized Australia about 65,000–50,000 years ago.[60] At the time, most of Southeast Asia formed one land mass known as Sunda. Sahul was the continental land mass of present-day Australia and New Guinea. Migration continued southeast on the coastal route to the straits between Sunda and Sahul.[61] This migration is believed to have happened about 50,000 years ago, before Australia and New Guinea were separated by rising sea levels.[62]

Some studies show that climate-induced changes in vegetation[63] "offer[] a new perspective on the possible impact of vegetation succession on the colonization of Homo sapiens on Southeast Asian islands." Other studies show that changes in the summer monsoon affected dispersal to South Asia since[64] "orbitally modulated summer monsoon rainfall and temperature increase in East Asia concurrent with Southeast African climate deterioration may have promoted the early H. sapiens dispersal out of Africa, to the more remote region(s) of East Asia, during the last interglacial." These studies provide evidence of the association between climate change and dispersal of humans across Asia.

In a later wave, modern humans spread across Europe about 45,000–40,000 years ago.[65] *Neanderthals* were already present in the area, and the arriving populations of anatomically modern humans interbred with these populations to a limited degree.[66] In this context, there is evidence for modern humans in northern Europe around 45,000 years ago,[67] in eastern Europe about 45,000 years ago,[68] in southern Europe between 45,000 and 43,000 years ago,[69] in northwestern Europe between 43,000 and 42,000 years ago,[70] and in the Arctic about 40,000 years ago.[71]

The spread of humans into Europe[72] "occurred when shifts in the North Atlantic meridional overturning circulation triggered a series of large and abrupt climate changes during the last glacial." The argument here is that the effect of the Heinrich Event[73] H5 climatic deterioration that occurred about 48,000 years ago was as extreme as that of a glacial maximum episode when most of Europe was deserted by *Neanderthals*. Heinrich H5 led to a similar demographic vacuum so that the incoming modern human populations had the opportunity to spread into and occupy large swaths of Europe before the *Neanderthals* were able to reoccupy this territory. This is also additional evidence that climate change contributed to dispersal into Europe.

Homo sapiens also colonized Siberia and Mongolia by 45,000–40,000 years ago. Scientists show that this migration was partly because[74] "major climate amelioration and pronounced forestation precipitated H. sapiens dispersal into Baikal Siberia 45 ka ago, as chronicled by the appearance of the Initial Upper Paleolithic." Parts of these populations in Siberia are the ones that migrated to the Americas during the Last Glacial Maximum. Some studies show that[75] "Nucleotide diversity analyses based on haplogroup A sequences suggest that Native Americans and Chukchi originated from a single migration to Beringia, probably from east Central Asia, that occurred ≈30,000 or ≈43,000 years ago." One possibility is that these early migrants moved when sea levels were significantly lowered along ice-free corridors that stretched between the Laurentide and Cordilleran ice sheets. Another proposed route is that, either on foot or using primitive boats, these groups migrated down the Pacific coast from North to South America. This also shows the connection between climate change and dispersal to Siberia initially and the Americas ultimately.

Besides the occupation of the Eastern Hemisphere of our planet, how humans dispersed to and settled in the Western Hemisphere is a question worthy of particular attention because of how separated the New World is from the Old. Scholars propose two alternative hypotheses to answer that question with the assumption that humans, somehow, moved from Asia to the Americas either by boat as seafarers across water or on foot as wanderers when the ice melted in the Bering Strait.

The Ice-Free-Corridor hypothesis assumes migration along an ice-free corridor during the Last Glacial Maximum or what is known as the Last Ice Age. The Bering Strait is the ocean passage that separates Northeast Asia from North America. This view suggests that at the end of the Last Ice Age, a Bering land bridge connected Siberia to Alaska. The theory posits that as the ice receded this land bridge would have allowed humans to cross and to live off plants and animals that were available on that bridge during their journey. At that time, humans were hunter-gatherers who would have depended on food sources close by to survive.

In this context, some studies attempt to provide evidence for such a hypothesis. For instance, reconstructing the flooding history of the Bering Strait for the last 50,000 years shows that[76] "humans migrated into the Americas as soon as the Bering Land Bridge allowed for their passage. If correct, such simultaneity implies a strong drive for migration among the ice-age human populations in Siberia." Other scholars refine the timing and geometry of sea level change in the Bering Strait during the last deglaciation and conclude that their[77] "sea level reconstructions predict an evolution of regional shorelines that provides a key boundary condition for studies of human migration into the Americas."

The issue with the Land Bridge theory is that there is evidence of human habitation in the Americas that predates the existence of the bridge since[78] "[t]he Ice-Free Corridor (IFC) has long played a key role in hypotheses about the peopling of the Americas. Earlier assessments of its age suggested that the IFC was available for a Clovis-first migration,[79] but subsequent developments now suggest a pre-Clovis occupation of the Americas that occurred before the opening of the IFC, thus supporting a Pacific coastal migration route instead." The evidence[80]

> from archaeology and ancient genomics, however, now suggests that pre-Clovis migrations occurred by at least ~15.5 to 16.0 ka or earlier than most recent assessments of the age of IFC opening at ~14 to 15 ka, lending support to the use of a Pacific coast migration route instead. Uncertainties in ages from the IFC used in these assessments, however, allow for an earlier IFC opening which would be consistent with the availability of the IFC as a migration route by ~15.5 to 16.0 ka. Here, we use 64 cosmogenic (10Be) exposure ages to closely date the age of the full opening of the IFC at 13.8 ± 0.5 ka. Our results thus clearly establish that the IFC was not available for the first peopling of the Americas after the Last Glacial Maximum, whereas extensive geochronological data from the Pacific coast support its earlier availability as a coastal migration route.

The coastal migration hypothesis is one of the two leading hypotheses on the settlement of the Americas at the time of the Last Glacial Maximum. This hypothesis proposes one or more migration routes involving the use of watercraft. Humans used these vessels to expand their habitat through the Kurile Island chain, the coast of Beringia, the archipelagos off the Western coast, down to Central and South America. Some scholars describe this journey as follows:[81]

> Upper Paleolithic populations moved from Asia to coastal regions along the northwestern Pacific Rim between ~45–30 ka. By ~30 ka these coastal populations developed a mixed maritime, nearshore, and terrestrial adaptation involving the use of boats, shell fishhooks for deep-water fishing, and a stemmed point and macroblade core technology. About 25–24 ka a subset of these coastal populations became isolated somewhere in the vicinity of the Japan/Paleo-Hokkaido, Sahkalin, Kuril (PSHK) region, developing genetically into the ancient Native American (ANA) populations that eventually settled the Americas. Between ~22–16 ka these ANA people began migrating by foot and boat along the southern Beringian coast and down the Alaskan and Canadian coastline into the Americas south of the continental ice sheets before eventually expanding inland.

A coastal migration route is now gaining wider acceptance with newly emerging evidence suggesting that people with boats sailed along the Pacific coast, hopping between islands, until Alaska and continuing south until Peru and Chile by 12,500 years ago or earlier. Findings[82] "from glacial geology and paleo-sea levels support the possibility of coastal migration from Beringia to the Pacific Northwest between about 14,000 and 10,000 BP, and preliminary paleoecological data suggest that the coastal landscape was in part vegetated and probably able to support a terrestrial fauna, including humans. The same cannot be said about the 'ice-free corridor.'"

To provide evidence for this hypothesis, scholars attempt to show that humans migrating along that route were able to find sufficient supplies to sustain themselves. For instance, a group of archaeologists and marine ecologists discuss the contribution of the kelp forest ecosystems in facilitating the migration of maritime people from Asia to the Americas near the end of the Pleistocene.[83] This is referred to as the Kelp Highway hypothesis which posits that[84] "kelp forests and other nearshore habitats sheltered similar suites of food resources that required minimal adaptive adjustments for migrating coastal peoples. With reduced wave energy, holdfasts for boats, and productive fishing, these linear kelp forest ecosystems may have provided a kind of 'kelp highway' for early maritime peoples colonizing the New World." A related paper concludes that a coastal route[85] "offered less ecological resistance than interior routes, providing a linear corridor entirely at sea level and essentially free of major obstructions after about 16,000 years ago. We show that North Pacific nearshore ecosystems—from Japan to Mexico—contained hundreds of species of edible shellfish, fish, marine mammals, birds, and seaweeds distributed more or less continuously over vast stretches of coast. A coastal route, including kelp forests and estuaries, would have provided a rich mix of marine, estuarine, riverine, and terrestrial resources."

Some scholars test various hypotheses to confirm the coastal theory. They specifically examine whether the earliest genetic antecedents of the ancient Native American population are found in the populations of Northeast Asia, that the lithic technologies in East Asia is similar enough to be the predecessor of those in the Americas, that the initial migrants employed true maritime technologies during their journey to the Americas, and that the Kelp forest increased significantly during the late Pleistocene under glacial conditions enabling migration by foragers who exploited the resources in that ecosystem. Based on the overwhelming genetic evidence[86]

> that the indigenous peoples of the Americas share ancestral origins in Northeast Asia, coupled with the recent discovery of multiple archaeological occurrences of humans south of North American continental ice sheets prior to an opening of an ice-free corridor, we logically conclude that the First Americans initially migrated from Asia via a coastal route of entry before ~16 ka. While our understanding of the paleoenvironmental context of the northern Pacific coastline is imperfect, the current state of knowledge about this region indicates that Pleistocene peoples had many opportunities to travel along lowered shorelines into the Americas.

This establishes that favorable climatic conditions also created a window of opportunity for the peopling of the New World, as much as it did in the Old.

3 Climate Window of Opportunity

The question that poses itself is why our ancestors left Africa to populate the entire world. Dispersal is argued to be associated with some sort of disturbance in climatic conditions. There are plenty of studies that assert that there is an association between climate change and human dispersal from Africa. Climate change influenced dispersal in two ways.

The first is in terms of its effects on factors that determine food supply which created an incentive for our ancestors to leave their initial habitat to another. Some suggest that[87] "increasing aridity and desiccation of biogeographic resources associated with Heinrich events could have rapidly rendered large parts of North, West, and East Africa unsuitable for hominin occupation, thereby potentially prompting them to relocate to more hospitable areas." Along the same vein, Benjamin Lieberman and Elizabeth Gordon point our attention to the role of climate in inducing humans to spread all over the world by asserting,[88] "What, then, propelled the ancestors of humans to begin the process of leaving the rain forests of Africa and moving to a much wider range of habitats? Tracking changes in climate helps answer that question. A shift in climate that led to the expansion of the rain forest would provide a greater range with abundant food, but a shift that reduced the area of the rain forest would diminish food supply."

The second influence of climate on dispersal is in terms of opening and closing corridors to facilitate the dispersal from one area to another. For instance, evolutionary ecologist Andrea Manica and other scholars present paleoclimatic reconstructions in combination with an estimate of the minimum amount of rainfall needed by hunter-gatherers to survive. The purpose of the study is to ascertain when, and along which paths, the expansions out of Africa would have been climatically feasible.[89] The analysis shows that[90] "exit routes and timings previously suggested based on archaeological and genetic data coincide with the presence of sufficiently wet corridors into Eurasia, indicating that palaeoclimatic conditions were an important factor in expansions out of Africa." In another contribution, Andrea Manica and other scholars explore the effect of past climate change on the demography of anatomically modern humans, exploiting the worldwide distribution of genetic variation in current populations, and find that[91] "the combinations of demographic parameters compatible with the current genetic makeup of worldwide populations indicate a clear effect of climate on past population densities."

These climatic shifts correlate with dispersal out of Africa since[92] "the first shift towards arid conditions at ~125 ka may have caused the first expansions of this species along this southern route into Arabia. The second major wave of expansion, this time through the 'Nile corridor' into the Levant, occurs after ~105 ka, when climate finally got drier and unstable."

3.1 Climate in the Cradle

To understand the stimulus for human dispersal from the cradle in East Africa, studies focus on recreating the climate in the lakes of Ethiopia. Some of these analyses focus specifically on the Chew Bahir basin in southern Ethiopia which is close to key fossil sites. Chew Bahir paleolake is well suited to explore whether strong environmental variability in the past influenced the exodus of hominin populations out of East Africa. Research in this field attempts to assess whether climate change episodes were coincident with waves of human dispersal. This is not intended to establish causality, as much as its purpose is to point our attention to the potential contribution of climate change as a facilitator of human dispersal.

In this context, a recreation of climate record from Chew Bahir shows stable humid conditions from around 620,000 to 275,000 years before present, which was interrupted by multiple abrupt and extreme hydroclimate perturbations.[93] This long period coincided with the emergence of high anatomical diversity in hominin groups. It was followed by a pattern of pronounced climatic cyclicity between 275,000 and 60,000 years before present, which was a crucial phase encompassing the transition to Middle Stone Age technologies and the emergence of *Homo sapiens* in East Africa. During the period between 60,000 and 10,000 years before present, several pronounced wet phases at Chew Bahir coincide with humid episodes in Northeast Africa and the Eastern Mediterranean. This potentially opened migration routes from the East African Rift System into the Levant. These continuous shifts in environmental conditions could have also contributed to the accumulation of cultural innovation over time which provided *Homo sapiens* with the means to expand beyond their initial habitat, and[94] "shaped adaptations and provided environmental opportunities facilitating modern human dispersal out of Africa."

Other paleoclimatic records from Chew Bahir show a long-term trend toward greater aridity between 200,000 and 60,000 years ago, punctuated by[95] "precession-driven wet-dry cycles." Wetter environmental conditions may have promoted human expansion into new territory, while dry spells may have led to[96] "spatial constriction and isolation of local human populations." During the wettest episode of the record, extensive lakes and connected hydrological networks that developed along the East African Rift System may have facilitated the long-distance dispersal of early modern humans. Since 60,000 years before present, a second mode of high-frequency climatic fluctuations is observed punctuating the predominant trend toward a drier climate. These[97]

> Documented wet phases at CHB,[98] comparable to other sedimentological records of northeastern Africa during the last 200–60 ka, indicate recurrent availability of favorable living conditions in the lowlands of the EARS[99] and

> adjacent regions for H. sapiens, which would have provided opportune corridors for our species to disperse into the Levant and Arabia. Increasing aridity in the lowlands of the southern Ethiopian rift valley starting during MIS 4 and intensifying aridity since 60 ka may have induced H. sapiens to develop, test and use new strategies to survive, including occupation of high mountain refugia and the development of new tools.

There is also a series of studies that point our attention to the observation that waves of human dispersal occurred during phases characterized by stable climate that followed unstable ones. Further evidence for environmental changes in lake sediment cores from Chew Bahir shows highly variable hydroclimate conditions from 116,000 to 66,000 years before present, with fast shifts from very wet conditions to extreme aridity.[100] This was followed by stable hydrological conditions between 58,000 and 32,000 years ago, which facilitated the development of more habitable ecosystems. This shift, from more to less variable hydroclimate, may account for the timing of later dispersal events out of Africa such that[101] "the optimal condition for AMH (anatomically modern humans) dispersal from Africa occurred ~58-32 kyr, a period of stable environments and abundant wildlife. Therefore, hydroclimate change may help explain the timing of AMH migration out of Africa."

Besides Chew Bahir paleolake in southern Ethiopia, some studies focus on Lake Tana in northern Ethiopia. Lake Tana is close to the earliest East African anatomically modern human sites Herto and Omo Kibish and to some dispersal routes. Scholars examine the proposal that periods of climate stability following those of abrupt transition from instability could have induced human dispersal.

Reconstructing a climate record of the past 150,000 years from Lake Tana, scholars identify four stable wet intervals between 150,000–144,000, 125,000–93,000, 82,000–73,000, and 42,000–34,000 years ago.[102] These conditions, which were preceded by an abrupt transition from unstable climate, could have presented[103] "long-lasting, relatively stable, moist, resource-rich conditions conducive to the demographic increase and range expansion of innovative populations into a wide range of habitats, including the Levant and Arabia." The long duration of some of these episodes could have also allowed multiple dispersal events across the southern route since the record[104] "shows interglacial conditions favorable for AMH increase and dispersal during the time windows suggested by recent paleontological, archaeological and genetic data, close to likely dispersal routes into SW Asia."

Along these lines, a two-stage hypothesis of hominin dispersal is proposed in which populations first accumulate high levels of climatic tolerance during highly variable climate phases and then use such acquired resilience for dispersal in subsequent low-variability phases.[105] This implies that dispersals are likely to occur during stable climatic phases that follow those of high climatic variability. Employing paleoclimatic data, a dispersal phase is identified in the Lake Tana record within a time bracket that fits well with the dating evidence for *Homo sapiens* occupation at the sites of Qafzeh and Skhul. Thus, the[106] "analyses of a precipitation evaporation proxy from Lake Tana pinpoint a likely dispersal phase from Ethiopia dating to between c. 112,550 and c. 96,975 years ago. The dating of this dispersal phase is consistent with early H. sapiens dispersal into the Levant, and also accords well with some dates for the 'southern route' out of Africa."

Other studies examine other lakes of the tropics such as Lake Malawi, Lake Tanganyika, and Lake Bosumtwi.[107] The record shows periods of extreme aridity between 135,000 and 75,000 years before present, when lakes' water volume was drastically diminished. The study also documents a shift to more humid conditions and an increase in water levels over tropical Africa after 70,000 years before present. Such climate change may have stimulated the expansion of early modern human populations since the[108] "climatic shift away from mainly arid conditions, identified by the dramatic rise in African lake levels following 70 kyr ago, coincides with the marked expansion of early modern human populations, suggested from studies of modern mtDNA inherent in maternal lineages and Y-chromosome analyses."

3.2 *Across the Deserts*

As much as the change in climate led to unfavorable living conditions in the initial habitat of humans, which deemed dispersal to another area a survival necessity, the environment also had to cooperate to make such step feasible. To disperse out of East Africa, it was essential for hominins to cross the deserts of the Sahara and the Arabian Peninsula. Thus, recreating the paleoclimate of the Sahara-Arabian space is critical in determining the contribution of these areas in the peopling of the planet. The dispersal of *Homo sapiens* out of Africa indicates that these populations were able to cross the arid Sahara-Arabian desert zone during humid periods. Understanding past climate change in these areas is, thus, essential to determine when these areas were arid or humid, to establish when it was possible for hominins to occupy and cross these areas, and to clarify the contribution of these deserts in forming barriers or corridors for the dispersal of hominins across them. In this context, Peter deMenocal and other scholars explore the factors that drove our species out of Africa with a reconstruction of the climate spanning the past 200,000 years.[109] The fossil and lithic data evidence suggests that warm and wet conditions that prevailed from 120,000 to 90,000 years ago could have facilitated early waves of human migration to cross the otherwise inhospitable Saharan or Arabian Deserts.

The Sahara Desert is considered by many to be the first obstacle to such human dispersals. Some scholars point our attention to the similarities in tool assemblages across the Sahara that imply that humans were able to cross that barrier through a humid corridor at one point in time such that[110]

> [t]he very widespread distribution of Middle Stone Age (MSA) Aterian assemblages across the Sahara and their precocious appearance in North Africa at the end of MIS 5 or earlier suggest a widespread dispersal of H. sapiens at this time. The absence of similar industries from the Nile Valley implies the existence of separate migrations along routes across the Sahara as far north as the Mediterranean coast. The similarity of Aterian assemblages in the Western Desert of Egypt and the Libyan Sahara, extending into coastal areas of Cyrenaica and Tunisia, implies a strong connection between the cultural traditions of these regions. Combining these observations with our evidence for continuous humid corridors through the central Sahara at the critical time, fed by strongly enhanced precipitation over the central Saharan watershed, we infer that northward dispersal from sub-Saharan Africa likely took place through regions that currently rank among the most arid on Earth.

Some scholars examine whether a Nile corridor has been used by hominins to cross the Sahara Desert.[111] In this context, an investigation of the zoogeography of the Sahara shows that more animals, many of which are aquatic, crossed via the desert than through the Nile route. The channeling of animals across the Sahara was possible because the area contained a series of linked lakes, rivers, and inland deltas during the Holocene humid period. The dating of lacustrine sediments[112] "show that the 'green Sahara' also existed during the last interglacial (~125 ka) and provided green corridors that could have formed dispersal routes at a likely time for the migration of modern humans out of Africa."

To cross from North Africa to Asia, humans had to overcome the obstacles of the Sinai Peninsula in the northwestern Egypt and the Negev Desert in the southern Levant. To show that a change in climatic conditions created an opportunity to cross these barriers, some scholars examine cave deposits or speleothems from the Negev desert.[113] The study shows a cluster of wet episodes between 140,000 and 110,000 years ago, which coincided with increased monsoonal precipitation in the southern parts of the Sahara-Arabian desert. The disappearance at that time of the desert barrier between Africa and the Levant, especially in the Sinai-Negev land bridge, created a climatic window for early dispersion from Africa to the Levant. This suggests that the[114] "episodic humid phase between 140 and 110 ka in the northern Saharan-Arabian Desert opened an important interglacial climatic window that allowed early modern humans to disperse out of Africa to other parts of the world."

Afterward, humans dispersed from the Levant to the Arabian interior. To evaluate the paleoclimatic context for hominin dispersals through the Levant and the Arabian Peninsula, some scholars use reconstructions of surface freshwater availability to confirm the presence of hydrological features such as lakes, wetlands, and rivers across these areas at the time.[115] This is to determine the feasibility of such dispersal given the available freshwater supplies on the way. Their analysis intimates the formation of a paleohydrological corridor, called the Tabuk Corridor, between the Levant and the Arabian interior during a couple of periods of MIS5. The authors also show that the archaeological sites in Arabia show similarities with Levantine assemblages which confirms that[116] "the Tabuk Corridor appears the most likely terrestrial route by which hominins and other mammal species could have dispersed into Arabia during the penultimate interglacial/glacial transition while remaining in proximity to critical freshwater resources."

Some studies focus on the Nefud desert in the northern part of the Arabian Peninsula. The Nefud is an erg which is a desert landform covered with sand and little or no vegetative cover. This desert is beneficial to these studies in many aspects since[117] "[a]lthough currently semi to hyper-arid, palaeolake deposits in interdune depressions demonstrate that significant climatic changes during the past episodically resulted in the Nefud being considerably wetter than at present." Thus, the Nefud could have acted at some point in time as another corridor in this journey to the Arabian interior.

In this context, some scholars examine Jubbah basin in the Nefud Desert and document a series of paleolake sequences associated with stone tool assemblages and vertebrate fossils.[118] Their findings show at least five hominin expansions into the Arabian interior, coinciding with brief windows of diminished aridity around 400,000, 300,000, 200,000, 130,000–75,000, and 55,000 years before present. The study also shows that the[119] "differences in material culture between these phases—with two phases of Acheulean technology and then three distinct forms of Middle Paleolithic—suggests that diverse hominin populations, and probably even species, were expanding into the region at different times."

Along the same lines, scholars describe the discovery of three archaeological sites situated along the shores of the Jubbah paleolake in the Nefud Desert with Middle Paleolithic stone tool assemblages.[120] These sites were situated in a grassland setting with some trees, which indicates that Middle Paleolithic hominins were able to penetrate deep into the interior of northern Arabia during ameliorated humid periods. Their[121] "paleoenvironmental analyses indicate that hominins were able to utilize and adapt to the marginal environment of the Nefud during humid periods." There was also another discovery of Middle Paleolithic assemblages in the Nefud Desert in a site located close to a substantial relict lake dated to 75,000 years ago.[122] This discovery indicates that these hominins penetrated deeply into the Arabian Peninsula to inhabit landscapes vegetated by grasses and some trees. This supports the hypothesis of expansion into Arabia during the final humid phase of MIS5, when environmental conditions were still favorable, showing that[123] "hominins were present in northern Arabia during pluvial periods."

Some studies focus on the effect of the monsoon rainfall on freshwater supplies in the Arabian interior. For instance, scholars examine whether the expansion into Arabia could have been facilitated by humid periods driven by incursions of monsoon rainfall. Terrestrial and marine core data show that incursions of the monsoon precipitation occurred at approximately 200,000–190,000, 170,000, 155,000, 130,000–120,000, 105,000–95,000, 85,000–75,000, and 60,000–55,000 years before present.[124] During these periods,[125] "the incursion of monsoon rainfall into the Arabian interior would have facilitated the movements of human populations through improved freshwater resources." This observed increase in humidity and the formation of freshwater lakes across the Nefud desert permitted the expansion into the Arabian interior. Others also confirm that southern Arabia experienced humid periods which could have[126] "facilitated a dispersal of AMH (anatomically modern humans) from east Africa across the Bab el Mandab and through southern Arabia."

In the same vein, examining terrestrial alluvial fan deposits from southeast Arabia provides evidence for increased monsoon precipitation which led to improved freshwater availability, the expansion of vegetation, and the activation of the drainage system during periods of MIS6, MIS5, and MIS3.[127] The development of freshwater systems during these periods offers multiple windows of opportunity for dispersal out of Africa during the late Pleistocene since the[128] "availability of freshwater in the southern dispersal zone during these periods would have been critical to the demographic expansion of early human populations."

After populating southwest Asia, humans dispersed to other areas around the world as shown before. Climatic factors were a critical component of that odyssey as discussed earlier.

Notes

1. M.H. Wolpoff, J.N. Spuhler, F.H. Smith, J. Radovcic, G. Pope, D. W. Frayer, R. Eckhardt, and G. Clark. "Modern Human Origins." Science, 241, 4867: 772–774, 1988.
2. Milford Wolpoff, John Hawks, and Rachel Caspari. "Multiregional, Not Multiple Origins." American Journal of Physical Anthropology, 112: 129–136 (2000).
3. Ibid.
4. Marta Lahr. "The Multiregional Model of Modern Human Origins: A Reassessment of its Morphological Basis." Journal of Human Evolution, 26, 1: 23–56, 1994.
5. Chris Stringer. "Out of Ethiopia." Nature, 423: 693–695, 2003. Alex Wilshaw. "Out of Africa Hypothesis." The International Encyclopedia of Biological Anthropology. Alex Wilshaw. "Origins of Modern Humans." The International Encyclopedia of Anthropology.
6. Chris Stringer. "Modern Human Origins: Progress and Prospects." Philosophical Transactions of the Royal Society B Biological Sciences, 357, 1420: 563–579, 2002.

7. Chris Stringer. "The Development of Ideas about a Recent African Origin for Homo Sapiens." Journal of Anthropological Sciences, 100: 5–18, 2022.
8. C. B. Stringer and P. Andrews. "Genetic and Fossil Evidence for the Origin of Modern Humans." Science, 239, 4845: 1263–1268, 1988.
9. Tim D. White, Berhane Asfaw, David DeGusta, Henry Gilbert, Gary D. Richards, Gen Suwa, and F. Clark Howell. "Pleistocene Homo Sapiens from Middle Awash, Ethiopia." Nature, 423: 742–747, 2003.
10. Rebecca L. Cann, Mark Stoneking, and Allan C. Wilson. "Mitochondrial DNA and Human Evolution." Nature, 325: 31–36, 1987. Mark Stoneking and Himla Soodyall. "Human Evolution and the Mitochondrial Genome." Current Opinion in Genetics & Development, 6, 6: 731–736, 1996. Mark Stoneking. "Mitochondrial DNA and Human Evolution." Journal of Bioenergetics and Biomembranes, 26, 3, 1994. Rebecca Louise Cann. "DNA and Human Origins." Annual Review of Anthropology, 17, 1: 127–143, 2003. Brigitte Pakendorf and Mark Stoneking. "Mitochondrial DNA and Human Evolution." Annual Review of Genomics and Human Genetics, 6: 165–183, 2005. Stringer, C. B., and P. Andrews. "Genetic and Fossil Evidence for the Origin of Modern Humans." Science 239: 1263–1268, 1988.
11. H.S. Wainscoat, A.V.S. Hill, A.L. Boyce, H. Flint, M. Hernandez, S.L. Them, H.M. Old, HR. Lynch, A.G. Falusi, D.H. Weatherall, and H.B. Clegg. "Evolutionary Relationships of Human Populations from an Analysis of Nuclear DNA Polymorphisms." Nature, 319, 491–493, 1986. H.S. Wainscoat, A.V.S. Hill, S.L. Thein, and J.B. Clegg. "Are We All Out of Africa? Reply." Nature, 322, 22, 1986.
12. Eleanor M. L. Scerri, Lounès Chikhi and Mark G. Thomas. "Beyond Multiregional and Simple Out-of-Africa Models of Human Evolution." Nature Ecology & Evolution, 3: 1370–1372, 2019.
13. Ibid.
14. Eleanor Scerri. "One species, many roots?" Nature Ecology and Evolution, 7: 975–976, 2023.
15. Eleanor M.L. Scerri, Mark G. Thomas, Andrea Manica, Philipp Gunz, Jay T. Stock, Chris Stringer, Matt Grove, Huw S. Groucutt, 1, Axel Timmermann, G. Philip Rightmire, Francesco d'Errico, Christian A. Tryon, Nick A. Drake, Alison S. Brooks, Robin W. Dennell, Richard Durbin, Brenna M. Henn, Julia Lee-Thorp, Peter deMenocal, Michael D. Petraglia, Jessica C. Thompson, Aylwyn Scally, and Lounès Chikhi. "Did Our Species Evolve in Subdivided Populations across Africa, and Why Does It Matter?" Trends in Ecology & Evolution, 33, 8: 582–594, 2018.

16. Eleanor M.L. Scerri and Manuel Will. "The Revolution that Still Isn't: The Origins of Behavioral Complexity in Homo Sapiens." Journal of Human Evolution, 179, 103358, 2023.
17. Chris Stringer, Henry Schwarcz, and Paul Goldberg. "ESR Dates for the Hominid Burial Site of Es Skhul in Israel." Nature, 338, 6218: 756–758, 1989.
18. Rainer Grun, Chris Stringer, Frank McDermott, Roger Nathan, Naomi Porat, Steve Robertson, Lois Taylor, Graham Mortimer, Stephen Eggins, Malcolm McCulloch. "U-series and ESR Analyses of Bones and Teeth Relating to the Human Burials from Skhul." Journal of Human Evolution 49: 316–334, 2005.
19. Ernesto Abbate and Mario Sagri. "Early to Middle Pleistocene Homo Dispersals from Africa to Eurasia: Geological, Climatic and Environmental Constraints." Quaternary International, 267: 3–19, 2012.
20. Quintana-Murci L., Semino O., Bandelt H.J., Passarino G., McElreavey K., and Santachiara-Benerecetti A.S. "Genetic Evidence of an Early Exit of Homo Sapiens from Africa through Eastern Africa." Nature Genetics, 23: 437–441, 1999.
21. Ibid.
22. Ernesto Abbate and Mario Sagri. "Early to Middle Pleistocene Homo Dispersals from Africa to Eurasia: Geological, Climatic and Environmental Constraints." Quaternary International, 267: 3–19, 2012.
23. Jon Hill, Alexandros Avdis, Geoff Bailey, and Kurt Lambeck. "Sea-level Change, Palaeotidal Modelling and Hominin Dispersals: The Case of the Southern Red Sea." Quaternary Science Reviews, 293, 107719, 2022.
24. Ibid.
25. Marine Isotope Stages (MIS) are alternating warm and cool periods in the Earth's paleoclimate. Working backward from the present, even-numbered stages represent cold glacial periods while odd-numbered stages represent warm interglacial intervals.
26. Genetic drift is the change in frequency of an existing gene variant in the population due to random chance.
27. Bastiaan Star and Hamish G. Spencer. "Effects of Genetic Drift and Gene Flow on the Selective Maintenance of Genetic Variation." Genetics, 194: 235–244, 2013.
28. Omkar Deshpande, Serafim Batzoglou, Marcus W. Feldman, and L. Luca Cavalli-Sforza. "A Serial Founder Effect Model for Human Settlement Out of Africa." Proceedings of the Royal Society B, 276: 291–300, 2009.

29. P. Mellars, K. C. Gori, M. Carr, P. A. Soares, and M. B. Richards. "Genetic and Archaeological Perspectives on the Initial Modern Human Colonization of Southern Asia." PNAS, 110: 10699–10704, 2013.
30. Paul Mellars. "Going East: New Genetic and Archaeological Perspectives on the Modern Human Colonization of Eurasia." Science, 313, 5788: 796–800, 2006.
31. M. Lahr and R. Foley "Multiple Dispersals and Modern Human Origins." Evolutionary Anthropology, 3: 48–60, 1994.
32. Axel Timmermann and Tobias Friedrich. "Late Pleistocene Climate Drivers of Early Human Migration." Nature, 538: 92–95, 2016.
33. Ibid.
34. R. Dennell and M.D. Petraglia. "The Dispersal of Homo Sapiens Across Southern Asia: How early, How Often, How Complex?" Quaternary Science Reviews 47: 15–22, 2012.
35. M.D. Petraglia, M. Haslam, D.Q. Fuller, N. Boivin, and C. Clarkson. "Out of Africa: New Hypotheses and Evidence for the Dispersal of Homo Sapiens Along the Indian Ocean Rim." Human Biology, 37: 288–311, 2010.
36. Reid Ferring, Oriol Oms, Jordi Agustí, Francesco Berna, Medea Nioradze, Teona Shelia, Martha Tappen, Abesalom Vekua, David Zhvania, and David Lordkipanidze. "Earliest Human Occupations at Dmanisi (Georgian Caucasus) Dated to 1.85–1.78 Ma." PNAS, 108, 26: 10432–10436, 2011.
37. Véronique Michel, Chuan-Chou Shen, Jon Woodhead, Hsun-Ming Hu, Chung-Che Wu, Pierre-Élie Moullé, Samir Khatib, Dominique Cauche, Marie-Hélène Moncel, Patricia Valensi, Yu-Min Chou, Sylvain Gallet, Anna Echassoux, François Orange, and Henry de Lumley. "New Dating Evidence of the Early Presence of Hominins in Southern Europe." Nature, 7: 10074, 2017.
38. Emanuel Vlček. "A New Discovery of Homo erectus in Central Europe." Journal of Human Evolution, 7, 3: 239–242, IN3–IN4, 243–251, 1978.
39. R. Garba, V. Usyk, L. Ylä-Mella, J. Kameník, K. Stübner, J. Lachner, G. Rugel, F. Veselovský, N. Gerasimenko, A. I. R. Herries, J. Kučera, M. F. Knudsen, and J. D. Jansen. "East-to-West Human Dispersal into Europe 1.4 Million Years Ago." Nature, 627: 805–810, 2024.
40. Eudald Carbonell, Jose´ M. Bermudez de Castro, Josep M. Pare´s, Alfredo Perez-Gonzalez, Gloria Cuenca-Bescos, Andreu Olle, Marina Mosquera, Rosa Huguet, Jan van der Made, Antonio Rosas, Robert Sala, Josep Vallverdu, Nuria Garcıa, Darryl E. Granger, Marıa Martinon-

Torres, Xose P. Rodrıguez, Greg M. Stock, Josep M. Verges, Ethel Allue, Francesc Burjachs, Isabel Caceres, Antoni Canals, Alfonso Benito, Carlos Dıez, Marina Lozano, Ana Mateos, Marta Navazo, Jesus Rodrıguez, Jordi Rosell, and Juan L. Arsuaga. "The First Hominin of Europe." Nature, 452: 465–469, 2008.

41. Zhaoyu Zhu, Robin Dennell, Weiwen Huang, Yi Wu, Shifan Qiu, Shixia Yang, Zhiguo Rao, Yamei Hou, Jiubing Xie, Jiangwei Han, and Tingping Ouyang. "Hominin Occupation of the Chinese Loess Plateau Since about 2.1 Million Years Ago." Nature, 559: 608–612, 2018.
42. Laurent Husson, Tristan Salles, Anne-Elisabeth Lebatard, Swann Zerathe, Régis Braucher, Sofwan Noerwidi, Sonny Aribowo, Claire Mallard, Julien Carcaillet, Danny H. Natawidjaja, Didier Bourlès, and ASTER team. "Javanese Homo erectus on the Move in SE Asia circa 1.8 Ma." Nature, Scientific Reports, 12, 19012, 2022.
43. F. Carotenuto N. Tsikaridze, L. Rook, D. Lordkipanidze, Laura Longo, Silvana Condemi, and P. Raia. "Venturing Out Safely: The Biogeography of Homo erectus Dispersal Out of Africa." Journal of Human Evolution, 95: 1–12, 2016.
44. Ibid.
45. Mateja Hajdinjak, Fabrizio Mafessoni, Laurits Skov, Benjamin Vernot, Alexander Hübner, Qiaomei Fu, Elena Essel, Sarah Nagel, Birgit Nickel, Julia Richter, Oana Teodora Moldovan, Silviu Constantin, Elena Endarova, Nikolay Zahariev, Rosen Spasov, Frido Welker, Geoff M. Smith, Virginie Sinet-Mathiot, Lindsey Paskulin, Helen Fewlass, Sahra Talamo, Zeljko Rezek, Svoboda Sirakova, Nikolay Sirakov, Shannon P. McPherron, Tsenka Tsanova, Jean-Jacques Hublin, Benjamin M. Peter, Matthias Meyer, Pontus Skoglund, Janet Kelso, and Svante Pääbo. "Initial Upper Palaeolithic Humans in Europe had Recent Neanderthal Ancestry." Nature, 592: 253–257, 2021.
46. David Reich, Nick Patterson, Martin Kircher, Frederick Delfin, Madhusudan R. Nandineni, Irina Pugach, Albert Min-Shan Ko, Ying-Chin Ko, Timothy A. Jinam, Maude E. Phipps, Naruya Saitou, Andreas Wollstein, Manfred Kayser, Svante Paabo, and Mark Stoneking. "Denisova Admixture and the First Modern Human Dispersals into Southeast Asia and Oceania." The American Journal of Human Genetics 89: 516–528, 2011.
47. Aurélien Mounier, and Marta Mirazón Lahr. "Deciphering African Late Middle Pleistocene Hominin Diversity and the Origin of Our Species." Nature Communication, 10, 1: 3406, 2019.

48. Mathew Stewart, Richard Clark-Wilson, Paul S Breeze, Klint Janulis, Ian Candy, Simon J Armitage, David B Ryves, Julien Louys, Mathieu Duval, Gilbert J Price, Patrick Cuthbertson, Marco A Bernal, Nick A Drake, Abdullah M Alsharekh, Badr Zahrani, Abdulaziz Al-Omari, Patrick Roberts, Huw S Groucutt, and Michael D Petraglia. "Human Footprints Provide Snapshot of Last Interglacial Ecology in the Arabian Interior." Science Advances, 6, 38, eaba8940, 2020.
49. John F Hoffecker and Ian T Hoffecker. "Technological Complexity and the Global Dispersal of Modern Humans." Evolutionary Anthropology, 26, 6: 285–299, 2017.
50. Li Jin, Peter Underhill, Vishal Doctor, Ronald Davis, Peidong Shen, Luca Cavalli-Sforza, and Peter Oefner. "Distribution of Haplotypes from a Chromosome 21 Region Distinguishes Multiple Prehistoric Human Migrations." PNAS, 96, 7: 3796–3800, 1999.
51. Simon Armitage, Sabah Jasim, Anthony Marks, Adrian Parker, Vitaly Usik, and Hans-Peter Uerpmann. "Hints of Earlier Human Exit from Africa." Science, 331, 6016: 453–456, 2011.
52. Veronica Fernandes, Farida Alshamali, Marco Alves, Marta D. Costa, Joana B. Pereira, Nuno M. Silva, Lotfi Cherni, Nourdin Harich, Viktor Cerny, Pedro Soares, Martin B. Richards, and Luisa Pereira. "The Arabian Cradle: Mitochondrial Relicts of the First Steps along the Southern Route out of Africa." The American Journal of Human Genetics, 90, 347–355: 2012.
53. Leonardo Vallini, Carlo Zampieri, Mohamed Javad Shoaee, Eugenio Bortolini, Giulia Marciani, Serena Aneli, Telmo Pievani, Stefano Benazzi, Alberto Barausse, Massimo Mezzavilla, Michael D. Petraglia, and Luca Pagani. "The Persian Plateau Served as Hub for Homo sapiens after the Main Out of Africa Dispersal." Nature, 15, 1882, 2024.
54. Melinda A. Yang. "A Genetic History of Migration, Diversification, and Admixture in Asia." Human Population Genetics and Genomics, 2, 1, 0001, 2022.
55. Chris Clarkson, Clair Harris, Bo Li, Christina M. Neudorf, Richard G. Roberts, Christine Lane, Kasih Norman, Jagannath Pal, Sacha Jones, Ceri Shipton, Jinu Koshy, M.C. Gupta, D.P. Mishra, A.K. Dubey, Nicole Boivin, and Michael Petraglia. "Human Occupation of Northern India Spans the Toba Super-eruption ~74,000 Years Ago." Nature Communications, 11, 96, 2020.

56. Sarah E. Freidline, Kira E. Westaway, Renaud Joannes-Boyau, Philippe Duringer, Jean-Luc Ponche, Mike W. Morley, Vito C. Hernandez, Meghan S. McAllister-Hayward, Hugh McColl, Clément Zanolli, Philipp Gunz, Inga Bergmann, Phonephanh Sichanthongtip, Daovee Sihanam, Souliphane Boualaphane, Thonglith Luangkhoth, Viengkeo Souksavatdy, Anthony Dosseto, Quentin Boesch, Elise Patole-Edoumba, Françoise Aubaile, Françoise Crozier, Eric Suzzoni, Sébastien Frangeul, Nicolas Bourgon, Alexandra Zachwieja, Tyler E. Dunn, Anne-Marie Bacon, Jean-Jacques Hublin, Laura Shackelford, and Fabrice Demeter. "Early Presence of Homo sapiens in Southeast Asia by 86–68 kyr at Tam Pà Ling, Northern Laos." Nature, 14, 3193, 2023.
57. K. E. Westaway, J. Louys, R. Due Awe, M. J. Morwood, G. J. Price, J. Zhao, M. Aubert, R. Joannes-Boyau, T. M. Smith, M. M. Skinner, T. Compton, R. M. Bailey, G. D. van den Bergh, J. de Vos, A. W. G. Pike, C. Stringer, E. W. Saptomo, Y. Rizal, J. Zaim, W. D. Santoso, A. Trihascaryo, L. Kinsley, and B. Sulistyanto. "An Early Modern Human Presence in Sumatra 73,000–63,000 Years Ago." Nature, 548: 322–325, 2017.
58. S. Park, J. Kim, Y. Lee, and J. Woo. "A Late Pleistocene Modern Human Fossil from the Gunang Cave, Danyang County in Korea." Quaternary International, 519: 82–91, 2019.
59. Tsutsumi Takashi. "MIS3 Edge-ground Axes and the Arrival of the First Homo sapiens in the Japanese Archipelago." Quaternary International, 248: 70–78, 2012.
60. James M. Bowler, Harvey Johnston, Jon M. Olley, John R. Prescott, Richard G. Roberts, Wilfred Shawcross, and Nigel A. Spooner. "New Ages for Human Occupation and Climatic Change at Lake Mungo, Australia." Nature, 421: 837–840, 2003. Chris Clarkson, Zenobia Jacobs, Ben Marwick, Richard Fullagar, Lynley Wallis, Mike Smith, Richard G. Roberts, Elspeth Hayes, Kelsey Lowe, Xavier Carah, S. Anna Florin, Jessica McNeill, Delyth Cox, Lee J. Arnold, Quan Hua, Jillian Huntley, Helen E. A. Brand, Tiina Manne, Andrew Fairbairn, James Shulmeister, Lindsey Lyle, Makiah Salinas, Mara Page, Kate Connell, Gayoung Park, Kasih Norman, Tessa Murphy, and Colin Pardoe. "Human Occupation of Northern Australia by 65,000 Years Ago." Nature, 547: 306–310, 2017.
61. James F. O'Connell, Jim Allen, Martin A. J. Williams, Alan N. Williams, Chris S. M. Turney, Nigel A. Spooner, Johan Kamminga, and Graham Brown. "When Did Homo Sapiens First Reach Southeast Asia and Sahul?" PNAS, 115, 34: 8482–8490, 2018.

62. Georgi Hudjashov, Toomas Kivisild, Peter A. Underhill, Phillip Endicott, Juan J. Sanchez, Alice A. Lin, Peidong Shen, Peter Oefner, Colin Renfrew, Richard Villems, and Peter Forster. "Revealing the Prehistoric Settlement of Australia by Y Chromosome and mtDNA Analysis." PNAS, 104, 21: 8726–8730, 2007.
63. Zaibao Yang, Yanli Lei, Yair Rosenthal, Tiegang Li, and Zhimin Jian. "Late Pleistocene Climate Induced Changes in Paleo-vegetation in Borneo: Possible Implications to human divergence." Quaternary Science Reviews, 267, 107109, 2021.
64. Hong Ao, Jiaoyang Ruan, María Martinón-Torres, Mario Krapp, Diederik Liebrand, Mark J. Dekkers, Thibaut Caley, Tara N. Jonell, Zongmin Zhu, Chunju Huang, Xinxia Li, Ziyun Zhang, Qiang Sun, Pingguo Yang, Jiali Jiang, Xinzhou Li, Xiaoxun Xie, Yougui Song, Xiaoke Qiang, Peng Zhang, and Zhisheng An. "Concurrent Asian Monsoon Strengthening and Early Modern Human Dispersal to East Asia during the Last Interglacial." PNAS 121, 3, e2308994121, 2024.
65. Cosimo Posth, Gabriel Renaud, Alissa Mittnik, Dorothee G. Drucker, Helene Rougier, Christophe Cupillard, Frederique Valentin, Corinne Thevenet, Anja Furtwangler, Christoph Wißing, Michael Francken, Maria Malina, Michael Bolus, Martina Lari, Elena Gigli, Giulia Capecchi, Isabelle Crevecoeur, Cedric Beauval, Damien Flas, Mietje Germonpre´, Johannes van der Plicht, Richard Cottiaux, Bernard Gely, Annamaria Ronchitelli, Kurt Wehrberger, Dan Grigorescu, Jirı´ Svoboda, Patrick Semal, David Caramelli, Herve´ Bocherens, Katerina Harvati, Nicholas J. Conard, Wolfgang Haak, Adam Powell, and Johannes Krause. "Pleistocene Mitochondrial Genomes Suggest a Single Major Dispersal of Non-Africans and a Late Glacial Population Turnover in Europe." Current Biology, 26: 827–833, 2016.
66. Arev P. Sümer, Hélène Rougier, Vanessa Villalba-Mouco, Yilei Huang, Leonardo N. M. Iasi, Elena Essel, Alba Bossoms Mesa, Anja Furtwaengler, Stéphane Peyrégne, Cesare de Filippo, Adam B. Rohrlach, Federica Pierini, Fabrizio Mafessoni, Helen Fewlass, Elena I. Zavala, Dorothea Mylopotamitaki, Raffaela A. Bianco, Anna Schmidt, Julia Zorn, Birgit Nickel, Anna Patova, Cosimo Posth, Geoff M. Smith, Karen Ruebens, Virginie Sinet-Mathiot, Alexander Stoessel, Holger Dietl, Jörg Orschiedt, Janet Kelso, Hugo Zeberg, Kirsten I. Bos, Frido Welker, Marcel Weiss, Shannon McPherron, Tim Schüler, Jean-Jacques Hublin, Petr Velemínský, Jaroslav Brůžek, Benjamin M. Peter, Matthias Meyer, Harald Meller,

Harald Ringbauer, Mateja Hajdinjak, Kay Prüfer, and Johannes Krause. "Earliest Modern Human Genomes Constrain Timing of Neanderthal Admixture." Nature, 2024.

67. Dorothea Mylopotamitaki, Marcel Weiss, Helen Fewlass, Elena Irene Zavala, Hélène Rougier, Arev Pelin Sümer, Mateja Hajdinjak, Geoff M. Smith, Karen Ruebens, Virginie Sinet-Mathiot, Sarah Pederzani, Elena Essel, Florian S. Harking, Huan Xia, Jakob Hansen, André Kirchner, Tobias Lauer, Mareike Stahlschmidt, Michael Hein, Sahra Talamo, Lukas Wacker, Harald Meller, Holger Dietl, Jörg Orschiedt, Jesper V. Olsen, Hugo Zeberg, Kay Prüfer, Johannes Krause, Matthias Meyer, Frido Welker, Shannon P. McPherron, Tim Schüler, and Jean-Jacques Hublin. "Homo sapiens Reached the Higher Latitudes of Europe by 45,000 years ago." Nature, 626: 341–346, 2024.
68. Jean-Jacques Hublin, Nikolay Sirakov, Vera Aldeias, Shara Bailey, Edouard Bard, Vincent Delvigne, Elena Endarova, Yoann Fagault, Helen Fewlass, Mateja Hajdinjak, Bernd Kromer, Ivaylo Krumov, João Marreiros, Naomi L. Martisius, Lindsey Paskulin, Virginie Sinet-Mathiot, Matthias Meyer, Svante Pääbo, Vasil Popov, Zeljko Rezek, Svoboda Sirakova, Matthew M. Skinner, Geoff M. Smith, Rosen Spasov, Sahra Talamo, Thibaut Tuna, Lukas Wacker, Frido Welker, Arndt Wilcke, Nikolay Zahariev, Shannon P. McPherron, and Tsenka Tsanova. "Initial Upper Palaeolithic Homo sapiens from Bacho Kiro Cave, Bulgaria." Nature, 581: 299–302, 2020.
69. Stefano Benazzi, Katerina Douka, Cinzia Fornai, Catherine C. Bauer, Ottmar Kullmer, Jirı´ Svoboda, Ildiko´ Pap, Francesco Mallegni, Priscilla Bayle, Michael Coquerelle, Silvana Condemi, Annamaria Ronchitelli, Katerina Harvati, and & Gerhard W. Weber. "Early Dispersal of Modern Humans in Europe and Implications for Neanderthal Behaviour." Nature, 479: 525–528, 2011.
70. Tom Higham, Tim Compton, Chris Stringer, Roger Jacobi, Beth Shapiro, Erik Trinkaus, Barry Chandler, Flora Groning, Chris Collins, Simon Hillson, Paul O'Higgins, Charles FitzGerald, and Michael Fagan. "The Earliest Evidence for Anatomically Modern Humans in Northwestern Europe." Nature, 479: 521–524, 2011.
71. Pavel Pavlov, John Inge Svendsen, and Svein Indrelid. "Human Presence in the European Arctic Nearly 40,000 Years Ago." Nature, 413: 64–67, 2001.
72. Ulrich C. Müller, Jörg Pross, Polychronis C. Tzedakis, Clive Gamble, Ulrich Kotthoff, Gerhard Schmiedl, Sabine Wulf, and Kimon Christanis. "The Role of Climate in the Spread of Modern Humans into Europe." Quaternary Science Reviews, 30: 273–279, 2011.
73. A Heinrich event is a phenomenon in which large groups of icebergs break off from the Laurentide ice sheet and cross the Hudson Strait into the North Atlantic.

74. Koji Shichi, Ted Goebel, Masami Izuho, and Kenji Kashiwaya. "Climate Amelioration, Abrupt Vegetation Recovery, and the Dispersal of Homo sapiens in Baikal Siberia." Science Advances, 9, eadi0189, 2023.
75. Sandro L. Bonatto and Francisco M. Salzano. "A Single and Early Migration for the Peopling of the Americas Supported by Mitochondrial DNA Sequence Data." PNAS, 94: 1866–1871, 1997.
76. Jesse R. Farmer, Tamara Pico, Ona M. Underwood, Rebecca Cleveland Stout, Julie Granger, Thomas M. Cronin, François Fripiat, Alfredo Martínez-García, Gerald H. Haug, and Daniel M. Sigman. "The Bering Strait was Flooded 10,000 Years Before the Last Glacial Maximum." PNAS, 120, 1, 2023.
77. T. Pico, J. X. Mitrovica, and A. C. Mix. "Sea Level Fingerprinting of the Bering Strait Flooding History Detects the Source of the Younger Dryas Climate Event." Science Advances, 6, eaay2935, 2020.
78. Jorie Clark, Anders E. Carlson, Alberto V. Reyes, Elizabeth C. B. Carlson, Louise Guillaume, Glenn A. Milne, Lev Tarasov, Marc Caffee, Klaus Wilcken, and Dylan H. Rood. "The Age of the Opening of the Ice-Free Corridor and Implications for the Peopling of the Americas." PNAS, 119, 14, e211855811, 2022.
79. The Clovis-First theory proposes that the Clovis people were the first to migrate to the Americas by crossing the Bering Land Bridge from Siberia to Alaska during the Last Ice Age, and then spread across the continent.
80. Ibid.
81. Loren Davis and David Madsen. "The Coastal Migration Theory: Formulation and Testable Hypotheses." Quaternary Science Reviews, 249, 106605, 2020.
82. Carole Mandryk, Heiner Josenhans, Daryl Fedje, and Rolf Mathewes. "Late Quaternary Paleoenvironments of Northwestern North America: Implications for Inland versus Coastal Migration Routes." Quaternary Science Reviews, 20, 1–3: 301–314, 2001.
83. Jon M. Erlandson, Michael H. Graham, Bruce J. Bourque, Debra Corbett, James A. Estes, and Robert S. Steneck. "The Kelp Highway Hypothesis: Marine Ecology, the Coastal Migration Theory, and the Peopling of the Americas." The Journal of Island and Coastal Archaeology, 2, 2: 161–174, 2007.
84. Ibid.
85. Jon M. Erlandson, Todd J. Braje, Kristina M. Gill & Michael H. Graham. "Ecology of the Kelp Highway: Did Marine Resources Facilitate Human Dispersal from Northeast Asia to the Americas?" The Journal of Island and Coastal Archaeology, Volume 10, 3: 392–411, 2015.

86. Loren G. Davis and David B. Madsen. "The Coastal Migration Theory: Formulation and Testable Hypotheses." Quaternary Science Reviews, 249, 106605, 2020.
87. Shannon L. Carto, Andrew J. Weaver, Rene´e Hetherington, Yin Lam, Edward C. Wiebe. "Out of Africa and Into an Ice Age: On the Role of Global Climate Change in the Late Pleistocene Migration of Early Modern Humans out of Africa." Journal of Human Evolution, 56: 139–151, 2009.
88. Benjamin Lieberman and Elizabeth Gordon. Climate Change in Human History: Prehistory to the Present. Bloomsbury, 2018. (PP. 12–13).
89. Robert M. Beyer, Mario Krapp, Anders Eriksson, and Andrea Manica. "Climatic Windows for Human Migration Out of Africa in the Past 300,000 Years." Nature Communications, 12, 4889, 2021.
90. Ibid.
91. Anders Eriksson, Lia Betti, Andrew D. Friend, Stephen J. Lycett, Joy S. Singarayer, Noreen von Cramon-Taubadel, Paul J. Valdes, Francois Balloux, and Andrea Manica. "Late Pleistocene Climate Change and the Global Expansion of Anatomically Modern Humans." PNAS, 109, 40: 16089–16094, 2012.
92. Martin H. Trauth, Andreas G.N. Bergner, Verena Foerster, Annett Junginger, Mark A. Maslin, and Frank Schaebitz. "Episodes of Environmental Stability versus Instability in Late Cenozoic Lake Records of Eastern Africa." Journal of Human Evolution, 87: 21–31, 2015.
93. Verena Foerster, Asfawossen Asrat, Christopher Bronk Ramsey, Erik T. Brown, Melissa S. Chapot, Alan Deino, Walter Duesing, Matthew Grove, Annette Hahn, Annett Junginger, Stefanie Kaboth-Bahr, Christine S. Lane, Stephan Opitz, Anders Noren, Helen M. Roberts, Mona Stockhecke, Ralph Tiedemann, Céline M. Vidal, Ralf Vogelsang, Andrew S. Cohen, Henry F. Lamb, Frank Schaebitz, and Martin H. Trauth. "Pleistocene Climate Variability in Eastern Africa Influenced Hominin Evolution." Nature Geoscience, 15: 805–811, 2022.
94. Ibid.
95. Frank Schaebitz, Asfawossen Asrat, Henry F. Lamb, Andrew S. Cohen, Verena Foerster, Walter Duesing, Stefanie Kaboth-Bahr, Stephan Opitz, Finn A. Viehberg, Ralf Vogelsang, Jonathan Dean, Melanie J. Leng, Annett Junginger, Christopher Bronk Ramsey, Melissa S. Chapot, Alan Deino, Christine S. Lane, Helen M. Roberts, Céline Vidal, Ralph Tiedemann, and Martin H. Trauth. "Hydroclimate Changes in Eastern Africa Over the Past 200,000 years may have Influenced Early Human Dispersal." Nature, Communications Earth & Environment, 2, 123, 2021.

96. Ibid.
97. Ibid.
98. Chew Bahir.
99. East African Rift System.
100. Finn A. Viehberg, Janna Just, Jonathan R. Dean, Bernd Wagner, Sven Oliver Franz, Nicole Klasen, Thomas Kleinen, Patrick Ludwig, Asfawossen Asrat, Henry F. Lamb, Melanie J. Leng, Janet Rethemeyer, Antoni E. Milodowski, Martin Claussen, and Frank Schaebitz. "Environmental Change During MIS 4 and MIS 3 Opened Corridors in the Horn of Africa for Homo Sapiens Expansion." Quaternary Science Reviews, 202: 139–153, 2018.
101. Ibid.
102. Henry F. Lamb, Richard Bates, Charlotte L. Bryant, Sarah J. Davies, Dei G. Huws, Michael H. Marshall, Helen M. Roberts, and Harry Toland. "150,000-year Palaeoclimate Record from Northern Ethiopia Supports Early, Multiple Dispersals of Modern Humans from Africa." Nature, Scientific Reports, 8, 1077, 2018.
103. Ibid.
104. Ibid.
105. Matt Grove, Henry Lamb, Helen Roberts, Sarah Davies, Mike Marshall, Richard Bates, and Dei Huws. "Climatic Variability, Plasticity, and Dispersal: A Case Study from Lake Tana, Ethiopia." Journal of Human Evolution 87: 32–47, 2015.
106. Ibid.
107. Christopher A. Scholza, Thomas C. Johnson, Andrew S. Cohen, John W. King, John A. Peck, Jonathan T. Overpeck, Michael R. Talbot, Erik T. Brown, Leonard Kalindekafe, Philip Y. O. Amoako, Robert P. Lyons, Timothy M. Shanahan, Isla S. Castaneda, Clifford W. Heil, Steven L. Forman, Lanny R. McHargue, Kristina R. Beuning, Jeanette Gomez, and James Pierson. "East African Megadroughts between 135 and 75 thousand Years Ago and Bearing on Early-modern Human Origins." PNAS, 104, 42: 16416–16421, 2007.
108. Ibid.
109. Jessica E. Tierney, Peter B. deMenocal, and Paul D. Zander. "A Climatic Context for the out-of-Africa Migration." Geology 45, 11: 1023–1026, 2017.
110. Anne H. Osborne, Derek Vance, Eelco J. Rohling, Nick Barton, Mike Rogerson, and Nuri Fello. "A Humid Corridor Across the Sahara for the Migration of Early Modern Humans Out of Africa 120,000 Years Ago." PNAS, 105, 43: 16444–16447, 2008.

111. Nick A. Drake, Roger M. Blench, Simon J. Armitage, Charlie S. Bristow, and Kevin H. White. "Ancient Watercourses and Biogeography of the Sahara Explain the Peopling of the Desert." PNAS, 108, 2: 458–462, 2011.
112. Ibid.
113. Anton Vaks, Miryam Bar-Matthews, Avner Ayalon, Alan Matthews, Ludwik Halicz, and Amos Frankin. "Desert Speleothems Reveal Climatic Window for African Exodus of Early Modern Humans." Geology, 35, 9: 831–834, 2007.
114. Ibid.
115. Paul S. Breeze, Huw S. Groucutt, Nick A. Drake, Tom S. White, Richard P. Jennings, Michael D. Petraglia. "Palaeohydrological Corridors for Hominin Dispersals in the Middle East ~250–70,000 Years Ago." Quaternary Science Reviews, 144: 155–185, 2016.
116. Ibid.
117. Paul S. Breeze, Huw S. Groucutt, Nick A. Drake, Julien Louys, Eleanor M.L. Scerri, Simon J. Armitage, Iyad S.A. Zalmout, Abdullah M. Memesh, Mohammed A. Haptari, Saleh A. Soubhi, Adel H. Matari, Muhammad Zahir, Abdulaziz Al-Omari, Abdullah M. Alsharekh, and Michael D. Petraglia. "Prehistory and Palaeoenvironments of the Western Nefud Desert, Saudi Arabia." Archaeological Research in Asia, 10: 1–16, 2017.
118. Huw S. Groucutt, Tom S. White, Eleanor M. L. Scerri, Eric Andrieux, Richard Clark-Wilson, Paul S. Breeze, Simon J. Armitage, Mathew Stewart, Nick Drake, Julien Louys, Gilbert J. Price, Mathieu Duval, Ash Parton, Ian Candy, W. Christopher Carleton, Ceri Shipton, Richard P. Jennings, Muhammad Zahir, James Blinkhorn, Simon Blockley, Abdulaziz Al-Omari, Abdullah M. Alsharekh, and Michael D. Petraglia. "Multiple Hominin Dispersals into Southwest Asia over the Past 400,000 Years." Nature, 597: 376–380, 2021.
119. Ibid.
120. Michael D. Petraglia, Abdullah Alsharekh, Paul Breeze, Chris Clarkson, Rémy Crassard, Nick A. Drake, Huw S. Groucutt, Richard Jennings, Adrian G. Parker, Ash Parton, Richard G. Roberts, Ceri Shipton, Carney Matheson, Abdulaziz al-Omari, Margaret-Ashley Veall. "Hominin Dispersal into the Nefud Desert and Middle Palaeolithic Settlement along the Jubbah Palaeolake, Northern Arabia." PLoS ONE 7, 11, e49840, 2012.
121. Ibid.
122. Michael D. Petraglia, Abdullah M. Alsharekh, Rémy Crassard, Nick A. Drake, Huw Groucutt, Adrian G. Parker, Richard G. Roberts. "Middle Paleolithic Occupation on a Marine Isotope Stage 5 Lakeshore in the Nefud Desert, Saudi Arabia." Quaternary Science Reviews 30:1555–1559, 2011.

123. Ibid.
124. Ash Parton, Tom S. White, Adrian G. Parker, Paul S. Breeze, Richard Jennings, Huw S. Groucutt, Michael D. Petraglia. "Orbital-scale Climate Variability in Arabia as a Potential Motor for Human Dispersals." Quaternary International, 382: 82–97, 2015.
125. Ibid.
126. Nick A. Drake, Paul Breeze, and Adrian Parker. "Palaeoclimate in the Saharan and Arabian Deserts During the Middle Palaeolithic and the Potential for Hominin Dispersals." Quaternary International, 300: 48–61, 2013.
127. Ash Parton, Andrew R. Farrant, Melanie J. Leng, Matt W. Telfer, Huw S. Groucutt, Michael D. Petraglia, and Adrian G. Parker. "Alluvial Fan Records from Southeast Arabia Reveal Multiple Windows for Human Dispersal." Geology, 43, 4: 295–298, 2015.
128. Ibid.

CHAPTER 5

Turbulence and Transition

1 Foraging for Food

From the emergence of humans until the advent of agriculture, hunting and gathering was the principal way of food procurement practiced by our ancestors. A gatherer is one leading a life in which food is obtained by foraging or gathering food from local natural sources such as wild plants. A hunter is one surviving by hunting game, or pursuing, trapping, and killing wild animals. Hunter-gatherers adopted diverse strategies depending upon the local environmental conditions. These included hunting big game or smaller animals, fishing, and gathering wild plants such as fruits, vegetables, tubers, seeds, and nuts. Hunter-gatherers combined a variety of these strategies to ensure a balanced diet. Most hunter-gatherers lived in temporary settlements, as they were dependent upon the abundance of food in the area, which if not plentiful would then have to relocate to another.

In this context, establishing settlements for prolonged periods was not a practical choice since their life depended upon access to large areas of land to find food essential for survival. Thus, hunter-gatherers were largely nomadic. However, some hunter-gatherer communities lived in environments with sufficiently abundant food that allowed them to be sedentary or semi-sedentary.[1] These conditions were rare, however, and most foraging groups had to relocate whenever the local food supply was depleted.

S. Khalifa, *Climate Change, Economic Channels, and Historical Junctures*, https://doi.org/10.1007/978-3-031-91867-4_5

In these cases, possessions are limited to what can be carried from one location to another.

Thus, hunter-gatherer communities tend to be egalitarian except for those settled ones. Egalitarianism in hunter-gatherer economies was attained because of direct access to resources with immediate return, mobility which prevents accumulation of property and material possessions, and the need for sharing to survive. In this context, anthropologist James Woodburn asserts that[2]

> [g]reater equality of wealth, of power and of prestige has been achieved in certain hunting and gathering societies than in any other human societies. These societies, which have economies based on immediate rather than delayed return, are assertively egalitarian. Equality is achieved through direct, individual access to resources; through direct, individual access to means of coercion and means of mobility which limit the imposition of control; through procedures which prevent saving and accumulation and impose sharing; through mechanisms which allow goods to circulate without making people dependent upon one another.

In a similar vein, the culture of sharing in hunter-gatherer societies impose rules that prescribe that the[3] "prey is redistributed eventually to all members of the community while everybody receives (an approximately) equal share." This ensured a largely egalitarian society such that[4] "[w]ealth inequality (measured with Gini coefficients) is moderate for most wealth types, matching what qualitative ethnographic research has generally indicated (if not the stereotype of hunter-gatherers as extreme egalitarians)." Others, however, argue that the origins of inequality can be traced to the resource-rich hunter-gatherer societies when they started to control access to defensible and clustered resource patches.[5] In this context, some[6] "ancient hunter-gatherers may have accumulated wealth and political clout by taking control of concentrated patches of wild foods."

Prehistoric hunter-gatherers often lived in small groups. Social groups were small because only a limited number of people can congregate without exhausting the resources in an area. Such small groups typically comprise either extended family units with kinship ties or a band of related ones. However, some scholars find evidence of cooperation between those not connected by blood in these communities since[7] "early humans may have formed ties with both kin and non-kin, based in part on their tendency to cooperate. These social networks may thus have contributed to the emergence of cooperation." Other scholars also find that cooperation in these communities was vital for subsistence. At that time, foragers engaged in[8] "large-scale communal hunts and constructed shared capital facilities; they made shared investments in improving the local environment; and they participated in warfare, formed enduring alliances, and established trading networks. Large-scale collective action often played a crucial role in subsistence."

Despite its obvious advantages, this way of life had some serious disadvantages. First, there was so much dependence on uncertain local food sources which implies that staying alive was a continuous challenge. Second, hunter-gatherers lived under the mercy of the elements including weather fluctuations, seasonal changes, game availability, animal migrations, or plant abundance. This implies that there was an unremitting reliance on the surrounding conditions for their food supply that they had no control over. Third, there was so much at stake if the increase in the number of people in the community expands beyond the carrying capacity of the land. This implies that the natural increase in population became an inevitable survival challenge to these communities. Fourth, hunter-gatherers had to constantly move to find food, limiting their ability to store surplus food that could have allowed them to smooth their consumption. Fifth, roaming around was not always feasible since children and old people had to be carried. Finally, everyone participated in acquiring food in hunter-gatherer societies, most of the time with no respite, to ensure survival. This left no other time for leisure, creative activities, or anything else.

2 Tied to the Land

That lifestyle obviously did not subsist, except for few patches of people that still practice hunting, gathering, and foraging in some parts of the world today. Humans found another way to survive, which is the cultivation of their food instead of chasing after it wherever it existed. This is another testament to human desire to control their destiny by having some say in the location and timing of food availability. The transition from foraging to farming, sometimes referred to as the Neolithic Revolution, was one of the most critical milestones in human history. The adoption of agriculture accomplished more, in the long run, to alter the world than any other human invention. Today, agriculture is the primary source of food procurement worldwide. The Neolithic, or New Stone

Age, is an archaeological period that corresponds to the final stage of the Stone Age. This dramatic transformation in our way of life, or revolution, occurred during that time period.

To be specific, the Neolithic Revolution refers to the wide-scale transition of human societies from a lifestyle of hunter-gatherers whose sustenance depended on foraging, or collecting wild plants and pursuing undomesticated animals, to a way of life that featured the cultivation of plants and the domestication of animals. Hunter-gatherers that had heretofore dominated human history became sedentary societies settled in their land where they cultivated their food. After 2,000,000 years of hunting and gathering, agriculture was invented in different parts of the world. Archaeologists agree that this occurred independently in the Levant and Fertile Crescent,[9] China,[10] the Andes, Mesoamerica,[11] and other locations.

In this context, this decisive development in human history provided the basis for densely populated settlements, specialization and division of labor, gender standards,[12] trade and commerce, art and architecture, centralized administrations, political structures, state formation, hierarchical ideologies,[13] property ownership,[14] writing alphabets, pottery, polished tools, metallurgy, mathematics, astronomy, urban planning, and countless other human achievements.

These societies changed their way of life through the cultivation of crops, the domestication of livestock, and the development of farming techniques which allowed the production of surplus food. Because food production became more efficient, it allowed some humans to direct their efforts into activities other than ones ensuring subsistence. The food surplus that early farmers were able to generate made possible for the first time in human history the establishment of a non-food production sector. The presence of non-food specialists, such as craftsmen and artisans, enabled creativity and innovation. Surplus food also led to episodes of accelerated population expansion, which is a phenomenon known as the Neolithic demographic transition.[15] These changes in both the tally and the talents of people were ultimately essential for the decisive emergence of civilizations.

In this context, some scholars provide evidence for the association between the duration of agricultural adoption and the emergence of complex societies. For instance, historian Peter Turchin and other scholars explore the factors that cause complex societies to rise and remain in some parts of the world compared to others.[16] Using data on the spatial and temporal distribution of the largest human groups over a 3000-year period, their analysis confirms that large-scale societies are more likely to occur in places where agriculture has been practiced for a longer period or where the productivity of agriculture is higher. This creates an opportunity for the institutional structures that facilitate large-scale organizations to emerge. Others also assert that the[17] "expansion of farming during the Holocene helped make possible the emergence of civilization, though the timing for the start of civilization varied greatly by region."

To be specific about this process, it was the introduction of farming that tied humans to the land. Food availability was determined by working the fields. Thus, settlement in proximity to these fields became imperative. Working the land goes through stages of land preparing, seed planting, sowing, fertilizing, irrigating, plowing, harvesting, and storing. This introduced the need for specialization and division of labor at each stage. It also created incentives for technological innovations that could simplify chores and enhance productivity. Those that practiced plow farming introduced gender norms pertaining to the appropriate role of men and women in this newly introduced production process.[18] Recording the production and calculating the output necessitated alphabets and numbers. This allowed for the introduction of ways of writing, reading, and counting. Settling in one area also made it essential to build dwellings for humans to inhabit, granaries for storage, and structures for agricultural and irrigation projects. This allowed the art of architecture and the tools of construction to develop over time.

Land and buildings implied that property ownership should be defined unequivocally and protected clearly to avoid potential expropriation. Thus, laws and institutional frameworks started to be formulated. Settled communities started developing nodes of human communities. Each discovered that an exchange of what they cultivate with what others produce makes everybody better off. Thus, trade transactions and commercial exchange were promoted between human settlements. To protect trade routes, laws needed to be drafted, law enforcement had to be deployed, and security systems had to be enforced.

To administer these isolated patches, a state had to be formed to impose rules at a higher level than the local one. Large-scale agriculture projects also necessitated centralized administrations, which in turn needed a hierarchical structure to function efficiently. The adoption of agriculture in river valleys was only possible through coordinated efforts in the construction of dikes, levees, dams, fields, plantations, orchards, and others. These collective actions led to the emergence of a centralized authority with immense powers leading to state formation,[19] autocratic governance,[20] and extractive institutions.[21]

Farming did not only shape institutions but also formulated cultural traits that were cherished by these societies. The advent of agriculture was accompanied by collectivist values because early farming was characterized by a high probability of predation from others and prevalence of infectious diseases. Thus, these societies became collectivist in nature to be able to deal with adversity.[22] Farming also increased affiliation with religious communities, which often offers the only source of social support beyond the family. This support is a sort of mutual insurance especially valuable in agricultural societies that usually encounter lots of uncertainty. Thus, a larger proportion of people are observed to organize in religious communities in economies that depend on rain-fed farming where output is reliant on rainfall fluctuations.[23]

Agriculture also had substantial consequences on health conditions and the spread of diseases. This is because settlements became densely populated, and living in proximity to each other allows infectiousness to run amok. In addition, the change in lifestyle and diet also caused health complications. Historian William McNeill asserts that[24] "[w]e should expect that human populations living in sedentary communities were therefore more thickly infested with worms and similar parasites than their hunting predecessors or contemporaries in the same climatic zones." Historian Jared Diamond and others argue that[25] "the most important infectious diseases of modern food-producing human populations also include diseases that could have emerged only within the past 11,000 years, following the rise of agriculture." In a similar vein, Jared Diamond also asserts that agriculture had an adverse effect on health conditions because[26]

> [f]irst, hunter-gatherers enjoyed a varied diet, while early farmers obtained most of their food from one or a few starchy crops. The farmers gained cheap calories at the cost of poor nutrition. (Today just three high-carbohydrate plants-wheat, rice, and corn-provide the bulk of the calories consumed by the human species, yet each one is deficient in certain vitamins or amino acids essential to life). Second, because of dependence on a limited number of crops, farmers ran the risk of starvation if one crop failed. Finally, the mere fact that agriculture encouraged people to clump together in crowded societies, many of which then carried on trade with other crowded societies, led to the spread of parasites and infectious disease.

Agriculture not only affects our way of production and creation of income but also affects the allocation of that income. One of the most important consequences of human settlement is laying the foundation of inequality. Sedentary life introduced property and land ownership. This allowed for the potential for appropriation of these assets and their transmission from one generation to another. This naturally led to disparities in the accumulation of wealth over time due to differences in innate ability, personal talents, hard work, ambition, risk taking, luck, and other factors. This is also because the existence of storable resources makes it easier for expropriation by others. The possession of crops, livestock, and dwellings that could be easily demarcated and defended also led to disparities in wealth. In this context, Walter Scheidel, in his effort to describe the factors that acted as equalizers in human history in *The Great Leveler*, states that forager egalitarianism was replaced with disparities after the transition to agriculture[27]

> led to what I call the "Great Disequalization," a transition to new modes of subsistence and new forms of social organization that eroded forager egalitarianism and replaced it with durable hierarchies and disparities in income and wealth. For these developments to occur, there had to be productive assets that could be defended against encroachment and from which owners could draw a surplus in a predictable manner. Food production by means of farming and herding fulfills both requirements and came to be the principal driver of economic, social, and political change.

In a similar vein, Chris Harman discusses the inception of class struggle as agriculture created an impetus for exploitation when storability tempted some to expropriate, while organization of labor entailed hierarchy that enticed leaders to oppress the ones they lead. He clarifies how farming contributed to economic divisions and class struggle as follows:[28]

> Groups with high prestige in preceding non-class societies would set about organizing labour needed to expand agricultural production by building irrigation works or cleaning vast areas of new land. They would come to see their own control of the surplus-and the use of some of it to protect themselves against natural vicissitudes-as in everyone's interest.

Economist Samuel Bowles and others endeavor to characterize and compare wealth disparities in different areas in the ancient world and find that[29] "wealth disparities generally increased with the domestication of plants and animals and with increased sociopolitical scale, using Gini coefficients computed over the single consistent proxy of house-size distributions." Samuel Bowles and other scholars also show that[30] "intergenerational transmission of wealth and wealth inequality are substantial among pastoral and small-scale agricultural societies (on a par with or even exceeding the most unequal modern industrial economies) but are limited among horticultural and foraging peoples (equivalent to the most egalitarian of modern industrial populations)." Along the same lines, Samuel Bowles and Jung-Kyoo Choi propose that[31] "farming and a new system of farming-friendly property rights nonetheless jointly emerged when they did. This Holocene revolution was not sparked by a superior technology. It occurred because possession of the wealth of farmers—crops, dwellings, and animals—could be unambiguously demarcated and defended. This facilitated the spread of new property rights that were advantageous to the groups adopting them."

Some scholars argue that agriculture did not only change human lives and livelihood at the time of adoption but also had a persistent effect that even influenced our current economic conditions. The argument is that this dramatic change had a lasting imprint on those societies that experienced it earlier than others. In other words, the earlier the transition to agriculture, the longer the period of accumulation of knowledge and foundation of institutions, the earlier the transition to industrialization, and the higher the level of current economic development. In support of these ideas, some scholars assert that the[32] "transition made possible the human population explosion, the rise of non-food-producing specialists, and the acceleration of technological progress that led eventually to the industrial revolution." Other scholars develop a Malthusian model for the evolution of human society from hunting-gathering to farming to industrialization.[33] Using cross-country data, the study finds evidence that[34] "an earlier transition to agriculture has a positive effect on the degree of industrialization in the modern era."

In addition, a study shows that some geographic factors and biogeographic conditions, or the distribution of heavy seeded plants and large domesticable animals, exerted influence on the location and timing of the transition to agriculture.[35] The evidence also indicates substantial effects of geography and biogeography on contemporary economic development. Economist Louis Putterman extends this analysis by introducing a new set of estimates for the year of transition to agriculture for a large set of countries.[36] The author argues that a better indicator of the time-since-transition in a country is a weighted average of the values applicable to the countries its people came from. The argument is that the transition to farming is associated with a[37] "lengthy development of human capabilities that are associated with the growth of civilizations." The analysis shows that this adjusted indicator achieves a better fit in the analysis than the one without the adjustment. This provides further evidence for the association between this transition thousands of years ago and current economic performance.

3 From Turbulence to Transition

Competing theories developed to ascertain the factors that drove societies to adopt that consequential change about 12,000 years ago. The fact that people transitioned from hunting and gathering to farming as a subsistence way of life never seemed to some scholars to be a logical choice. To archaeologists and anthropologists, hunting and gathering in a world of plenty and limited population is a less demanding and more flexible activity compared to farming. These issues notwithstanding, the adoption of agriculture was a turning point in our history. Drastically changing how we produce our food and determine our subsistence does not seem a natural choice unless something equally radical leads to it. Thus, some posit that this transition was a consequence of a necessity rather than a calculated choice. This led some scholars to ascribe this to a fundamental shift in climate at a certain period that made farming easier. Quaternary scientist Herbert Edgar Wright Jr. asserts that the[38] "domestication of plants and animals constituted a real revolution, resulting in major control of the environment, followed by rapidly accelerated cultural changes. The chronological coincidence of climatic change and the agricultural revolution cannot be denied."

In this context, some argue that the advent of agriculture was triggered by an increase in climatic fluctuations shortly before the first archaeological evidence for agriculture. Survival of hunter-gatherers was harder with harsher winters and drier summers. Those adversely affected by these climatic fluctuations reacted by storing wild foods to smooth their consumption. This, in turn, forced them to abandon their nomadic ways, as they had to settle most of the year adjacent to their stationary granaries, either stocking them or drawing from them. While these newly formed sedentary communities continued hunting and gathering, sedentarism and food storage made it easier for them to eventually adopt farming. This hypothesis is tested against a global dataset of climate conditions and Neolithic adoption dates.[39] The study finds that the introduction and adoption of agriculture were faster in locations exposed to higher climate seasonality, such that one extra standard deviation of temperature seasonality is associated with adopting agriculture 1500 years earlier.

Some other theories were also developed to explain the association between climate turbulence and this critical transition. Some of these theories argue that humans, plants, and animals were forced to live together in small spaces, due to climatic factors, that led to inevitable domestication. This is referred to as the Oasis Theory. Other theories argue that humans had to resort to areas where climate allowed the cultivation of food. This is referred to as the Hilly Flanks Theory.

The Oasis Theory posits that both North Africa and the Near East experienced a prolonged period of drought, with higher temperatures and decreased precipitation. As the climate got warmer and drier at the end of the Pleistocene, people, plants, and beasts became packed in few and increasingly limited fertile areas. The aridity, thus, drove these organisms to congregate together at what looks like oases. This contiguity forced human communities into close contact with plants and animals, created a closer familiarity with plants and animals, and finally forced these communities to learn to raise crops and to domesticate animals. The Hilly Flanks Theory proposes another potential explanation. The Hilly Flanks refer to the upland areas surrounding the Fertile Crescent. These include the foothills of the Zagros Mountains, the Taurus Mountains, and the highland parts of the Levant. The theory posits that the transition to agriculture began in these Hilly Flanks which received enough rainfall for rain-fed farming without the need for irrigation. This view is also predicated on the fact that many of the progenitors of domesticated crops had their natural habitats in the Hilly Flanks.

These theories do not make claims about causality, as much as they intend to show that the concurrence of climate change episodes and the advent and adoption of agriculture cannot be a mere coincidence. These studies intend instead to highlight the potential contribution of climate change to this drastic historical turn of events.

4 The Adoption of Agriculture

There is a plethora of studies that examine the association between climate change and the adoption of agriculture and others that explore the connection between these climatic fluctuations and the diffusion of agriculture from the frontier to other parts of the world. To provide evidence for the association between climate turbulence and this transition, we refer to some scientific work that attempted to reconstruct climate records around the time the data shows evidence for settlement of farming communities.

Some of these studies focus on the reconstruction of climatic conditions near Lake Huleh Valley and Tell Abu Hureyra. The former attracted human settlement in the Levant from early prehistoric times, where archaeological remains were found at the southern end of the valley. The first permanent settlement in the valley, Ain Mallaha, dates from 9000 to 10,000 years ago. In that site, the[40] "Eynan people settled in the vicinity of the Hula Lake and the vast adjacent wetland area, and exploited a wide array of resources and habitats, as reflected by the plant and faunal remains at the site."

The latter is an archaeological site in the Euphrates valley in Syria. Tell Abu Hureyra was inhabited between 13,000 and 9000 years ago and was home to some of the world's earliest known farmers. This rendered the Tell one of the most pertinent sites in the study of the origins of agriculture. The site is also significant because the inhabitants of Abu Hureyra started out as hunter-gatherers but gradually shifted to farming. In this context, the excavation in this site uncovered two villages.[41] In the first, inhabitants foraged vegetation and hunted local wildlife between 11,500 and 10,000 before present. In the second, inhabitants employed a more sophisticated ways of food production, the cultivation of grain crops, and the pasturing of sheep, goats, cattle, and pigs around 9700–7000 before present. New evidence from the site[42] "suggests that systematic cultivation of cereals in fact started well before the end of the Pleistocene by at least 13000 years ago." Other evidence suggests deliberate cultivation of cereals by the Natufian culture at Tell Abu Hureyra more than 14,000 years ago.[43]

4.1 *The Pleistocene*

Studies, in this context, focus on climatic conditions that led to the emergence of the Natufian culture in the Pleistocene. The Natufian is a Late Epipaleolithic[44] culture of the Levant dating between 15,000 and

11,500 years ago. This culture was unique as it supported a sedentary or semi-sedentary population even before the advent of agriculture. Natufian communities may have been the earliest settlers in the world.

Some studies show a particularly warm and humid period around 14,500 years before present that created favorable conditions for settlement. A paleoclimate reconstruction for the entire Epipaleolithic period was conducted by some scholars using pollen record collected from the archaeological site of Jordan River Dureijat located on the banks of Lake Hula.[45] This record shows that the wettest and warmest period of the record was approximately between 14,900 and 13,000 years before present with peak values at 14,500 years before present. This warm and humid interval coincides with the onset of the Natufian culture and the emergence of sedentary life in the Hula Valley and the entire southern Levant taking advantage of favorable climatic conditions. Thus, the data indicate that the early Natufian[46] "emerged during a time of favorable climatic conditions and abundant resource availability. Such conditions may have augmented the capability of the first sedentary communities to face the environmental and subsistence challenges that surely accompanied early sedentism and population increase."

It is argued that this first step toward settlement led to another one toward the domestication of animals and plants. Along the lines of this intuition, some research shows that this warm and wet period eventually induced adaptations that may have led to domestication of plants and animals. For instance, some scholars compare paleoenvironmental data with archaeological evidence for human occupancy and population change in southwest Asia between 16,000 to 9000 years before present.[47] The authors find that abrupt warming transitions around 14,500 and 11,700 years before present may have acted as triggers for cultural change at the start of the Natufian and the succeeding Pre-Pottery Neolithic cultures. These periods[48] "of rapid warming and wetting-up of the climate followed by climatic reversals prompted a range of human adaptive responses, including some that with hindsight we might view as evolutionary 'false starts' and dead ends, but others that eventually led to domestication of selected plants and animals."

This last study also points our attention to the warming that occurred at 11,700 years before present which coincides with the end of the Younger Dryas. The Younger Dryas, which occurred between 12,900 and 11,700 years before present, was a rebound to glacial conditions that reversed the gradual climatic warming after the Last Glacial Maximum.

The Younger Dryas was[49] "an ~1,300-y period of extreme climate that dramatically reversed the course of global warming that brought the last Ice Age to a close." The abrupt end of the Younger Dryas marks the beginning of the current Holocene epoch.[50] The Younger Dryas, as an intense global cooling and drying event, has been attributed a compelling role in the advent and adoption of agriculture in the Levant. Some scholars show that the[51] "various lines of evidence demonstrate cold, wet conditions during the Geometric Kebaran/Mushabian period (14,000-12,800/12,500 B.P.) preceding the Natufian, a dry spell during the very Early Natufian, a steady increase in arboreal pollen during the Early Natufian, and an ensuing drier period in the Late Natufian (Younger Dryas)."

Along these lines, archaeologist Harvey Weiss and climatologist Raymond Bradley state,[52] "About 12,000 years ago, the Natufians abandoned seasonally nomadic hunting and gathering activities that required relatively low inputs of labor to sustain low population densities and replaced these with new labor-intensive subsistence strategies of plant cultivation and animal husbandry." To understand what induced the Natufians to change their lifestyle so drastically, the authors assert the role of climate change during the Younger Dryas:[53]

> Following the end of the last glacial period, when southwest Asia was dominated by arid steppe vegetation, a shift to increased seasonality (warm, wet winters and hot, dry summers) led to the development of an open oak terebinth parkland of woods and wild cereals across the interior Levant and northern Mesopotamia. This was the environment exploited initially by the hunting and gathering Natufian communities. When cooler and drier conditions abruptly returned during the Younger Dryas, the harvests of wild resources dwindled, and foraging for these resources could not sustain Natufian subsistence. They were forced to transfer settlement and wild cereals to adjacent new locales where intentional cultivation was possible.

Examining whether the Younger Dryas led to human adaptations that contributed to the development of agriculture, some scholars use a new pollen core extracted from Lake Huleh and plant remains from Tell Abu Hureyra to recreate the climate in the Levant during that period.[54] Their data show that in response to the onset of drier climatic conditions during the Younger Dryas, forest gave way to grassland steppe. The stresses associated with this change in climate and vegetation induced the inhabitants of Abu Hureyra to adjust their hunting and gathering behavior and contributed to the subsequent development of agriculture in that area. Thus, it is no coincidence that the[55] "transition from Epipaleolithic to Neolithic and from hunting and gathering to farming happened at about the same time, just as the Younger Dryas had run its course. We suggest that the disruption that took place in Epipaleolithic patterns of adaptation acted as a powerful incentive for the peoples of the Levant to develop new modes of subsistence."

Some scholars also use evidence collected from Abu Hureyra to show the pressures that drove the sedentary hunter-gatherers to start growing their caloric staples.[56] Their evidence indicates that hunter-gatherers at Abu Hureyra first started cultivating crops due to a steep decline in wild plants that had served as staple foods for a long time. The decline in these staples is attributable to a sudden change to dry and cold climate during the Younger Dryas. The evidence, thus, suggests that the[57] "primary trigger appears to have been the critically reduced availability of key wild plant staples during the arid conditions of the Younger Dryas climatic episode. This early inception of cultivation then set the scene for the development and rapid spread of integrated agro-pastoral economies in the early Holocene."

4.2 *The Holocene*

The Holocene Epoch is the last of the two epochs that constitute the Quaternary Period. The preceding and substantially longer sequence of alternating glacial and interglacial ages is the Pleistocene. Some studies focus on the Early Holocene to examine whether the transition to agriculture was essential during that period. This is because some scholars find that the onset of wetter and warmer conditions in the early Holocene favored the earliest development of village life as the[58] "newly organized Early Natufian societies changed their settlement pattern, experienced a population increase in response to their sedentism, and as a result overexploited their environment."

This point of view argues that it is the climate stability of the Holocene that triggered the adoption of agriculture in some areas. This shift[59] "toward a warmer and far more stable climate during the Holocene created favorable conditions for a major shift during the Neolithic, or New Stone Age. The New Stone Age, which began about 12,000 years ago in the Fertile Crescent, did not erase the practice of foraging or eliminate hunter-gatherers, but it initiated a decisive shift toward the paramount use of domesticated crops and animals." Thus, it was the stable Holocene climate, not the instability in the Late Pleistocene, that led to the emergence of agriculture because[60] "[i]n the last ice age, climate fluctuations and low CO_2 concentrations made agriculture impossible. In the climatically quiet Holocene, the competitive advantage of agricultural subsistence led to its dominance everywhere, albeit after thousands of years of cultural evolution."

In the opinion of the proponents of this view, stable Holocene climate allowed the evolution of agriculture in vast areas with its warm and wet climate.[61] This is since prehistoric populations tended to grow quickly to overwhelm the carrying capacity of the environmental surroundings and the sufficiency of the prevailing subsistence system. Communities that discover more intensive subsistence strategies will increase in number and exert pressure on smaller populations with less intensive strategies. Such intergroup competition favored the advent and diffusion of agriculture in the Holocene. Thus, the stability and[62]

> the reduction in climate variability, increase in CO_2 content of the atmosphere, and increases in rainfall rather abruptly changed the earth from a regime where agriculture was impossible everywhere to one where it was possible in many places. Since groups that use efficient, plant-rich subsistence systems will normally out-compete groups that make less efficient use of land, the Holocene has been characterized by a persistent, but regionally highly variable, tendency toward subsistence intensification.

In addition to the Levant and the Fertile Crescent, there is some evidence of the contribution of climate change to the adoption of agriculture in Mesoamerica,[63] in the Andes such that[64] "the emergence of agriculture (ca. 1500 B.C.) and the collapse of the Tiwanaku civilization (ca. A.D. 1100) coincided with periods of abrupt, profound climate change," and in the transitional area between the Tibetan Plateau and the Loess Plateau of China.[65] All this evidence seems to confirm that climate change played an essential role in this transition process wherever it occurred.

5 The Diffusion of Agriculture

Climate change did not only contribute to the advent of agriculture, but some scholars argue that it could have affected the diffusion of agriculture to other areas such as the Aegean and southeast Europe. In this context, when climate became unfavorable in an agricultural adoption area, farmers opt to take their practice somewhere else.

In an insightful study pertaining to the diffusion of agriculture, some scholars argue that climatic volatility induced foragers to change their ways eventually.[66] To the extent that climatic shocks did not wipe out the underlying subsistence resource base, societies that were frequently pushed to exploit their habitats accumulated knowledge complementary to farming practices. This facilitated the adoption of agriculture when this technology was diffused from the Neolithic frontier. In contrast, extremely volatile or stationary environments were less conducive to the adoption of agriculture. In one hand, societies facing stable climatic conditions were not sufficiently nudged to exploit their habitats. On the other hand, extreme climatic shocks prevented the type of experimentation that was essential for the accumulation of knowledge that is considered complementary to farming. Along the lines of this intuition, some economists find that societies that faced climatic fluctuations adopted survival strategies by accumulating knowledge integral to farming, which facilitated the adoption of agriculture when the opportunity arose.[67] Consistent with the predictions of their theory, the empirical analysis demonstrates a highly statistically significant association between the standard deviation of temperature and the timing of transition to agriculture.

5.1 8.2 ka Climate Event

Some studies focus on the major abrupt cooling climate event that occurred 8200 years before present called the 8.2 ka event. The event was characterized by a sudden decline in global warming. However, the cooling was significantly less pronounced than the Younger Dryas. The total duration of this climate event was roughly 150 years.[68] This is considered the largest climatic anomaly during the Holocene, which is a period otherwise characterized by a stable climate as discussed earlier. The event may have been caused by the collapse of the Laurentide Ice Sheet of North America.[69] This event is observed in a[70] "large number of high-resolution climate proxies in the Northern Hemisphere, and in many cases corresponds to markedly cold and arid conditions."

Some scholarly work shows the consequences of this climatic event on farming communities in the Near East. For instance, comparing the paleoclimate record with changes in architectural, archaeozoological, and archaeological records in the excavated area of the site of Çatalhöyük-East in central Anatolia shows significant changes in husbandry and consumption practices by early farmers.[71] Other scholars test the hypothesis that the abrupt climate change during the 8.2 ka event contributed to the spread of farming into communities in southeast Europe.[72] This study was motivated by the observation that the large and long-flourishing settlement at Çatalhöyük-East was deserted quite abruptly around 8200 years before present. The authors speculate that the aridity during that climate event led to inconsistencies in the water supply of the large settlement. This prompted the spread of early farmers out of Anatolia, into many areas in southeast Europe. Thus, the introduction of farming[73] "to South-East Europe occurs in all study regions (Thrace, Macedonia, Thessaly, Bulgaria) near 8200 cal yr BP. We observe major disruptions of Neolithic cultures in the Levant, North Syria, South-East Anatolia, Central Anatolia and Cyprus, at the same time. We conclude that the 8200 cal yr BP aridity event triggered the spread of early farmers, by different routes, out of West Asia and the Near East into Greece and Bulgaria."

5.2 *Rapid Climate Change*

Other studies focus on the effect of episodes of Rapid Climate Change on the diffusion of agriculture. Rapid Climate Change refers to the repetitive pattern of global cooling anomalies. According to some scientists,[74] "paleoclimate records reveal as many as six periods of significant rapid climate change during the time periods 9000–8000, 6000–5000, 4200–3800, 3500–2500, 1200–1000, and 600–150 cal yr B.P. Most of the climate change events in these globally distributed records are characterized by polar cooling, tropical aridity, and significant atmospheric circulation changes."

In this context, scholars explore the social impact of these climate cold anomalies in the Eastern Mediterranean during the Early and Middle Holocene.[75] The authors conclude that the initial domestication of plants and animals in the Levant was not associated with Rapid Climate Change episodes. However, the study identified a coincidence between some of these events and the spread of early farming from Anatolia to Southeast Europe. Along the same lines, another study investigates critical archaeological turnover events in the Aegean-Levantine area that coincide with Rapid Climate Change events.[76] Simulations with the use of paleoclimatic proxy data, with emphasis on sea-surface temperature reconstructions and a cave speleothem stable oxygen isotope record from Lebanon, show that these cold climatic events are associated with the diffusion of the agricultural way of life. This is since[77] "both the abrupt onset of moist conditions at around 10.2 ka BP, and the return to milder climatic conditions immediately following the 8.6-8.0 ka BP RCC, are suggestive drivers of a rapid, punctuated mode of Neolithic dispersal."

Some scholars also explore the impact of Rapid Climate Change on communities in the Aegean and Southeast Europe.[78] The study focuses on determining the dates for the introduction of farming in the Aegean, its further dispersal into Southeast Europe, and its coincidence with the beginning and end of Rapid Climate Change conditions. The study proposes two chronological steps:[79]

> The first comprises a land-based dispersal of the Neolithic from Central Anatolia to the Aegean and southern Marmara region, and probably – also by the sea-based coastal route from the Near East. This first step, which dates (abbreviated) to ~6600 calBC (i.e. the onset of RCC-conditions) appears to have been consolidated within a few decades, although this remains to be validated. The second step took Neolithic lifestyles away from the Aegean littoral all the way to north-eastern Hungary, starting at ~6050 calBC (i.e. towards the end of RCC-conditions); this step was completed within 200 years. We infer that these processes can partly be explained by a mitigation of climate-induced biophysical and social hazards.

To examine the spread of farming from the Aegean to the Balkans, and to present a possible explanation for the locational preferences apparent in the pathways used by Neolithic communities during their initial venture into the area, some scholars compare the current natural environments in that area with the corresponding prehistoric settlement patterns.[80] The study shows that the earliest Neolithic groups would first appear in areas with mild conditions like those in the Mediterranean. Before venturing further into the Balkans and introducing an economy based on farming and stockbreeding, the Neolithic package had to be adapted first to the harsh winter conditions of that area. Only following this period of climatic adaptation was it possible to apply the Neolithic lifestyle to the areas of Thrace, Walachia, Dobrudzha, and the Carpathian Basin. The available data[81] "show that the adaptation period is identical to the timespan of Rapid Climate Change (RCC: 6550-6050 calBC) as defined in previous studies."

Some studies, however, argue that Rapid Climate Change was a contributor, not a main factor, in some of the consequential changes of the time. Comparing climate reconstructions with archaeological data does not support[82] "a direct influence of Early Holocene RCCs on the process of Neolithization and its cultural dispersal." However, climate change had an indirect effect through the stress it exerted on the existing subsistence structures:[83]

> In this view, climate variability, leading to increased stress or amelioration of background environmental conditions, appears to accelerate and force existing cultural and subsistence dynamics, which were however not directly attributed to the climatic change itself. Climate variability thus acts as a stimulus that continuously interacted with technological and cultural adaptations of complex societies, fostering the evolution of new and multifaceted adaptive strategies that progressively increased the resilience of ancient populations and modified the way they interacted with their environment.

Notes

1. Lisa Maher, Tobias Richter, Danielle Macdonald, Matthew Jones, Louise Martin, and Jay Stock. "Twenty-Thousand-Year-Old Huts at a Hunter-Gatherer Settlement in Eastern Jordan." PLoS ONE, 7, 2: e31447, 2012.
2. James Woodburn. "Egalitarian Societies." Man, 17, 3: 431–451, 1982.
3. Rabindra Nath Chakraborty. "Sharing Culture and Resource Conservation in Hunter-Gatherer Societies." Oxford Economic Papers, 59, 1: 63–88, 2007.
4. Eric Alden Smith, Kim Hill, Frank Marlowe, David Nolin, Polly Wiessner, Michael Gurven, Samuel Bowles, Monique Borgerhoff Mulder, Tom Hertz, and Adrian Bell. "Wealth Transmission and Inequality Among Hunter-Gatherers." Current Anthropology, 51, 1: 19–34, 2010.
5. Eric Alden Smith and Brian Codding. "Ecological Variation and Institutionalized Inequality in Hunter-Gatherer Societies." PNAS, 118, 13, e2016134118, 2021.

6. Heather Pringle. "The Ancient Roots of the 1%." Science, 344, 6186: 822–825, 214.
7. Coren L. Apicella, Frank W. Marlowe, James H. Fowler, and Nicholas A. Christakis. "Social Networks and Cooperation in Hunter-Gatherers." Nature, 481: 497–501, 2012.
8. Robert Boyd and Peter Richerson. "Large-Scale Cooperation in Small-Scale Foraging Societies." Evolutionary Anthropology, 31, 4: 175–198, 2022.
9. Ofer Bar-Yosef and Anna Belfer-Cohen. "The Origins of Sedentism and Farming Communities in the Levant." Journal of World Prehistory, 3: 447–498, 1989.
10. David Cohen. "The Beginnings of Agriculture in China: A Multiregional View." Current Anthropology, 52, S4, 2011.
11. Bruce Smith. "The Origins of Agriculture in the Americas." Evolutionary Anthropology, 3, 5: 174–184, 1994.
12. Alba Masclans, Caroline Hamon, Christian Jeunesse, and Penny Bickle. "A Sexual Division of Labour at the Start of Agriculture? A Multi-Proxy Comparison Through Grave Good Stone Tool Technological and Use-Wear Analysis." PLOS ONE, 16, 4, e024913, 2021. Masclans Latorre A, Bickle P, and Hamond C. "Sexual Inequalities in the Early Neolithic? Exploring Relationships Between Sexes/Genders at the Cemetery of Vedrovice Using Use-Wear Analysis, Diet and Mobility." Journal of Archaeological Method and Theory, 28: 232–273, 2021. Per Frederiksson and Satyendra Gupta. "Irrigation and Gender Roles." Journal of Development Economics, 163, 103076, 2023. Per Frederiksson and Satyendra Gupta. "The Neolithic Revolution and Contemporary Sex Ratios." Economics Letters, 173: 19–22, 2018.
13. Joram Mayshar, Omer Moav, and Luigi Pascali. "The Origin of the State: Land Productivity or Appropriability?" Journal of Political Economy, 130, 4, 2022.
14. Samuel Bowles and Jung-Kyoo Choi. "The Neolithic Agricultural Revolution and the Origins of Private Property." Journal of Political Economy, 127, 5, 2019. Samuel Bowles and Jung-Kyoo Choi. "Coevolution of Farming and Private Property During the Early Holocene." PNAS, 110, 22: 8830–8835, 2013.
15. Jean-Pierre Bouquet-Appel. "When the World's Population Took Off: The Springboard of the Neolithic Demographic Transition." Science, 333, 6042: 560–561, 2011. Jean-Pierre Bocquet-Appel. "Paleoanthropological Traces of a Neolithic Demographic Transition." Current Anthropology, 43: 637–650, 2002. Jean-Pierre Bouquet-Appel. "The Demographic Impact of the Agricultural System in Human History." Current Anthropology, 50, 5: 657–660, 2009. Bocquet-Appel, Jean-Pierre, and

Stephan Naji. "Testing the Hypothesis of a Worldwide Neolithic Demographic Transition: Corroboration from American Cemeteries." Current Anthropology, 47, 2: 341–365, 2006.

16. Thomas E. Currie, Peter Turchin, Edward Turner, and Sergey Gavrilets. "Duration of Agriculture and Distance from the Steppe Predict the Evolution of Large-scale Human Societies in Afro-Eurasia." Nature, Humanities and Social Sciences Communications, 7, 34, 2020.
17. Benjamin Lieberman and Elizabeth Gordon. Climate Change in Human History: Prehistory to the Present. Bloomsbury, 2018. (P. 45).
18. Alberto Alesina, Paula Giuliano, and Nathan Nunn. "On the Origins of Gender Roles: Women and the Plough." Quarterly Journal of Economics, 128, 2: 469–530, 2013.
19. Bang Petersen, M. and Skaaning, S. E. "Ultimate Causes of State Formation: The Significance of Biogeography, Diffusion, and Neolithic Revolutions." Historical Social Research, 35, 3: 200–226, 2010.
20. Ola Olsson and Christopher Paik. "A Western Reversal Since the Neolithic? The Long-Run Impact of Early Agriculture." The Journal of Economic History, 80, 1: 100–135, 2020.
21. Christopher Paik. "Historical Underpinnings of Institutions: Evidence from the Neolithic Revolution." Princeton Working Paper, 2011.
22. Ola Olsson and Christopher Paik. "Long-Run Cultural Divergence: Evidence from the Neolithic Revolution." Journal of Development Economics, 122: 197–213, 2016.
23. Philipp Ager and Antonio Ciccone. "Agricultural Risk and the Spread of Religious Communities." Journal of the European Economic Association, 16, 4: 1021–1068, 2018.
24. William McNeill. Plagues and Peoples. Anchor Books, 1976. (P. 61).
25. Nathan Wolfe, Claire Panosian Dunavan, and Jared Diamond. "Origins of Major Human Infectious Diseases." Nature, 447: 279–283, 2007.
26. Jared Diamond. "The Worst Mistake in the History of the Human Race." Discover, April 30, 1999.
27. Walter Scheidel. The Great Leveler: Violence and the History of Inequality from the Stone Age to the Twenty-First Century. Princeton University Press, 2018. (P. 33).
28. Ibid. (P. 25).
29. Timothy A. Kohler, Michael Smith, Amy Bogaard, Gary Feinman, Christian Peterson, Alleen Betzenhauser, Matthew Pailes, Elizabeth Stone, Anna Marie Prentiss, Timothy J. Dennehy, Laura J. Ellyson, Linda Nicholas, Ronald Faulseit, Amy Styring, Jade Whitlam, Mattia Fochesato, Thomas A. Foor, and Samuel Bowles. "Greater Post-Neolithic Wealth Disparities in Eurasia than in North America and Mesoamerica." Nature, 551: 619–623, 2017.

30. Monique Borgerhoff Mulder, Samuel Bowles, Tom Hertz, Adrian Bell, Jan Beise, Greg Clark, Ila Fazzio, Michael Gurven, Kim Hill, Paul L. Hooper, William Irons, Hillard Kaplan, Donna Leonetti, Bobbi Low, Frank Marlowe, Richard McElreath, Suresh Naidu, David Nolin, Patrizio Piraino, Rob Quinlan, Eric Schniter, Rebecca Sear, Mary Shenk, Eric Alden Smith, Christopher von Rueden, and Polly Wiessner. "Intergenerational Wealth Transmission and the Dynamics of Inequality in Small-Scale Societies." Science, 326, 5953: 682–688, 2009.
31. Samuel Bowles and Jung-Kyoo Choi. "Coevolution of Farming and Private Property During the Early Holocene." PNAS, 110, 22: 8830–8835, 2013.
32. Ola Olsson and Douglas Hibbs. "Geography, Biogeography, and Why some Countries are Rich, and others are Poor." PNAS, 101, 10: 3715–3720, 2004.
33. Angus C. Chu and Rongxin Xu. "From Neolithic Revolution to Industrialization." Macroeconomic Dynamics, 28: 699–717, 2024.
34. Ibid.
35. Ola Olsson and Douglas Hibbs. "Biogeography and Long-Run Economic Development." European Economic Review, 49, 4: 909–938, 2005.
36. Louis Putterman. "Agriculture, Diffusion and Development: Ripple Effects of the Neolithic Revolution." Economica, 75, 300: 729–748, 2008.
37. Ibid.
38. H. E. Wright, Jr. "Environmental Changes and the Origin of Agriculture in the Near East." BioScience, 20: 210–212+217, 1970.
39. Andrea Matranga. "The Ant and the Grasshopper: Seasonality and the Invention of Agriculture." The Quarterly Journal of Economics, 139, 3: 1467–1504, 2024.
40. Florent Rivals, Rivka Rabinovich, Hamoudi Khalaily, François Valla, and Anne Bridault. "Seasonality of the Final Natufian Occupation at Eynan/ Ain Mallaha (Israel): An Approach Combining Dental Ageing, Mesowear and Microwear." Archaeological and Anthropological Sciences, 12, 232, 2020.
41. Andrew Moore, Gordon Hillman, and Anthony Legge. Village on the Euphrates: From Foraging to Farming at Abu Hureyra. Oxford: Oxford University Press, 2000.
42. Hillman, Gordon, Hedges, Robert, Moore, Andrew, Colledge, Susan, Pettitt, Paul "New Evidence of Lateglacial Cereal Cultivation at Abu Hureyra on the Euphrates." The Holocene, 11, 4: 383–393, 2016.
43. Amaia Arranz-Otaegui, Lara Gonzalez Carretero, Monica N. Ramsey, Dorian Q. Fuller, and Tobias Richter. "Archaeobotanical Evidence Reveals the Origins of Bread 14,400 Years Ago in Northeastern Jordan." PNAS, 115, 31: 7925–7930, 2018.

44. In archaeology, the Epipaleolithic is the period between the Upper Paleolithic and the Neolithic during the Stone Age.
45. Dafna Langgut, Rachid Cheddadi, and Gonen Sharon. “Climate and Environmental Reconstruction of the Epipaleolithic Mediterranean Levant (22.0–11.9 ka cal. BP).” Quaternary Science Reviews, 270, 107170, 2021.
46. Ibid.
47. Neil Roberts, Jessie Woodbridge, Andrew Bevan, Alessio Palmisano, Stephen Shennan, and Eleni Asouti. “Human Responses and Non-responses to Climatic Variations During the Last Glacial-Interglacial Transition in the Eastern Mediterranean.” Quaternary Science Reviews, 184: 47–67, 2018.
48. Ibid.
49. Hai Cheng, Haiwei Zhang, Christoph Spötl, Jonathan Baker, Ashish Sinha, Hanying Li, Miguel Bartolomé, Ana Moreno, Gayatri Kathayat, Jingyao Zhao, Xiyu Dong, Youwei Li,Youfeng Ning, Xue Jia, Baoyun Zong, Yassine Ait Brahim, Carlos Pérez-Mejías, Yanjun Cai, Valdir F. Novello, Francisco W. Cruz, Jeffrey P. Severinghaus, Zhisheng An, and R. Lawrence Edwards. “Timing and Structure of the Younger Dryas Event and Its Underlying Climate Dynamics.” PNAS, 117, 38: 23408–23417, 2020.
50. R. B. Alley, D. A. Meese, C. A. Shuman, A. J. Gow, K. C. Taylor, P. M. Grootes, J. W. C. White, M. Ram, E. D. Waddington, P. A. Mayewski, and G. A. Zielinski. “Abrupt Increase in Greenland Snow Accumulation at the End of the Younger Dryas Event.” Nature, 362 (6420): 527–529, 1993. R.Alley. “The Younger Dryas Cold Interval as Viewed from Central Greenland.” Quaternary Science Reviews, 19, 1: 213–226, 2000. W. Dansgaard, J. W. C. White, and S.J. Johnsen. “The Abrupt Termination of the Younger Dryas Climate Event.” Nature, 339 (6225): 532–534, 1989.
51. Ofer Bar-Yosef and Francois Valla. “The Natufian Culture and the Origin of the Neolithic in the Levant.” Current Anthropology, 31, 4: 433–436, 1990.
52. Harvey Weiss and Raymond Bradley. “What Drives Societal Collapse?” Science, 291, 5504: 609–610, 2001.
53. Ibid.
54. Andrew Moore and Gordon Hillman. “The Pleistocene to Holocene Transition and Human Economy in Southwest Asia: The Impact of the Younger Dryas.” American Antiquity, 57, 3: 482–494, 1992.
55. Ibid.
56. Gordon Hillman, Robert Hedges, Andrew Moore, Susan Colledge and Paul Pettitt. “New Evidence of Late Glacial Cereal Cultivation at Abu Hureyra on the Euphrates.” The Holocene, 11: 383–393, 2001.

57. Ibid.
58. Ofer Bar-Yosef and Anna Belfer-Cohen. "The Origins of Sedentism and Farming Communities in the Levant." Journal of World Prehistory, 3, 4: 447–498, 1989.
59. Benjamin Lieberman and Elizabeth Gordon. Climate Change in Human History: Prehistory to the Present. Bloomsbury, 2018. (P. 37).
60. Peter J. Richerson, Robert Boyd, and Robert L. Bettinger. "Constraints on the Development of Agriculture." Current Anthropology, 50, 5: 627–631, 2009.
61. Peter J. Richerson, Robert Boyd, and Robert L. Bettinger. "Was Agriculture Impossible during the Pleistocene but Mandatory during the Holocene? A Climate Change Hypothesis." American Antiquity, 66, 3: 387–411, 2001.
62. Ibid.
63. Gerald A. Islebe, Nuria Torrescano-Vall, Mirna Valdez-Hernández, Alicia Carrillo-Bastos, and Alejandro A. Aragón-Moreno. "Maize and Ancient Maya Droughts." Nature, Scientific Reports, 12, 22272, 2022.
64. Michael W. Binford, Alan L. Kolata, Mark Brenner, John W. Janusek, Matthew T. Seddon, Mark Abbott, and Jason H. Curtis. "Climate Variation and the Rise and Fall of an Andean Civilization." Quaternary Research, 47, 2: 235–248, 1997.
65. Liu Fenggui, Zhang Yili, Feng Zhaodong, Hou Guangliang, Zhou Qiang, and Zhang Haifeng. "The Impacts of Climate Change on the Neolithic Cultures of Gansu-Qinghai Region During the Late Holocene Megathermal." Journal of Geographical Sciences, 20, 3: 417–430, 2010.
66. Quamrul Ashraf and Stelios Michalopoulos. "Climatic Fluctuations and the Diffusion of Agriculture." The Review of Economics and Statistics, 97, 3: 589–609, 2015.
67. Ibid.
68. Takuro Kobashi, Jeffrey P. Severinghaus, Edward J. Brook, Jean-Marc Barnola, and Alexi M. Grachev. "Precise Timing and Characterization of Abrupt Climate Change 8200 Years Ago from Air Trapped in Polar Ice." Quaternary Science Reviews, 26: 1212–1222, 2007.
69. Christopher R. W. Ellison, Mark R. Chapman, and Ian R. Hall. "Surface and Deep Ocean Interactions During the Cold Climate Event 8200 Years Ago." Science, 312, 1929, 2006. D. C. Barber, A. Dyke, C. Hillaire-Marcel, A. E. Jennings, J. T. Andrews, M. W. Kerwin, G. Bilodeau, R. McNeely, J. Southon, M. D. Morehead, and J.-M. Gagnon. "Forcing of the Cold Event of 8200 Years Ago by Catastrophic Drainage of Laurentide Lakes." Nature, 400: 344–348, 1999.

70. Bernhard Weninger, Eva Alram-Stern, Eva Bauer, Lee Clare, Uwe Danzeglocke, Olaf Jöris, Claudia Kubatzki, Gary Rollefson, Henrieta Todorova, and Tjeerd van Andel. "Climate Forcing Due to the 8200 cal yr. BP Event Observed at Early Neolithic Sites in the Eastern Mediterranean." Quaternary Research, 66, 3: 401–420, 2006.
71. Mélanie Roffet-Salque, Arkadiusz Marciniak, Paul J. Valdes, Kamilla Pawłowska, Joanna Pyzel, Lech Czerniak, Marta Krüger, C. Neil Roberts, Sharmini Pitter, and Richard P. Evershed. "Evidence for the Impact of the 8.2-ky BP Climate Event on Near Eastern Early Farmers." PNAS, 115, 35:l 8705–8709, 2018.
72. Bernhard Weninger, Eva Alram-Stern, Eva Bauer, Lee Clare, Uwe Danzeglocke, Olaf Jöris, Claudia Kubatzki, Gary Rollefson, Henrieta Todorova, Tjeerd van Andel. "Climate Forcing due to the 8200 cal yr. BP Event Observed at Early Neolithic Sites in the Eastern Mediterranean." Quaternary Research, 66: 401–420, 2006.
73. Ibid.
74. Paul A. Mayewski, Eelco E. Rohling, J. Curt Stager, Wibjorn Karlen, Kirk A. Maasch, L. David Meeker, Eric A. Meyerson, Francoise Gasse, Shirley van Kreveld, Karin Holmgren, Julia Lee-Thorp, Gunhild Rosqvist, Frank Rack, Michael Staubwasser, Ralph R. Schneider, and Eric J. Steig. "Holocene Climate Variability." Quaternary Research, 62: 243–255, 2004.
75. Bernhard Weninger, Lee Clare, Eelco J. Rohling, Ofer Bar-Yosef, Utz Böhner, Mihael Budja, Manfred Bundschuh, Angelica Feurdean, Hans-Georg Gebel, Olaf Jöris, Jörg Linstädter, Paul Mayewski, Tobias Mühlenbruch, Agathe Reingruber, Gary Rollefson, Daniel Schyle, Laurens Thissen, Henrieta Todorova, and Christoph Zielhofer. "The Impact of Rapid Climate Change on Prehistoric Societies During the Holocene in the Eastern Mediterranean." Documenta Praehistorica, XXXVI: 7–59, 2009.
76. Eelco J. Rohling, Gianluca Marino, Katharine M. Grant, Paul A. Mayewski, and Bernhard Weninger. "Model for Archaeologically Relevant Holocene Climate Impacts in the Aegean-Levantine Region (easternmost Mediterranean)." Quaternary Science Reviews, 208: 38–53, 2019.
77. Ibid.
78. Bernhard Weninger, Lee Clare, Fokke Gerritsen, Barbara Horejs, Raiko Krauß, Jörg Linstädter, Rana Özbal, and Eelco J. Rohling. "Neolithisation of the Aegean and Southeast Europe during the 6600–6000 calBC period of Rapid Climate Change." Documenta Praehistorica, 41: 1–31, 2014.
79. Ibid.

80. Raiko Krauß, Elena Marinova, Hanne De Brue, and Bernhard Weninger. "The Rapid Spread of Early Farming from the Aegean into the Balkans via the Sub-Mediterranean-Aegean Vegetation Zone." Quaternary International, XXX: 1–18, 2017.
81. Ibid.
82. Eleonora Regattieri, Luca Forti, Russell N. Drysdale, Giorgio Mannella, John C. Hellstrom, Cecilia Conati Barbaro, Daniele Morandi Bonacossi, and Andrea Zerboni. "Neolithic Hydroclimatic Change and Water Resources Exploitation in the Fertile Crescent." Nature, Scientific Reports, 13, 45, 2023.
83. Ibid.

CHAPTER 6

The Last Straw

Humans had little choice but to settle after adopting an agricultural way of life. Once settled, small communities started to turn into villages. Different villages interacted with each other through trade transactions and commercial exchange. Prosperity and surplus food allowed for an increase in population, an expansion of settlements, and the subsequent rise of urban centers and cities. This transpired way of life eventually needed a political, economic, and social structure above the local level. Chiefdoms and states had to be formed to administer the affairs of these societies, to ensure security, to promulgate laws, and to defend territories.[1] When states are formed, leadership had to be chosen in some form of kingship or a monarchy. That developed into dynasties which are associated with hereditary succession, in which a sovereign rule for life and the power of the position pass to their progeny or a member of their family when they pass away. Some of these kingdoms became empires when the monarchs expanded their territories and dominions to increase their power and wealth. Some of these empires reached an awe-inspiring pinnacle at some point in time before they started receding back. Whatever is left now, be it monuments, ruins, or temples, stands as a testament to their ingenuity and creativity.

S. Khalifa, *Climate Change, Economic Channels, and Historical Junctures*, https://doi.org/10.1007/978-3-031-91867-4_6

1 Climate Change and the Dawn of Civilization

Before discussing how climate change acted as a lasting blow to some of these societies, it is also necessary to understand how it served as a stimulus for the dawn of civilization. Historian Susan Wise Bauer in *The History of the Ancient World: From the Earliest Accounts to the Fall of Rome* discusses the cradle of civilization in what is known as the Fertile Crescent. In her account, the dawn of civilization emerged as[2] "the climate began to warm, and the ice caps began to melt-a process that geologists assign to the five thousand years between 11,000 and 6000 BC." The author associates this with settlement and emergence of agriculture:[3]

> Perhaps, as the ice sheets retreated and the herds of meat-providing animals moved north and grew thinner, the hunters who followed these herds gave up the full-time pursuit of meat and instead harvested the wild grains that grew in the warmer plains, shifting residence only when the weather changed (as the native North Americans in modern Canada were still doing when Jacques Cartier showed up). May be these former nomads progressed from harvesting wild grain to planting and tending it, and finally gave up travelling altogether in favor of full-time village life. Well-fed men and women produced more babies. Sickles and grinding stones, discovered from modern Turkey down to the Nile valley, suggest that as those children grew to adulthood, they left their overpopulated villages and travelled elsewhere, taking their farming skills with them and teaching them to others.

The challenges that accompanied these changes laid the foundations of civilized life. In this context, civilization emerged in the Fertile Crescent[4] "not because it was an Edenic place overflowing with natural resources, but because it was so hostile to settlement that a village of any size needed careful management to survive. Farmers had to cooperate in order to construct the canals and reservoirs needed to capture floodwaters. Someone needed to enforce that cooperation and oversee the fair division of the limited water. Someone had to make sure that farmers, who grew more grain than their families needed would sell food to the nonfarmers (the basket makers, leatherworkers, and carpenters) who grew no grain themselves. Only in an inhospitable and wild place is this sort of bureaucracy-the true earmark of civilization-needed."

Climate change coincided with the emergence of the earliest centers of civilization.[5] These climatic changes[6] "are attributed to several factors, such as variations in sunstroke, and some large volcanic eruptions, amplified by feedback mechanisms between oceanic and atmospheric circulations. This turning point, since 6,000 years B.P., corresponds more or less to the emergence of the first major centers of civilization." Thus, climate change altered the environment in such a way that communities had to adapt by adopting farming and establishing human settlements. To administer agricultural activities and human settlements, and the complex web of ties that developed accordingly, some level of organization and hierarchical leadership was needed. This paved the way for states to be formed, for sovereigns to be ordained to govern peoples and territories, and for the formation of sophisticated societal structures. These political, economic, social, and cultural entities became the bedrocks for complex societies and great civilizations.

This is essential to allow us to see that climatic fluctuations are not necessarily an adverse disruptive event that could drive societies into disintegration but could also be an impetus for societies to muster their power to blossom. Thus, climate change was, in some cases, a stimulus for societies to develop, flourish, and grow.

2 Climate Change and Societal Collapse

The question that comes to the fore is what happened to some of these ancient kingdoms and empires. The causes of the collapse of these societies are an issue of intense debate.[7] Societal collapse is the fall of a complex human society. A collapsing society may revert to a more primitive state, may get absorbed into a stronger society, or may completely disappear as its members abandon their long-established settlements. According to Jared Diamond, a collapse of society is[8] "a local drastic decrease in human population numbers and/or in political, economic, or social complexity. Collapse can even reach the point that human population completely disappears over a considerable area."

Scholars have long pondered the causes behind such a dismal end. Possible causes of a societal collapse include various factors such as a natural catastrophe, climate deterioration, warfare, domestic strife, pestilence, famine, economic collapse, population explosion, demographic decline, or mass migration. Discussing each is essential to understand why these events could lead to that bleak outcome. Natural disasters, if sudden and severe, could lead to physical destruction and human casualties on such a scale that recovering from it becomes impossible. Being embroiled in warfare with another entity, especially if there is an imbalance of power or if the conflict continues for such a long time, could overwhelm the state fiscally, could cause a shrinkage in the territory under its control, and could lead to mass killings of its finest. Domestic strife leads to large-scale destruction and casualties and could create a fissure in the social fabric by tearing any cohesion left for a society to keep functioning. Changes in climate could lead to variations in the surrounding habitat upon which humans depend to secure their vital needs for survival. The spread of diseases, if unchecked, could ravage communities who get deprived of their productive capacity. Infectiousness could also create social tensions due to the fear of contagion. Hunger, starvation, or an extreme lack of food due to famine could also cause the deaths of scores and debilitation of those who survive. Drastic demographic changes, in the form of population explosions, could also affect the fine balance between the carrying capacity of the land and the growth in demand for what the land can offer. Mass migration could cause a contraction in the labor force, abandonment of cities and towns, and decreasing the tax base upon which the state coffers depend. A combination of these factors can also come together to drive these societies into oblivion. These factors may cascade into one another and build up to a point that could overwhelm any effort that would otherwise have preserved continuity.

Amid all these factors that could lead to societal collapse, climate change looms large. This is because climate change can precipitate a collapse or could push a society, already on the brink due to other factors, over the cliff. Sometimes, climate changes its tempo and deviates from its usual patterns. These fluctuations may be natural or due to ongoing human activities that could have a lasting effect on the surrounding environment. These sudden, or gradual, shifts are invariably accompanied by a change in everything that steady climate patterns have established heretofore. When sudden, shocks take societies by surprise that their ability to contain its repercussions and to adjust to its consequences becomes very limited. When slow, societies find no alternative but to change their ways drastically to be able to survive in an altered environment than the one they are accustomed to. Not only that, but climate change can also trigger all these other factors that have been identified by scholars as determinants of societal collapse.

Societies, on some of these occasions, face climatic fluctuations that disrupt their way of life, disturb their livelihood, distort their production capacity, and diminish their chances of survival. The ability of societies to adjust is critical in these situations, since a change in climate offers no alternative but either to adapt to the new surroundings, depart the area completely, or perish altogether. Thus, societies facing these challenges have to choose either to react creatively or to be relegated to the dustbin of history.

The effect of climate and its fluctuations on humanity cannot be understated. Thus, this chapter, and the following ones, are dedicated to the effect of climate change on societies that turned into great civilizations, and polities that grew into kingdoms and empires. These chapters tell the stories of how some of these societies dealt with the climatic shock they had to endure, and how these environmental blows acted as the last straw that sent some of these historical structures into a past reference rather than a present existence. This narrative will be complemented by historical, archaeological, anthological, anthropological, and scientific evidence that confirms how climate fluctuations can be connected to these dramatic historical junctures.

This association can be confirmed by new scientific techniques that allow us to study history not only from the writings on the monuments, the narratives of historians, or the content of folkloric tales, but also from the perspective of newly introduced scientific tools of radiocarbon dating, dendrochronology, stratigraphy, ice core analysis, genomic sequencing, and others. These types of analyses are conducted to show how climate change contributed to the collapse of some of these complex societies, given the caveats that were highlighted in some studies. For instance, a group of scholars show examples of societies that have survived some of these episodes of climate change through resilience and resourcefulness. These examples show that[9] "the past does not reveal that societies and communities inevitably succumbed when confronted with climate change and variability. Our case studies suggest that a combination of continuity and flexibility characterized many—perhaps most—social responses to shifting climatic conditions."

On the other hand, climate change also acted as the last straw of social evolution and advancement. Not only that, but it led in some cases to complete societal collapse. Historian Malcolm Weiner states,[10] "How societies respond to major climate events together with contemporary developments in other dimensions, including migrations, weapons and warfare, modes of transport, and plagues, determine societal survival or collapse." In another article, he also asserts that[11]

> [a]rmed with DNA analysis of the movements of human populations, animals, and pathogens; strontium isotope analysis documenting the movements of people over the course of individual lifetimes; analyses of past climates through beryllium as well as oxygen isotope analysis, together with the drilling of deep lake, sea, glacier, and cove cores, and the study of annual growth of tree rings, among other scientific advances, we can look back upon the history of humankind as never before. Five causes of collapse appear paramount: major episodes of climate change, crises-induced mass migrations, pandemics, dramatic advances in methods of warfare and transport, and human failings in crises including societal lack of resilience and the madness, incompetence, cultic focus, or ignorance of rulers.

This indicates that the final effect of climate change depends largely on how societies choose to act or react to it. It could be a death sentence in some cases or a stimulus for change and a trigger for survival strategies in others. Thus, there is no deterministic societal outcome for climate anomalies. The consequences of climatic events also depend on other factors that could cause a society to be ripe for collapse. Thus, any climate shock can act as a last straw and not the primary cause in these cases.

In this context, some scholars discuss the contribution of climate change to societal collapse by asserting that[12] "[h]istorical and archeological research suggests that past societal collapses have rarely been the result of direct climate perturbations but instead were more commonly attributable to a combination of stressors. However, this does not mean that the risk of climate collapse is overstated." This implies that climate change could be the main cause of collapse, one of the culprits leading to societal breakdown, or the last straw that pushed that society over the edge given the contribution of other factors. In the following exposition in the coming chapters, there will be examples where climate change was the critical factor contributing to the collapse of that society. In other cases, we will see that a combination of factors, including climate change, caused the final breakdown of that society. While in yet other cases, there are other factors that pushed a society to the edge. Then, a climate shock acted as the last straw in pushing that society over the edge.

Societal collapse due to climate fluctuations can be brought about through several channels. Climate change could lead to fluctuations in precipitation or variations in temperature and humidity. These changes can diminish agricultural productivity and cause a shortage in food supply. This is because crop cultivation depends critically on soil quality, the availability of water, and a specific combination of climatic features that allow crops to grow in a particular area. Crop loss can also be caused by unseasonal droughts in some cases and unexpected flooding in others. These disasters, caused sometimes by climate change, can destroy the harvest and hinder the ability of farmers to cultivate. The ensued severe food shortages can lead to hunger, starvation, and even famine. The lack of food could push people to go in search of greener pastures if possible or to perish altogether if not. Either way could lead to societal collapse.

Climate change could lead to extreme weather that expresses itself in the form of hurricanes, tornadoes, blizzards, cyclones, tsunamis, typhoons, droughts, wildfires, floods, and others. These are climate-induced natural disasters that some societies cannot remain intact if they encounter them. Some of these events cause scores of casualties, deaths, destruction, and human suffering on a wide scale. Since some of these societies were vulnerable because of the lack of proper preparation either to contain the disaster or to deal with its consequences, they had to suffer the ruinous ramifications of these harsh expressions of the wrath of nature. This could also lead to societal collapse.

Climate change could also lead to war, internal strife, and violent conflict due to the contest over scarce resources. This becomes more acute especially if such society, with overpopulation and dense settlements, surpasses the carrying capacity of their habitat. The carrying capacity of an ecosystem is the maximum number of people that a specific environment can sustainably support given the available resources. Members of a community could turn on each other to overtake the resources left after a climatic shift. This could also turn one society that became bereft of resources due to the climatic shock, to attempt to put their hands on the bounty of other societies. These conflicts could lead to societal collapse due to the amount of death and destruction left in their wake.

Climate change could lead to a human exodus, as people decide to leave for another area that promises a better life. The ensuing potential population displacement could strip societies of the bulk of its people and labor force. This adversely affects not only productivity in the short run due to the shortfall in the workforce, but also its ability to sustain itself in the long run because of the potentially intense population contraction. Large-scale abandonment of urban centers and cities could also lead to the collapse of the institutional structures upon which the complex society was founded.

Climate change could also lead to the spread of diseases and the outbreak of epidemics. These health crises could cause mass casualties, malfunctioning of societal structures, and desertion of the contaminated and infected areas. The loss of life of workers could adversely affect labor supply and lead subsequently to lower productivity. The efforts to contain a disease, and to provide medical care for the infected, could also inflict a deep wound on the coffers of the state. These occurrences could also contribute to societal collapse.

For all these and other factors, climate change can be a critical factor in societal collapse, the fall of kingdoms and empires, and the demise of civilizations. Climate change also[13]

> interacts with other anthropogenic stressors such as changes in land use, loss of biodiversity, nutrient imbalances, pollution, and an overuse of available resources that are crossing the planetary safety boundary limits and operating as a possible catastrophic mix. This mix may exacerbate society vulnerabilities and cause multiple indirect stresses such as economic damage, loss of land and water, and food insecurity that can merge into system-wide synchronous failures. These cascading effects are not only biophysical or biogeochemical, but they also affect human society, generating conflicts, political instability, systemic financial risks, the spread of infectious diseases and the risk of spillover.

Thus, the contribution of climate change to civilization cannot be underestimated. The following sections, in this chapter, will focus on the channels through which climate change can lead to the collapse of complex societies. The following chapters, after this one, will focus on some stories highlighting the effect of climate change on the fate of some nations, kingdoms, and empires. This will start with the 4.2 ka event which refers to the aridification event that occurred 4200 years ago. That climate event has been hypothesized to have caused the collapse of the Old Kingdom on the banks of the Nile, the Akkadian Empire located between the Tigris and Euphrates, the Indus Valley Civilization along the Indus, and the Liangzhu culture in the Yangtze River Valley.

This will be followed by a discussion of the 3.2 ka event, or the Late Bronze Age crisis, which coincides with a widespread drought. That was a time of sweeping societal collapse in the circum-Mediterranean of the Mycenaean, the Hittite, the Minoan, the Canaanite, and others. The discussion continues with societal collapse in the Americas before Columbus.

This includes the collapse of the Tiwanaku, the Maya, the Ancestral Pueblo, the Easter Island, and Cahokia. Then, we continue to cover stories of societal collapse that occurred during the common era which include that of the Roman Empire, the Khmer Empire, and a long list of Chinese dynasties. Finally, we discuss the Little Ice Age crisis and the transformations to the political, economic, and social structures that occurred during that time but still affect us today. Before we delve into the stories of these cases of societal collapse, we continue discussing in detail the channels through which climate change could lead to this lamentable outcome.

3 Climate, Conflict, and Collapse

One of the critical channels between climate change and societal collapse is conflict. Whether it is internal strife or conflict with other societies, these cycles of violence can lead to societal collapse due to the death toll of those in the battlefields, civilian casualties, the funds needed to attend to the injured, the strain on the coffers of the state due to defense spending, the destruction of productive facilities, and the demolition of infrastructures, structures, and dwellings.

3.1 Climate of Conflict

Climate fluctuations can create conducive conditions for conflict through multiple channels. Climate change can increase the propensity for aggressive and hostile behavior, can lead to violent competition over scarce resources and fresh water supply, can decrease the opportunity cost of conflict, can cause political instability due to food shortages or the increase in food price inflation, can shrink the government budget limiting its ability to spend to be able to sidestep the potential for conflict, can increase inequalities leading to distributive conflict, can cause refugee crises as people flee from the climate stricken area to another, can cause the spread of diseases, and can increase the incidence of natural disasters. A combination of these channels allows the fluctuations in climate to lead to conflict and subsequently societal collapse. We discuss each of these in full detail.

First, climate change is said to increase the likelihood of individual violence due to some underlying physiological or psychological factors. Deviations of temperatures from the average increase hostility, aggressiveness, and violence by elevating the level of discomfort. Along these lines, psychologist Craig Anderson and others argue,[14] "Hot weather and violence go hand in hand. This fact can be derived from a variety of sources, from a variety of centuries, and from a variety of continents." Craig Anderson and others also show a positive association between temperature and serious deadly assault.[15] In another contribution, Craig Anderson and Andreas Miles-Novelo find few ways that global warming exacerbates aggression.[16] Along the lines of their intuition, uncomfortable warm temperatures increase violent thoughts and combative feelings. When in an irritable state, even a trivial provocation can trigger excessively aggressive reactions. Climate change can also lead to conditions known for creating violence-prone adults, such as growing up in poverty, inadequate prenatal and childhood nutrition, dysfunctional families, exposure to war and conflicts, low levels of education, and being exposed to climate change–induced disasters. In addition, climate anomalies may alter an individuals' capacity to reasonably and correctly interpret events, possibly leading to aggression triggered by misjudgment.

Second, an individual's incentive to rebel rises as income and economic opportunities dwindle. This implies that the opportunity cost of conflict decreases, which induces individuals to engage in such violent actions.[17] In this context, when climatic shocks cause economic productivity to decline, the value of engaging in conflict increases compared to that of participating in standard economic activities. Adverse climate shocks and the ensuing deterioration in economic conditions also make it easier for armed militias to recruit combatants from an expanding pool of frustrated unemployed young people who find themselves without a source of income.

Third, climate change could increase the likelihood of intragroup violence due to the scarcity of renewable resources such as freshwater, fertile arable land, forests, and fisheries. Adverse climatic conditions, coupled with overpopulation, reduce the accessible resources to sustain human livelihood. This scarcity increases competition between groups over the limited resources, potentially leading to conflict. Some scholars also propose that scarcity, especially of shared resources across borders, can lead to interstate conflict. For instance, political scientist Thomas Homer-Dixon provides evidence that[18] "environmental scarcity causes violent conflict. This conflict tends to be persistent, diffuse, and sub-national." He also discusses the different channels that environmental change could lead to conflict by stating,[19] "Countries may fight over dwindling supplies of water and the effects of upstream pollution. In developing countries, a sharp drop in food crop production could lead to internal strife across urban-rural and nomadic-sedentary cleavages."

Fourth, adverse climatic conditions can lead to a spike in food prices by dramatically diminishing crop yields. Any disruption in the agricultural sector can seriously affect food security, especially for the poorest segments of society. Some scholars suggest that transitory shocks are sufficient to solve collective action problems and to mobilize crowds for political ends. Thus, higher food prices due to climatic shocks could lead to incidences of political violence in the form of protests and riots. This is especially the case in urban settings where residents lack access to cheap substitutes. In addition, heightened uncertainty about food supply can force communities to find alternative strategies which often clash with the needs of other communities also facing increased sustenance pressures. This could lead to conflict between these groups.

Fifth, output contractions due to adverse climate shocks could also diminish the government budget through a steep decline in tax collection. Limited funds curtail a government's capacity to provide goods and services to the public, keep political promises, secure alliances, build patronage networks, and buy off opposition. This makes it easier for opponents to instigate political action to overthrow the incumbent from office. This situation could also hamper a government's ability to wage a counterinsurgency, or suppress rebellion or political resistance, due to diminished funds in its coffers. This situation could lead to prolonging the duration of a domestic conflict.

Sixth, climate-driven economic downturns are likely to have a disproportionate effect that could exacerbate actual or perceived economic inequality. This is because the poorer segments of society are either less prepared to absorb the consequences of the shock or more susceptible to its economic repercussions. These detrimental shocks which produce wider disparities could increase resentment and exasperation toward the state or create tensions across social classes. This could induce individuals to participate in rebellious actions that aim to redistribute economic wealth and political power. Thus, income inequality could enhance the likelihood of distributive conflict.[20]

Seventh, climate change can cause many people to flee from their homelands and evacuate their areas. The influx of environmental evacuees is likely to overburden the economies and the resource base of the recipient. For instance, refugees may compete with native inhabitants over land, jobs, housing, health care, educational opportunities, and social services.

In addition, this migration could lead to conflict by stirring ethnic tensions, especially when the newcomers and the residents belong to different ethnolinguistic groups.[21] Faced with sudden shocks brought about or compounded by climate change, people will be displaced from rural areas into urban centers to search for better life. This new trend will accelerate urbanization, adding to problems of urban poverty, population density, social strife, and heightened criminality. Others will cross borders in the hope that a new land will offer better prospects. In either case, those leaving non-viable areas will often go to areas that are already only barely viable, potentially leading to conflict.[22] Thus,[23] "People living in lesser developed countries may be more likely to leave affected areas, which may cause conflict in receiving areas."

Eighth, climate change could significantly affect fresh water supply. The conflict risk rises if water resources are also inadequate because of poor management that wastes water by inappropriate use and inadequate conservation. This issue could also be politicized seeking a scapegoat on whom to blame for these shortages leading to sociopolitical instability. Conflicting claims to water resources have also been a feature in numerous conflicts as some rivers are shared between countries. In this case, the source country's increase in the usage of water could limit the amount available to other riparian nations. This also could lead to conflict on the banks of the river valley.

Ninth, climate change poses significant hazards to human health due to the spread of diseases which, if unaddressed, could lead to epidemics. Large epidemics could alter the power balance and impact the relationships between communities based on their ability to adapt and deal with this type of adversity. This could potentially lead to some level of instability or conflict as well.

Tenth, climate change could increase the incidence of natural disasters. These catastrophes lead to casualties, deaths, and destruction, putting pressure on already stretched resources. Severe heat waves and water shortages will also have an adverse effect on safe drinking water and sanitation that will disproportionately affect the poorest communities. Failure by the state to ensure these basic public health care aspects is a fundamental factor in eroding the social contract between state and citizens leading to political instability or even violent conflict.

3.2 *From Volatility to Violence*

There are several studies that attempt to examine the association between climate change and conflict. For instance, environmental scholars Marshall Burke, Solomon Hsiang, and Edward Miguel synthesize various studies on the effect of climate change on conflict.[24] The authors find that deviations from weather patterns systematically increase the likelihood of different types of conflict including crimes, demonstrations, and civil war. Findings from the[25] "growing body of rigorous research in economics, as well as from political science and other disciplines that use modern econometric analytical approaches, indicate that adverse climatic events increase the risk of violence and conflict, at both the interpersonal level and the intergroup level, in societies around the world and throughout history."

In another attempt to carry out a comprehensive synthesis of the growing literature on climate and conflict, the previous scholars show that deviations from typical precipitation and temperature systematically increase the prospect of conflicts including violent crime, intergroup conflict, political instability, institutional breakdown, and the collapse of civilizations.[26] In this context, findings from[27] "a growing corpus of rigorous quantitative research across multiple disciplines suggest that past climatic events have exerted considerable influence on human conflict. This influence appears to extend across the world, throughout history, and at all scales of social organization."

Along the same vein, scientists Marshall Burke and Solomon Hsiang examine 50 quantitative studies on whether violent conflict and sociopolitical instability are associated with changes in climate.[28] The authors confirm the findings of these studies and conclude,[29] "Studies best positioned to make rigorous causal claims overwhelmingly indicate strong linkages between climatic anomalies and conflict and social instability. Furthermore, this growing literature demonstrates that climate's influence on security persists in both historical and modern periods, is generalizable to populations around the globe, arises from climatic events that are both rapid and gradual, and influences numerous types of conflict that range across all spatial scales." Marshall Burke and a group of scholars assess the current understanding of the connection between climate and conflict, based on the judgments of experts from diverse disciplines.[30] These experts agree that climate change affected armed conflict within countries, even though other drivers, such as low socioeconomic development and poor state capabilities, are judged to be substantially more influential.

Solomon Hsiang and other scholars argue that planetary-scale climate changes, estimated by El Niño Southern Oscillation, are associated with conflict.[31] In this context, the probability of conflict throughout the tropics doubles during El Niño years compared to La Niña years such that the[32]

> ENSO has a proximate influence on a variety of climatological variables, each of which may plausibly influence how conflict-prone a society is. Precipitation, temperature, sunlight, humidity and ecological extremes can adversely influence both agrarian and non-agrarian economies. In addition, ENSO variations affect natural disasters, such as tropical cyclones, and trigger disease outbreaks. All of these have adverse economic effects, such as loss of income or increasing food prices, and it is thought that economic shocks can generate civil conflict through a variety of pathways. Furthermore, altered environmental conditions stress the human psyche, sometimes leading to aggressive behaviour. We hypothesize that El Niño can simultaneously lead to any of these adverse economic and psychological effects, increasing the likelihood of conflict.

In addition, Edward Miguel, Shanker Satyanath, and Ernest Sergenti find that lower economic growth, driven by falling rainfall, is strongly associated with higher likelihood of conflict.[33] In a related article, Edward Miguel and Shanker Satyanath reconfirmed their original findings that adverse economic shocks, driven by falling rainfall, increase the likelihood of conflict in sub-Saharan Africa.[34]

Some studies argue that the effect of climate change on conflict depends on other factors. For instance, political scientist Vally Koubi and other scholars propose that climate change may increase the risk of conflict, under specific circumstances but not necessarily in a systematic way and unconditionally.[35] Vally Koubi shows that climatic conditions breed conflict in fertile grounds, such as areas dependent on agriculture, and in combination with other factors such as a low level of economic development and political marginalization.[36] Vally Koubi and others study whether the causality linking climatic conditions and armed conflict is contingent on the political system.[37] Their study finds weak support for the hypothesis that non-democratic countries are more likely to experience civil conflict when economic conditions deteriorate due to climatic fluctuations.

On the other hand, there are some studies that find that there is no association between climate change and conflict. For instance, contrary to other studies that examine the effect of rainfall annual growth rates on conflict, economist Antonio Ciccone explores the effect of lagged and current rainfall levels.[38] The author shows that negative rainfall shocks do not increase the onset and incidence of conflict in sub-Saharan Africa. In another study, Antonio Ciccone examines the effect of weather and weather-driven transitory income changes on the onset and incidence of conflict.[39] The author finds that adverse transitory income shocks, driven by rainfall fluctuations, actually lower the risk of conflict. Antonio Ciccone, Vally Koubi, and a group of scholars find no evidence of a convergence of findings on the effect of climate variability and conflict.[40] But the authors conclude that "this commentary should not be taken to imply that climate has no influence on armed conflict. Rather, we argue—in line with recent scientific reviews—that research to date has failed to converge on a specific and direct association between climate and violent conflict."

In light of all these conflicting views, it is likely that there is a plethora of economic, social, cultural, political, and historical factors that could prepare the ground for conflict. Climate change in this context can act as the last straw that pushes a society that is on the edge, due to these other factors, into conflict. It is also possible that climate change does not instigate conflict, but it could contribute to the ferocity and duration of such conflict.

4 Climate, Capacity, and Collapse

Climate change can lead to food shortages in multiple ways. This could be by altering the predictable weather patterns upon which cultivation depends, by adversely affecting the water supply needed for farming, or by causing disasters that destroy the harvest. Some of these factors impede a society's ability to produce to begin with, while others wreak havoc on the output even when society is able to produce. These shortages in food supply, if sufficiently intense, could lead to some form of societal collapse.

Climate fluctuations can alter the pattern of rainfall and cause deviations from average temperatures and humidity. These departures from the mean can adversely affect agricultural yield since cultivation depends on predictable seasonal patterns of precipitation and temperature overtime. Climatic fluctuations can also affect water availability which can hinder irrigation. Thus, climate change can decrease agricultural productivity leading to food shortages.

Climate change can also lead to disasters in various forms. These unexpected events can destroy the harvest since some crops are not designed to survive droughts and extreme heat waves. Most plants will also perish with intense flooding due to heavier than usual precipitation. This could also lead to lower food production and diminished agricultural yield.

All these factors imply a connection between climate change and food supply. To provide evidence for the association between climate change and agricultural productivity, some scholars find that anthropogenic climate change leads to a significant decline in global agricultural total factor productivity.[41] Other scholars show that[42] "the effects of climate change may undermine agricultural systems and disrupt food supply, which can lead to economic shocks, socio-political instability as well as starvation, migration and conflict."

The climate-induced food shortfall can lead to widespread hunger and potentially famine in extreme cases. Lower caloric intake and lack of nutrition can cause the spread of diseases due to immunodeficiency. Starvation can cause deaths when no alternative exists, or to evacuation of the area if such an option is feasible. The shortage can also lead to a spike in prices which affect disproportionately the poorer members of a community who might not be able to afford the same consumption basket as before. In any of these cases, societal collapse can easily ensue.

It is also possible that the population increases beyond the carrying capacity of their habitat. As the population expands and available technology makes it easier to exploit the resource base, environmental diminishing returns become unavoidable. At some point, a threshold is crossed where the output of the land becomes insufficient to satisfy the demands of the mouths that must be fed. Societal complexity is then potentially threatened if such a society, already on the edge of a cliff, is faced with a climate shock.

5 Climate, Catastrophe, and Collapse

Climate change is also associated with a higher intensity of natural catastrophes. For instance, the United Nations claims,[43] "Climate change is affecting the hydrological cycle and increasing the frequency and intensity of storms. Over 90 per cent of disasters are weather-related, including drought and aridification, wildfires, pollution and floods. They lead to death, injury, loss of livelihoods and displacement and place a huge burden on societies, economies and the environment." In another report, the United Nations concludes that[44] "from 1970 to 2019, these natural hazards accounted for 50 per cent of all disasters, 45 per cent of all reported deaths and 74 per cent of all reported economic losses. There were more than 11,000 reported disasters attributed to these hazards globally, with just over two million deaths and $3.64 trillion in losses." In this context, we need first to comprehend how climate change can cause these natural disasters. Then, we can attempt to ascertain the effect of these catastrophic events on afflicted communities that could possibly take the form of societal collapse in some cases.

On the one hand, increasing temperatures makes droughts more likely to occur. This is because warmer temperatures enhance evapotranspiration. Evaporation is a type of vaporization that occurs on the surface of a liquid as it transforms into gas, which decreases surface water. Transpiration is the process of water dispersal through a plant which dries out vegetation. These two processes are exacerbated by warming trends. In addition, as average temperatures warm above freezing earlier in the year, snowmelt occurs sooner and faster than usual. This process results in a shorter period during which soils and plants stay moist. Thus, climate change increases the odds of worsening drought conditions.

In this context, some scientists show a large contribution of anthropogenic warming to an emerging megadrought in North America such that the[45] "atmosphere and ocean anomalies that drove past megadroughts very likely dwarfed those that occurred during 2000–2018, but superposition of the 2000–2018 climate dynamics on background anthropogenic soil drying put an otherwise moderately severe soil-moisture drought onto a trajectory characteristic of the megadroughts of 800–1600 CE. Critical to the megadrought-like trajectory of the 21st-century event were enhanced evaporative demand, early snowpack loss, and a broad spatial extent, all promoted by anthropogenic warming."

Climate change also alters the timing of water availability which could lead to wildfires due to dried vegetation. For wildfires to take place, an alignment of a few factors is essential. These include high temperatures, low humidity, strong wind, in addition to lack of moisture in soil, trees, shrubs, grasses, and forest debris. Drier conditions cause vegetation to become more flammable. All these factors have strong direct or indirect ties to climate change. Some scientists find that[46] "due to global warming, the global area with frequent fire-prone conditions would increase by 29%, mostly in Boreal (+111%) and Temperate (+25%) zones, where there may also be a significant lengthening of the potential fire season."

Climate change can also increase the intensity of storms and extreme weather events. As temperature increases, which intensifies evaporation, so does the transfer of heat from the oceans to the air. As more water is evaporated into the atmosphere, more powerful storms develop. As storms sail across warm oceans, they pull in more water vapor and heat. That means there will be stronger wind, heavier rainfall, and more flooding when the storm hits land. Some scholars estimate a[47] "US $143 billion per year of the costs of extreme events is attributable to climatic change. The majority (63%), of this is due to human loss of life."

Climate change could also cause more intense flooding. This is because warming produces more moisture in the atmosphere. Heavier precipitation than usual could lead to intense disastrous flooding. In addition, storm surge occurs when water rises above normal levels and is pushed inland by wind. The increase in sea level is triggered by warming due to climate change, since warmer ocean water expands and land ice melts. This can also lead to more flooding, especially in coastal areas. Some scholars find that climate change[48] "remains a smaller but still important driver in flood exposure."

In addition to comprehending how climate change can induce these natural disasters, we also need to know how these drastic events can contribute to societal collapse. For instance, there is a plethora of studies that explores the effect of natural disasters on economic outcomes.[49] The intuition is based on the effects of disasters on factors of production such as physical capital, human capital, and technological progress. These are inputs into the production process, without which output cannot be produced. Thus, these factors determine economic activity, productivity, and economic growth. In this context, physical capital refers to the structures and equipment used in the production process. Human capital refers to the level of educational attainment and health conditions in a population. Technology is what determines how we transfer these inputs into output. The idea is that to be able to produce we need workers with a high level of knowledge and in good health who will use equipment and tools in the production process. Output will be determined by the amount of human capital and physical capital incorporated in the process, in addition to the adopted production technology that can enhance productivity even with the use of the same amounts of inputs.

Natural disasters can cause substantial physical damage to the stricken area. Destruction of property, infrastructure, production structures, and manufacturing plants lowers the stock of physical capital which may impair a country's productive potential. Thus, the ability to produce will be drastically curtailed if the disaster damages or destroys completely the productive facilities in that area.

Natural disasters can also decrease human capital especially if there is a substantial loss of life due to epic disastrous events that hit without warning. Another potential impact on educational attainment comes from the damage caused by these disasters to instructional facilities. Destruction of schools can force students out of their classrooms, which adversely affects the level of educational attainment that they otherwise would have obtained. In addition, when families lose a source of income due to a disaster, some children will drop out of school to join the labor force to decrease the household expenses and to compensate for the decline in the family's income. This increases the level of child labor.

Human capital considers overall health conditions as well. Natural disasters also have a detrimental effect on physical health and mental wellness. The emotional, psychological, and physical effects will continue to have their toll on afflicted people well after the occurrence of a natural disaster. Some survivors suffer permanent physical incapacitation that might adversely affect their productivity. Disasters could also psychologically handicap those who endure these traumatic situations. Workers who suffer from these disaster psychological syndromes may not be as productive as they were before their traumatic experience.

Thus, these disasters have a tremendous economic impact, costing these areas immense damage and scores of casualties and human suffering. They can also have a long-lasting effect that varies depending on the country's ability to absorb the initial shock, to contain its aftermath, and to recuperate from its repercussions. These incidents claim lives, intensify the spread of diseases, destroy dwellings and infrastructure, cause an exodus of the population from the stricken area, and impose a huge economic burden on societies. All these factors, if sufficiently intense, can lead to societal collapse.

6 Climate, Pestilence, and Collapse

Climate change can lead to the spread of infectious diseases, which could in turn lead to societal collapse. The change in climate leads to ecological changes that may affect the lifecycles of disease pathogens, vectors, and hosts. A pathogen is anything that can cause disease, such as an infectious agent or some other microorganism. A vector is any agent that carries a pathogen into another living organism. Humans and animals act as hosts in these cases. Climate change can affect the interaction between these elements, leading to an increase in the rate of infectiousness.

For instance, climate change can increase the breeding rates of disease vectors and the longevity of the agents they carry, causing them to be more infectious. Climatic fluctuations could also lead to behavioral changes in human hosts that make them more likely to be exposed to an infection. This can occur in such a way to increase the transmission of diseases, leading to enormous amounts of sickness and deaths. A detailed discussion of these issues is relegated to a later chapter.

In this context, some scholars show that there are several ways that climate change can spread infectious diseases which include[50] "the slow rise in temperature; changes in environmental conditions that increase the dispersal of disease vectors such as mosquitoes, rodents, and ticks; and the sudden appearance of extreme events such as floods, which contaminate drinking-water sources and trigger the displacement of humans and animals, which can carry and transmit pathogens." Other scholars find that more than half of the[51] "infectious diseases confronted by humanity worldwide have been at some point aggravated by climatic hazards."

Some scientists described the connection between climate change and diseases by asserting that increases[52] "in temperature decrease generation times for pathogens and vectors, in turn increasing disease spread and the potential for outbreaks; however, the effects of temperature on infectious disease are often nonlinear and vary by parasite, host, and vector, depending on species' thermal optima and disease ecology." In this context, extreme climate events such as[53]

> heat waves or deluges, modify disease pressure through induced stress responses and lowered host immunity. Extreme heat and drought can additionally have indirect effects on host immunological competence—for example, via food shortages. Extreme climate events also affect transmission dynamics. For instance, in environments with little water, droughts lead to more hosts congregating around scarce water sources, facilitating transmission of waterborne or environmentally transmitted diseases. Flash floods that cause damage to wastewater and potable water infrastructure can lead to an increase in transmission of waterborne pathogens in people.

The spread of diseases leads to labor shortages causing a decline in worker output. This negatively affects productivity and economic activity. Deaths, due to the spread of disease, can lead to a sudden decline in the population which affects both the number of producers and consumers. This adversely affects overall economic activities. The restrictions imposed on society to contain the spread of the disease can also lead to a decline in production activities, human mobility, and commercial exchange. If the level of disease infectiousness is intense, these factors can lead to societal collapse.

Notes

1. Timothy K. Earle. "Chiefdoms in Archaeological and Ethnohistorical Perspective." Annual Review of Anthropology, 16: 279–308, 1987.
2. Susan Wise Bauer. The History of the Ancient World: From the Earliest Accounts to the Fall of Rome. W. W. Norton & Company, 2007. (P. 4).
3. Ibid. (P. 6).
4. Ibid. (P. 7).
5. Malaize Bruno. "Climate Change and Ancient Civilizations." Encyclopedia of the Environment. June 1, 2020.
6. Ibid.
7. Danilo Brozovic. "Societal Collapse: A Literature Review." Futures, 145, 103075, 2023.
8. Jared Diamond. "Ecological Collapses of Past Civilizations." Proceedings of the American Philosophical Society, 138, 3: 363–370, 1994.
9. Dagomar Degroot, Kevin Anchukaitis, Martin Bauch, Jakob Burnham, Fred Carnegy, Jianxin Cui, Kathryn de Luna, Piotr Guzowski, George Hambrecht, Heli Huhtamaa, Adam Izdebski, Katrin Kleemann, Emma Moesswilde, Naresh Neupane, Timothy Newfield, Qing Pei, Elena Xoplaki, Natale Zappia. "Towards a Rigorous Understanding of Societal Responses to Climate Change." Nature, 591: 539–550, 2021.
10. Malcolm Weiner. "The Interaction of Climate Change and Agency in the Collapse of Civilizations ca. 2300–2000." BC. Radiocarbon, 56(4): S1–S16, 2014.
11. Malcolm Weiner. "The Collapse of Civilizations." Paper, Belfer Center for Science and International Affairs, Harvard Kennedy School, 2018.
12. Daniel Steel, Tyler DesRoches, and Kian Mintz-Woo "Climate Change and the Threat to Civilization." PNAS, 119, 42, e221052511, 2022.
13. Josep Peñuelas and Sandra Nogué. "Catastrophic Climate Change and the Collapse of Human Societies." National Science Review, 10: nwad082, 2023.
14. Craig Anderson, Kathryn B. Anderson, Nancy Dorr, Kristina M. DeNeve, and Mindy Flanagan. "Temperature and Aggression." Advances in Experimental Social Psychology, 32: 63–133, 2000.

15. Craig Anderson, Brad Bushman, and Ralph Groom. "Hot Years and Serious and Deadly Assault: Empirical Tests of the Heat Hypothesis." Journal of Personality and Social Psychology, 73, 6, 1213–1223, 1997.
16. Craig Anderson and Andreas Miles-Novelo. "Climate Change and Psychology: Effects of Rapid Global Warming on Violence and Aggression." Current Climate Change Reports, 5:36–46, 2019.
17. Sylvain Chassang and Gerard Padro i Miquel. "Economic Shocks and Civil War." Quarterly Journal of Political Science, 4, 3: 211–228, 2009.
18. Thomas F. Homer-Dixon. "Environmental Scarcities and Violent Conflict: Evidence from Cases." International Security, Summer, 19, 1: 5–40, 1994
19. Thomas F. Homer-Dixon. "On the Threshold: Environmental Changes as Causes of Acute Conflict." International Security, 16, 2: 76–116, 1991.
20. Christopher Cramer. "Does Inequality Cause Conflict?" Journal of International Development, 15, 4: 397–412, 2003.
21. Cemal Eren Arbatli, Quamrul H. Ashraf, Oded Galor, and Marc Klemp. "Diversity and Conflict." Econometrica, 88: 727–797, 2020.
22. Nathan Nunn and Eoin McGuirk. "Transhumant Pastoralism, Climate Change and Conflict in Africa." The Review of Economic Studies, 92, 1: 404–441, 2025.
23. Rafael Reuveny. "Climate Change-induced Migration and Violent Conflict." Political Geography, 26, 6: 656–673, 2007.
24. Marshall Burke, Solomon Hsiang, and Edward Miguel. "Climate and Conflict." Annual Review of Economics, 7: 577–617, 2015.
25. Ibid.
26. Marshall Burke, Solomon Hsiang, and Edward Miguel. "Quantifying the Influence of Climate on Human Conflict." Science, 341, 1235367, 2013.
27. Ibid.
28. Solomon Hsiang and Marshall Burke. "Climate, Conflict, and Social Stability: What Does the Evidence Say?" Climatic Change, 123: 39–55, 2014.
29. Ibid.
30. Katharine J. Mach, Caroline M. Kraan, W. Neil Adger, Halvard Buhaug, Marshall Burke, James D. Fearon, Christopher B. Field, Cullen S. Hendrix, Jean-Francois Maystadt, John O'Loughlin, Philip Roessler, Jürgen Scheffran, Kenneth A. Schultz, and Nina von Uexkull. "Climate as a Risk Factor for Armed Conflict." Nature, 571: 193–199, 2019.
31. Solomon Hsiang, Kyle Meng, and Mark Cane. "Civil Conflicts are Associated with the Global Climate." Nature, 476: 438–441, 2011.
32. Ibid.
33. Edward Miguel, Shanker Satyanath, and Ernest Sergenti. "Economic Shocks and Civil Conflict." Journal of Political Economy, 112, 4: 725–753, 2004.

34. Edward Miguel and Shanker Satyanath. "Re-examining Economic Shocks and Civil Conflict." American Economic Journal: Applied Economics, 3, 4: 228–232, 2011.
35. Thomas Bernauer, Tobias Bohmelt, and Vally Koubi. "Environmental Changes and Violent Conflict." Environmental Research Letters, 7, 015601, 2012.
36. Vally Koubi. "Climate Change and Conflict." Annual Review of Political Science, 22: 343–360, 2019.
37. Vally Koubi, Thomas Bernauer, Anna Kalbhenn, and Gabriele Spilker. "Climate Variability, Economic Growth, and Civil Conflict." Journal of Peace Research, 49, 1: 113–127, 2012.
38. Antonio Ciccone. "Economic Shocks and Civil Conflict." American Economic Journal: Applied Economics, 3, 4: 215–227, 2011.
39. Antonio Ciccone. "Estimating the Effect of Transitory Economic Shocks on Civil Conflict." Review of Economics and Institutions, 4, 2: 1–14, 2013.
40. H. Buhaug, J. Nordkvelle, T. Bernauer, T. Böhmelt, M. Brzoska, J. W. Busby, A. Ciccone, H. Fjelde, E. Gartzke, N. P. Gleditsch, J. A. Goldstone, H. Hegre, H. Holtermann, V. Koubi, J. S. A. Link, P. M. Link, P. Lujala, J. O'Loughlin, C. Raleigh, J. Scheffran, J. Schilling, T. G. Smith, O. M. Theisen, R. S. J. Tol, H. Urdal, and N. von Uexkull. "One Effect to Rule Them All? A Comment on Climate and Conflict." Climatic Change, 127: 391–397, 2014.
41. Ariel Ortiz-Bobea, Toby R. Ault, Carlos M. Carrillo, Robert G. Chambers, and David B. Lobell. "Anthropogenic Climate Change Has Slowed Global Agricultural Productivity Growth." Nature Climate Change, 11: 306–312, 2021.
42. C. E. Richards, R. C. Lupton, and J. M. Allwood. "Re-framing the Threat of Global Warming: An Empirical Causal Loop Diagram of Climate Change, Food Insecurity and Societal Collapse." Climatic Change, 164: 49, 2021.
43. https://www.unep.org/topics/fresh-water/disasters-and-climate-change
44. https://news.un.org/en/story/2021/09/1098662
45. A. Park Williams, Edward R. Cook, Jason E. Smerdon, Benjamin I. Cook, John T. Abatzoglou, Kasey Bolles, Seung H. Baek, Andrew M. Badger, and Ben Livneh. "Large Contribution from Anthropogenic Warming to An Emerging North American Megadrought." Science, 368: 314–318, 2020.
46. Martín Senande-Rivera, Damián Insua-Costa, and Gonzalo Miguez-Macho. "Spatial and Temporal Expansion of Global Wildland Fire Activity in Response to Climate Change." Nature Communication, 13, 1208, 2022.

47. Rebecca Newman, and Ilan Noy. "The Global Costs of Extreme Weather that are Attributable to Climate Change." Nature Communications, 14, 6103, 2023.
48. Justin S. Rogers, Marco P. Maneta, Stephan R. Sain, Luke E. Madaus, and Joshua P. Hacker. "The Role of Climate and Population Change in Global Flood Exposure and Vulnerability." Nature Communications, 16, 1287, 2025.
49. Ilan Noy. "The Macroeconomic Consequences of Disasters." Journal of Development Economics, 88: 221–231, 2009. Eduardo Cavallo, Sebastian Galiani, Ilan Noy, and Juan Pantano. "Catastrophic Natural Disasters and Economic Growth." The Review of Economics and Statistics, 95(5): 1549–1561, 2013. Mark Skidmore and Hideki Toya. "Do Natural Disasters Promote Long Run Growth?" Economic Inquiry, 40 (4): 664–687, 2002. Hideki Toya and Mark Skidmore. "Economic Development and the Impacts of Natural Disasters." Economics Letters, 94: 20–25, 2007. Thomas Fomby, Yuki Ikeda, and Norman Loayza. "The Growth Aftermath of Natural Disasters." Journal of Applied Econometrics, 28: 412–434, 2012. Norman Loayza, Eduardo Olaberria, Jamele Rigolini, and Luc Christiansen. "Natural Disasters and Growth: Going Beyond the Averages." World Development, 40 (7): 1317–1336, 2012. Eric Strobl. "The Economic Growth Impact of Natural Disasters in Developing Countries: Evidence from Hurricane Strikes in the Central American and Caribbean Regions." Journal of Development Economics, 97: 130–141, 2012. Eric Strobl, Luisito Bertinelli and Preeya Mohan. "Hurricane Damage Risk Assessment in the Caribbean: An Analysis Using Synthetic Hurricane Events and Nightlight Imagery." Ecological Economics, 124(C): 135–144, 2016. Eric Strobl and Preeya Mohan. "A Hurricane Wind Risk and Loss Assessment of Caribbean Agriculture." Environment and Development Economics, 22(1): 84–106, 2017. Eric Strobl, Preeya Mohan and Bazoumana Ouattara. "Decomposing the Macroeconomic Effects of Natural Disasters: A National Income Accounting Perspective." Ecological Economics, 146(C): 1–9, 2018.
50. Tulio de Oliveira and Houriyah Tegally. "Will Climate Change Amplify Epidemics and Give Rise to Pandemics?" Science, 381, 6660, 2023.
51. Camilo Mora, Tristan McKenzie, Isabella M. Gaw, Jacqueline M. Dean, Hannah von Hammerstein, Tabatha A. Knudson, Renee O. Setter, Charlotte Z. Smith, Kira M. Webster, Jonathan A. Patz, and Erik C. Franklin. "Over Half of Known Human Pathogenic Diseases Can be Aggravated by Climate Change." Nature, Climate Change, 12: 869–875, 2022.
52. Alaina Pfenning-Butterworth, Lauren B. Buckley, John M. Drake, Johannah E. Farner, Maxwell J. Farrell, Alyssa-Lois M. Gehman, Erin

A. Mordecai, Patrick R. Stephens, John L. Gittleman, and T. Jonathan Davies. "Interconnecting Global threats: Climate Change, Biodiversity Loss, and Infectious Diseases." The Lancet. Planetary Health, 8, 4: e270–e283, 2024.

53. Ibid.

CHAPTER 7

4200 Years Before Present

1 The 4.2 ka Event

The first example of the effect of climatic fluctuations on societal collapse is the 4.2 ka event. This refers to the severe climate event of aridification that occurred 4200 calibrated years before present. The evidence for the 4.2 ka climatic drought event comes from different parts of the world. For instance, there is evidence from southeastern Arabia that shows that[1] "[l]ake sediment geochemical analyses record precipitation minima at 8200, 5000 and 4200 cal yr BP that coincide with Bond events in the North Atlantic." From the Northern Red Sea, the evidence shows that the[2] "timing and strength of the reconstructed environmental changes around 4200 cal yr BP suggest that this event is the regional expression of a major drought event, which is widely observed in the neighboring regions, and which strongly affected Middle East agricultural civilizations." Evidence form the Dead Sea indicates that the[3] "arid events in the Holocene Dead Sea appear to coincide with major breaks in the Near East cultural evolution (at ~ 8.6, 8.2, 4.2, 3.5 cal kyr BP)." These are among other evidence collected from other areas as well. Thus, there is a consensus[4] "that some type of drying event happened around 4,200 years ago across an extended area that had an impact on the people living there." This event had drastic consequences for some of the civilizations that existed at the time.

S. Khalifa, *Climate Change, Economic Channels, and Historical Junctures*, https://doi.org/10.1007/978-3-031-91867-4_7

The 4.2 ka event has been hypothesized to have caused the collapse of civilizations that flourished along the banks of rivers such as the Old Kingdom on the Nile River, the Akkadian Empire on the Tigris and Euphrates, the Harappan Civilization on the Indus River, and the Liangzhu culture on the Yangtze River. A river valley civilization is one situated beside and draw sustenance from a river. Civilizations tended to blossom in river valleys due to several factors. The most obvious is access to a reliable source of water for drinking, agriculture, and other needs. Plentiful water and the enrichment of the soil due to annual floods makes it possible to grow excess crops beyond what was needed for subsistence. This allowed for some members of the community to engage in non-farming activities and to support the foundations of urban centers and states. Using boats as a means of shipping also provides an easy and efficient way to transport people and products, allowing for the promotion of commercial exchange and central control of outlying areas.

In addition, riverine nations became highly stratified hydraulic societies. This is because river valleys provide the ideal environment for irrigation agriculture which was carried out on a scale that necessitated a high level of organization, a refined division of labor, a sophisticated administration of scarce water, and supervision of workers by the elite. This paved the way for social hierarchy and the creation of extractive institutions. Historian Karl Wittfogel proposes,[5] "In the core areas of Oriental society, the despotic state fulfilled vital economic functions by operating the large hydraulic enterprises, 'heavy water works.'" These factors contributed to the creation of states and empires.

However, the utter dependence and complete reliance on a river also implies that any shock that disrupts water flow will also adversely affect all these other foundations on which a civilization depends. A climatic shock can always be an example of such disruption as seen in this chapter using a collection of scientific evidence to support this view.

This chapter will discuss the stories of these societies including their greatest achievements, their contributions to humanity, and the final collapse they faced. The discussion will also incorporate scientific studies that provide evidence for the coincidence between climate change during that era and the ensuing societal collapse. This is not intended to invoke causality into this discussion as much as it aims at pointing our attention to the contribution of climate change, in addition to other factors, to the tragic destiny of these societies.

2 Calamity Between Tigris and Euphrates

Climatic factors played a critical role in making Mesopotamia the cradle of civilization. According to some scholars, the predictable flooding pattern along the Tigris and the Euphrates turned some of the surrounding land especially fertile and ideal for growing crops. That made it a prime spot for the transition to agriculture. Societies developed independently in Lower Mesopotamia, where the early civilization of Sumer flourished, and Upper Mesopotamia. In Lower Mesopotamia, the earliest cities developed on the margins of a great marsh where water was easily accessible for irrigation. In Upper Mesopotamia, the rainfall was reliable enough that farmers did not have to do much irrigation.

Climate shifts contributed further to the development of Mesopotamia. Around 4000 BCE,[6] "climates slowly became drier and the rivers more unpredictable." Due to these new conditions, the[7] "marsh retreated from Lower Mesopotamia, leaving behind settlements now surrounded by lands that needed to be irrigated, requiring added work, and possibly greater coordination." Because Mesopotamians had to work harder and in a more organized way, they gradually developed a more elaborate system of governance. In this context, the famed Sumerian agrarian system and its city-states were the outcome of adaptation to these adverse conditions. In Upper Mesopotamia, by contrast, people coped with a drier climate by going in the opposite direction. That area witnessed a retreat to a less complex social structure in the form of small-scale villages.

Mesopotamia eventually saw the rise of empires such as that of Acadia and Babylonia. Akkad was the seat of the Akkadian empire, which was the first political entity and empire in history that followed the long-lived civilization of Sumer. No one knows the exact location of Akkad, but some surmise it was established at the closest point between the Tigris and the Euphrates.[8] This polity started with Sargon the Great who unified Mesopotamia and then founded an empire that extended over a vast expanse of land from the Mediterranean Sea to the Persian Gulf. He was one of the earliest of the world's great empire builders, conquering parts of Syria, Anatolia, and Elam in western Iran. Sargon is known from the tales that followed his death, and not from the writings during his lifetime. The lack of contemporaneous records is attributed to the fact that the capital city of Akkad has never been located and excavated. This empire, however, stabilized the area it dominated allowing for strides in art, literature, language, and religion. There were also other achievements in the technology of agriculture, the art of architecture, and the construction of roads to connect cities and facilitate commerce.

The empire, however, stretched to include other entities that had long histories as independent political powers. These would periodically attempt to reassert their desire for independence throughout the era of the Akkadian Empire. These tendencies had to be suppressed by the rulers to keep the empire intact. For instance, Sargon's son and successor Rimush spent the early years of his reign restoring order to his empire when some areas rebelled after Sargon's demise. Most of his short tenure was consumed in consolidating the empire founded by his father. According to historian Samuel Noah Kramer,[9] "Sargon was followed by his son Rimush, who found his empire torn by revolts and rebellions. In bitter battles involving tens of thousands of troops, he conquered, or rather reconquered, the cities of Ur, Umma, Adab, Lagash, Der, and Kazallu, as well as the countries of Elam and Barahshi. He reigned, however, only nine years, and was followed by his 'elder brother'—perhaps his twin—Manishtushu, who continued in the same military and political pattern."

The successor Manishtushu also had to quell rebellions across the empire before resuming the business of ruling and leading campaigns to distant lands. He also launched great projects throughout the empire and is thought to have initiated the reconstruction of the Ishtar Temple at Nineveh, which was considered a very impressive feat of architecture at the time.[10] He was able to consolidate his authority over cities incorporated into the nascent state that led to a transformation of the perception of kingship culminating in the deification of his successor.[11]

Manishtushu was succeeded by his son Naram-Sin who also had to carry on with the tradition of suppressing insurgencies within the empire before he could begin to govern. Once he was given the chance, however, the empire flourished under his command. He expanded the boundaries of the empire, kept order within, increased commercial exchange, and campaigned with his army beyond the Persian Gulf. Naram-Sin also consolidated direct royal control over the various city-states by appointing some of his sons as key provincial governors, and his daughters as high priestesses. His spectacular achievements, considered the epitome of the Akkadian Empire, were described by historian Samuel Noah Kramer as follows:[12]

> Manishtushu reigned fifteen years and was followed by his son Naram-Sin who raised Agade to new heights of power and glory, only to see it come to

> a bitter and tragic end. His military successes were numerous and prodigious: he defeated a powerful coalition of rebellious kings from Sumer and the surrounding lands; he conquered the region to the west as far as the Mediterranean Sea and the Taurus and Amanus ranges; he extended his dominion into Armenia and erected his statue of victory near modern Dierbakir; he fought the LuUubi in the northern Zagros ranges and commemorated his victory with a magnificent stele; he turned Elam into a partially Semitized vassal-state and constructed numerous buildings in Susa; he brought booty from Magan after defeating its king Manium, whom some scholars have identified with the renowned Menes of Egypt. No wonder that he felt himself powerful enough to add the epithet 'Icing of the four quarters' to his titulary and that he was presumptuous enough to have himself deified as "the god of Agade".

Nevertheless, a widespread insurrection by a large coalition of city-states occurred at some point in his reign. Because of the tremors this brought upon his empire, later generations would associate him with The Curse of Agade. According to the curse, the King attracted the ire of God Enlil by plundering a temple. This was believed to have caused the end of the Akkadian empire after plague, famine, and conquest left Akkad in ruin. As such, it was a victim of one king's misguided arrogance before the omnipotent Gods.

Naram-Sin was succeeded by his son, Shar-Kali-Sharri, whose reign was not smooth from the outset. Like his predecessors, he had to expend a great deal of time and energy putting down rebellions after his father's death. Unlike his predecessors, he seemed to lack the ability to maintain order within and to prevent further attacks on the empire from without. In these circumstances, it was the Gutian invasion which was most credited with the ultimate collapse of the Akkadian Empire and the dark age that ensued.

Recent studies, however, claim that it was most likely climate change which caused famine that weakened the empire to the point where the invasions and insurgencies which were crushed in the past, could no longer be dealt with so easily. After Shar-Kali-Sharri's death, the area fell into anarchy with no king able to claim dominance for long. Climate change obviously acted as the last straw in the case of an empire that expanded to a point when attempting to preserve it by its leader became a recurrent theme at the beginning of their reign. This is especially the case as it conquered other peoples, who took advantage of the period of one emperor succeeding another to proclaim their demands for independence with the hope that the new ruler is not sufficiently strong yet to suppress them. This took a heavy toll on the empire, at a time when the means to communicate across a vast expanse of land was limited, and thus the ability to enforce complete control was largely constrained.

To show the connection between climate change and the fall of the first empire in human history, we go back to some studies that use the latest scientific advances to provide evidence for the proposed fluctuations in climate before the collapse. In this context, archaeologist Harvey Weiss and a group of scholars conducted excavations in Tell Leilan Acropolis, an archaeological site which was used as an administrative center under the control of the Akkadian empire.[13] The excavations yielded architectural, faunal, and floral data which show that there was a marked increase in aridity and wind circulation at 2200 BCE.[14] This abrupt change is argued to have caused a considerable degradation of land use conditions, the abandonment of Tell Leilan, and the eventual collapse of the Akkadian empire. Thus, after[15] "four centuries of urban life, this abrupt climatic change evidently caused abandonment of Tell Leilan, regional desertion, and collapse of the Akkadian empire based in southern Mesopotamia. Synchronous collapse in adjacent regions suggests that the impact of the abrupt climatic change was extensive."

2.1 *The Basin Area*

The first stream of studies focuses on examining the Tigris-Euphrates basin. In this context, climate scientists Peter de Menocal and Heidi Cullen show that[16] "much of the observed interannual–decadal variability in Middle Eastern climate and Tigris–Euphrates streamflow is physically linked to a well-known, natural mode of climate variability—the North Atlantic Oscillation." Along these lines, Peter de Menocal continues in another article to show that the[17] "onset of sudden aridification in Mesopotamia near 4100 calendar yr B.P. coincided with a widespread cooling in the North Atlantic." He associates that change in climate with societal collapse since the[18] "stratigraphic level representing the collapse at Tell Leilan, northeast Syria, is overlain by a thick (- 100 cm) accumulation of wind-blown silts, which was devoid of artifacts, suggesting a sudden shift to more arid conditions. Social collapse evidently occurred despite archaeological evidence that the Akkadians had implemented grain storage and water regulation technologies to buffer themselves against the large interannual variations in rainfall that characterize this region."

Other scholarly work attempts to explain the connection between the sudden aridity and the decline in agricultural yield, thus highlighting the economic channel between climate change and societal collapse. For instance, a group of scholars conduct precipitation simulations that show that the annual mean water outflow from the Tigris-Euphrates basin steadily decreased in 2000 BCE, in the months of peak flow of the wet season.[19] This shift to a drier climate is likely to have been amplified by feedback effects from the soil. The loss in soil moisture leads to a decline in the atmospheric water content over the land. This, in turn, lowers precipitation causing a decrease in vegetation coverage and a shift to a more drought tolerant types. This further diminishes the water vapor available in the atmosphere due to the decrease in evapotranspiration. The authors argue that this cycle eventually led to lower agricultural yields with drastic social consequences since settlements were abandoned earlier where rainfall was lower. These results[20]

> show that long-term drivers produced a shift to a more arid climate, showing minima in both precipitation and river flow at 2000 BCE, whilst temperatures were colder at 2250 BCE. These changes were sufficient to have a negative impact on the natural vegetation in Mesopotamia, suggesting that this climate change would have also impacted the agriculture sustaining local communities. We suggest that the combined effects of climate change and land mismanagement would lead to shortages of water and food, which may have contributed to social disruption and the collapse of the Akkadian Empire.

2.2 *The Surrounding Area*

Besides the basin area, some scholars searched for evidence for climate change from the surrounding area. The Gulf of Oman proved useful in this endeavor. This is because the Gulf is directly downwind of Mesopotamian dust source areas and archaeological sites of the Akkadian empire. In this context, Peter de Menocal and other scholars document changes in aridity using analyses of a marine sediment core from the Gulf of Oman.[21] Their data show[22] "a very abrupt increase in eolian dust and Mesopotamian aridity, accelerator mass spectrometer radiocarbon dated to 4025 ± 125 calendar yr B.P., which persisted for ~300 yr." This sudden change in climatic conditions was associated with societal collapse since the[23] "[g]eochemical correlation of volcanic ash shards between the archeological site and marine sediment record establishes a direct temporal link between Mesopotamian aridification and social collapse, implicating a sudden shift to more arid conditions as a key factor contributing to the collapse of the Akkadian empire."

Some scholars attempt to reconstruct wintertime temperatures and hydrological changes from fossil corals, that lived between 4500 and 2900 years before present, sampled from the Gulf of Oman.[24] The data show that the area witnessed a significant change in seasonality during the 4200-year climatic event. This change led to an abrupt intensification of surface winds causing aridification during winter, which is a critical season for agriculture in Mesopotamia. This wind system is known as a shamal which is a northwesterly wind that blows over Iraq and the Persian Gulf mostly in the summer but sometimes in the winter. Thus, their[25] "fossil coral records provide new evidence that frequent winter shamals and a prolonged cold winter season contributed to the collapse of the Akkadian Empire."

Moving from the Gulf of Oman to neighboring Iran, some scholars present a stalagmite record spanning the period from 5200 to 3700 years ago.[26] A stalagmite is a rock formation that grows from the floor of a cave. The stalagmite was collected from an Iranian site at which interannual rainfall fluctuations today is positively correlated with that in north Mesopotamia. The study finds two periods of dust events, one of which occurred around the time of the 4200-climate event, such that[27]

> [t]he second period of heightened dust flux, suggested to be of greater magnitude and/or larger regional extent, occurs within decadal-scale error of the decline of the Akkadian empire and abandonment of advanced urban settlements in north Mesopotamia [4.19 ± 0.02 (1σ) ka], strengthening the case for association between societal and environmental change. Comparison with the sample's stable isotope record and regional speleothem and marine paleoclimate records supports the idea that both periods of switched on dust activity coincide with periods of drier climate, and that the later 290-y period beginning at 4.26 ± 0.066 (1σ) ka was more extreme in magnitude than the earlier shorter period.

Some scholars saw the possibility of constructing the climate of the area not only using samples collected from different areas near the Persian Gulf, but also from those close to the Mediterranean. Reconstructing paleoclimatic conditions for the Eastern Mediterranean, through an oxygen and carbon isotopic record in a speleothem from Soreq Cave in the Levant, also show evidence of dry conditions around the time of the collapse of the Akkadian empire.[28] A speleothem is a geological formation by mineral deposits that accumulate over time in natural caves and underground caverns. According to this speleothem,[29] "several short-lived decadal- to centennial-scale climatic events were identified. Dry events occurred at 6650–6600 yr BP, 6250–6180 yr BP, 5700–5600 yr BP, 5250–5170 yr BP and 4200–4050 yr BP. The last two events coincide with the cultural collapse of the Uruk society in Mesopotamia and the Akkadian Empire."

3 Famine on the Banks of the Nile

It was on the banks of the Nile that some of the greatest human achievements were erected and continue to stand the test of time till the present moment. Some of the significant events that occurred in that part of the world were attributed to climatic factors. These include the settlement of humans on the Nile valley, the emergence of civilization, and the collapse of kingdoms with the ensuing societal tumult. In the beginning, the valley used to witness intense flooding which did not allow humans to settle. At that time, communities strayed away from the fierce water currents in the valley into the Sahara area that happened to be grassy at the time. Eventually, drier weather deprived the Sahara of the water. Thus, people shifted away from the bareness of the desert back to the fertility of the valley. Historian Susan Wise Bauer explains this process as follows:[30]

> Every year, when heavy rains poured down on the southern mountains, the gathered waters cascaded down the length of the Nile, northwards to the Mediterranean, and rushed far out over the surrounding land. The flooding was so violent that few groups of hunters and gatherers dared to linger. Instead, they lived in the more hospitable lands to the east and west: settling close to the shores of the Red Sea and wandering through the Sahara. In those milder, wetter years, the Sahara was grassy and watered. Archaeologists have discovered leaves, trees, and the remains of game animals beneath the sands.

She continues to describe the effects of climate change on how people populated the valley due to the fluctuations in precipitation and variations in inundation:[31]

> But the hotter, dryer weather patterns that changed the Mesopotamian plain also withered the Sahara. The people of the Sahara journeyed east, towards the well-watered Nile valley. Thanks to the decreasing rains, the Nile flood had become more moderate; the refugees found that they could manage the yearly inundation, digging reservoirs to hold the water at flood-time, and canals to irrigate their fields in drier months. They built settlements on the banks, planted grains in the dark silt left by the floods, and hunted the wildlife of the marshes: wild cattle, ibex, crocodiles, hippopotami, fish, and birds. Other peoples travelled over from the western shores of the Red Sea to join them. They were still full-time residents of the Nile valley: the first Egyptians.

After humans settled in the valley, eventually civilization emerged due to the need to survive in an arid area where the Nile is the only source of water. The administration of the Nile water to irrigate necessitated a level of organization that led eventually to the establishment of political, economic, social, cultural, and institutional structures that were not common at the time. One of the first manifestations of this civilizational development is the Old Kingdom. That period is known for the sweeping political transformation when a group of independent states came to be provinces directly under the control of a centralized government at the capital Memphis. This paved the way for a new period in the history of Egypt where state formation, political centralization, economic specialization, and social stratification became integral to life on the banks of the Nile. The written records of the Old Kingdom are scarce. Instead, the narrative of the era is literally written in stone because it is through the inscriptions on the pillars of the monuments that scholars have been able to construct a history thereafter.

The era of the Old Kingdom of Egypt is also known as the "Age of the Pyramids" when the three wonders of the ancient world were constructed under the Kings Khufu, Khafre, and Menkaure. The Old Kingdom is[32] "possibly unparalleled in world history for the amount of construction they undertook." This Kingdom followed the Early Dynastic Period known for the Pyramid of King Djoser at Saqqara which was the first step pyramid ever built in Egypt. This wondrous feat was constructed after the pioneer Imhotep revolutionized architecture and construction in Egypt by building the king's tomb out of stone. New evidence coming out shows how these timeless wonders were established. For instance, hydraulic force is found to have been used to assist in building the step pyramid of Saqqara and potentially in erecting other similar structures of the time.[33] These pyramids were also built along an extinct Nile branch at the foothills of the Western Desert Plateau. The so-called Ahramat Branch was used as a transportation waterway for workmen and building materials to the pyramids' sites.[34]

These achievements would not have been possible without the consolidation of political power by the Pharaohs, and their close circle and intimate clique, to be able to allocate such enormous resources to build their own personal tombs. The Old Kingdom started with the fourth dynasty during a period when centralization was at its epitome. Thousands of workers, immense resources, and disproportionate provisions have been dedicated to the construction of these elaborate royal mortuaries and burial sites of kings. This certainly came at the expense of general living conditions and other projects and potential fiscal outlays that would have been more temporally beneficial to the public. These unparalleled construction projects, however, also imply a high degree of sophistication that include an unprecedented bureaucratic efficiency to oversee the organization and division of labor, a strong centralized government that can force everyone to comply with its draconian decrees, and great technological achievements in construction, surveying, geometry, and astronomy. In this context, most[35] "of the 20-some kings compelled thousands of laborers to quarry, transport, put in place, and decorate vast quantities of stone in order to construct royal mortuary monuments. They diverted enormous resources from the entire country for this purpose, filling a 70-kilometer-long stretch of the desert edge along the west bank of the Nile near modern Cairo with huge monuments still awe-inspiring today despite the ravages of time." The Great Pyramid of Giza was nothing less than a wonder to marvel at for all eternity such that the[36] "size boggles the mind: it was 146 meters high (479 feet) by 230 meters at the base (754 feet). We estimate that it contained 2,300,000 blocks of stone with an average weight of 2 and 3/4 tons some weighing up to 16 tons."

This was the case in the fourth dynasty. Afterward, the fifth and sixth dynasties experienced a dissolution of central authority of the Pharaohs in favor of priesthoods who began to grow in power primarily through their hold over those same funerary practices. As mortuary priests served increasing number of tombs, wealth was transferred away from the court to the clergy. Decentralization worked also in favor of local officials who were empowered in their localities, rendering the central government inconsequential and diminishing the place of the Pharaoh in the political arena. This continued such that[37]

> [t]owards the end of the Sixth Dynasty, royal power declined rapidly, due largely to the unsustainable charge on the royal exchequer of maintaining the funerary monuments of previous kings and making gifts to nobles of mortuary equipment and endowments of offerings. The endowing of mortuary priests who served increasing numbers of tombs transferred wealth away from the king to the priesthood. At the same time, the power of provincial governors grew until they became barons of their own fiefdoms.

These provincializing tendencies of the fifth and sixth dynasties can be shown by the increasing number of officials who lived in the provinces, who held local offices, and who emphasized local concerns in their inscriptions. On the other hand, the splendor of the cemeteries at the capital decreased with some tombs decorated only in their subterranean parts indicating that security could not be ensured above ground. This marked the beginning of the end of the Old Kingdom.

Historians attribute the collapse of the old Kingdom to a few factors. These include the burden brunt by Egyptians in building the pyramids of some Pharaohs, who Egyptians detested wholeheartedly according to some ancient accounts. The second factor is that these Pharaohs had tested the limits of their divine prerogatives by imposing their utmost tyrannical will on the populace to complete such futile yet impressive structures. In addition, royal power declined due largely to the unsustainable charge on the state coffers of maintaining the funerary monuments of former kings. The third factor is that divine kings needed to marry a peer-divinity to maintain the godlike nature in their line of succession, which led to incest. Inbreeding of blood relations tends to reproduce a limited genetic pool. Therefore, damage in the genes of the royals was more likely to show up eventually. Besides all these factors, it was the drought that was the last straw.

Egyptologists, historians, and other scholars have been seeking explanations for the crisis in Egypt 4200 years before present. A significant factor in the fall and demise of the Old Kingdom was the occurrence of lower-than-average inundation events that led to a decline in agricultural output. A succession of low inundations due to a prolonged period of abnormally low precipitation in the source of the Nile caused severe drought toward the end of the sixth dynasty. Thus, after[38] "the wasteful

Fourth Dynasty squandering of Egyptian lives and money, the weakness of the royal family's genes, and the natural self-limiting nature of the pharaoh's divinity, drought provided the final push over the edge." Thus, climate change was the last straw in this case as well.

When these drought conditions were at a peak, it brought famine which the government could not do much to alleviate as it coincided with the decay of central political authority. At that point,[39] "it only required a slight change in climate for people to starve and society to shake to its core. This happened in Egypt at the end of the 'Old Kingdom', when a fall in the level of the Nile floods caused difficulties with irrigation." The Old Kingdom ended with the sixth dynasty as no ruler powerful enough came to the throne to lead the people. Local officials took care of their own communities and had no resources, nor felt the responsibility, to assist the rest of the country. Given the[40] "environmental problems of increasing aridity and lower Nile floods, the state was even unable to meet the basic subsistence needs of many of its subjects, but it was probably not organized to coordinate any large-scale redistribution of food." As the sixth dynasty passed away, Egypt slowly tumbled into an era classified by scholars as the First Intermediate Period. Harvey Weiss describes these dire conditions as follows:[41]

> At the end of the Sixth Dynasty and between 2250 and 2045 BCE, the First Intermediate Period saw the abrupt politico-economic fragmentation and end of the Old Kingdom's generation and deployment of Nile inundation cereal harvests. Symbolized later with the onset of "70 kings in 70 days," this period witnessed division of the Old Kingdom state into northern and southern domains, termination of pyramid construction, major abandonment of Nile delta settlements, abandonment of the Memphis capital, temple complexes, and "The White House" royal treasury, and abandonment of the Nile-distributed royal centers (Egyptian ḥwt) for goods, labor, and tax collection—all while provincial elites were being empowered.

Egyptologist Barbara Bell argues that the drought acted as a last straw in a situation where only a central government could have handled. The fact that the trend of provincialization prevailed ensured that no coordinated effort in the entire country could have dealt with the drought and the subsequent famine since the[42] "dire famine, due to prolonged (on the historic, though very brief on the geologic, time scale) failure of the rains over the central and eastern African sources of the Nile—a sort of 'exclamation point' emphasizing the ending of the Neolithic Wet Phase—was the crisis that shattered a weakened central government utterly unable to cope with the problem, and decimated the Egyptian people." She also supplies a treasure trove of ancient texts and inscriptions referring to the famine in what she dubbed the first dark ages of Egypt. In the habit of ancient Egyptians who sought nothing more than to commemorate their heroic actions, some have written about their success in the face of calamity that struck the entire country. For instance, a very telling writing on the tomb of military commander Ankhtifi states,[43] "All of Upper Egypt was dying of hunger (hkr), to such a degree that everyone had come to eating his children, but I managed that no one died of hunger in this nome."

However, to provide evidence for the change in climate that brought about the end of a great kingdom, we cannot depend only on texts written on remnants and ruins. We must also resort to research that uses scientific tools to provide evidence for the occurrence of climate change during the period that preceded the collapse. This evidence comes first from the source of the Nile, in the lakes of the Ethiopian highlands, and second from its sink, in the Egyptian Nile Delta, before the river discharges its water into the sea.

3.1 Sediment at the Source

Starting from the source of the Nile, scholars reconstruct the climatic conditions of the time using data collected from Lake Tana, which is Ethiopia's largest lake and the source of the Blue Nile. The Blue Nile is one of the tributaries of the lower Nile in Egypt. The high discharge of the Blue Nile contributes over half of the lower Nile water flow and most of its transported sediment. In this context, some scholars propose that the prolonged low Nile waterflow from the sources may have crushed ancient Egyptians.[44] To prove their argument, paleoclimatic records from Lake Tana were compared with data from the Nile delta. This allows a better comprehension of the history of the Nile basin, from the dominant sediment source in the Ethiopian highlands to the ultimate sink in the Mediterranean. The comparison shows that there is a concurrence between the evidence of drought and the fall of the Old Kingdom such that[45]

> [s]eismic and proxy evidence indicates a short term low stand of Lake Tana and a decline in catchment runoff beginning around 8.5 cal kyr BP, which

may mark aridification caused by the movement of the ITCZ[46] to the south, culminating with a period of intense dryness at 4.2 cal kyr BP. Drought in the headwaters of the Blue Nile at this time coincides with the collapse of the Old Kingdom in Ancient Egypt, and may, through reduced Nile floods, have contributed to this societal shift.

3.2 *Evidence from the Valley*

Besides the source, scholars also use data from the debris left from the flooding of the Nile on its banks. For example, excavations in western Saqqara supplied data which enabled a reconstruction of climate during the Old Kingdom, especially at its initial and final phases.[47] In this context, traces of thick diluvial deposits were found inside the tombs discovered in the western part of Saqqara, mainly in shafts or burial chambers from the late sixth dynasty. Even though winter precipitation was presumably common at that time, the most unusual at the site was their intensity and the proof of a protracted wet period recorded at the end of the Old Kingdom. At the end of that wet period, there was a swift change into an extremely dry climate with the occasional occurrence of strong stormy winds that transported sand and debris. The authors conclude that their investigation prove that[48] "climate change in Egypt in the 3rd millennium BC has been expressed not only by aridification and low floods of the Nile but also by heavy rainfall periods. All these reasons resulted presumably in the rapid collapse of the Old Kingdom at about 4200-4100 cal BP. Low floods of the Nile must have been firstly a consequence of decreased summer precipitation in the Ethiopian Highlands and the resulting low discharges in the Blue Nile drainage basin."

Other studies provide evidence for climate change during that period by focusing on the human reaction to fluctuations in flooding.[49] Examination of structures erected at the time on the island of Elephantine assumes that construction took into consideration the maximum inundation level of the Nile to ensure their safety from flooding. Thus, it is possible to estimate changes in the flood levels for the Old Kingdom using the archaeological evidence of the altitude of the buildings on the island. The author finds that the[50] "1st Dynasty fortress was built 96 m above sea level (a.s.l.), buildings of the 2nd Dynasty were erected lower, close to 94 m a.s.l., which has been interpreted as an indication of falling flood levels. 4th and 5th Dynasty occupation is situated just a little bit lower at about 93.5 m a.s.l." Alternatively, the latest excavations[51] "showed that during the 6th

Dynasty simple buildings were constructed on top of fluvial sediments, at 92 m a.s.l." This is considered another piece of evidence for creeping drought conditions over time.

Evidence for climate fluctuations in ancient times can also be brought about by looking at the fragments of flora and fauna in the valley. In the context of the South Abusir project, Egyptologist Miroslav Bárta and Entomologist Ales Bezdek examine beetles' fragments to study climate change.[52] The use of beetles can be justified by the fact that they represent approximately 40% of all animal species found in terrestrial and freshwater-brackish environments, they are habitat specific, they are dependent on some climatic factors, their climate dependency can be determined from the distribution data of modern specimens, they respond rapidly to environmental stress, and dead beetles are well-preserved in waterlogged or desiccated sediments. The study shows that many beetle species discovered in tomb complexes in Abusir can be associated with a dry and salty environment such that[53] "there is evidence already from the early Sixth Dynasty which indicates that there existed desert to the west of the Lake of Abusir." Not only that, but this evidence[54] "starts to appear in the reign of Teti. This may indicate that a major climate decline started even earlier than previously thought. Two independent sources seem to fully support the notion of a continuous worsening of the climate conditions at the end of the Old Kingdom."

In another study, Miroslav Bárta discusses other evidence from specimens collected in South Abusir.[55] During sampling activities at the former Lake Abusir, the team was able to collect evidence of molluscs dated to the Old Kingdom. The evidence[56] "for molluscs shows that many of them may be connected again with slow flowing or stagnant waters." The analysis of small vertebrae species in the area also confirms a[57] "clear and unbiased picture of an environment where cultivated and inundated areas were meeting sharply with approaching desert environment which we so much believe characterized the Sixth Dynasty and the end of the Old Kingdom."

3.3 *Data from the Delta*

Evidence for climate change can also be sought from sediment analysis sampled from the sink of the Nile. Sediment is a solid substance, which consists of minerals or the remains of plants and animals, that is transported from one location into another. The Nile Delta is the end of the journey of the river. Sediments from the Nile Delta proved indispensable for scholars searching for evidence of climate change in ancient Egypt, as much as those from the source of the Nile in the Ethiopian lakes. In this context, anthropologist Fekri Hassan shows that sediments from the Nile Delta indicate a drying of the delta floodplain[58]

> sediments obtained from drilling the subsurface sediments of the Delta revealed a distinctly thin layer of reddish-brown silt dating to 2250-2050 BCE. This layer indicates that the delta floodplain dried up for a long period of time, allowing iron reddish-brown iron oxides to accumulate at the surface. There is also compelling evidence from the ongoing drilling program at Memphis of dry conditions represented by the encroaching desert sand that began to engulf the Old Kingdom settlement during the First Intermediate Period.

In another contribution, Fekri Hassan also concludes that the[59] "collapse of centralized government about 2200 BC (3700 uncalibrated radiocarbon years bp) coincides with reduced Nile flood discharge, invasion of the Nile Valley by dune sand, and possibly degradation of the Delta floodplain as revealed by proxy data in Egypt. At the same time lower lake levels, a reduction of arboreal vegetation, and onset of cooler conditions in equatorial Africa strongly indicate drier conditions that severely diminished water supply to the Nile tributaries."

Along the same vein, geoarchaeologist Jean Daniel-Stanley and other scholars present new geological data from sediment cores collected in the Nile delta.[60] The information obtained from these sediment cores indicate that paleoclimatic conditions changed considerably from about 4200 to 4000 years before present, showing a decrease in vegetative cover and an increase in erosion rate accompanying a marked fall in rainfall. Their data substantiate the hypothesis that a drying trend and failure of Nile flow played a critical role in the demise of the Old Kingdom. These paleoclimatic events and the[61] "systematic changes in both the annual flood and baseflow of the river Nile, which we document here with new geoscience data, are simultaneous with the end of the Old Kingdom in Egypt within our time resolution."

Compositional and textural characteristics of coastal to offshore deposits of the Nile delta also allow scientists to determine to what extent climate change altered the sedimentation of the Nile. In this context, Jean-Daniel Stanley examines the composition of the deposits that record changes in sediment transported by the Nile and discharged into the delta around the end of the fifth millennium before present.[62] The author finds a period of lower Nile floods at that time as evidenced by sediment loads of altered composition and texture in the Nile Delta and its coastal margin. The[63] "numerous altered sediment compositional and textural patterns in lower Egypt that are reviewed here are attributed largely to lower Nile flood levels ca. 4200 to 4000 years BP that responded primarily to a period of increased aridity, altered rainfall patterns, and reduced Nile flows that affected NE Africa."

Some scholars posit that the provenance pattern of Nile sediments can be used as a proxy for paleoclimatic changes. The Nile River is made up of two main tributaries, the Blue Nile and the White Nile, which cut through different geologic terrains and climatic zones. Because changes in the rate of erosion in a catchment area are controlled to a certain extent by climatic conditions, it is expected that information on Nile sediment provenance can help define changes in the paleoclimate of East Africa. Along these lines, Jean Daniel-Stanley and a group of scholars conduct such an investigation in the Nile Delta and find that[64] "[t]he marked minimum in 87Sr/86Sr at 4200–4500 yr B.P. is coincident with the end of the Old Kingdom in Egypt and provides independent evidence that demise of the Old Kingdom might have been associated with an extended period of catastrophic low floods."

Examining the floral varieties in the delta also proved valuable in reconstructing the climate of the area in that era. In this context, ecological changes may have developed due to lower river flow. The argument is that a low Nile should have caused changes to the distribution and abundance of plant life along the river. Along these lines, Jean Daniel-Stanley and other scholars present a 7000-year palynologic[65] record from the Burullus Lagoon in the Nile Delta to examine changes in terrestrial delta vegetation that likely reflect fluctuations in Nile water flow.[66] The authors propose that the abundance of Cyperaceae pollen is a marker of rainfall and the resultant Nile flow. The study shows that decreases in Cyperaceae pollen, interpreted as an indicator of diminished Nile flow, occurred at around 6000–5500, 5000, 4200, and 3000 years before present. The[67] "timing of three (ca. 5000, 4200, and 3000 cal. yr B.P.) of the four low Cyperaceae pollen events in the study coincides with documented periods of extreme regional droughts that also affected Middle Eastern civilizations."

A lower river implies that inundation carries less water. Consequently, fewer nutrients are deposited on to the land while a greater amount of nutrients stay in the river. This would change the environmental conditions of the river and subsequently the surrounding ecosystems. Along the lines of this intuition, four plants characteristic of Pharaonic times are examined to explore how they may have reacted to such climatic changes.[68] Papyrus and *Phragmites* are proposed as plants that would benefit from a situation where the river retains nutrients, whereas *Typha* and Lotus display characteristics that benefit less. Thus, a drought would lead to more Papyrus and *Phragmites* in the water stream than *Typha* and Lotus. The analysis shows that climatic changes led to[69] "conditions that promoted growth of the Papyrus marshes and Phragmites reed beds." This implies that the Marshes of Edfu may have developed as a consequence of the bloom of Papyrus and *Phragmites* due to the retention of nutrients within the Nile.

All this evidence supports the hypothesis that climate change coincided and contributed to the collapse of the Old Kingdom of Egypt. It was the last straw that broke the camel's back, after the weakening of a state that was able at one point in time to establish such wonders as we still see today in the Giza Plateau.

4 Lamentable Fate of Liangzhu

The Liangzhu was the last Neolithic culture in the Yangtze Delta of China that lasted between 3400 and 2250 BCE. This culture was particularly known for jade artifacts and icons which have always been synonymous with Chinese culture.[70] Jade work was so time-consuming that only a few could afford it. Jade objects of the time have been found only in the tombs of the wealthy, which is an indication of class hierarchy and social stratification.

The Liangzhu site, southwest of Shanghai, was home to an ancient city with the oldest known use of an elaborate water system and large hydraulic engineering structures. The ruins of the walled city of Liangzhu show signs of technological advancements in agriculture and aquaculture. These include navigable canals, dams, dikes, and water reservoirs. Historian Bin Liu and other scholars state,[71] "Together with the well-excavated remains of Liangzhu city and its rice fields, the new findings represent one of the largest efforts of hydraulic landscape engineering in the ancient world." They also add that[72] "[a]rchaeological surveys and excavations can now portray the impressive extent and structure of dams, levees, ditches, and other landscape-transforming features, supporting the ancient city of Liangzhu, with an estimated size of about 300 ha."

This hydraulic system is an indication of a specific political structure that prevailed as well. The[73] "large-scale public works and remarkable grave goods at Liangzhu are products of what may be the earliest state society in East Asia." This is because[74] "it represented an opportunity to consolidate political power. This political aspect cannot be observed directly in an ancient archaeological context without written records, yet it can be inferred through the numbers of functional elements in the Liangzhu hydraulic landscape, the scale and complexity of labor organization, and associated religious beliefs potentially reflecting social order and political authority."

This highly sophisticated and complex culture, however, suddenly disappeared. Archaeological evidence suggests that Liangzhu city was abandoned, and the culture collapsed at about 4300 years ago. This was most likely due to flooding which destroyed people's homes that were built near waterways. A typical Liangzhu community preferred to live on the banks of rivers, and recovered boats and oars indicate proficiency with watercraft. On the other hand, this flooding event also helped preserve the culture. Many of the jades produced during that era have stayed pristine as they were buried under silt consistently with flooding. There is also evidence of a severe drought that followed afterwards, consistently with the 4200-climatic event.

To provide evidence for the climatic fluctuations that contributed to the collapse of such a sophisticated culture, some scholars present paleoclimatic records using speleothems from Shennong and Jiulong caves near the Yangtze Delta.[75] Their data show that the Liangzhu culture declined within a short and anomalously wet period between about 4345 and 4324 years before present. This supports the hypothesis that the city was abandoned after wide-scale flooding and inundation. However, the authors show that this was followed by a drought that dealt the final blow to this culture such that the collapse[76] "might have been caused by flooding and inundation between 4345 ± 32 yr B.P. and 4324 ± 30 yr B.P., a megadrought starting at 4000 ± 47 yr B.P. and a subsequent volatile climate may have resulted in the final demise of the Neolithic culture in the YRD (Yangtze River Delta)."

These changes had a drastic effect on the economic basis of this culture and its agricultural output and[77] "was immediately followed by an abrupt decline in the rice-based agriculture, suggesting that the prolonged period of ENSO dominated like climate condition may have caused the collapse of Liangzhu culture in eastern China." This implies that climate change dealt a double blow, through flooding and drought conditions, to the economic structure upon which this culture depended completely. No society can survive this unscathed.

5 Disaster and Abandonment in the Indus Valley

The Indus Valley Civilization flourished in the northern part of the Indian subcontinent. It stretched along the Indus River and then in all directions outward. This is commonly known as the Harappan Civilization where the designation comes from the ancient city of Harappa, the discovery of which was the first indication that any such civilization existed.

As other sites were excavated, a high degree of sophistication became clear. Unlike cities of other cultures which usually develop from rural communities, the cities of this civilization had been well designed and purposefully constructed prior to full habitation. Furthermore, they reflect conformity which indicates the presence of a strong central government with an efficient bureaucracy and urban planning capabilities to be able to construct such elaborate cities. Historian John Keay describes the apparent similarity and impression of cultural uniformity of Harappan sites as follows:[78]

> The ubiquitous bricks, for instance, are all of standardized dimensions, just as the stone cubes used by the Harappans to measure weights are also standard and based on the modular system. Road widths conform to a similar module; thus, streets are typically twice the width of side lanes, while the main arteries are twice or one and a half times the width of streets. Most of the streets so far excavated are straight and run either north-south or east-west. City plans therefore conform to a regular grid pattern and appear to have retained this layout through several phases of building.

The cities of the ancient Indus were also noted for their intricate drainage, sewage disposal, and elaborate water supply systems. As an illustration, Mohenjo-Daro, which was the largest settlement of this civilization, had an estimated population of at least 40,000 people.[79] Excavations show evidence in this city of[80] "a sophisticated system for supplying water and expelling sewage. Water came from more than 700 wells and supplied not only domestic demands but also a system of private baths and a Great Bath for public use. Drains and sewers were carefully constructed to facilitate the removal of waste."

The history of the Indus Valley Civilization is divided into early, mature, and late Harappan periods. By the early phase, villagers had domesticated several crops. Early Harappan communities eventually turned into urban centers by the time the mature Harappan phase started, along with some rural urban migration at the time.[81] The early phase was also characterized by trade networks with other civilizations of the time in Egypt and Mesopotamia. The mature Harrapan phase was characterized by the construction of great cities and widespread urbanization. Agricultural surplus at the time paved the way for the development of more than 1000 settlements that have been discovered. Although some houses were larger than others, there is no evidence of palaces. All the houses had access to water, sanitation systems, and drainage facilities. This gives the impression of a society with relatively low wealth concentration and higher level of egalitarianism.[82]

The late Harappan phase marked the decline of this civilization when cities have been abandoned amidst evidence of violence. For instance, anthropologist Gwen Robbins Schug and other scholars find that the[83] "prevalence and patterning of cranial injuries, combined with striking differences in mortuary treatment and demography among the three burial areas indicate interpersonal violence in Harappan society was structured along lines of gender and community membership." This period also witnessed the spread of infectious diseases, violent behavior, and a breakdown of urban networks with an expansion of rural ones.[84]

Climate change is considered the culprit to such societal collapse, especially the recorded changes in the monsoon system. The slow southward shift of the monsoons across Asia initially allowed the Indus valley to develop by taming the floods of the river and its tributaries. Flood-supported farming, the use of irrigation techniques and canals, and dedicating different areas for cattle grazing and crops led to large agricultural surpluses. Eventually, the Indus Valley climate grew significantly cooler and drier due to a general weakening of the monsoon at that time. As the monsoon kept shifting southwards, aridity increased, leading to erratic and less extensive flooding which decreased the water supply. This made inundation-agricultural less tenable. The inhabitants then migrated toward the Ganges basin, where they established smaller villages and isolated farms. The lower surplus produced in these small communities did not allow the development of trade and urbanization, and the cities eventually died.

Paleoclimate reconstructions show that[85] "hydro-climatic stress due to a weakened monsoon system may have impacted urban centers like Harappa by the end of the third millennium B.C. The impact of environmental change was compounded by concurrent disruptions to the regional interaction sphere. Climate, economic, and social changes contributed to the disintegration of this civilization after 1900 B.C." These climatic events that led to the end of the Indus Valley Civilization occurred against a backdrop of global changes such that the[86] "[m]acro-regional paleohydrological records sensitive to the strength of the Indian Monsoon generally show increasing aridity and variability over this period consistent with the changes in insolation and the Pacific Ocean. Evidence also exists for a pronounced increase in aridity in the late Holocene and a particularly steep drought at 4200 cal BP." This caused the ultimate demise of this civilization during the 4200-climatic event. Along these lines, archaeologists Harvey Weiss and Michael Staubwasser state:[87]

> The 4.2 ka event apparently displaced the Mediterranean westerlies and possibly the Indian monsoon, thereby reducing the seasonal precipitation necessary for rainfed cereal agriculture. A cultural response to the 4.2 ka climate event may also be seen within the Harappan civilization centered around the Indus valley into the Makran (West Pakistan) and Northwest India. A transition from an urbanized (mature or urban Harappan) to a rural (post-urban) society is well documented beginning at approximately at 3950 cal yr BP. At the end of the third millennium and the beginning of the second millennium BC, the Great Bath and Granary at Mohenjo-Daro were abandoned, settlement in Sindh, the Indus-Sarasvati valley and the Baluchi highlands collapsed and shifted east to the headwaters of the Sarasvati and south to the Saurashtra Peninsula.

To provide evidence for the association between climate change and the collapse of the Indus Valley Civilization, we go back to some scholarly work that has been conducted in this area. The evidence is collected from seas and lakes in or around the Harappan territory, in addition to the Himalayas where the rivers of the area originate.

5.1 *Sea Evidence*

Some studies focus on evidence collected from the Arabian Sea, especially marine planktonic foraminifera,[88] which are highly sensitive to water column structure and marine conditions. These, in turn, are influenced by climatic factors. Therefore, they are valuable in reconstructing certain climate parameters.[89]

To reconstruct climate in the Indus valley during the last 6000 years, Michael Staubwasser and other scholars examine marine planktonic oxygen isotopes from the Arabian Sea.[90] The record shows that the most prominent climate change event occurred 4200 years before present. Opposing isotopic trends across the northern Arabian Sea surface at that time indicate a fall in annual rainfall over the Indus River watershed and a decrease in its discharge. This adversely affected farming and life in the Indus valley, deeming large city life unsustainable. Thus, cultural centers[91] "such as the large cities of Mohenjo-Daro and Harappa, were almost completely abandoned while locations in northern India grew in population. The concordance of Harappan habitat tracking with the 4.2 ka Indus discharge event suggests a causal relationship."

In a related article, Michael Staubwasser and other scholars examine a record of a planktonic foraminifera from the northeast Arabian Sea.[92] A stronger monsoon is shown to have coincided with the urban Harappan period between 4500 and 4300 years ago. Weaker summer and winter monsoons, causing an abrupt reduction in rainfall and in the Indus River discharge, were followed by an end of the urbanized phase. These findings provide evidence that[93] "the initial growth of large Indus urban centers coincided with increased winter rainfall, whereas the contraction of urbanism and change in subsistence strategies followed a reduction in rainfall of both seasons."

To present a reconstruction of the Indian summer and winter monsoon in the Arabian Sea for the last 6000 years, some scholars use records collected from the continental margin of Pakistan including planktonic foraminifers.[94] Changes in the planktonic community indicate strong winter monsoon conditions between 4500 and 3000 years ago, which were contemporaneous with weakness in the summer monsoon. The latter change has been considered detrimental to the inundation agriculture practiced along the Indus and its tributaries. Aided by an analysis of Harappan archaeological site distribution, these climatic changes explain the relocation of people from summer flood-deficient river valleys to the Himalayan plains with plentiful winter rain and reliance on rainfed crops. This[95] "coordinated climate reorganization may have helped trigger the metamorphosis of the urban Harappan civilization into a rural society through a push–pull migration from summer flood-deficient river valleys to the Himalayan piedmont plains with augmented winter rains."

5.2 *Lake Evidence*

Lake hydrology is sensitive to changing precipitation and evaporation. Therefore, some studies use records extracted from lakes to reconstruct the paleoclimate of an area. A higher evaporation over precipitation usually indicates drier conditions. To evaluate past changes in the intensity of the Indian summer monsoon in the last 6500 years, some scholars report an oxygen isotope record from sediments of paleolake Kotla Dahar, which was adjacent to some Indus settlements.[96] Their analysis shows a peak in the evaporation over precipitation ratio in the lake catchment related to a weakening of the summer monsoon occurring at around 4100 years before present. The[97] "drought event 4.1 ka on the northwestern Indian plains is within the radiocarbon age range for the beginning of Indus de-urbanization, suggesting that climate may have played a role in the Indus cultural transformation."

To infer past changes in the hydrology of paleolake Karsandi of Thar Desert, in the vicinity of several Indus settlements, some scholars estimate the isotopic values of gypsum hydration water in the lake sediments.[98] Due to its low solubility in water, gypsum is shown to have precipitated from the lake water with drier climate conditions and higher hydrologic rates of evaporation over precipitation. The authors show that this type of evidence for climate change coincide with the initial expansion of the urban phase and the subsequent contraction of the Harappan civilization. This is since[99] "[m]onsoon rainfall intensified further between 5.0 and 4.4 ka BP, during the period when Indus urban centers developed in the western Thar Desert margin and on the plains of Haryana to its north. Drier conditions set in sometime after 4.4 ka BP, and by ~3.9 ka BP an eastward shift of populations had occurred. Our findings provide evidence that climate change was associated with both the expansion and contraction of Indus urbanism along the desert margin in northwest India."

5.3 *Himalayas Evidence*

Other studies reconstruct climate using evidence collected from the Himalayas. This was an area influenced primarily by the Indian summer monsoon supplemented by the winter monsoon. The Harappan civilization flourished along the Indus-Ghaggar-Sarasvati River Valleys.[100] Part of the system originates from the glaciers of the Garhwal in the Himalayas. Thus, data collected from the Himalayas proved valuable in providing evidence for drought conditions at the time. Some of these studies show a trend toward aridification in the fluvial landscapes of the Harrapan from approximately 5000 years before present.[101] This trend intensified such that the[102] "Himalayan rivers in Punjab stopped incising upstream on the alluvial plain, while sedimentation slowed downstream." The gradual decrease in flood intensity, due to the fall in monsoon precipitation, caused these rivers to dry out. This hydroclimatic stress adversely affected both inundation and rainfed farming that supported urbanization leading to settlement downsizing and large-scale abandonment. The[103] "preservation of numerous archaeological sites at locations seemingly vulnerable to flooding, erosion, or burial suggest that, as aridity intensified, monsoon-augmented floods became less frequent and/or less intense."

In this context, Quaternary scientist Bahadur Kotlia and other scholars present a reconstruction of hydroclimate variability between 5200 and 3000 years before present using a lake sediment core recovered from Deoria Tal, which is a closed basin lake located in the Garhwal Himalaya.[104] An abrupt shift in elemental concentrations and sediment density is documented indicating the onset of lake drawdown at 4200 years before present. This finding sheds light on[105] "the temporal relationship between hydroclimate anomalies and large scale deurbanization, population decrease and the spatial contraction of Indus civilization in northern India between 4500 and 3000 cal yr BP. This record suggests that the onset of de-urbanization and the deterioration of the Indus civilization at ~ 4200 cal yr BP coincided with largest hydroclimate anomaly evidenced in the Garhwal Himalaya during the last five millennia."

As much as the 4200-climate event was the catalyst for such societal failure, the process continued for a while until the final collapse which also coincided with climatic changes from 3700 to 3000 years before present. In this context, Bahadur Kotlia and other scholars present a climatic record between 4000 and 1900 years before present based on a stalagmite from Dharamjali Cave in Kumaun Himalaya.[106] The authors document five sudden drought events around 3400, 3200, 3000, 2500–2400, and 2100 years before present. A gradual decline in precipitation from about 3700 to 3000 years ago coincides with the disintegration of the Harappan civilization along the Indus-Ghaggar-Sarasvati valleys. Thus, the increasing aridity and droughts[107] "between ~3.7 and 3.0 ka BP contributed to the gradual decline in the Harappan civilization, its breakdown in steps and complete collapse around ~3.0 ka BP. During this period, the shift of Harappan settlements from large urban cities to lesser villages as well as migration of population may have also been a result of limited resources brought on by mounting aridity and scarcity of water."

To conclude, the[108] "close temporal relationship between these large-scale hydroclimatic changes and the intervals marking the significant sociopolitical developments of the Indus Valley and Vedic civilizations suggests a plausible role of climate change in shaping the important chapters of the history of human civilization in the Indian subcontinent." This evidence highlights the role climate change played in disturbing the economic structure of this civilization, causing life to be unsustainable in the urban areas which were supported by an agricultural sector whose productivity was disrupted by a drought that was caused by weakened monsoon conditions.

Notes

1. Adrian G. Parker, Andrew S. Goudie, Stephen Stokes, Kevin White, Martin J. Hodson, Michelle Manning, and Derek Kennet. "A Record of Holocene Climate Change from Lake Geochemical Analyses in Southeastern Arabia." Quaternary Research, 66, 3, 465–476, 2006.
2. Helge W. Arz, Frank Lamy, and Jürgen Pätzold. "A Pronounced Dry Event Recorded Around 4.2 ka in Brine Sediments from the Northern Red Sea." Quaternary Research, 66, 3: 432–441, 2006.
3. Claudia Migowski, Mordechai Stein, Sushma Prasad, Jörg F.W. Negendank, and Amotz Agnon. "Holocene Climate Variability and Cultural Evolution in the Near East from the Dead Sea Sedimentary Record." Quaternary Research, 66, 3: 421–431, 2006.
4. Michael Marshall. "Did a Mega Drought Seed Global Chaos 4200 Years Ago?" Nature, 601: 498–450, 2022.
5. Karl Wittfogel. "Oriental Despotism." Sociologus, 3, 2: 96–108, 1953.
6. Hervé Reculeau. "Climate, Environment and Agriculture in Assyria: In the 2nd Half of the 2nd Millennium BCE." Harrassowitz, 2011.
7. Ibid.
8. Christophe Wall-Ramona. "An Areal Location of Agade." Journal of Near Eastern Studies, 49, 3: 205–245, 1990. Harvey Weiss. "Kish, Akkad and Agade." Journal of the American Oriental Society, 95, 3: 434–453, 1975.
9. Samuel Noah Kramer. The Sumerians. The University of Chicago Press. 1963. (P. 61).
10. Julian Reade. "The Ishtar Temple at Nineveh." Iraq, 67, 1: 347–390, 2005.

11. Melissa Eppihimer. "Assembling King and State: The Statues of Manishtushu and the Consolidation of Akkadian Kingship." American Journal of Archaeology, 114, 3, 2010.
12. Samuel Noah Kramer. The Sumerians. The University of Chicago Press. 1963. (P. 62).
13. Harvey Weiss, Lauren Ristvet, and Thomas Guilderson. "The Dynamics of State Development and Imperialization at Third Millennium Tell Leilan, Syria." Orient Express, 21, 2, 2004.
14. H. Weiss, M.-A. Courty, W. Wetterstrom, F. Guichard, L. Senior, R. Meadow and A. Curnow. "The Genesis and Collapse of Third Millennium North Mesopotamian Civilization." Science, 261, 5124: 995–1004, 1993.
15. Ibid.
16. Heidi Cullen and Peter de Menocal. "North Atlantic Influence on Tigris-Euphrates Streamflow." International Journal of Climatology, 20: 853–863, 2000.
17. Peter de Menocal. "Cultural Responses to Climate Change during the Late Holocene." Science, 292, 5517: 667–673, 2001.
18. Ibid.
19. Evangeline Cookson, Daniel J. Hill, and Dan Lawrence. "Impacts of Long-Term Climate Change During the Collapse of the Akkadian Empire." Journal of Archaeological Science, 106: 1–9, 2019.
20. Ibid.
21. H. Cullen, P. de Menocal, S, Hemming, G. Hemming, F. Brown, T. Guilderson, and F. Sirocko. "Climate Change and the Collapse of the Akkadian Empire: Evidence from the Deep Sea." Geology, 28, 4: 379–382, 2000.
22. Ibid.
23. Ibid.
24. Takaaki K. Watanabe, Tsuyoshi Watanabe, Atsuko Yamazaki, and Miriam Pfeiffer. "Oman Corals Suggest that a Stronger Winter Shamal Season Caused the Akkadian Empire (Mesopotamia) Collapse." Geology, 47, 12: 1141–1145, 2019.
25. Ibid.
26. Stacy A. Carolin, Richard T. Walker, Christopher C. Day, Vasile Ersek, R. Alastair Sloan, Michael W. Deed, Morteza Talebian, and Gideon M. Henderson. "Precise Timing of Abrupt Increase in Dust Activity in the Middle East Coincident with 4.2 ka Social Change." PNAS, 116, 1: 67–72, 2019.
27. Ibid.
28. Miryam Bar-Matthews and Avner Ayalon. "Mid-Holocene Climate Variations Revealed by High-Resolution Speleothem Records from Soreq

Cave, Israel and their Correlation with Cultural Changes." The Holocene, 21, 1: 163–171, 2011.
29. Ibid.
30. Susan Wise Bauer. The History of the Ancient World: From the Earliest Accounts to the Fall of Rome. W. W. Norton & Company, 2007. (P. 22).
31. Ibid. (P. 22, 23).
32. Marc Van De Mieroop. A History of Ancient Egypt. Wiley-Blackwell, 2010. (P. 52).
33. Xavier Landreau, Guillaume Piton, Guillaume Morin, Pascal Bartout, Laurent Touchart, Christophe Giraud, Jean-Claude Barre, Cyrielle Guerin, Alexis Alibert, Charly Lallemand. "On the Possible Use of Hydraulic Force to Assist with Building the Step Pyramid of Saqqara." Plos One, 19, 8, e0306690, 2024.
34. Eman Ghoneim, Timothy J. Ralph, Suzanne Onstine, Raghda El-Behaedi, Gad El-Qady, Amr S. Fahil, Mahfooz Hafez, Magdy Atya, Mohamed Ebrahim, Ashraf Khozym, and Mohamed S. Fathy. "The Egyptian Pyramid Chain was Built Along the Now Abandoned Ahramat Nile Branch." Nature, Communications Earth and Environment, 5, 233, 2024.
35. Ibid. (P. 52).
36. Ibid. (P. 58).
37. Barbara Watterson. The Egyptians. Wiley-Blackwell, 1997. (P. 52).
38. Susan Wise Bauer. The History of the Ancient World: From the Earliest Accounts to the Fall of Rome. W. W. Norton & Company, 2007. (P. 117).
39. Chris Harman. A People's History of the World. Verso, 2008. (P. 35).
40. Kathryn Bard. State Collapse in Egypt in the Late Third Millennium B.C. Annali dell'Università degli studi di Napoli "L'Orientale." Rivista del Dipartimento di Studi Asiatici e del Dipartimento di Studi e Ricerche su Africa e Paesi Arabi, 1994.
41. Harvey Weiss. "Pyramid Building and Collapse." PNAS, 119, 37, e221248311, 2022.
42. Barbara Bell. "The Dark Ages in Ancient History. I. The First Dark Age in Egypt." American Journal of Archaeology, 75(1): 1–26, 1971.
43. Ibid.
44. Michael H. Marshall, Henry F. Lamb, Dei Huws, Sarah J. Davies, Richard Bates, Jan Bloemendal, John Boyle, Melanie J. Leng, Mohammed Umer, and Charlotte Bryant. "Late Pleistocene and Holocene Drought Events at Lake Tana, the Source of the Blue Nile." Global and Planetary Change, 78: 147–161, 2011.
45. Ibid.

46. The Inter-Tropical Convergence Zone (ITCZ) is a band of clouds and low pressure that encircles the equator when winds from the Northern and Southern Hemispheres converge.
47. Fabian Welc and Leszek Marks. "Climate Change at the End of the Old Kingdom in Egypt around 4200 BP: New Geoarchaeological Evidence." Quaternary International, 324: 124–133, 2014.
48. Ibid.
49. Nadine Moeller. "The First Intermediate Period: A Time of Famine and Climate Change?" Ägypten und Levante / Egypt and the Levant, 15: 153–167, 2005.
50. Ibid.
51. Ibid.
52. Miroslav Bárta and Ales Bezdek. "Beetles and the decline of the Old Kingdom: Climate change in ancient Egypt." In book: Chronology and Archaeology in Ancient Egypt (The Third Millennium B.C.). Czech Institute of Egyptology, Faculty of Arts, Charles University, Prague Editors: Hava Vymazalová, Miroslav Bárta.
53. Ibid.
54. Ibid.
55. Miroslav Bárta. "In Mud Forgotten: Old Kingdom Palaeoecological Evidence from Abusir." Studia Quaternaria, 30(2): 75–82, 2013.
56. Ibid.
57. Ibid.
58. Fekri Hassan. Droughts, Famine, and the Collapse of the Old Kingdom: Re-reading Ipuwer. In The archaeology and art of ancient Egypt: Essays in honor of David B. O'Connor I, ed. Zahi Hawass and Janet Richards, pp. 357–377. Cairo: Supreme Council of Antiquities.
59. Fekri Hassan. Nile Floods and Political Disorder in Early Egypt. In Third Millennium BC Climate Change and Old World Collapse, ed. H. Nüzhet Dalfes, George Kukla, Harvey Weiss, pp. 1–23. Berlin-Heidelberg: Springer.
60. Jean-Daniel Stanley, Michael D. Krom, Robert A. Cliff, and Jamie C. Woodward. "Short Contribution: Nile Flow Failure at the End of the Old Kingdom, Egypt: Strontium Isotopic and Petrologic Evidence." Geoarchaeology, 18, 3: 395–402, 2003.
61. Ibid.
62. Jean-Daniel Stanley. "Egypt's Nile Delta in Late 4000 Years BP: Altered Flood Levels and Sedimentation, with Archaeological Implications." Journal of Coastal Research, 35, 5: 1036–1050, 2019.
63. Ibid.
64. Jean-Daniel Stanley, Michael D. Krom, Robert A. Cliff, and Jamie C. Woodward. "Nile River Sediment Fluctuations Over the Past 7000 yr

and their Key Role in Sapropel Development." Geology, 30, 1: 71–74, 2002.

65. Palynology is the study of micro-organisms and microscopic fragments of mega-organisms.
66. Jean Daniel-Stanley, Christopher Bernhardt, and Benjamin Horton. "Nile Delta Vegetation Response to Holocene Climate Variability." Geology, 40, 7: 615–618, 2012.
67. Ibid.
68. John William Burn. "A River in Drought: Consequences of a Low Nile at the End of the Old Kingdom." Environment and Ecology Research, 6, 5: 446–460, 2018.
69. Ibid.
70. Tsui-Mei Huang. "Liangzhu – a Late Neolithic Jade-Yielding Culture in Southeastern Coastal China." Antiquity, 66, 250: 75–83, 1992.
71. Bin Liu, Ningyuan Wang, Minghui Chen, Xiaohong Wu, Duowen Mo, Jianguo Liu, Shijin Xu,and Yijie Zhuan. "Earliest Hydraulic Enterprise in China, 5,100 years ago." PNAS, 114, 52: 13637–13642, 2017.
72. Ibid.
73. Colin Renfrew and Bin Liu. "The Emergence of Complex Society in China: The Case of Liangzhu." Antiquity, 92, 364: 975–990, 2018.
74. Bin Liu, Ningyuan Wang, Minghui Chen, Xiaohong Wu, Duowen Mo, Jianguo Liu, Shijin Xu,and Yijie Zhuan. "Earliest Hydraulic Enterprise in China, 5,100 years ago." PNAS, 114, 52: 13637–13642, 2017.
75. Haiwei Zhang, Hai Cheng, Ashish Sinha, Christoph Spötl, Yanjun Cai, Bin Liu, Gayatri Kathayat, Hanying Li, Ye Tian, Youwei Li, Jingyao Zhao, Lijuan Sha, Jiayu Lu, Binglin Meng, Xiaowen Niu, Xiyu Dong, Zeyuan Liang, Baoyun Zong, Youfeng Ning, Jianghu Lan, and R. Lawrence Edwards. "Collapse of the Liangzhu and other Neolithic Cultures in the Lower Yangtze Region in Response to Climate Change." Science Advances, 7, eabi9275, 2021.
76. Ibid.
77. Chun-Hai Li, Yong-Xiang Li, Yun-Fei Zheng, Shi-Yong Yu, Ling-Yu Tang, Bei-Bei Li, and Qiao-Yu Cui. "A High-Resolution Pollen Record from East China Reveals Large Climate Variability near the Northgrippian-Meghalayan Boundary (around 4200 years ago) Exerted Societal Influence." Palaeogeography, Palaeoclimatology, Palaeoecology, 512, 26: 156–165, 2018.
78. John Keay. India: A History. Grove Press, 2010 (P. 9).
79. https://www.bbc.com/travel/article/20221114-pakistans-lost-city-of-40000-people
80. M. Jansen. "Water Supply and Sewage Disposal at Mohenjo-Daro." World Archaeology, 21, 2: 177–192, 1989.

81. Benjamin Valentine, George D. Kamenov, Jonathan Mark Kenoyer, Vasant Shinde, Veena Mushrif-Tripathy, Erik Otarola-Castillo, and John Krigbaum. "Evidence for Patterns of Selective Urban Migration in the Greater Indus Valley (2600–1900 BC): A Lead and Strontium Isotope Mortuary Analysis." PLOS ONE, 10, 4, e0123103, 2015.
82. Adam S. Green. "Killing the Priest-King: Addressing Egalitarianism in the Indus Civilization." Journal of Archaeological Research, 29, 2: 153–202, 2020.
83. Gwen Robbins Schug, Kelsey Gray, V. Mushrif-Tripathy, and A.R. Sankhyan. "A Peaceful Realm? Trauma and Social Differentiation at Harappa." International Journal of Paleopathology, 2, 2–3: 136–147, 2012.
84. Gwen Robbins Schug, K. Elaine Blevins, Brett Cox, Kelsey Gray, and V. Mushrif-Tripathy. "Infection, Disease, and Biosocial Processes at the End of the Indus Civilization." PLOS ONE, 8, 12, e84814, 2013.
85. Ibid.
86. Glen MacDonald. "Potential Influence of the Pacific Ocean on the Indian Summer Monsoon and Harappan Decline." Quaternary International, 229: 140–148, 2011.
87. Michael Staubwasser and Harvey Weiss. "Holocene Climate and Cultural Evolution in Late Prehistoric–early Historic West Asia." Quaternary Research, 66: 372–387, 2006.
88. Plankton are organisms found in water that are unable to propel themselves against a current. Foraminifera are single-celled organisms that are the most abundant in many marine environments.
89. Tonke Strack, Lukas Jonkers, Marina C. Rillo, Helmut Hillebrand, and Michal Kucera. "Plankton Response to Global Warming is Characterized by Non-uniform Shifts in Assemblage Composition Since the Last Ice Age." Nature Ecology and Evolution, 6: 1871–1880, 2022. Lukas Jonkers, Helmut Hillebrand, and Michal Kucera. "Global Change Drives Modern Plankton Communities Away from the Pre-industrial State." Nature, 570: 372–377, 2019.
90. M. Staubwasser, F. Sirocko, P. M. Grootes, and M. Segl. "Climate change at the 4.2 ka BP Termination of the Indus Valley Civilization and Holocene South Asian Monsoon Variability." Geophysical Research Letters, 30, 8: 14–25, 2003.
91. Ibid.
92. Alena Giesche, Michael Staubwasser, Cameron A. Petrie, and David A. Hodell. "Indian Winter and Summer monsoon Strength over the 4.2 ka BP event in Foraminifer Isotope Records from the Indus River Delta in the Arabian Sea." Climate of the Past, 15: 73–90, 2019.
93. Ibid.

94. Liviu Giosan, William D. Orsi, Marco Coolen, Cornelia Wuchter, Ann G. Dunlea, Kaustubh Thirumalai, Samuel E. Munoz, Peter D. Clift, Jeffrey P. Donnelly, Valier Galy, and Dorian Q. Fuller. "Neoglacial Climate Anomalies and the Harappan Metamorphosis." Climate of the Past, 14: 1669–1686, 2018.
95. Ibid.
96. Yama Dixit, David A. Hodell, and Cameron A. Petrie. "Abrupt Weakening of the Summer Monsoon in Northwest India ~4100 yr ago." Geology, 42 4: 339–342, 2014.
97. Ibid.
98. Yama Dixit, David A. Hodell, Alena Giesche, Sampat K. Tandon, Fernando Gázquez, Hari S. Saini, Luke C. Skinner, Syed A. I. Mujtaba, Vikas Pawar, Ravindra N. Singh, and Cameron A. Petrie. "Intensified Summer Monsoon and the Urbanization of Indus Civilization in Northwest India." Nature, Scientific Reports, 8, 4225, 2018.
99. Ibid.
100. Anirban Chatterjee, Jyotiranjan S. Ray, Anil D. Shukla, and Kanchan Pande. "On the Existence of a Perennial River in the Harappan Heartland." Nature, Scientific Reports, 9, 17221, 2019.
101. Liviu Giosan, Peter D. Clift, Mark G. Macklin, Dorian Q. Fuller, Stefan Constantinescu, Julie A. Durcan, Thomas Stevens, Geoff A. T. Duller, Ali R. Tabrez, Kavita Gangal, Ronojoy Adhikari, Anwar Alizai, Florin Filip, Sam Van Laningham, and James P. M. Syvitski. "Fluvial Landscapes of the Harappan Civilization." PNAS, 109, 26, E1688–E1694, 2012.
102. Ibid.
103. Ibid.
104. E. A. Niederman, D. F. Porinchu, and B. S. Kotlia. "Hydroclimate Change in the Garhwal Himalaya, India at 4200 yr BP Coincident with the Contraction of the Indus civilization." Nature, Scientific Reports, 11, 23082, 2021.
105. Ibid.
106. Bahadur S. Kotlia, Anoop K. Singh, Lalit M. Joshi, Kamini Bisht. "Precipitation Variability over Northwest Himalaya from ~4.0 to 1.9 ka BP with Likely Impact on Civilization in the Foreland Areas." Journal of Asian Earth Sciences, 162: 148–159, 2018.
107. Ibid.
108. Gayatri Kathayat, Hai Cheng, Ashish Sinha, Liang Yi, Xianglei Li, Haiwei Zhang, Hangying Li, Youfeng Ning, R. Lawrence Edwards. "The Indian Monsoon Variability and Civilization Changes in the Indian Subcontinent." Science Advances, 3, e1701296, 2017.

CHAPTER 8

The Late Bronze Age Crisis

1 The 3.2 ka Event

The Bronze Age is so-called because of the widespread use of bronze in making weapons and tools at the time. It followed the Stone Age after the discovery of bronze, which was produced by smelting copper and alloying it with tin. One of the earliest tin bronze artifacts is dated to the mid-fifth millennium BCE.[1] An ancient civilization is deemed to be part of the Bronze Age if it either produced bronze, used it in the production of items, or traded other items for bronze from producing areas. Bronze is much harder and more durable than other metals of the time, allowing Bronze Age civilizations to gain a technological advantage.

This era saw the emergence of civilizations around the Mediterranean basin that are best known for their advances in culture, language, religion, art, technology, architecture, politics, warfare, and trade. The Mediterranean is known for its temperate climate that is comfortable to live in. The favorable climate of the area also provides adequate rainfall for farming activities and for the cultivation of bountiful crops. In addition, there was no severe spread of diseases since the[2] "Mediterranean landscape, as it evolved toward civilization, remained a relatively healthy place for human beings." Living in proximity to the coastline also allows for easy transportation of products and commercial exchange around the Mediterranean basin. This was particularly a time of the development of trade networks, such that a truly globalized economy existed in which

S. Khalifa, *Climate Change, Economic Channels, and Historical Junctures*, https://doi.org/10.1007/978-3-031-91867-4_8

several ancient civilizations depended on each other for raw materials and traded final products. Because such connectivity was[3] "driven by the necessity to gain access to remote resources and technological skills, Bronze Age societies established communication links that ranged from the Baltic to the Mediterranean and from the Atlantic to the Black Sea." To ensure a smooth exchange, these civilizations[4] "incorporated natural pathways such as coastal sea routes, rivers, and mountain passes, as well as trails and built roads, to form a 'network of networks' that facilitated a great diversity of physical modes and motivations for transport and travelling."

Before the dramatic end of such a system around 1200 BCE, the Mediterranean hosted some of the world's most advanced civilizations such that[5]

> [i]n the Aegean, the Mycenaean culture was flourishing with powerful urban centres such as Mycenae and Tiryns in Argolis, Pylos in Messenia, Athens in Attica, Thebes and Orchomenus in Boeotia, Iolkos in Thessaly, and Knossos in Crete. The Hittites had carved out a vast empire encompassing a large part of Anatolia, the north-western region of Syria, and extending eastward into Upper Mesopotamia. In the Levant, the Canaanite coastal cities were prospering through trade from Egypt to Mesopotamia, and Canaan was the sphere of interest of the Egyptian and Hittite empires. In Egypt, the New Kingdom was at its height during the prosperous reign of Seti I (first regnal year: 1307–1296 cal yr BC; historical date 1295–1279 BC) and Ramses II (first regnal year: 1292–1281 cal yr BC; historical date 1279–1213 BC). However, around 1200 BC, at the end of the LBA, the Eastern Mediterranean civilization declined or collapsed.

These civilizations suffered a sudden societal collapse toward the end of the Bronze Age. This event is referred to as the 3.2 ka event or the "Late Bronze Age Crisis." The collapse was a time of widespread societal upheaval that occurred approximately between 1200 and 1150 BCE. This sudden, violent, and disruptive breakdown adversely affected a large area of the Eastern Mediterranean, especially in Southeast Europe and the Near East. At that time, cities were destroyed or abandoned, whole civilizations disintegrated, diplomatic and trade ties were severed, writing systems vanished, and there were widespread devastation and death on a scale never seen before. When the collapse had run its course, the Mediterranean entered a dark age. Historian Eric Cline describes this dramatic end by stating that by that time[6]

> the Bronze Age in the Aegean, Egypt, and Near East had lasted nearly 2000 years, from approximately 3000 B.C. to just after 1200 B.C. When the end came, as it did after centuries of cultural and technological evolution, most of the civilized and international world of the Mediterranean regions came to a dramatic halt in a vast area stretching from what is now Italy to Afghanistan and from Turkey down to Egypt. Large empires and small kingdoms, which had taken centuries to evolve, collapsed rapidly. These included the Mycenaeans on mainland Greece and the Minoans on Crete, the Hittites in Anatolia (modern Turkey), the Assyrians, Babylonians, and Mitannians in Mesopotamia (modern Iraq and inland northern Syria), the Cypriots on Cyprus, and the Canaanites in the Levant (modern coastal Syria, Lebanon, Israel, and Jordan), and, of course, the Egyptians.

This collapse attracted the attention of other historians who attempted not only to depict it but also to offer an assortment of explanations on how such fate could befall so many entities at the same time. In this context, historian Walter Scheidel describes the Late Bronze Age Crisis in detail as follows:[7]

> Nobody would have predicted the rapid collapse of this state system in the decades after 1200 BCE. All over the region cities suffered damage or wholesale destruction-in Greece, Anatolia, Syria, and Palestine. Just after 1200 BCE, the Hittite empire failed, and its capital city Hattusa was partly destroyed and abandoned. The important city of Ugarit on the Syrian coast was wiped out a few years later, as were other cities farther inland. Cities such as Meggido followed suit. In Greece, the mighty palaces were destroyed one by one. What rebuilding took place in some of them was undone near the end of the century. Farther south, the Egyptian state lost control of Palestine and from about 1100 began to unravel, torn between the priestly elite of Thebes in the south and assorted dynasts in the Nile delta. Assyria did not escape unscathed, either. To various degrees, institutions of rule and extraction fell apart, cities disappeared or survived much diminished, the use of writing retreated, and empires splintered into statelets and city-states. Output and exchange declined, and social complexity was diminished.

The precise cause of the Bronze Age Collapse has been debated by scholars. Some of the primary causes advanced for this denouement include a combination of climate change causing drought and famine,[8] invasions by the Sea Peoples,[9] natural catastrophes in the form of earthquakes,[10] and internal warfare and political instability. Some even suggested a combination of these factors claiming that[11] "the inhabitants could have survived one disaster, such as an earthquake or a drought, but they could not survive the combined effects of earthquake, drought, and invaders all occurring in rapid succession. A 'domino effect' then ensued, in which the disintegration of one civilization led to the fall of others."

Climate change, however, was emphasized as a culprit by some scholars since the evidence connecting the drought to societal collapse[12] "suggests that the Late Bronze Age crisis was a long and complex spiral of decline that coincided with the onset of a ~300-year drought event, 3200 years ago." This is further confirmed by Benjamin Lieberman and Elizabeth Gordon who describe the Late Bronze Age Crisis as an event that was caused by numerous stressors, of which the drought was a critical one.[13]

> Along with singular natural disasters, internal problems, and external attacks, climate change was a possible cause of stress for the late Bronze Age societies of the Mediterranean and the Levant. A sequence of temperature increases in the Northern Hemisphere, followed by temperature decreases and increased aridity during the early Iron Age resulted in a "hydrological anomaly," or less available water between 1200 and 850 BCE. Records of vegetation from the Nile River Delta point to a series of regional droughts, including the ones around 4200 and 3000 ybp (2250 and 1050 BCE), that would have affected civilizations in the region.

There are several studies that endeavor to provide evidence for climate change during the 3.2 ka event. For instance, some scholars present paleoclimate records from the coasts of Syria and Cyprus which were at the heart of these ancient civilizations of the circum-Mediterranean at the time.[14] The climatic proxy based on a pollen record from Hala Sultan Tekke, Larnaca Salt Lake, indicates an abrupt climate change-driven famine along the Cypriot coast during the crisis. Climate reconstruction from Gibala-Tell Tweini, which was a thriving trade center on the coast of the Ugarit Kingdom in Syria, also indicates that drought conditions prevailed at the time of the crisis. By combining data from coastal Cyprus and Syria, this study[15] "shows that the LBA (Late Bronze Age) crisis coincided with the onset of a ca. 300-year drought event 3200 years ago. This climate shift caused crop failures, dearth and famine, which precipitated or hastened socio-economic crises and forced regional human migrations at the end of the LBA in the Eastern Mediterranean and southwest Asia." This is not an attempt to propose that the drought was the primary cause of collapse during that time. Along with other factors, a protracted drought such as the one observed in the paleoclimatic records cannot be discarded or considered trivial given its effect on agricultural productivity and food availability. This is but another example of how climate change can act as a last straw in the process of societal collapse.

This chapter discusses the stories of some of these civilizations that lived through this climatic event, but did not come out unscathed, in addition to studies that attempt to explain the association between such events and climate change. The examples of societal collapse include the stories of the Minoan in Crete, the Mycenaean in the Peloponnese, the Hittite in Anatolia, the Canaanite in the Levant, and the Kassites in Babylonia.

2 In the Cradle of European Culture

The Minoan civilization prospered on the island of Crete in the Eastern Mediterranean during the Middle Bronze Age. The term Minoan is derived from the name of the mythical King Minos, who the Greeks believed to have ruled Knossos of Crete in the distant past. This civilization evolved to become the forerunner to that of ancient Greece.[16] With the spread of their ideas, through contact with other cultures, the Minoans made an impactful contribution to the development of European culture.

The Minoans, as seafaring people, were also in contact with others throughout the Aegean. There is evidence associating them with other European populations since the[17] "Minoans show the strongest relationships with Neolithic and modern European populations and with the modern inhabitants of the Lassithi plateau." In addition, the early farmers[18] "from Crete shared the same ancestry as other contemporaneous Neolithic Aegeans."

Minoan settlements, tombs, and cemeteries have been found all over Crete, but the principal palace sites were in Knossos, Phaistos, Malia, and Zakros. At each of these sites, enormous complex palace structures probably acted as local administrative centers. While some of these sites seem to have been politically and economically connected, it is not clear whether there was a unified consolidated polity. The art of the time also contains no clear depiction of a monarch. This is quite unusual, given the fascination of ancient civilizations with commemorating their rulers. Small towns, villages, and farms were spread around the territory seemingly controlled by a single palace. Roads connected these isolated settlements to each other and to the core center.

The Minoan era is divided into Early, Middle, and Late periods. The Early period saw a gradual shift from clan-based society living in villages toward a more urbanized one as settlements expanded and became more complex. Minoans also spread from fertile plains toward highland sites and islands as they were more able to exploit less hospitable terrain. The Middle period saw the emergence of the so-called Proto-palatial structure as the first palaces were built at sites which had been used for communal ceremonies before. This period also witnessed the development of their writing system especially the Cretan hieroglyphic.[19] The Late period was an eventful time that saw profound changes with ambitious building projects, bustling international trade, and exertive artistic expressions.

This was, however, disrupted by the eruptions of the Thera volcano which was one of the largest in recorded history.[20] These eruptions caused a tsunami killing thousands of people along the shorelines of the Eastern Mediterranean, destructive earthquakes emanating from the epicenter near the volcano, and eruption-induced climatic fluctuations.[21] Coastal settlements were, thus, abandoned in favor of defensible locations on higher ground.

The causes for the subsequent demise of this civilization continue to be debated. The factors proposed include the invasion and occupation by the Mycenaeans, seismic activities and earthquakes that destroyed the palaces, the eruption of Thera whose volcanic ash covered the entire island destroying crops and killing animals, a tsunami that killed thousands on the shorelines, and finally climate change. None of the theories that have been invoked to stress a natural disaster, however, is consistent with the observed gradual decline that occurred afterward. Only climate change seems plausible in producing such a gradual trend. Drier conditions, at the time, would have affected water availability and agricultural activity. This would have threatened the economic basis upon which this civilization depended.

To provide support for the hypothesis that climate change may have been the culprit for the slow but steady demise of the Minoan, some scholars use proxy El Niño Southern Oscillations and precipitation reconstruction data to present evidence for drier conditions in Crete.[22] El Niño Southern Oscillation is a phenomenon that takes place in the Pacific Ocean. During normal conditions, often referred to as La Niña, there are cold surface temperatures in the eastern Pacific and warm ones in the western part. The continual accumulation of warm water in the west increases the surface elevation. Eventually, the warm pool of surface water sloshes back to cover the tropical Pacific. Then we have El Niño, which is characterized by a large warm spot over the tropical Pacific Ocean. This surface warming is large enough to interact with the atmosphere to bring about significant weather changes all over the world. Such event could have induced drier conditions at the time of the crisis. In this context, El Niño[23] "may have been much stronger at the time of the Minoans. Thus, it is highly probable that the area of Crete experienced drier conditions from 1450 to 1200 BC and even later. For communities that strongly depended on water and agriculture in order to survive, the cumulative effect of these drier conditions could have been devastating and may have led to a slow decline bringing the population below a critical threshold that will allow it to exist and thrive." Thus, even though[24] "ENSO originates in the tropical Pacific through interactions between the ocean and the atmosphere, but its environmental and socioeconomic impacts are felt worldwide."

Another group of scholars recreated the climate of the time by examining the deposits from the tsunami that followed the Thera eruption.[25] This is because these fossiliferous deposits are formed instantaneously and therefore have the potential to offer snapshots of past climates. This is done by trapping elements of a civilization such as construction items, art works, and domestic artifacts, as well as living organisms which have perished in the tsunami. Thus, studying the sedimentary deposits formed by the tsunami may provide access to several climatic variables.

Focusing on the tsunami fossiliferous deposits from the coast of Crete, the archaeological content and the radiocarbon dating of pottery fragments and mollusc shells indicate that this tsunami[26] "corresponds to a climatic period globally warm during the middle Holocene, which is called 'Minoan' because it covers the period of rise and fall of this civilization in Crete." This climatic deterioration[27] "with increasing warming and drying most likely had a drastic and lasting impact on the quality and quantity of food resources on the island. These results should be taken into account to analyze the social and political changes that took place during this period of the Minoan civilization." This indicates that there is evidence of drier conditions that could have upset the economic balance upon which this society depended upon for its sustenance.

3 The Collapse of the Palace Economy

The Mycenaean civilization blossomed in the last phase of the Bronze Age in Ancient Greece. Named after the city of Mycenae, the Mycenaeans expanded their influence to dominate most of mainland Greece, throughout the Peloponnese, and across the Aegean. The Mycenaeans also extended commercial ties and trade relations to other Bronze Age cultures in such places as the Levant, Cyprus, Anatolia, Sicily, and Egypt. They were influenced by the Minoans whose culture spread from Crete to cover the wider Aegean. The Mycenaean is considered the first advanced and distinctive civilization in mainland Greece with its palatial states, urban planning, artworks, and writing system.

The Mycenaeans were dominated by a warrior elite class in a network of palace-centered states. At the head of this society was the king, known as a Wanax, which is a Greek word for lord or leader. A large palace complex has been found at many of the Mycenaean centers. These complexes were built around a large central hall, known as Megaron. The whole palace complex was surrounded by a fortification wall of large blocks. In contrast to these elaborate structures, the commoners lived in modest mud-brick houses which had stone foundations. This stratification of society continued untethered over time.[28] Other structures include terracing of farming lands and damns for flood containment. This is evidence of a rural agricultural system intended to support complex urban centers.

By 1100 BCE, however, most Mycenaean sites have been downsized to mere villages. The causes behind the demise of such civilization are also much debated. Suggestions submitted by scholars include earthquakes, volcanoes, a tsunami, overpopulation, internal social strife and political unrest, invasion from foreign tribes such as the Sea Peoples, climate change, or a combination of some or all these factors. Some scholars, however, cite Aristotle on the possibility of a link between climate change and the collapse of the Mycenaean:[29]

> "This has happened in Greece to the land about Argos and Mycenae. In the time of the Trojan war, Argos was marshy and able to support few inhabitants only, while Mycenae was good land and therefore the more famous. Now the opposite is the case for the reason given above: for Mycenae has become unproductive and completely dry while the Argive land that was once marshy and unproductive is now under cultivation". Aristotle leaves no doubt on what was known at his time about a climatic change in the Argolid area; he also puts his finger to the emigration and resettlement at a

> deteriorated district and his whole discussion is to be compared with the evidence known at present on the depopulation and the complex figure of immigration which occurred during the Mycenaean decline period.

To examine the association between episodes of climate change and the collapse of the Palatial economy, some scholars reconstruct the climate of the area using evidence collected from the Gialova Lagoon in the Southwest Peloponnese. This shallow coastal ecosystem offers an uncommon setting to study past hydroclimate changes. This is because its hydrological system has been largely determined by the amount of precipitation and evaporation, especially after its isolation from the sea approximately 3300 years before present. In addition, the lagoon contains continuous sediments due to its sheltered location that record the environmental conditions at the time of deposition. The area also functioned as one of the critical centers of the ancient Mycenaean civilization between 3600 and 3000 calibrated years before present.

In this context, reconstructing the climate of the Eastern Mediterranean based on a sediment core from the Gialova Lagoon shows a dry period around the time the Mycenaean collapsed. The evidence shows that there are[30] "two major shifts from dry and/or warm periods at ca 3600-3000 cal BP and ca 1700-1300 cal BP, to wet and/or cold episodes at ca 3000-2700 cal BP and ca 1300-900 cal BP." In another attempt to shed light on the evolution of the lagoon and the associated coastal paleoenvironmental changes, another study also documents dry conditions during the time of the Mycenaean collapse. During the late[31] "Holocene period (3300-2500 yrs BP) a big decline at the Rb/Sr ratio was recorded indicating dry conditions. This can be correlated with the 3500-2500 yrs BP Period of Rapid Climate Change (RCC) that has been recorded for the Mediterranean region and the end of the Mycenaean state development."

The Gialova Lagoon is also located near the ancient city of Pylos, the seat of the kingdom of King Nestor. Thus, another study attempts to depict the climate background to the destruction of the nearby Palace of Nestor at Pylos which functioned as the central administrative center of the area.[32] Data from a stalagmite sampled from Mavri Trypa Cave in the Peloponnese shows a brief period of drier conditions around 3200 years before present. The increasing aridity may have disrupted the agricultural system that was likely operating close to its limit at the time, by decreasing crop yields. This clear trend[33]

> towards drier conditions caused reduced agricultural output, hampering the restoration of a central authority or the formation of new social elites. Small-scale subsistence agriculture however, persisted in the area. For the first time, there are indications that climate may be one mechanism behind the process that led to the failure of the Mycenaean way of life in Pylos and there is strong evidence that developing aridity following the destruction of the Palace made it difficult for social elites to reform and for the palatial system to be reestablished.

Some studies examine other lakes in the area to offer a more profound picture of the environmental history of the Peloponnese, going beyond the capabilities of climate reconstruction based on a single lake. For instance, some scholars present four lacustrine sediment archives from the Peloponnese in Stymphalia, Asea, Pheneos, and Kaisari.[34] Their data indicate that Pheneos and Kaisari experienced a drying trend during the transition phase from about 3200–2800 years before present, while evidence from Stymphalia and Asea show a short dry peak about 3200 years before present. These[35] "climatic changes may have been only one factor in a multi-causal interaction network that contributed to but did not cause social transformations." In yet another example, climate change is proposed as a contributor and not the sole cause of societal collapse. This does not underestimate the role of climate change in these social processes, as much as it sheds light on its contribution to historical developments that have been largely brushed aside in some circles.

Some studies attempt to explain the economic transmission channels through which climate change led to such societal collapse of the Palatial economy. For that purpose, a study uses a collection of sources of information including stable oxygen-isotope speleothem records, stable carbon isotope chronologies from pollen records in Greece, sea surface temperatures from Mediterranean sediment cores, dinocysts and foraminifera from Mediterranean sediment cores, paleotemperature proxies from Greenland ice cores, and solar irradiance data derived from Beryllium in ice cores.[36] This data indicates that the Early Iron Age was more arid than the preceding Bronze Age. This is because the Mediterranean Sea surface temperatures cooled rapidly during the Late Bronze Age, limiting the influx of moist into the atmosphere and decreasing precipitation over land. These climatic changes could have affected Palatial centers that were dependent upon high levels of agricultural productivity to support urban populations. Lower agricultural yield, due to lower precipitation, would have made higher-density populations in these centers unsustainable. The Greek dark ages followed since such[37] "climatic pressures would have influenced social tensions, and eventually led to competition for limited resources. This climatic change could have influenced the systems collapse of complex society in the Eastern Mediterranean, as well as influence the population declines, urban abandonments, and long-distance migrations associated with the period."

To show the dependency of these urban centers on supplies from the agricultural sector, some scholars determine the annual sustenance demands of each settlement and whether the resources exploited to satisfy the needs of society were deficient when environmental conditions deteriorated.[38] The study shows that the large sites did not have sufficient space in their surroundings to supply them with the vital amount of food, and thus they depended on supplies from the hinterland. Dry climatic conditions exacerbated this dependency situation and added to the vulnerability of the overall system. In this case,[39] "External stresses, as mirrored in a dry scenario, are very likely to have aggravated this situation, threatening the food-security of the large sites and the overall power balance."

4 Disaster in Ancient Anatolia

Not so far from the Aegean, another civilization survived and thrived in Anatolia. The Hittites occupied ancient Anatolia prior to 1700 BCE, developed a culture originating from the indigenous Hatti people, and expanded their territories into an empire which competed with and even challenged ancient Egypt. The duration of the Hittite civilization was divided into the Old Kingdom and the New Kingdom.

The Old Kingdom lasted from 1700 to 1500 BCE. The beginning was marked by the sacking and burning of the city of Hattusa by King Anitta of the neighboring Kingdom of Kussara in 1700 BCE. Not long after, however, the city was rebuilt by another King of Kussara named Hattusili I. He founded a unified kingdom with the support of his extended family. Once this was accomplished, his sons rebelled against him using the resources of the territories he had placed them in charge of. This excerpt from the Edict of Telepinu illustrates the unification of the Hittites under his command and the challenges he faced afterward:[40]

> Hattusili was king, and his sons, brothers, in-laws, family members, and troops were all united. Wherever he went on campaign he controlled the

> enemy land with force. He destroyed the lands one after the other, took away their power, and made them the borders of the sea. When he came back from campaign, however, each of his sons went somewhere to a country, and in his hand the great cities prospered. But, when later the princes' servants became corrupt, they began to devour the properties, conspired constantly against their masters, and began to shed their blood.

On his deathbed, Hattusili I chose his grandson as heir. Unlike his grandfather, Mursili I attacked other kingdoms solely for the loot and not to sequester their land to expand his own kingdom. Mursili's brother-in-law, Hantili, conspired to assassinate him and take the throne with the assistance of his son-in-law Zidanta. They were successful in their conspiracy. Hantili ruled for approximately 30 years but seems to have accomplished little in that time. Having grown weary of watching Hantili enjoy the throne, Zidanta assassinated him and killed his heirs. Afterward, Zidanta I became king for ten uneventful years until he was assassinated by his son Ammuna. Ammuna was king for 20 years and, during that time, proved to be worse than his predecessors. The vast kingdom fell apart as more provinces defied central command, and Ammuna did little to stop the insurgency or to placate these territories in any way.

After Ammuna died, apparently of natural causes which is unusual for the dynasty, he was succeeded by a son who continued on the throne for five years until he was deposed in 1460 BCE by a younger son, or son-in-law, named Telepinu.[41] He was the last king of the Old Kingdom, after which the Hittites enter a dark age about which little is known. Telepinu is known for his proclamation which boasts of past glories but also laments the sad state of the kingdom. The Telepinu Edict is significant as it allowed historians to reconstruct a succession of Hittite Kings and to recount some critical episodes of that era.

The history of the Hittites resumes with the New Kingdom which lasted until 1200 BCE. This era begins with King Suppiluliuma I who assumed the throne about 1344 BCE. The Hittite empire attained its peak under his command. Even before occupying the throne, he distinguished himself as a military commander. Once he became king, he continued with the consolidation and expansion of the empire in Anatolia and Syria.[42] He was succeeded by his son, Mursili II, who followed in his father's footsteps and set about securing the borders of the empire and expanding them by conquering tribes which had long proved challenging. Even though he was greeted with contempt by his enemies and faced insurgencies early on, since he was perceived to be inexperienced who only became king due to the early death of his older brother, he proved more than a match for his successful father in his military escapades and diplomatic exploits.

After a long reign of 25 years, Mursili II passed away leaving the throne to his son Muwatalli II who is known for facing Pharaoh Ramesses II of Egypt at the battle of Kadesh. Hittite prosperity was largely dependent on the control of trade routes in Syria and the Levant. This was threatened by the Egyptian incursion into that area under Ramesses II. The confrontation was[43]

> an attempt to restore the vassalage of Kadesh to Egypt and to stem Hittite influence in Syria. That the campaign was expected to lead to major military operations, is clearly indicated by the preparations taken by both parties. The Hittites are said to have secured the support of various people settled in Asia Minor, in addition to Naharin, Carchemish, Ugarit, and a host of others. The Egyptian report does not wish to acknowledge that the Hittites had a voluntary following, and thus ascribes the gathering of this alliance to great financial inducement offered by the Hittite king: 'He left no silver in his land, he stripped it of all its possessions and gave them to all the foreign countries in order to bring them with him to fight.' The preparations by Ramesses II were no less extensive and seem likewise to have required great expenditure.

The Hittite army advanced south to confront the Egyptians. The two armies engaged each other close to the archaeological site of Kadesh. The outcome of the battle is uncertain, though some believe that the timely arrival of Egyptian reinforcements prevented the Hittites from attaining victory. The Egyptians forced the Hittites to take refuge in the fortress of Kadesh, but their own losses prevented them from sustaining the siege.

After a few more kings, and repeated attacks by the Sea Peoples and the Kaska tribe, the Hittite empire declined and eventually fell to the Assyrians. The Assyrians destroyed whatever they could not utilize and stamped the area with their own culture. The end of settlement at Hattusa itself has been a key topic of historical scrutiny. A victim of attacks by the Sea Peoples or local Anatolian raiders, archaeological findings indicate that the city was abandoned by the royal administration and only later was it set ablaze.

The final collapse and abandonment of Hattusa and the central Hittite administration was seismic in scale, and climate change was proposed as a culprit. The incessant power struggle between the heirs of the empire and the continuous attacks by the outsiders hoping that the domestic strife provides an advantageous window of opportunity for their attacks, in addition to the weakness of the rulers who did not contribute much to the empire, are all causes behind the vulnerability of the empire to a last straw. That came in the form of climate change. Thus, climate change was not the only factor that strained this society to the limit, but instead was the feather that broke the camel's back. One back that was already bearing the brunt of the weight of too many other factors.

To examine the causes of the collapse, archaeologist Sturt Manning and others use data that measure moisture levels to investigate whether there was a catastrophic prolonged multiyear drought across central Anatolia around the time of the collapse of the Hittite empire in the Late Bronze Age.[44] Their examination of tree ring width and stable isotope records provides evidence for an unusually severe continuous dry period accompanied by harvest declines from around 1198 to 1196 BCE that would have severely challenged existing adaptation strategies. Large[45] "land-locked centres and territories reliant on regional grain production and specialized animal husbandry (such as Hattusa and the core Hittite realm, along with the Empire's overall subsistence and tax base infrastructure) may have been particularly vulnerable in such circumstances (despite various other loci being able to adapt and survive)."

5 The Plight of the Canaanite

Canaan was a civilization that developed in the Levant. The earliest habitation was close to the location of the city of Jericho during the Paleolithic or the Old Stone Age. The people there were primarily hunter-gatherers as the land proved largely inhospitable for agriculture, but slowly they were turning to farming and herding activities.[46] This early rural community would then grow into the city which became one of the oldest urban centers in the entire area. During the Early Bronze Age, other cities and permanent settlements were founded.[47]

Searching for the origins of the people who occupied the southern Levant show that this[48] "Canaanite-related ancestry derived from mixture between local Neolithic populations and eastern migrants genetically related to Chalcolithic Iranians." A genomic study on the origins of farming in the Near East also shows that[49] "the first farmers of the southern Levant (Israel and Jordan) and Zagros Mountains (Iran) were strongly genetically differentiated, and each descended from local hunter–gatherers. By the time of the Bronze Age, these two populations and Anatolian-related farmers had mixed with each other and with the hunter–gatherers of Europe to greatly reduce genetic differentiation." Another genomic study by archaeologist Israel Finkelstein and other scholars shows that these[50] "individuals, who share the 'Canaanite' material culture, can be modeled as descending from two sources: (1) earlier local Neolithic populations and (2) populations related to the Chalcolithic Zagros or the Bronze Age Caucasus."

The Levant was absorbed into the Akkadian Empire by Sargon the Great around 2300 BCE. During that time, urban centers blossomed in the area, and trade flourished with other nations that the Canaanites were in contact with such as Egypt, Asia Minor, and Mesopotamia. Because of its geographic location, the Levant[51] "served as cross-roads for trade and exchange throughout much of antiquity. International routes connecting Mesopotamia, Egypt, Asia Minor, and the Aegean ran directly through Canaan, Transjordan, and Syria–Lebanon, which together form the region known today as the Levant." After the fall of the Akkadian empire, commerce in the area stalled.

This period is marked by the abandonment of cities and a rebound to a lifestyle based on farming villages and semi-nomadic herding. Some scholars attribute this crisis to the 4.2 ka climate event. Even though[52] "the 4.2 ka BP event also corresponds to a drier period, a different climate pattern emerges in the central-southern Levant, with two arid phases framing a wetter period, suggesting a W-shaped event." Other studies suggest that the[53] "first urban culture of southern Levant collapsed and the first period of urbanisation of Canaan (Early Bronze Age I-III) terminated at around 4200 yrs BP. The Canaanites abandoned their walled cities, dispersed and underwent pastoralisation." This dramatic end occurred when[54] "precipitation greatly diminished after 4200 yrs BP in a littoral zone of eastern Mediterranean."

Cities, however, reemerged again during the Middle Bronze Age. At that time, the Canaanite-Phoenicians developed the first alphabetic writing system that was inspirational to other nations in the area. The Phoenicians[55] "inspired all the alphabetic writing systems of their neighbors. In the Near East, the Hebrew and Aramaic scripts derived from the Phoenician. Of major importance to Europe was the adoption of the Phoenician alphabet by the Greeks, either directly from Phoenicians or through intermediaries in Syria or Anatolia."

This period also saw the resumption of relations with other nations, especially nearby Egypt. Commerce had first been established between the Canaanite port city of Byblos and Egypt around 4000 BCE. Commerce between Egypt and the city-states of Canaan was interrupted by the arrival of the Hyksos who occupied parts of Egypt. Eventually, Pharaoh Ahmose I ousted the Hyksos out of Egypt and pursued them from Canaan to Syria, leaving a swath of destruction in his wake. In his effort to ensure no other foreigners ever gained a foothold in Egypt, Ahmose I created a buffer zone to protect his country. This initiated the age of the Egyptian Empire in Palestine.[56] Canaan was naturally absorbed into that empire.[57]

The area continued to flourish under the Egyptians in the early stages of the Late Bronze Age. But Egypt's rule became precarious afterward. Ramses II was able to maintain control over the area after the stalemated Battle of Kadesh against the Hittites. Soon thereafter, the Hittites successfully took over the northern Levant. Egypt's withdrawal from the southern Levant was a protracted process lasting some 100 years from the late thirteenth century to the end of the twelfth century BCE. Egypt's withdrawal was most likely a product of the internal political turmoil. In this process, some Egyptian garrisons stationed in the southern Levant were abandoned without destruction, but others were demolished.[58]

Canaan continued to prosper until about 1250–1150 BCE. Around 1250 BCE, some catastrophic event struck Canaan, demolishing cities and displacing the population. This Late Bronze Age crisis was a time of disintegration since the[59] "balkanization of the southern Levant is founded on significant structural variation between settlement and polities on the Coastal Plain, the Central Hills, and the Jordan Rift."

Climate change, in the form of drought conditions, seems to be culpable as well in this outcome. Dry conditions devastate agricultural activities leading to famine, which is typically followed by depopulation and urban abandonment. Archaeologist Israel Finkelstein and other scholars conclude that[60] "the withdrawal of Egypt from Canaan was part of a broader, longer and gradual process that lasted for over a century, possibly related to predicaments brought about by a period of dry climate in the period between 1250–1100 BCE." Israel Finkelstein and Dafna Langgut also assert that the[61] "major dry period traced in the Sea of Galilee and Zéelim pollen diagrams in the ~1250–1100 BCE time interval seems to have played a role in the 'crisis years' at the end of the Late Bronze Age."

To establish the connection between climate change and the collapse in the Levant, Israel Finkelstein, Dafna Langgut, and other scholars examine several datasets that include faunal and flint records from the ancient city of Megiddo, the pollen diagram of the Sea of Galilee, and the ancient DNA study of Bronze Age cattle in the Levant.[62] These datasets provide evidence of grain growing in Canaan at the latter half of the thirteenth century and the twelfth century BCE. The efforts to expand dry farming in Canaan[63] "were probably related to the dry climate event in the later phases of the Late Bronze Age." Textual evidence also suggests that the Egyptian administration in Canaan initiated the extension of dry farming to stabilize the situation in the southern areas of the Levant and to supply grain to the northern areas which were badly stricken by the climate crisis. The records,[64] "including the textual evidence for droughts and famine, assemble to the same period of time, c. 1250–1100 BCE."

To reconstruct the impact of past climate change on the vegetation of the southern Levant, Israel Finkelstein, Dafna Langgut, and Thomas Litt conduct a pollen analysis of a core drilled from the Sea of Galilee.[65] Their analysis indicates that the driest event of the record occurred between 1250 and 1100 BCE at the end of the Late Bronze Age. Textual evidence from several places in the ancient Near East also attests to drought and famine conditions during that time. Archaeological evidence also indicates that the crisis occurred during the same period of the destruction of urban centers, contraction of other sites, hoarding activities, and changes in settlement patterns. This is because[66]

> [c]old spells in the northern areas of the eastern Mediterranean and decrease in precipitation across the entire region had devastating effects on agriculture productivity and grazing opportunities. Such climatic pressure led to increased food prices and to social tensions due to competition for limited recourses. Groups in the north were forced to move to lands with more hospitable conditions in search of food, leaving a path of destruction and disorder and causing disruption in trade. Pastoral nomads, who depended on surplus grain in the sedentary communities, were especially vulnerable. The long-term climatic changes influenced the stability of the organized kingdoms in the region and led to systemic collapse of the previously well-integrated complex societies in the eastern Mediterranean, depopulation of large areas, urban abandonments and long-distance migration.

6 The Last Blow to Babylonia

Babylon was an ancient city located on the Euphrates in southern Mesopotamia. The earliest known mention of Babylon as a small town appears on a clay tablet from the time of the Akkadian Empire. Conflict between Gutians and the Akkadian Empire has been considered one of the factors in the collapse of the latter. After the disintegration of that empire, this part of Mesopotamia was controlled by the Gutians for a few decades. This was followed by the Third Dynasty of Ur that ruled over the whole of Mesopotamia including the town of Babylon which was a provincial center at the time. That was the last Sumerian dynasty which came to power in Mesopotamia. After the collapse of the Third dynasty of Ur, Babylon became the nucleus of a small kingdom or an independent city-state. This was established in the late nineteenth century BCE by an Amorite King. His successors consolidated its status until one of their kings, Hammurabi, conquered the surrounding city-states and promoted Babylon to be the capital of a kingdom comprising southern Mesopotamia and parts of Assyria. Thus, he founded the Old Babylonian Empire in the eighteenth century BCE and declared himself king.[67] Southern Mesopotamia became known as Babylonia.

Hammurabi is known for the issuance of the Code of Hammurabi, which was one of the first law codes to place emphasis on the physical punishment of the perpetrator, and prescribing penalties for each crime, rather than the earlier concept of compensating the victim of the crime. According to some scholars, the purpose of the promulgation of these laws was to consolidate his power over various territories that came under his control because[68] "[w]hether the work was done by a commission or was entrusted to a single jurist, the glory of the achievement belonged to the king, who combined the authority of his personal sovereignty with a supernatural sanction derived from the gods."

However, the short-lived empire waned under Hammurabi's son. In the context of the turmoil that followed, the city passed to the control of the Kassites in the sixteenth century BCE who established a dynasty lasting for centuries. The Kassites have been attempting to penetrate Mesopotamia but were repulsed by Hammurabi's son. However, they secured holdings within the Tigris-Euphrates valley on the northern frontiers of Babylonia. They eventually gained control of Babylonia in the sixteenth century BCE and established a dynasty based first in that city and later shifted to the new city of Dur-Kurigalzu. The Kassite kings appear to have been members of a small military aristocracy.

In the early fourteenth century BCE, a three-way power structure was established in the area between the Kassites, Hittites, and Assyrians. At the same time, Elam was exerting pressure from the east and Egypt from the south. At the peak of their power, the Kassites conquered Elam under Kurigalzu I in the mid-fourteenth century BCE. That ruler is the one behind the construction of the new capital city, Dur-Kurigalzu which contained many palaces and temples to worship the Babylonian gods.[69] Elam, however, struck the final blow at Kassite power in Babylonia which was already weakened by local insurrection. The Elamites conquered Babylonia in the twelfth century BCE. Afterward, Mesopotamia fell into a dark age which was a time of fending off the Aramaean invasions and crop failures leading to hunger and famine.[70] Aramaeans were tribes that occupied Aram in Syria and some areas of Mesopotamia. The wanderer nomad Aramaeans invaded Babylon when the son of Nebuchadnezzar, the great king who triumphed over Elam at some point, lost his throne to an Aramaean usurper.

Some scholars argue that the[71] "dramatic political, military, and socioeconomic setbacks of Assyria and Babylonia in these 'dark centuries' were ultimately due to an adverse change in climate." About 1200 BCE, a notable warming occurred in the Near East which lasted until about 900 BCE. In that part of the world, winters are the principal seasons for precipitation. Thus, warm winters tend to produce lower amounts of rainfall. The change to a warmer climate is bound to have an adverse effect on both local cultivation on which the settlers count on and the steppe vegetation on which the nomads depend. Thus, the nomad invasions were primarily due to famines simultaneously affecting both the settled areas and the outlying nomad habitats. These raiders were most likely to attack the settled areas of Assyria and Babylonia in times of famine when they were unable to procure food by peaceful means, and when the inhabitants of Assyria and Babylonia were weaker and unable to defend themselves because of the compounded hardships caused by climate change. Thus, the change in climate provided an incentive for the invaders to conquer while heightening the vulnerability of the conquered.

Notes

1. Miljana Radivojevic, Thilo Rehren, Julka Kuzmanovic-Cvetkovic, Marija Jovanovic, and J. Peter Northover. "Tainted Ores and the Rise of Tin Bronzes in Eurasia, c. 6500 Years Ago." Antiquity, 87, 338: 1030–1045, 2013.
2. William H. McNeill. Plagues and Peoples. Anchor Books, 1976. (P. 118).
3. Kristian Kristiansen and Paulina Suchowska-Ducke. "Connected Histories: The Dynamics of Bronze Age Interaction and Trade 1500–1100 BC." Proceedings of the Prehistoric Society, 81: 361–392, 2015.
4. Ibid.
5. David Kaniewski, Elise Van Campo, Joel Guiot, Sabine Le Burel, Thierry Otto, and Cecile Baeteman. "Environmental Roots of the Late Bronze Age Crisis." PLOS ONE, 8, 8, e71004, 2013.
6. Eric Cline. 1177 B.C. The Collapse of Bronze Age Civilization. Biblical Archaeology Review, Summer 2022.
7. Walter Scheidel. The Great Leveler: Violence and the History of Inequality from the Stone Age to the Twenty-First Century. Princeton University Press, 2018. (P. 270).
8. David Kaniewski, Elise Van Campo, Joel Guiot, Sabine Le Burel, Thierry Otto, and Cecile Baeteman. "Environmental Roots of the Late Bronze Age Crisis." PLOS ONE, 8, 8, e71004, 2013.
9. David Kaniewski, Elise Van Campo, Karel Van Lerberghe, Tom Boiy, Klaas Vansteenhuyse, Greta Jans, Karin Nys, Harvey Weiss, Christophe Morhange, Thierry Otto, and Joachim Bretschneider. "The Sea Peoples, from Cuneiform Tablets to Carbon Dating." PLOS One, 2011, 6, 6, e20232, 2011.
10. Eric Cline and Amos Nur. "Poseidon's Horses: Plate Tectonics and Earthquake Storms in the Late Bronze Age Aegean and Eastern Mediterranean." Journal of Archaeological Science, 27: 43–63, 2000.
11. Eric Cline. 1177 B.C. The Year Civilization Collapsed. Princeton University Press, 2015. (P. 165).
12. David Kaniewski, Joël Guiot, and Elise Van Campo. "Drought and Societal Collapse 3200 Years Ago in the Eastern Mediterranean: a Review." WIREs Climate Change, 2015.
13. Benjamin Lieberman and Elizabeth Gordon. Climate Change in Human History: Prehistory to the Present. Bloomsbury, 2018 (P. 56).
14. David Kaniewski, Elise Van Campo, Joel Guiot, Sabine Le Burel, Thierry Otto, and Cecile Baeteman. "Environmental Roots of the Late Bronze Age Crisis." PLOS ONE, 8, 8, e71004.
15. Ibid.

16. Iosif Lazaridis, Alissa Mittnik, Nick Patterson, Swapan Mallick, Nadin Rohland, Saskia Pfrengle, Anja Furtwängler, Alexander Peltzer, Cosimo Posth, Andonis Vasilakis, P. J. P. Mcgeorge, Eleni Konsolaki-Yannopoulou, George Korres, Holley Martlew, Manolis Michalodimitrakis, Mehmet Özsait, Nesrin Özsait, Anastasia Papathanasiou, Michael Richards, Songül Alpaslan Roodenberg, Yannis Tzedakis, Robert Arnott, Daniel M. Fernandes, Jeffery R. Hughey, Dimitra M. Lotakis, Patrick A. Navas, Yannis Maniatis, John A. Stamatoyannopoulos, Kristin Stewardson, Philipp Stockhammer, Ron Pinhasi, David Reich, Johannes Krause, and George Stamatoyannopoulos "Genetic Origins of the Minoans and Mycenaeans." Nature, 548: 214–218, 2017.
17. Jeffery R. Hughey, Peristera Paschou, Petros Drineas, Donald Mastropaolo, Dimitra M. Lotakis, Patrick A. Navas, Manolis Michalodimitrakis, John A. Stamatoyannopoulos, and George Stamatoyannopoulos. "A European Population in Minoan Bronze Age Crete." Nature Communications, 4, 186, 2013.
18. Skourtanioti, Eirini; Ringbauer, Harald; Gnecchi Ruscone, Guido Alberto; Bianco, Raffaela Angelina; Burri, Marta; Freund, Cäcilia; Furtwängler, Anja; Gomes Martins, Nuno Filipe; Knolle, Florian; Neumann, Gunnar U.; Tiliakou, Anthi; Agelarakis, Anagnostis; Andreadaki-Vlazaki, Maria; Betancourt, Philip; and Hallager, Birgitta P. "Ancient DNA Reveals Admixture History and Endogamy in the Prehistoric Aegean". Nature, Ecology & Evolution, 7, 2: 290–303, 2003.
19. Silvia Ferrara, Barbara Montecchi, and Miguel Valério. "The Making of a Script: Cretan Hieroglyphic and the Quest for Its Origins." Bulletin of the American Schools of Oriental Research, 386, 2021.
20. Sturt W. Manning, Christopher Bronk Ramsey, Walter Kutschera, Thomas Higham, Bernd Kromer, Peter Steier, and Eva M. Wild. "Chronology for the Aegean Late Bronze Age 1700–1400 B.C." Science, 312: 565–569, 2006.
21. P.E. LaMoreaux. "Worldwide Environmental Impacts from the Eruption of Thera." Environmental Geology, 26: 172–181, 1995.
22. A. A. Tsonis, K. L. Swanson, G. Sugihara, and P. A. Tsonis. "Climate Change and the Demise of Minoan Civilization." Climate of the Past, 6: 525–530, 2010.
23. Ibid.
24. Michael McPhaden, Stephen Zebiak, and Michael Glantz. "ENSO as an Integrating Concept in Earth Science." Science, 15, 314, 5806: 1740–1705, 2006.
25. Christophe Lécuyer, François Atrops, Romain Amiot, Delphine Angst, Valérie Daux, Jean-Pierre Flandrois, François Fourel, Kevin Rey, Aurélien Royer, Magali Seris, Alexandra Touzeau, and Denis–Didier Rousseau.

"Tsunami Sedimentary Deposits of Crete Records Climate during the 'Minoan Warming Period' (≈3350 yr BP)." The Holocene, 28, 6: 914–929, 2018.

26. Ibid.
27. Ibid.
28. Giampaolo Graziado. "The Process of Social Stratification at Mycenae in the Shaft Grave Period: A Comparative Examination of the Evidence." American Journal of Archaeology, 95, 3: 403–440, 1991. Giampaolo Graziadio. "The Chronology of the Graves of Circle B at Mycenae: A New Hypothesis." American Journal of Archaeology, 92, 3, 1988.
29. Ch. S. Zerefos and E. C. Zerefos. "Climatic Change in Mycenaean Greece: A Citation to Aristotle." Archiv für Meteorologie, Geophysik und Bioklimatologie, Serie B, 26: 297–303, 1978.
30. Christos Katrantsiotis Malin E. Kylander, Rienk Smittenberg, Kweku K.A. Yamoah, Martina Hattestrand, Pavlos Avramidis, Nichola A. Strandberg, Elin Norstrom. "Eastern Mediterranean Hydroclimate Reconstruction over the Last 3600 Years Based on Sedimentary n-alkanes, their Carbon and Hydrogen Isotope Composition and XRF Data from the Gialova Lagoon, SW Greece." Quaternary Science Reviews, 194: 77–93, 2018.
31. Alexandros Emmanouilidis, Christos Katrantsiotis, Elin Norstrom, Jan Risberg, Malin Kylander, Taariq Ali Sheik, George Iliopoulos, and Pavlos Avramidis. "Middle to Late Holocene Palaeoenvironmental Study of Gialova Lagoon, SW Peloponnese, Greece." Quaternary International, 476: 46–62, 2018.
32. Martin Finné, Karin Holmgren, Chuan-Chou Shen, Hsun-Ming Hu, Meighan Boyd, and Sharon Stocker. "Late Bronze Age Climate Change and the Destruction of the Mycenaean Palace of Nestor at Pylos." PLOS ONE, 2017.
33. Ibid.
34. Joana Seguin, Pavlos Avramidis, Annette Haug, Torben Kessler, Arndt Schimmelmann, and Ingmar Unkel. "Reconstruction of Palaeoenvironmental Variability Based on an Inter-comparison of Four Lacustrine Archives on the Peloponnese (Greece) for the last 5000 years." E&G Quaternary Science Journal, 69: 165–186, 2020.
35. Ibid.
36. Brandon Drake. "The Influence of Climatic Change on the Late Bronze Age Collapse and the Greek Dark Ages." Journal of Archaeological Science, 39: 1862–1870, 2012.
37. Ibid.
38. Daniel Knitter, Gerrit Günther, Wolfgang Berengar Hamer, Torben Keßler, Joana Seguin, Ingmar Unkel, Erika Weiberg, Rainer Duttmann, and Oliver

Nakoinz. "Land Use Patterns and Climate Change—a Modeled Scenario of the Late Bronze Age in Southern Greece." Environmental Research Letters, 14, 125003, 2019.

39. Ibid.
40. Marc Van De Mieroop. A History of the Ancient Near East ca. 3000–323 BC. Blackwell Publishing, 2007. (P. 120).
41. Siim Mõttus. "On the Lineage of King Telepinu." Studia Antiqua et Archaeologica, 25, 2: 249–259, 2019.
42. Hans Gustav Güterbock. "The Deeds of Suppiluliuma as Told by His Son, Mursili II." Journal of Cuneiform Studies, 10, 2: 41–68, 1956.
43. Hans Goedicke. "Considerations on the Battle of Ḳadesh." The Journal of Egyptian Archaeology, 52: 71–80, 1966.
44. Sturt W. Manning, Cindy Kocik, Brita Lorentzen, and Jed P. Sparks. "Severe Multi-year Drought Coincident with Hittite Collapse Around 1198–1196 BC." Nature, 614: 719–739, 2023.
45. Ibid.
46. Patricia L. Fall, Lee Lines, and Steven E. Falconer. "Seeds of Civilization: Bronze Age Rural Economy and Ecology in the Southern Levant." Annals of the Association of American Geographers, 88, 1: 107–125, 1998. Steven E. Falconer. "Rural Responses to Early Urbanism: Bronze Age Household and Village Economy at Tell el-Hayyat, Jordan." Journal of Field Archaeology, 22, 4: 399–419, 1995.
47. Christophe Nicolle. "Beyond Urbanization, Regional Settlement Pattern in South-Eastern Levant During the Early Bronze Age." Levant, 55, 1: 26–45, 2023.
48. Marc Haber, Claude Doumet-Serhal, Christiana Scheib, Yali Xue, Petr Danecek, Massimo Mezzavilla, Sonia Youhanna, Rui Martiniano, Javier Prado-Martinez, Michal Szpak, Elizabeth Matisoo-Smith, Holger Schutkowski, Richard Mikulski, Pierre Zalloua, Toomas Kivisild, and Chris Tyler-Smith. "Continuity and Admixture in the Last Five Millennia of Levantine History from Ancient Canaanite and Present-Day Lebanese Genome Sequences." The American Journal of Human Genetics, 101: 274–282, 2017.
49. Iosif Lazaridis, Dani Nadel, Gary Rollefson, Deborah C. Merrett, Nadin Rohland, Swapan Mallick, Daniel Fernandes, Mario Novak, Beatriz Gamarra, Kendra Sirak, Sarah Connell, Kristin Stewardson, Eadaoin Harney, Qiaomei Fu1, Gloria Gonzalez-Fortes, Eppie R. Jones, Songül Alpaslan Roodenberg, György Lengyel, Fanny Bocquentin, Boris Gasparian, Janet M. Monge, Michael Gregg, Vered Eshed, Ahuva-Sivan Mizrahi, Christopher Meiklejohn, Fokke Gerritsen, Luminita Bejenaru, Matthias Blüher, Archie Campbell, Gianpiero Cavalleri, David Comas, Philippe Froguel, Edmund Gilbert, Shona M. Kerr, Peter Kovacs, Johannes

Krause, Darren McGettigan, Michael Merrigan, D. Andrew Merriwether, Seamus O'Reilly, Martin B. Richards, Ornella Semino, Michel Shamoon-Pour, Gheorghe Stefanescu, Michael Stumvoll, Anke Tönjes, Antonio Torroni, James F. Wilson, Loic Yengo, Nelli A. Hovhannisyan, Nick Patterson, Ron Pinhasi, and David Reich. "Genomic Insights into the Origin of Farming in the Ancient Near East." Nature, 536: 419–424, 2016.
50. Lily Agranat-Tamir, Shamam Waldman, Mario A.S. Martin, David Gokhman, Nadav Mishol, Tzilla Eshel, Olivia Cheronet, Nadin Rohland, Swapan Mallick, Nicole Adamski, Ann Marie Lawson, Matthew Mah, Megan Michel, Jonas Oppenheimer, Kristin Stewardson, Francesca Candilio, Denise Keating, Beatriz Gamarra, Shay Tzur, Mario Novak, Rachel Kalisher, Shlomit Bechar, Vered Eshed, Douglas J. Kennett, Marina Faerman, Naama Yahalom-Mack, Janet M. Monge, Yehuda Govrin, Yigal Erel, Benjamin Yakir, Ron Pinhasi, Shai Carmi, Israel Finkelstein, Liran Carmel, and David Reich. "The Genomic History of the Bronze Age Southern Levant." Cell, 181: 1146–1157, 2020.
51. Eric Cline. "Trade and Exchange in the Levant." Near Eastern Archaeology: A Reader, edited by Suzanne Richard, Penn State University Press, 360–366, 2003.
52. David Kaniewski, Nick Marriner, Rachid Cheddadi, Joël Guiot, and Elise Van Campo. "The 4.2 ka BP Event in the Levant." Climate of the Past, 14: 1529–1542, 2018.
53. Michal E. Bieniada. "Intermediate Bronze Age in Southern Levant (4200–4000 BP) – Why Did Four Cities in Transjordan Survive Urban Collapse?" Studia Quaternaria, 33, 1: 5–10, 2016.
54. Ibid.
55. Marc van de Mieroop. A History of the Ancient Near East, ca. 3000–323 BC. Wiley-Blackwell, 2015. (P. 222).
56. James Weinstein. "The Egyptian Empire in Palestine: A Reassessment." Bulletin of the American Schools of Oriental Research, 241: 1–28, 1981.
57. James Weinstein. "Egyptian Relations with Palestine in the Middle Kingdom." Bulletin of the American Schools of Oriental Research, 217: 1–16, 1975.
58. Jesse Michael Millek. "Destruction and the Fall of Egyptian Hegemony Over the Southern Levant." Journal of Ancient Egyptian Interconnections, 19, 1: 1–21, 2018.
59. Stephen H. Savage and Steven E. Falconer. "Spatial and Statistical Inference of Late Bronze Age Polities in the Southern Levant." Bulletin of the American Schools of Oriental Research, 330: 31–45, 2003.
60. Israel Finkelstein, Eran Arie, Mario A.S. Martin, and Eli Piasetzky. "New Evidence on the Late Bronze/Iron I Transition at Megiddo: Implications

for the End of the Egyptian Rule and the Appearance of Philistine Pottery." Ägypten und Levante/Egypt and the Levant, 27: 261–280, 2017.

61. Israel Finkelstein and Dafna Langgut. "Dry Climate in the Middle Bronze I and its Impact on Settlement Patterns in the Levant and Beyond: New Pollen Evidence." Journal of Near Eastern Studies, 73, 2: 219–234, 2014.
62. Israel Finkelstein, Dafna Langgut, Meirav Meiri, and Lidar Sapir-Hen. "Egyptian Imperial Economy in Canaan: Reaction to the Climate Crisis at the End of the Late Bronze Age." Ägypten und Levante/Egypt and the Levant, 27: 249–260, 2017.
63. Ibid.
64. Ibid.
65. Israel Finkelstein, Dafna Langgut, and Thomas Litt. "Climate and the Late Bronze Collapse: New Evidence from the Southern Levant, Tel Aviv, 40:2, 149–175, 2013.
66. Ibid.
67. Ardalan Khwshnaw. "A New Old Babylonian Date List with Hammurapi Year Names." Journal of Studies in History and Archeology, 84: 665–686, 2023.
68. George E. Vincent. "The Laws of Hammurabi." American Journal of Sociology, 9, 6: 737–754, 1904.
69. T. Clayden. "Kurigalzu I and the Restoration of Babylonia." Iraq, 58:109–121, 1996.
70. Frans van Koppen. "The Old to Middle Babylonia Transition: History and Chronology of the Mesopotamian Dark Age." Ägypten und Levante/ Egypt and the Levant, 20: 453–463, 2010.
71. J. Neumann and S. Parpola. "Climatic Change and the Eleventh-Tenth Century Eclipse of Assyria and Babylonia." Journal of Near Eastern Studies, 46, 3: 161–182, 1987.

CHAPTER 9

Climate and Collapse Before Columbus

Climate change had an indelible mark on communities that lived in the Americas before the arrival of Christopher Columbus. This chapter discusses the rise of these societies, their greatest achievements, their contributions to humanity, and how the fluctuations in climate led some to their eventual demise. Examples of societal collapse in this chapter include the stories of the Tiwanaku culture, the Maya, the Ancestral Pueblo, the Easter Island, and Cahokia.

1 Climate and Collapse in the Andes

1.1 Tiwanaku and Its Sphere of Influence

The city of Tiwanaku was the capital of an empire that lasted between 100 and 1000 CE.[1] The city became the center of one of the most influential of the Andean cultures.[2] The Tiwanaku empire, at its epitome, dominated the Altiplano plains in the central Andes and extended from the coast of present-day Peru to parts of Bolivia and Chile. However, Tiwanaku was not an empire in the traditional sense because it lacked some features that we usually associate with this type of polity. For instance, we find no defensive structures at any Tiwanaku site, no royal burials or other evidence of a ruling dynasty, no formal social hierarchy, and no evidence of state-controlled pathways or outposts. However, Tiwanaku had its sphere of

S. Khalifa, *Climate Change, Economic Channels, and Historical Junctures*, https://doi.org/10.1007/978-3-031-91867-4_9

influence. There were cultural offshoots, out of the core area in the Lake Titicaca basin, where highland people imitated the Tiwanaku style in their temples, ceramics, and cemeteries. To prove the clout of this culture, the genomes from individuals in the Titicaca basin show that[3] "the ritual center of Tiwanaku revealed high diversity, including individuals with primarily local genetic ancestry and those with foreign admixture or provenance from as far as the Amazon."

Despite the deep connections with these enclaves, there is little evidence that Tiwanaku leaders controlled the territory or the people within. With few exceptions, the influence of Tiwanaku outside the Lake Titicaca Basin was soft power that blossomed into an enduring cultural hegemony.[4] Some even suggest that it was religious ideology and ritual practices that shaped the cultural processes which fostered the emergence of the Tiwanaku and the political connections between these diverse societies.[5]

In examining their political structure, anthropologists John Janusek and Scott Smith suggest that the[6] "Tiwanaku political influence was selective and focused on developing relationships with riverine communities in order to gain access to caravan circuits. Rather than a core area of continuous control, these processes created a shifting political mosaic rooted in fluid politico-religious webs." John Janusek also postulates that Tiwanaku leaders[7] "facing profound social diversity and enduring local identities, emphasized incorporative strategies of integration, leaving a great deal of productive management and sociopolitical organization in the hands of local groups." In yet another article, John Janusek states that the noncentralized craft production[8] "indicates that they emphasized a corporate political strategy, leaving a great deal of economic management, and therefore power over production, in the hands of local groups." A group of scholars also propose that the Tiwanaku polity is far from a highly centralized hierarchical state but is, instead, a system of settlement enclaves with different ties to the capital.[9]

Situated at a high altitude near the shores of the Lake Titicaca basin, Tiwanaku was the highest city in the ancient world. The city center was surrounded by a trench on three sides which linked with Lake Titicaca on the fourth side of the city. There were residential areas surrounding the center that show social stratification. Elite domiciles were adorned with high adobe walls surrounding a courtyard, while some other buildings were constructed from finely cut stone blocks. The humbler structures were erected using desiccated mud bricks on cobblestone foundations. The city[10] "had been carefully designed as an imposing ceremonial core, spatially aligned according to cosmological principles and surrounded by a huge moat that restricted access and that was meant to give the center the appearance of a sacred island." The architecture, art, and urban layout of Tiwanaku would exert a tremendous influence on the later Inca civilization. Inca cities took some inspiration from the city of Tiwanaku in their architecture and infrastructure.

Tiwanaku developed an agricultural system based upon irrigation. There is clear evidence for large-scale crop production to support the urban population of the city. Irrigation was conducted via canals, aqueducts, and dikes which brought water from the lake. The ample agricultural yield, especially potatoes and quinoa,[11] allowed for sustained population growth. The Tiwanaku developed unique farming techniques known as[12] "flooded-raised fields." A raised field is a cultivated elevation typically surrounded by water-filled ditches, that allow farmers to control critical factors such as rainfall, frost, and flooding. Anthropologist Alan Kolata states that the[13] "raised fields of the Pampa Koani were clearly an effective indigenous technique for intensifying food production in an otherwise unpromising agricultural landscape."

This system of intensive agriculture was a prime economic strategy of the Tiwanaku state that was devised and administered by a hierarchically organized central government, especially[14] "the intensification of agricultural production through large-scale reclamation of flat land along the margins of Lake Titicaca." Thus, the organization of agricultural production in Tiwanaku depended on both a hydrological technology and a degree of political centralization such that[15] "(1) the technology of Tiwanaku intensive agricultural production turned on the creation of an artificial regional hydrological regime of canals, aqueducts, and groundwater regulation articulated with massive raised-field systems, and (2) the organization of agricultural production in this core territory entailed structured, hierarchical interaction between urban and rural settlements characterized by a substantial degree of political centralization and the mobilization of labor by social principles that reached beyond simple kinship relations."

The Tiwanaku entity, however, collapsed around 1000 CE. Tiwanaku city was abandoned possibly as late as 1100 CE. The downfall of the center[16] "was accompanied by agricultural collapse in its hinterland. Cities disappeared from the Lake Titicaca basin for several centuries, as political fragmentation and localized economic activity became the norm." Population also shrank and whoever is left withdrew into settlements with extensive defensive fortifications that indicate violent conditions. Some scholars estimate the timing of collapse between 1010 and 1050 CE concluding that[17]

> monument building ended ~AD 720 (the median of the ending boundary). Around ~AD 910, burials in tombs ceased as violent deaths began, which we document for the first time in this paper. Ritualized murders are limited to the century leading up to ~AD 1020. Our clearest proxy for social networks breaking down is a precise estimate for the end of permanent residence, ~AD 1010 (970–1050, 95%). This major inflection point was followed by visitors who used the same ceramics until ~AD 1040. Temporary camps lasted until roughly ~AD 1050. These four events suggest a rapid, city-wide collapse at ~AD 1010–1050, lasting just ~20 years.

1.2 Drought and the Demise

The collapse of the Tiwanaku culture was likely due to excessive drought brought about by climate change. In this context, historian Walter Schiedel describes the climate change–induced collapse amid social upheaval, destruction, violence, and political breakdown by stating,[18] "Climate change in the form of severe drought is thought to have undermined Tiwanaku's complex structures of control. Its state collapse, taking rulers, nobles, and their ceremonial center with it. The capital city itself was abandoned in stages and had completely emptied by 1000 CE. Archaeologists have unearthed tell-tale signs of extensive violence." Along the same vein, Benjamin Lieberman and Elizabeth Gordon describe the consequences of the prolonged dry spell by stating that[19] "the society of Tiwanaku thrived centuries on the shores of Lake Titicaca before a long dry period started in the eleventh century. The capital of an empire, Tiwanaku contained numerous ceremonial sites, including temples and pyramids. Terraced fields surrounded the capital. This large and complex society declined and came to an end in the eleventh and twelfth centuries. In one scenario, the state saw its power erode and ultimately declined because of a decrease in precipitation."

In his revelations of the Americas before Columbus, Charles Mann elaborates on the effect of climate change on the Tiwanaku and Wari by stating that in 1000 CE[20] "both societies were reeling from a succession of terrible droughts. Perhaps eighty years earlier, dust storms had engulfed the high plains, blackening the glaciers in the peaks above. (Ice samples, dug out in the 1990s, suggest the assault.) Then came a run of punishing dry spells, many more than a decade in duration, interrupted by gigantic floods."

To provide evidence for the proposed association between climate change and the collapse of Tiwanaku, we refer to some scholarly work which aim to establish such a connection. These studies specifically focus on information collected from Lake Titicaca. To show evidence for the severe drought conditions that decreased the lake water level and affected the practice of raised field farming in the basin, Alan Kolata and John Janusek examine lake and ice cores from the area.[21] Their record documents a drought which[22] "caused the shores of Lake Titicaca to recede for kilometers, and local water tables to drop far below the surface. Decreasing lake levels effectively stranded huge tracts of raised fields and rendered their hydraulic sustaining systems inoperable, particularly in inland areas." Because of the specific nature of their farming structure, the decline in water levels due to drought conditions was a complete blow to the sustainability of such a system.

In a similar vein, Alan Kolata, John Janusek, and others conduct a study of Lake Titicaca basin and the surrounding Altiplano that span 3500 years.[23] Their paleolimnological[24] evidence demonstrates that the collapse of the Tiwanaku coincided with periods of abrupt climate change toward increased aridification, which is inferred from lake-level variation and estimates of drainage basin water levels deduced from lake-sediment cores. Their archaeological evidence establishes spatial and temporal patterns of agricultural field use showing that[25] "large urban and rural populations had become dependent upon raised-field systems that relied on abundant water. Increased aridity induced declining agricultural production, progressive raised-field abandonment, population dispersal, and ultimately Tiwanaku cultural collapse."

To study the collapse of Tiwanaku through the lens of its agricultural history, Alan Kolata and Charles Ortloff examine paleoenvironmental data derived from the Quelccaya ice cap of southern Peru and sediment cores from Lake Titicaca.[26] The data provides evidence that the collapse of intensive agriculture was caused by changes in climatic conditions in the Andes in the form of a significant decrease in average precipitation and a chronic drought that persisted until 1400 CE. This led to the deterioration and the ultimate abandonment of its agricultural systems, both in its core in the Andean Altiplano and its economic dominions. Thus, the Tiwanaku empire[27] "experienced collapse of its agricultural base after AD

1000 due to a dramatic decline in mean annual precipitation commencing around AD 950."

Studying how societies reacted to the drastic environmental changes in the Andes, with an emphasis on the period between 500 and 1500 BCE, Alan Kolata and Tom Dillehay show that the prolonged drought adversely affected agricultural productivity leading to abandonment of land, evacuation of cities, and disintegration of political structures.[28] In the specific case of Tiwanaku, these[29] "protracted drought conditions induced region-wide failure of agricultural infrastructure; the only effective response to this crisis was state collapse and the migration of human populations."

Some scholars focus on the amounts of lake water that the Tiwanaku depended upon for agriculture, to determine the variations that may have affected their agricultural production. To identify a new chronology of lake-level variations, geologist Mark Abbott and others examine sediment cores collected from the southern basin of Lake Titicaca.[30] The analysis indicates the timing of five periods of low lake level, some of which coincided with the collapse of this civilization. Their data show that[31] "[t]he final low lake stand is coincident with the decline of raised-field agriculture and the collapse of Tiwanaku culture."

In a similar vein, Mark Abbott and other scholars reconstruct hydrologic changes in nearby Lake Orurillo to compare periods of increased aridity to archaeological data on the timing of the Tiwanaku collapse.[32] Their data show that the[33] "drought and the prolonged, centennial scale aridity phase preserved in the isotopic record of Lake Orurillo corresponds with the collapse of Tiwanaku civilization and lasts until ca.1250 CE. This interval of aridity was the longest and most severe period of reduced precipitation throughout the lake's 4000-year sedimentary archive." This is because the raised fields, with a complex system of water channeling, sustained dense populations throughout the basin. A protracted period of aridity would erode the economic underpinnings of the Tiwanaku society by limiting the amount of land amenable to irrigation and lowering agricultural output per unit. Although these systems were buffered against short periods of lower precipitation, they could not sustain production through centennial-scale droughts. The gradual[34]

> reduction of lake and groundwater levels profoundly disrupted the production of agricultural systems and eventually threatened the functioning and the legitimacy of the Tiwanaku state. The length and regional severity of the aridity phase is a crucial component of the collapse: short arid periods

> undoubtably occurred prior to the MCA;[35] however, centuries of lower precipitation throughout the central Andes were impossible to overcome. The collapse of Tiwanaku was thus ultimately a result of a centennial scale arid period driven by global teleconnections that resulted in a regionally coherent signal of reduced precipitation.

Despite the abundance of evidence on the contribution of drought to the destiny of this culture, there is one study that posits that[36] "a careful scrutiny of the data from ice cores and lake sediments persuades the author that no such drought can be inferred: the evidence for climatic change is of quite a different scale and order to the archaeological changes and cannot be used as an explanation of social events." Weighing the plethora of studies that provide evidence for the drought-induced social disruption against such a cautionary tale leads us to lean on the side of the former but to also err on the side of caution with hopes that future studies can settle this issue between the two views to one's satisfaction.

2 Climate Change in Mesoamerica

2.1 The Maya of Mesoamerica

The Maya is an indigenous people of Mesoamerica. The designation comes from the ancient city of Mayapán, the last capital of the Maya in the Yucatán Peninsula. The Maya settled in villages as early as the so-called Pre-Classic Period from approximately 2000 BCE to 250 CE.[37] This was followed by the Classic period which lasted from about 250 CE until 900 CE. Before the Spanish conquest of Mexico and Central America, the Maya developed one of the greatest civilizations in the Western Hemisphere. There are hundreds of Maya sites spread across five countries that include present-day Mexico, Belize, El Salvador, Guatemala, and Honduras. The civilization is noted for its art, architecture, writing, mathematics, and astronomy.

There is evidence for the development of agriculture and the subsequent settlement in villages as far as 2000 BCE. The Mayas developed a swidden agricultural system since[38] "it seems only reasonable to conclude that the development of concentrations and such centers began under conditions of extensive-as opposed to intensive-agricultural practices, probably largely swidden agriculture." In such a system, forests were cleared to make way for crop cultivation. However, soil fertility deteriorated rapidly, which necessitated slash-and-burn techniques to replenish the land.[39] Slash-and-burn is a farming technique in which existing vegetation is cut down and burned off before new seeds are sown. To increase soil fertility, farmers also had to implement types of wetland cultivation such as raised and channeled fields, terraces, and forest gardens. This is since the evidence indicates that the[40] "large number of well-defined ground patterns reported in other areas in the central Maya lowlands are probably vestiges of Maya wetland cultivation." It is also found that the Mayas practiced intensive cultivation in some areas since[41] "[r]emnants of terraces and raised fields are common through-out southern Campeche and Quintana Roo, indicating that the Rio Bec region was inhabited by sophisticated, intensive cultivators." Aerial surveys of the southern Maya lowlands also[42] "suggest that large areas were drained by ancient canals that may have been used for intensive cultivation."

At its epitome, this civilization had several cities each with a population between 5000 and 50,000, containing temples, pyramids, palaces, courts, and plazas. Using Laser Imaging Detection and Ranging techniques, scholars find that[43] "[m]ore than 775 ancient Maya settlements are identified within the MCKB (Mirador-Calakmul Karst Basin of Guatemala), and 189 more in the surrounding karstic ridge, which we condensed into 417 ancient cities, towns, and villages of at least six preliminary tiers based on surface area, volumetrics, and architectural configurations." The city centers included ceremonial structures and administrative complexes, surrounded by a sprawl of residential areas. Different parts of a city were linked by causeways. City buildings included palaces, pyramid-temples, ceremonial courts, and structures specially aligned for astronomical observation.[44] These city-states were also connected by an intricate trade network. Estimates of the Gini index indicates higher values in the core Maya area, implying higher inequality, and[45] "notably lower values in peripheral areas, including coastal zones and the Western lowlands."

Among their many achievements, the Mayas developed a highly sophisticated system of hieroglyphic writing. Some members of the elite were literate, as the Maya developed the most advanced writing system in pre-Columbian America. Samples of[46] "carbonized wood that are closely associated with the writing have calibrated radiocarbon dates of 200 to 300 B.C. This early Maya writing implies that a developed Maya writing system was in use centuries earlier than previously thought."

The political system, however, never integrated the entire Maya cultural space into a single state or empire. Throughout its history, the Maya area contained a combination of statelets and chiefdoms. These polities fluctuated greatly in their ties with each other and were engaged in a complex web of rivalries, periods of dominance or submission, vassalage ties, and alliances. The[47] "identification of 72 Maya polities with sufficiently accurate dates of formation and termination, support a model of Maya polities based on Middle Preclassic origins, punctuated phases of development, multiple cycles of expansion and collapse, and weaker political stability for more complex polities."

After 900 CE, the Maya civilization perished precipitously, leaving the cities and ceremonial centers vacant and overcome with jungle vegetation. In that period, there was widespread political collapse leading to violence and social strife,[48] the abandonment of cities, and a northward shift of populations. Some scholars suggest that armed conflicts and the exhaustion of farming land were responsible for the sudden decline. Other scholars propose other factors stating:[49]

> The Maya Lowlands and Maya society also contained numerous potential triggers to initiate system release or collapse. These triggers included droughts, hurricanes, and volcanic eruptions (capable of choking or fouling reservoirs in the EIR), all of which could generate system-stressing crop failures and population movements. The political system itself also likely generated triggering events in the form of warfare spawned by interpolity competition among prestige-obsessed dynasts.

2.2 Climate and Collapse

By the time the Spaniards conquered the area in the early sixteenth century, most of the Maya domain had become village-dwelling farmers. Thus, the[50] "Maya heartland entered a kind of Dark Ages. Many of the greatest cities emptied, as did much of the countryside around them. Incredibly, some of the last inscriptions are gibberish, as if scribes had lost the knowledge of writing and were reduced to meaningless imitation of their ancestors."

This denouement is also attributed partly to climate change. There was a series of studies that documents drought conditions coincident with the period of collapse. In this context, the[51] "vegetation composition shows the driest conditions of the last 3800 at 960 cal yr BP (ca. 1000 AD), coincident with the demise of Classic Maya civilization." An analysis of precipitation changes in the Holocene shows that social turmoil is[52] "associated with periods of reduced precipitation and fall into time periods of extended droughts related to the Maya Late Classic and the Little Ice Age."

To comprehend the connection between the drought and the demise of this civilization, it is essential to understand how the Maya got so close to surpassing the carrying capacity of their ecosystem with their extreme farming practices before the last blow. In this context, the[53] "Maya packed by the millions into land poorly suited to intensive farming, were dangerously close to surpassing the capacity of their ecosystems. The drought, possibly caused by a mega-Niño, pushed the society, already so close to the edge, over the cliff." In addition to these farming practices, the Maya also cut down the forests using wood for fuel and land for cultivation. Such loss of tree cover would have caused[54] "large-scale erosion and floods. With their fields disappearing beneath their feet and a growing population to feed, Maya farmers were forced to exploit ever more marginal terrain with ever more intensity. The tottering system was vulnerable to the first good push, which came in the form of a century-long dry spell that hit Yucatán between 800 and 900 A.D. Social disintegration followed thereafter."

This combination of a relentless drought and a society that pushed itself to the brink was a recipe for calamity. Caused by a shift in climate,[55] "[a]n arid period with several intense droughts weakened a society that had already pushed the limits of its environment. Mayans adapted to their landscape over many centuries, but their large population and deforestation made them less resilient to drought." The aridity that was caused by the drought overwhelmed the ability of the Mayas to adapt to it as they did in earlier episodes since[56] "[t]he Mayan cities of the Yucatán and Central America proved highly sensitive to reductions in rainfall of some 40 percent. Drought was most intense in the regions that displayed the strongest evidence of collapse. Mayan societies had previously shown resilience to dry periods, but greater social complexity and more severe drought overwhelmed their capacity to adapt."

Along the same lines, Walter Scheidel offers the demise of this civilization as an example for societal collapse due to environmental degradation, drought, in addition to other factors.[57]

> Yet in the end, loss of social complexity was widespread and severe. In Tikal, one of the biggest cities, building activity ended by 830 CE, and may be 90 percent of the population is thought to have left or have been lost eighty

> years later. Other major sites were likewise abandoned: the largest cities were most heavily affected while smaller settlements experienced greater continuity. Once again, the causes behind this downfall are contested. Modern explanations suggest that collapse may have been an overdetermined outcome as multiple factors interacted in undermining Mayan societies—most notably endemic warfare, population pressure, and environmental degradation and drought.

Thus, this episode of climate change undermined the power of the rulers as it stripped them from their ability to provide for their subjects. This is since the basis for royal power rested in what they provided their subjects in times of need, especially water during the annual drought season through a complex system of water distribution. In the face of[58] "rulers losing their powers due to drought, people left. Without their labor, support and services, the foundation of royal power crumbled; it was too inflexible and little suited to adapting to change." In addition, these kings[59] "monopolized artificial reservoirs and other water sources during annual drought, providing the means to exact tribute from subjects. Climate change undermined the institution of rulership when existing ceremonies and technology failed to provide sufficient water."

2.3 *The Evidence Speaks Volumes*

To provide evidence for the effect of climate change on the Maya, some scholars examine the lakes of the Yucatán Peninsula, especially Salpeten, Punta Laguna, and Chichancanab. These lakes are ideal for such studies because they have hydrologic characteristics that is conducive for the reconstruction of the paleoclimate of the area, they lose most of their water to evaporation which is determined by climatic conditions, they provide a powerful tool for inferring past drought history, and they are close to the archaeological sites of the Mayas, in addition to other characteristics that make them appropriate for this type of analysis.

Some studies show that the drought conditions occurred in interspersed episodes that gradually overwhelmed the civilization not because of its intensity but because the carrying capacity of the Yucatán Peninsula was up to its limits. To provide a detailed overview of climate variability during the last 1500 years, paleoclimatologist Martín Medina-Elizalde and others study a stalagmite from the area.[60] Their climate record shows that eight severe droughts, lasting from 3 to 18 years, correspond to major depopulation and city abandonment events of the Maya. The number and short duration of the drought events, when precipitation declined by 52% to 36%, explain why the collapse of the Mayan civilization occurred over 150 years and not abruptly. The potential implications[61] "of these successive droughts; decreased environmental carrying capacity, increased inter-state rivalry for resources, famine, disease, and popular dissent from 'divine' rulership that failed to prevent recurrent drought, may have slowly weakened the Classic Maya socio-political system, while the more benign intervals between these droughts allowed the civilization to partially recover and linger."

Martín Medina-Elizalde and Eelco Rohling present paleoclimate records from the Yucatán Peninsula using data from Lake Chichancanab and Punta Laguna.[62] Their analysis shows that the droughts were caused by a 40% decline in annual precipitation, due to a decrease in summer season tropical storm frequency and intensity. This decline in precipitation was considerable, but not as severe as would be implied by other proposed mechanisms. If these episodes of drier climate contributed to the fate of the Classic Maya,[63] "then this would imply that the ecological carrying capacity of the Yucatan Peninsula is highly sensitive to precipitation reductions." This is another indication that the drought was the last straw when the carrying capacity was at its limits.

Some scholars focus on Lake Chichancanab to be able to recreate climatic conditions in the area during the time of the demise. To reconstruct a continuous record of Holocene climate change for the central Yucatán Peninsula, scientists David Hodell, Jason Curtis, and Mark Brenner use temporal variations in oxygen isotope and composition in a sediment core from Lake Chichancanab.[64] The study shows that the period between 800 and 1000 CE was the driest of the middle to late Holocene and coincided with the collapse of the Maya civilization. Although others have suggested that[65] "drought may have played a role in the classic Maya collapse, results from Lake Chichancanab provide the first unambiguous evidence for climate drying between AD 800 and 1000." To provide a direct estimate of the magnitude of this drought, David Hodell, Jason Curtis, Mark Brenner, and others reconstruct the past isotopic composition of water in Lake Chichancanab.[66] The authors find a drastic decline in precipitation and humidity at the Terminal Classic Period compared to present climatic conditions such that[67] "annual precipitation decreased between 41 and 54% (with intervals of up to 70% rainfall reduction during peak drought conditions) and that relative humidity declined by 2 to 7% compared to present-day conditions."

Examining whether these climatic conditions were an extended period of drought, or a series of dry events separated by episodes of wet conditions, is essential to understand the gradual societal collapse that occurred at the time. Along these lines, David Hodell, Jason Curtis, and Mark Brenner present records from sediment cores taken along a depth transect in Lake Chichancanab.[68] Their data show that the drought events that coincided with the demise of the Maya civilization between 750 and 1050 CE was not a single long megadrought but rather consisted of a series of dry events separated by intervening periods of moister conditions. Their estimate is that the Terminal Classic Drought[69] "lasted from ca 770 to 1100 AD and was comprised of two drought phases (ca 770–870 AD and 920–1100 AD) and an intervening 50-year period (ca 870–920 AD) of more mesic conditions. Within each of the dry phases, climate was marked by alternating dry and moist conditions with an interval of drought recurrence of about 50 years."

This evidence for the frequent arid events needed to be confirmed from other lakes in the area as well. In this context, David Hodell, Jason Curtis, and Mark Brenner reconstruct climate change on the Yucatán Peninsula during the past 3500 years using a sediment core from Punta Laguna in Mexico.[70] The authors show that the climate during the latter part of that period was persistently dry, with exceptionally arid events around 862, 986, and 1051 CE. This interval of frequent drought was documented at several other localities in Mexico and Central America where the[71] "second drought at 862 +- 50 A.D. coincides with the collapse of Classic Maya civilization between 800 and 900 A.D." Evidence for the drought was also found in an examination of a 4000-year sediment core from Lake Salpeten in Guatemala by David Hodell, Jason Curtis, Mark Brenner, and Michael Rosenmeier.[72] In tropical lakes with little surface outflow, variations in the oxygen isotopic ratio of lake water are determined by changes in the rate of evaporation relative to the combined inputs of precipitation and surface and groundwater inflow. Extended periods of enhanced evaporation, or decreased precipitation and surface and groundwater inflow, increase the oxygen isotopic ratios of lake water. In this context, the authors find evidence of increased oxygen isotope composition, indicating diminished lake levels that are coincident with the Terminal Classic Maya demographic decline between 800 and 900 CE.

As much as the timing of the dry events matter, determining the location was also equally critical given that the collapse did not occur at the same time in Maya lowlands. To assess variations in water availability and land use in the northern and southern Maya lowlands, David Hodell, Jason Curtis, Mark Brenner, and other scholars examine two sediment cores from Lakes Chichancanab and Salpeten.[73] The study shows that drying conditions occurred more intensely in the southern lowlands than in the northern ones during the Terminal Classic period. This is consistent with earlier, more pronounced, and more persistent societal decline in the south. The record also shows a shift from extensive to intensive agriculture and water conservative maize cultivation that was instigated by a drying climate. These agricultural adaptations were initially successful[74] "but that more severe droughts during the Terminal Classic, as well as the increased complexity of Late Classic societies, made adaptation to climate change less effective."

Other scholars also use evidence collected from the Caribbean area to complement those collected from the Yucatán Peninsula. For instance, sediments collected from the Cariaco Basin of the southern Caribbean show that the collapse occurred during an extended dry period, punctuated by more intense multiyear droughts at approximately 810, 860, and 910 CE.[75] The intervals[76] "of peak drought were brief, each lasting between 3 and 9 years, but they occurred during an extended period of reduced overall precipitation that may have already pushed the Maya system to the verge of collapse."

Along the same vein, a climate rainfall record for the past 2000 years from a stalagmite collected from the Yok Balum Cave in Belize suggests that high rainfall and increased agricultural productivity favored unprecedented population expansion and the proliferation of political centers between 440 and 660 CE. This was followed by a drying trend between 660 and 1000 CE that triggered the[77] "balkanization of polities, increased warfare, and the asynchronous disintegration of polities, followed by population collapse in the context of an extended drought between 1020 and 1100 C.E." Another stalagmite from the Macal Chasm cave in western Belize indicates that a series of droughts, which lasted from 700 to 1135 CE, coincided with the collapse of the civilization.[78] This adds[79] "to a growing body of evidence suggesting that severe dryness affected a broad region of Mesoamerica and contributed to the collapse of the Maya civilization during the Late Classic period."

Despite the abundance of evidence on the critical contribution of climate change to the collapse of this society that was beyond the carrying capacity of the land, some studies offer a cautionary tale. Using Lidar Survey technology, a group of scholars found indications that communities in some parts of the Maya Lowlands likely had an abundance of crops and were not struggling for scarce resources when Maya civilization collapsed.[80] The study finds that "[b]eyond meeting basic subsistence needs, agricultural production in multiple areas permitted surpluses likely for the purposes of tribute, taxation, and marketing." This directs our attention to the many ways that these societies navigated the complex challenges of competing statelets and a climate in flux. According to these scholars, the drought-induced disintegration does not necessarily capture the entire story in the Maya domains. However, this also does not discredit the other evidence for the climate change contribution to the collapse given that this specific study focuses only on particular communities and cannot be generalized to the entire Maya territory.

3 Climate Backdrop to Puebloan Culture

The Ancestral Puebloans were an ancient Native American culture that occupied the area where the boundaries of the present-day American states of Arizona, New Mexico, Colorado, and Utah intersect. The people and their culture are often referred to as Anasazi.[81] The farmer Ancestral Puebloans and their nomadic neighbors were often hostile to each other. This is the source of the term Anasazi, which is a Navajo word meaning "enemy ancestors." Ancestral Pueblo culture lasted from approximately 100 to 1600 CE. This is typically divided into multiple periods including the Basketmaker II (100–500 CE), the Basketmaker III (500–750 CE), Pueblo I (750–950 CE), Pueblo II (950–1150 CE), Pueblo III (1150–1300 CE), and Pueblo IV (1300–1600 CE).

The Basketmaker II economy featured hunting wild animals, gathering wild plants, and some corn cultivation. Puebloans, at that time, typically lived in caves or in shallow pit houses. The Basketmaker III period is marked by the increasing reliance on farming, including the introduction of new crops and the domestication of turkey.[82] To support their agricultural activities to sustain a growing population, the Puebloans set the foundations for irrigation projects in the form of water reservoirs and check dams. Continued population growth[83] "coupled with increasing uncertainty in annual rain-fall patterns provided a framework within which some Mesa Verde inhabitants invested increasing labor into soil and water conservation and construction of other permanent improvements on agricultural lands."

During the Pueblo I period, most structures shifted above ground. That was the time when Kivas, the circular chambers used henceforth for ceremonial purposes, became critical community features.[84] The construction of the kivas, which was an arduous undertaking for these communities,[85] "would have been the tangible symbol of community integration, cooperation, and common belief." While many communities in the Pueblo I period were quite large, the Pueblo II period is characterized by a greater diversity of settlements. During Pueblo I and II eras, the population grew fast due to a consistent precipitation pattern which supported agricultural production.[86] The Pueblo III period was the time of the so-called great cliff dwellings. Villages were built in sheltered recesses in the face of cliffs. The population became concentrated in large communities, while many villages and hamlets were abandoned. During that period, agriculture continued to be the primary economic activity, and craftsmanship achieved its finest quality.

Ancestral Puebloans, however, abandoned their communities by about 1350 CE. The ancestral Pueblo world[87] "experienced great transitions between A.D. 1150 and A.D. 1300/1350 (Pueblo III period). The geographic extent of the ancestral Pueblo world decreased as parts of southern Nevada and eastern New Mexico were abandoned by Puebloan populations." This geographic contraction[88] "continued after A.D. 1350 with the abandonment of previously inhabited portions of southern Colorado, southeastern Utah, and much of northeastern Arizona."

The factors that contributed to the abandonment include environmental ones, especially the Great Drought that occurred during the period from 1276 to 1299 CE which caused widespread crop failure. The coincidence[89] "during the A.D. 1250-1300 interval of a primary hydrologic-aggradation minimum with a major drought would have had important adaptive consequences for Anasazi populations." This led to adverse conditions where the[90] "Mesa Verde peoples abandoned the four corners area, probably moving to the Rio Grande Valley of New Mexico, where large-scale irrigation could be practiced."

Even though climatic anomalies are thought to have triggered wide-scale transformations of various ancient societies, they rarely seem to be the sole cause. Instead, slow internal developments often make societies less resilient over time, setting them up for failure.[91] Along the lines of this intuition, some scholars use annual time series data of building activity to demonstrate that dramatic transformations of Puebloan cultures were preceded by signals of slowing down. Their results[92] "resonate with archaeological evidence that successful Puebloan societies repeatedly lost resilience in a persistent pattern until at least the early 1200s." Such loss of resilience implies that eventually even inconsequential adverse events could trigger a drastic societal transformation. Other scholars also confirm that there is[93]

> no single, simple cause for this depopulation. Instead, it was a cascade of events that included climate-induced immigration from peripheral regions resulting in over population of the VEP study area, in turn generating resource depletion that was exacerbated by a decline in maize productivity that affected both carbohydrate and protein intakes. These changes provoked conflict, which in turn induced more scarcity. As these societies began to lose population, they also functioned less successfully and became vulnerable to aggression. In the end, violence and famine provided potent motives for departure.

To recreate the climatic backdrop for the entire Pueblo period, some scholars use a stalagmite from a cave in the Guadalupe Mountains of New Mexico.[94] The data show a period of increased frequency of droughts from 1260 to 370 years before 2000 CE. The swift transition to increasing aridity was associated with greater urbanization and the establishment of pueblo population centers. Not only did climate change contribute to the development of this culture, but also to its eventual demise. Data also shows a drier condition during the Late Holocene that correlates with the archaeological record of cultural changes in the form of dwelling abandonment and population displacement.[95] The timing[96] "of the onset of significantly drier conditions, represented by no stalagmite growth from 670 to 460 years B.P., is also coincident with the Pueblo IV period of significant abandonment of higher elevation dwellings and population redistribution to river areas."

As familiar by now, climate change is seldom the sole cause for societal collapse. There is usually a set of factors that lower the immunity of society to any climate shock. Once that shock occurs, the society that lacks resilience succumbs without resistance. This, however, does not undermine the contribution of climate shocks to the final fate of these societies and in no way should be used as a pretext to discard such climatic factors as inconsequential.

4 Climate Shock to the Easter Island

The Easter Island is a territory of present-day Chile in the southeastern Pacific Ocean. The island is most famous for its 1000 monumental statues, called moai, which were built by the early Rapa Nui people who inhabited the island from about 1200 CE. According to archaeologists Terry Hunt and Carl Lipo,[97] "Radiocarbon dates for the earliest stratigraphic layers at Anakena, Easter Island, and analysis of previous radiocarbon dates imply that the island was colonized late, about 1200 A.D." The settlement was followed by a rapid population growth as the[98] "first settlers arrived from other Polynesian islands around 1200 a.d. Their numbers grew quickly, perhaps at about three percent annually, which would be similar to the rapid growth shown to have taken place elsewhere in the Pacific."

The inhabitants created a thriving culture, as evidenced by the island's numerous enormous stone moais and other artifacts. However, this society eventually collapsed. The causes of such a collapse are attributed to either an ecocide or a genocide scenario. According to some scholars, the ecocide hypothesis[99] "assumes a punctuated demographic crash caused by the abrupt reduction and replacement of native palm forest by grasslands, ultimately driven by unchecked population growth coupled with social instability as the per-capita food productivity decreased." Alternatively, the other view that advocates[100] "a 'genocide hypothesis' assumes that the Rapa Nui society did not collapse until European contact in the early eighteenth century."

According to the former view, land clearing by cutting trees for cultivation and the introduction of the Polynesian rat led to gradual deforestation. Thus, the people of Easter Island destroyed their forest, degraded their island's topsoil, wiped out their plants, and drove their animals to extinction. As a result of this self-inflicted environmental devastation, its complex society collapsed, descending into internal strife and self-destruction.

This self-destructive behavior was also connected to a change in climate. To examine the causes of such a societal collapse, ecologist Nils Stenseth and other scholars develop population dynamic models that integrate feedback between climatic, demographic, and ecological factors that underlined the trajectory of this culture.[101] Their analysis shows that the[102] "combination of positive population growth rates and a gradual increasing long-term trend in La Niña conditions (which causes droughts on the island) could explain the extensive deforestation as agriculture production increased the demand for farming lands, linked also to soil erosion and exhaustion." Their results support the hypothesis that the[103] "Rapa Nui experienced a long-term climatic trend towards drier conditions since the initial colonization of the island. This, concomitant with a gradual decrease in rainfall and island productivity, explains the process of expansion and demographic collapse experienced by the Rapa Nui society."

According to the other view, the culture and the environment of the island[104] "were destroyed to all intents by European slave traders, whalers, and colonists." In this context, Terry Hunt and Carl Lipo assert that the shrinkage in population was associated more with foreign invasion than forest logging.[105] This is because[106] "during the period of deforestation (about A.D. 1250 to 1650, based on many radiocarbon dates), the island's population grew even though the forest declined. The first and only sign of sustained decline in the population, so vital to the 'ecocide' thesis, came from A.D. 1750 to 1800, after the arrival of the first European visitors. On Rapa Nui, like so many other places in the New World and the Pacific, European germs decimated the native population that had only limited immunity to Old World diseases." Along the same vein, Terry Hunt and Carl Lipo add,[107] "A pre-contact demographic collapse remains untested, undemonstrated archaeologically. The historic slave-trading, epidemic diseases, intensive sheep ranching, and tragic population collapse—indeed the genocide of the Rapanui People—is well documented and has been recognized for a long time."

Given the two views, and the evidence corroborating them, it seems sensible not to endorse one and discard the other. These two opinions do not have to be mutually exclusive. It is very likely that a combination of environmental degradation in the form of soil erosion, climate shock in the form of drier conditions, and contact with foreigners in the form of European invasion, led to the calamity that struck this society in Easter Island.

5 Calamity in Cahokia City

Cahokia was the largest settlement in North America before the European conquest, and its cultural domain covered most of what is now Central and Southeastern United States. Evidence from the Horseshoe Lake in the Central Mississippi shows that agricultural activity began in the area at 450 CE and intensified over the following centuries. In this context, fast forest clearance[108] "was followed closely by the proliferation of indigenous seed crops of the Eastern Agricultural Complex beginning ca. 450 CE, centuries before the emergence of Cahokia at 1050 CE. Agricultural intensification that included the use of maize (Zea mays subsp. mays) followed this initial clearance, with peak land use intensity between 900 and 1200 CE." This culture flourished soon after the adoption of agriculture until 1350 CE.

The inhabitants of the complex left only symbols on pottery, copper, wood, and stone. There were no written records left for scholars to study. But the elaborately planned community, especially by these mound builders, reveals a complex and sophisticated society. These earthen mounds required a lot of work including digging and conveyance by hand using woven baskets. This led some scholars to conclude that building mounds in such a way entailed a central authority capable of delegating tasks and overseeing other construction aspects, including logistics, food supply, housing, and work shifts. The articulately planned city with ceremonial plazas around these mounds, and houses connected by pathways and courtyards, suggests that the location served as a central pilgrimage city. These earthen mounds may have also served to elevate the chiefs or priests above the common people and place them closer to the sun, which was worshipped by the community as the source of life. It is also thought that these mounds were built to focus spiritual power in a central location. The chiefs or priests performed rituals on these mounds to harness this power to protect the people and to ensure plentiful rainfall and bountiful harvest.

Cahokia became the most important center of the Mississippian culture which comprised of settlements along major waterways across that part of the present-day United States. Strategically located near the confluence of the Mississippi and other rivers, it maintained commercial ties with communities as far away as the Great Lakes to the north and the Gulf Coast to the south. Some estimates claim the city had a population of almost 50,000 at its peak with much more living in farming villages that supplied the urban center with its essential needs. This forgotten city of Cahokia is even described by some as[109]

> more than just a stupendous pile of earth or a ceremonial site where scattered tribes congregated once in a while. Nearly everywhere they dug, archaeologists found homes—indicating that thousands of people had once lived in the community—and many of these homes had been built within a very brief span of time. In fact, the whole city seemed to spring to life almost overnight around 1050, a phenomenon now referred to as a "big bang."

> People streamed in from surrounding areas, built houses, and quickly constructed the infrastructure of a new city—including several mounds with buildings on top and a grand plaza the size of 45 football fields, used for everything from sporting events to communal feasts to religious celebrations.

The population of Cahokia began to decline and eventually the site was abandoned by 1350 CE. Some scholars suggest environmental stresses as a culprit for this denouement. Explanations include multidecadal drought, fluctuations in seasonal precipitation, changes in the intensity and frequency of Mississippi River flooding, environmental degradation due to deforestation, and resource overexploitation. Some scholars even declare:[110]

> Intensifying midcontinental socio-political instability and warfare between 1250–1350 CE corresponded with drier positive PNA-like conditions, culminating in the staggered abandonment of many major Native American river valley settlements and large urban centers between 1350–1450 CE during an especially severe warm-season drought. We hypothesize that this sustained drought interval rendered it difficult to support dense populations and large urban centers in the midcontinental US by destabilizing regional agricultural systems, thereby contributing to the host of socio-political factors that led to population reorganization and migration in the midcontinent and neighboring regions shortly before European contact.

To evaluate the contribution of flooding, drought, and environmental degradation in Cahokia's demographic decline, some scholars compare fecal stanol data from the Horseshoe Lake adjacent to the Cahokia site with oxygen stable-isotope and paleoenvironmental data from the same sediment cores.[111] Fecal stanols are organic molecules that originate in the guts of humans and may linger in sediment for a long time. These provide evidence of trace human waste and are used as a proxy for population change over time.[112] The authors find that both dry conditions during the growing season and a large flood event were crucial factors in Cahokia's population decline about 1150 CE. This is because[113] "decreased warm season precipitation, coupled with a natural disaster in the form of a Mississippi River flood around 1150 CE, would have created stress for the Cahokia system atop cultural problems such as economic decline and political strife that cannot be measured through sedimentary analysis."

To provide evidence for the occurrence and timing of the flooding, some scholars report a paleoecological record from the Horseshoe Lake.[114]

The study indicates a flooding that occurred around 1200 CE leading to[115] "declining agricultural activity, coeval with the decreasing population size and diminishing cultural prominence of Cahokia." Other scholars use floodwater sediments deposited in two floodplain lakes and find that the[116] "return of large floods after A.D. 1200, driven by waning midcontinental aridity, marks the onset of sociopolitical reorganization and depopulation that culminate in the abandonment of Cahokia and the surrounding region by A.D. 1350."

To provide evidence for the occurrence and timing of the drought, some scholars rely on tree-ring-based reconstructions of climate and show that Cahokia witnessed exceptional growth between 1050 and 1130 CE but underwent intense stress by 1150 CE when[117] "the Cahokians had abandoned one or more of their agricultural support centers, including the large Richland farming complex, suggesting that the middle-12th-century drought did, indeed, impact the Cahokia region." In a similar vein, examining tree-ring based records of climate change for the Mississippi valley show that the development of Cahokia occurred during the wettest period from 1150 to 1100 CE, while the subsequent 150 years witnessed a series of prolonged droughts.[118] This contributed to the abandonment of the farming complex that was an integral part of Cahokia's agricultural base when[119] "people began exiting Cahokia and, by the end of the Stirling phase (A.D. 1200), Cahokia's population had decreased by about 50 percent, and by A.D. 1350, Cahokia and much of the central Mississippi valley had been abandoned."

Notes

1. Erik Marsh. "A Bayesian Re-Assessment of the Earliest Radiocarbon Dates from Tiwanaku, Bolivia." Radiocarbon, 54, 2: 203–218, 2012.
2. Erik Marsh. "The Founding of Tiwanaku." Ñawpa Pacha, 32, 2: 169–188, 2012.
3. Danijela Popović, Martyna Molak, Mariusz Ziółkowski, Alexei Vranich, Maciej Sobczyk, Delfor Ulloa Vidaurre, Guido Agresti, Magdalena Skrzypczak, Krzysztof Ginalski, Thiseas Christos Lamnidis, Nathan Nakatsuka, Swapan Mallick, and Mateusz Baca. "Ancient Genomes Reveal Long-range Influence of the Pre-Columbian Culture and Site of Tiwanaku." Science Advances, 7: eabg7261, 2021.
4. John Janusek. "Tiwanaku and its Precursors: Recent Research and Emerging Perspectives." Journal of Archaeological Research, 12, 2: 121–183, 2004.

5. John Janusek. "The Changing 'Nature' of Tiwanaku Religion and the Rise of an Andean State." World Archaeology, 38, 3: 469–492, 2006.
6. John Janusek and Scott Smith. "Political Mosaics and Networks: Tiwanaku Expansion into the Upper Desaguadero Valley, Bolivia." World Archaeology, 46, 5: 681–704, 2014.
7. John Janusek. "Out of Many, One: Style and Social Boundaries in Tiwanaku." Latin American Antiquity, 13, 1: 35–61, 2002.
8. John Janusek. "Craft and Local Power: Embedded Specialization in Tiwanaku Cities." Latin American Antiquity, 10, 2: 107–131, 1999.
9. Timothy L. McAndrews, Juan Albarracin-Jordan, and Marc Bermann. "Regional Settlement Patterns in the Tiwanaku Valley of Bolivia." Journal of Field Archaeology, 24, 1: 67–83, 1997.
10. Walter Schiedel. The Great Leveler: Violence and the History of Inequality from the Stone Age to the Twenty-First Century. Princeton University Press, 2018. (PP. 276–277).
11. Melanie J. Miller, Iain Kendall, José M. Capriles, Maria C. Brunoe, Richard P. Evershed, and Christine A. Hastorf. "Quinoa, Potatoes, and Llamas Fueled Emergent Social Complexity in the Lake Titicaca Basin of the Andes." PNAS, 118, 49, e2113395118, 2021.
12. Alan Kolata and Charles Ortloff. "Thermal Analysis of Tiwanaku Raised Field Systems in the Lake Titicaca Basin of Bolivia." Journal of Archaeological Science, 16, 3: 233–263, 1989.
13. Alan Kolata. "Tiwanaku and its Hinterland." Source: Archaeology, 40, 1: 36–41, 1987.
14. Alan Kolata. "The Agricultural Foundations of the Tiwanaku State: A View from the Heartland." American Antiquity, 51, 4: 748–762, 1986.
15. Alan Kolata. "The Technology and Organization of Agricultural Production in the Tiwanaku State." Latin American Antiquity, 2, 2: 99–125, 1991.
16. Walter Schiedel. The Great Leveler: Violence and the History of Inequality from the Stone Age to the Twenty-First Century. Princeton University Press, 2018. (P. 278).
17. Erik J. Marsh, Alexei Vranich, Deborah Blom, Maria Bruno, Katharine Davis, Jonah Augustine, Nicole C. Couture, Santiago Ancapichun, Kelly J. Knudson, Danijela Popović, and Gianni Cunietti. "The Center Cannot Hold: A Bayesian Chronology for the Collapse of Tiwanaku." PLOS ONE, 18, 11, e0288798, 2023.
18. Walter Schiedel. The Great Leveler: Violence and the History of Inequality from the Stone Age to the Twenty-First Century. Princeton University Press, 2018. (P. 277).
19. Benjamin Lieberman and Elizabeth Gordon. Climate Change in Human History: Prehistory to the Present. Bloomsbury, 2018. (P. 98).

20. Charles Mann. 1491. Vintage Books, 2005. (P. 25).
21. John Wayne Janusek and Alan L. Kolata. "Top-down or Bottom-up: Rural Settlement and Raised Field Agriculture in the Lake Titicaca Basin, Bolivia." Journal of Anthropological Archaeology, 23: 404–430, 2004.
22. Ibid.
23. Alan Kolata, John Janusek, Mark Abbott, Michael Binford, Mark Brenner, Matthew Siddon, and Jaso Curtis. "Climate Variation and the Rise and Fall of an Andean Civilization." Quaternary Research, 47: 235–248, 1997.
24. Paleolimnology is a scientific discipline which reconstructs the past environments of inland waters such as lakes and streams using the geologic record.
25. Ibid.
26. Alan Kolata and Charles Ortloff. "Climate and Collapse: Agro-Ecological Perspectives on the Decline of the Tiwanaku State." Journal of Archaeological Science, 20: 195–221, 1993.
27. Ibid.
28. Alan Kolata and Tom Dillehay. "Long-term Human Response to Uncertain Environmental Conditions in the Andes." PNAS, 101, 12: 4325–4433, 2004.
29. Ibid.
30. Mark Abbott, Michael Binford, Mark Brenner, and Kerry Kelts. "3500 14C yr High-Resolution Record of Water-Level Changes in Lake Titicaca, Bolivia/Peru." Quaternary Research, 47: 169–180, 1997.
31. Ibid.
32. T. Elliott Arnold, Aubrey L. Hillman, Mark B. Abbott, Josef P. Werne, Steven J. McGrath, and Elizabeth N. Arkush. "Drought and the Collapse of the Tiwanaku Civilization: New Evidence from Lake Orurillo, Peru." Quaternary Science Reviews, 251, 106693, 2021.
33. Ibid.
34. Ibid.
35. Medieval Climate Anomaly.
36. Michael Callaway. "Ice-cores, Sediments and Civilisation Collapse: A Cautionary Tale from Lake Titicaca." Antiquity, 79, 306: 778–790, 2005.
37. Norman Hammond, Duncan Pring, Rainer Berger, V. R. Switsur, and A. P. Ward. "Radiocarbon Chronology for Early Maya Occupation at Cuello, Belize." Nature, 260, 5552: 579–581, 1976.
38. Don E. Dumond. "Swidden Agriculture and the Rise of Maya Civilization." Southwestern Journal of Anthropology, Winter, 17, 4: 301–316, 1961.
39. Nicholas P. Dunning, Armando Anaya Hernández, Timothy Beach, Christopher Carr, Robert Griffin, John G. Jones, David L. Lentz, Sheryl Luzzadder-Beach, Kathryn Reese-Taylor, and Ivan Šprajc. "Margin for

Error: Anthropogenic Geomorphology of Bajo Edges in the Maya Lowlands." Geomorphology, 331: 127–145, 2019. N. P. Dunning, T. Beach, P. Farrell, and S. Luzzadder-Beach, "Prehispanic Agrosystems and Adaptive Regions in the Maya Lowlands" in Precolumbian Water Management: Ideology, Ritual, and Politics, L. J. Lucero, B. W. Fash, Eds., University of Arizona Press, 2006.

40. B. L. Turner and Peter D. Harrison. "Prehistoric Raised-Field Agriculture in the Maya Lowlands." Science, 213, 4506: 399–405, 1981.
41. B. L. Turner. "Prehistoric Intensive Agriculture in the Mayan Lowlands." Science, 185, 4146: 118–124, 1974.
42. Adams, R. E. W., W. E. Brown, and T. Patrick Culbert. "Radar Mapping, Archaeology, and Ancient Maya Land Use." Science, 213, 4515: 1457–1463, 1981.
43. Richard D. Hansen, Carlos Morales-Aguilar, Josephine Thompson, Ross Ensley, Enrique Hernández, Thomas Schreiner, Edgar Suyuc-Ley, and Gustavo Martínez. "LiDAR Analyses in the Contiguous Mirador-Calakmul Karst Basin, Guatemala: An Introduction to New Perspectives on Regional Early Maya Socioeconomic and Political Organization." Ancient Mesoamerica: 1–40, 2022.
44. Ivan Šprajc. "Astronomy, Architecture, and Landscape in Prehispanic Mesoamerica." Journal of Archaeological Research, 26: 197–251, 2018. Ivan Šprajc. "Astronomical Correlates of Architecture and Landscape in Mesoamerica." In: Ruggles, C. (eds) Handbook of Archaeoastronomy and Ethnoastronomy. Springer, New York, 2015. Ivan Šprajc. "Astronomical Aspects of Group E-type Complexes and Implications for Understanding Ancient Maya Architecture and Urban Planning." PLOS ONE, 16, 4: e0250785, 2021.
45. Whittaker Schroder, Timothy Murtha, Charles Golden, Madeline Brown, Robert Griffin, Kelsey E. Herndon, Shanti Morell-Hart, and Andrew K. Scherer. "Regional Household Variation and Inequality across the Maya Landscape." Journal of Anthropological Archaeology, 72, 101552, 2023.
46. William Saturno, David Stuart, Boris Beltrán. "Early Maya Writing at San Bartolo, Guatemala." Science, 311, 5765: 1281–1283, 2006.
47. Claudio Cioffi-Revilla and Todd Landman. "Evolution of Maya Polities in the Ancient Mesoamerican System." International Studies Quarterly, 43, 4: 559–598, 1999.
48. David Webster. "The Not So Peaceful Civilization: A Review of Maya War." Journal of World Prehistory, 14, 1: 65–119, 2000.
49. Nicholas P. Dunning, Timothy P. Beach, and Sheryl Luzzadder-Beach. "Kax and Kol: Collapse and Resilience in Lowland Maya Civilization." PNAS, 109, 10: 3652–3657, 2012.

50. Charles Mann. 1491. Vintage Books, 2005. (P. 26).
51. Nuria Torrascano-Valle, Gerald Islebe, and Alejandro Aragon-Moreno. "A ~ 3800-yr, High-Resolution Record of Vegetation and Climate Change on the North Coast of the Yucatan Peninsula." Review of Palaeobotany and Palynology, 178: 35–42, 2012.
52. Vela-Pelaez A.A., Torrescano-Valle N., Islebe G.A, Mas J.F., Weissenberger H. "Holocene Precipitation Changes in the Maya Forest, Yucatán Peninsula, Mexico." Palaeogeography, Palaeoclimatology, Palaeoecology, 505: 42–52, 2018.
53. Charles Mann. 1491. Vintage Books, 2005. (P. 27).
54. Ibid. (P. 277).
55. Benjamin Lieberman and Elizabeth Gordon. Climate Change in Human History: Prehistory to the Present. Bloomsbury, 2018. (P. 93).
56. Ibid. (PP. 93–94).
57. Walter Schiedel. The Great Leveler: Violence and the History of Inequality from the Stone Age to the Twenty-First Century. Princeton University Press, 2018. (P. 274).
58. Lisa Lucero, Vernon Scarborough, and Joel Gunn. "Climate Change and Classic Maya Water Management." Water, 3: 479–494, 2011.
59. Lisa Lucero. "The Collapse of the Classic Maya: A Case for the Role of Water Control." American Anthropologist, 104, 3:814–826, 2002.
60. Martín Medina-Elizalde, Stephen J. Burns, David W. Lea, Yemane Asmerom, Lucien von Gunten, Victor Polyak, Mathias Vuille, Ambarish Karmalkar. "High Resolution Stalagmite Climate Record from the Yucatán Peninsula Spanning the Maya Terminal Classic Period." Earth and Planetary Science Letters, 298: 255–262, 2010.
61. Ibid.
62. Martín Medina-Elizalde and Eelco J. Rohling. "Collapse of Classic Maya Civilization Related to Modest Reduction in Precipitation." Science, 335: 956–959, 2012.
63. Ibid.
64. David Hodell, Jason Curtis and Mark Brenner. "Possible Role of Climate in the Collapse of the Maya Civilization." Nature, 375: 391–394, 1995.
65. Ibid.
66. Nicholas P. Evans, Thomas K. Bauska, Fernando Gázquez-Sánchez, Mark Brenner, Jason H. Curtis, and David A. Hodell. "Quantification of Drought During the Collapse of the Classic Maya Civilization." Science, 361: 498–501, 2018.
67. Ibid.
68. David Hodell, Jason Curtis and Mark Brenner. "Terminal Classic Drought in the Northern Maya Lowlands Inferred from Multiple

Sediment Cores in Lake Chichancanab (Mexico)." Quaternary Science Reviews 24: 1413–1427, 2005.

69. Ibid.
70. David Hodell, Jason Curtis and Mark Brenner. "Climate Variability on the Yucatan Peninsula (Mexico) during the Past 3500 Years, and Implications for Maya Cultural Evolution." Quaternary Research, 46: 37–47, 1996.
71. Ibid.
72. David Hodell, Jason Curtis, Mark Brenner, and Michael Rosenmeier. "A 4000-Year Lacustrine Record of Environmental Change in the Southern Maya Lowlands, Peten, Guatemala." Quaternary Research, 57: 183–190, 2002.
73. Peter M. J. Douglas, Mark Pagani, Marcello A. Canuto, Mark Brenner, David A. Hodell, Timothy I. Eglinton, and Jason H. Curtis. "Drought, Agricultural Adaptation, and Sociopolitical Collapse in the Maya Lowlands." PNAS, 112, 18: 5607–5612, 2015.
74. Ibid.
75. Gerald H. Haug, Detlef Gunther, Larry C. Peterson, Daniel M. Sigman, Konrad A. Hughen, and Beat Aeschlimann. "Climate and the Collapse of Maya Civilization." Science, 299: 1731–1735, 2003.
76. Ibid.
77. Douglas J. Kennett, Sebastian F. M. Breitenbach, Valorie V. Aquino, Yemane Asmerom, Jaime Awe, James U.L. Baldini, Patrick Bartlein, Brendan J. Culleton, Claire Ebert, Christopher Jazwa, Martha J. Macri, Norbert Marwan, Victor Polyak, Keith M. Prufer, Harriet E. Ridley, Harald Sodemann, Bruce Winterhalder, Gerald H. Haug. "Development and Disintegration of Maya Political Systems in Response to Climate Change." Science, 338: 788–791, 2012.
78. James W. Webster, George A. Brook, L. Bruce Railsback, Hai Cheng, R. Lawrence Edwards, Clark Alexander, Philip P. Reeder. "Stalagmite Evidence from Belize Indicating Significant Droughts at the Time of Preclassic Abandonment, the Maya Hiatus, and the Classic Maya Collapse." Palaeogeography, Palaeoclimatology, Palaeoecology, 250: 1–17, 2007.
79. Ibid.
80. Charles Golden, Andrew K. Scherer, Whittaker Schroder, Timothy Murtha, Shanti Morell-Hart, Juan Carlos Fernandez Diaz, Socorro del Pilar Jiménez Álvarez, Omar Alcover Firpi, Mark Agostini, Alexandra Bazarsky, Morgan Clark, G. Van Kollias III, Mallory Matsumoto, Alejandra Roche Recinos, Joshua Schnell, and Bethany Whitlock. "Airborne Lidar Survey, Density-Based Clustering, and Ancient Maya

Settlement in the Upper Usumacinta River Region of Mexico and Guatemala." Remote Sensing, 13, 4109, 2021.

81. Harry Walters and High Rogers. "Anasazi and Anaasazi: Two Words and Two Cultures." Kiva, 66, 3: 17–326, 2001.
82. Cyler Conrad. "Contextualizing Ancestral Pueblo Turkey (Meleagris Gallopavo spp.) Management." Journal of Archaeological Method and Theory, 29: 624–665, 2022. Cyler Conrad, Emily Lena Jones, Seth D. Newsome, and Douglas W. Schwartz. "Bone Isotopes, Eggshell and Turkey Husbandry at Arroyo Hondo Pueblo." Journal of Archaeological Science: Reports, 10: 566–574, 2016.
83. Michael Adler. "Land Tenure, Archaeology, and the Ancestral Pueblo Social Landscape." Journal of Anthropological Archaeology, 15: 337–371, 1996.
84. Michael Adler. "Why is a Kiva? New Interpretations of Prehistoric Social Integrative Architecture in the Northern Rio Grande Region of New Mexico." Journal of Anthropological Research, 49, 4: 319–346, 1993.
85. Michael A. Adler and Richard H. Wilshusen. "Large-Scale Integrative Facilities in Tribal Societies: Cross-Cultural and Southwestern US Examples." World Archaeology, 22, 2: 133–146, 1990.
86. Nancy M. Mahoney, Michael A. Adler, and James W. Kendrick. "The Changing Scale and Configuration of Mesa Verde Communities." Kiva, 66, 1: 67–90, 2000.
87. Michael A. Adler, Todd Van Pool and Robert D. Leonard. "Ancestral Pueblo Population Aggregation and Abandonment in the North American Southwest." Journal of World Prehistory, 10, 3: 375–438, 1996.
88. Ibid.
89. Jeffrey S. Dean, Robert C. Euler, George J. Gumerman, Fred Plog, Richard H. Hevly, and Thor N. V. Karlstrom. "Human Behavior, Demography, and Paleoenvironment on the Colorado Plateaus." American Antiquity, 50, 3: 537–554, 1985.
90. Robert C. Euler, George J. Gumerman, Thor N. V. Karlstrom, Jeffrey S. Dean, and Richard H. Hevly. "The Colorado Plateaus: Cultural Dynamics and Paleoenvironment." Science, 205, 4411: 1089–1101, 1979.
91. Marten Scheffer, Egbert H. van Nesa, Darcy Bird, R. Kyle Bocinsky, and Timothy A. Kohler. "Loss of Resilience Preceded Transformations of pre-Hispanic Pueblo Societies." PNAS, 118, 18, e2024397118, 2021.
92. Ibid.
93. Timothy A. Kohler, Mark D. Varien, Aaron M. Wright, and Kristin A. Kuckelman. "Mesa Verde Migrations: New Archaeological Research and Computer Simulation Suggest Why Ancestral Puebloans Deserted the Northern Southwest United States." American Scientist, 96, 2: 146–153, 2008.

94. Viktor Polyak, Yemane Asmerom, and Matthew Lachniet. "Climatic Backdrop for Pueblo Cultural Development in the Southwestern United States." Nature, Scientific Reports, 12, 8723, 2022.
95. Vitor Polyak and Yemane Asmerom. "Late Holocene Climate and Cultural Changes in the Southwestern United States." Science, 294: 148–151, 2001.
96. Ibid.
97. Terry Hunt and Carl Lipo. "Late Colonization of Easter Island." Science, 311, 5767: 1603–1606, 2006.
98. Terry Hunt. "Rethinking the Fall of Easter Island." American Scientist, 94: 412–419, 2006.
99. M. Lima, E. M. Gayo, C. Latorre, C. M. Santoro, S. A. Estay, N. Cañellas-Boltà, O. Margalef, S. Giralt, A. Sáez, S. Pla-Rabes, and N. Chr. Stenseth. "Ecology of the Collapse of Rapa Nui Society." Proceedings of the Royal Society B, 287, 2020.
100. Ibid.
101. M. Lima, E. M. Gayo, C. Latorre, C. M. Santoro, S. A. Estay, N. Cañellas-Boltà, O. Margalef, S. Giralt, A. Sáez, S. Pla-Rabes, and N. Chr. Stenseth. "Ecology of the Collapse of Rapa Nui Society." Proceedings of the Royal Society B, 287, 2020.
102. Ibid.
103. Ibid.
104. Benny Peiser. "From Genocide to Ecocide: The Rape of Rapa Nui." Energy & Environment, 16, 3/4, SPECIAL ISSUE: "Institutions, Progress, Affluence, Technology and the Environment": 513–539, 2005.
105. Terry Hunt and Carl Lipo. "Ecological Catastrophe and Collapse: The Myth of 'Ecocide' on Rapa Nui (Easter Island)" PERC Research Paper 12/3, 2012.
106. Ibid.
107. Terry Hunt and Carl Lipo. "Chronology, Deforestation, and 'Collapse': Evidence vs. Faith in Rapa Nui Prehistory." Rapa Nui Journal, 21, 2: 85–97, 2007.
108. Samuel Munoz, Sissel Schroeder, David Fike, and John Williams. "A Record of Sustained Prehistoric and Historic Land Use from the Cahokia Region, Illinois, USA". Geology, 42, 6: 499–502, 2014.
109. Glenn Hodges. "America's Forgotten City." National Geographic, January 2011.
110. Broxton W. Bird, Jeremy J. Wilson, William P. Gilhooly III, Byron A. Steinman, and Lucas Stamps. "Midcontinental Native American Population Dynamics and Late Holocene Hydroclimate Extremes." Nature, Scientific Reports, 7, 41628, 2017.

111. A.J. White, Lora R. Stevens, Varenka Lorenzi, Samuel E. Munoz, Sissel Schroeder, Angelica Cao, and Taylor Bogdanovich. "Fecal Stanols Show Simultaneous Flooding and Seasonal Precipitation Change Correlate with Cahokia's Population Decline." PNAS, 116, 12: 5461–5466, 2019.
112. A.J. White, Lora R. Stevens, Varenka Lorenzi, Samuel E. Munoz, Carl P. Lipo, and Sissel Schroeder. "An Evaluation of Fecal Stanols as Indicators of Population Change at Cahokia, Illinois." Journal of Archaeological Science, 93: 129–134, 2018.
113. A.J. White, Lora R. Stevens, Varenka Lorenzi, Samuel E. Munoz, Sissel Schroeder, Angelica Cao, and Taylor Bogdanovich. "Fecal Stanols Show Simultaneous Flooding and Seasonal Precipitation Change Correlate with Cahokia's Population Decline." PNAS, 116, 12: 5461–5466, 2019.
114. Samuel E. Munoz, Sissel Schroeder, David A. Fike, and John W. Williams. "A Record of Sustained Prehistoric and Historic Land use from the Cahokia Region, Illinois, USA." Geology, 42, 6: 499–502, 2014.
115. Ibid.
116. Samuel E. Munoz, Kristine E. Gruley, Ashtin Massie, David A. Fike, Sissel Schroeder, and John W. Williams. "Cahokia's Emergence and Decline Coincided with Shifts of Flood Frequency on the Mississippi River." PNAS, 112, 20: 6319–6324, 2015.
117. Larry V. Benson, Michael S. Berry, Edward A. Jolie, Jerry D. Spangler, David W. Stahle, and Eugene M. Hattori. "Possible Impacts of Early-11th-, Middle-12th-, and Late-13th-Century Droughts on Western Native Americans and the Mississippian Cahokians." Quaternary Science Reviews, 26: 336–350, 2007.
118. Larry Benson, Timothy Pauketat, and Edward Cook. "Cahokia's Boom and Bust in the Context of Climate Change." American Antiquity, 74, 3:467–483, 2009.
119. Ibid.

CHAPTER 10

Climate Change in the Common Era

The common era is an alternative to the Anno Domini notation of the Gregorian calendar. This period witnessed several climatic events including the Roman Warm Period, the Late Antique Ice Age, the Medieval Warm Period, and the Little Ice Age for which we are dedicating the following chapter. Some of these events coincided with episodes of societal collapse. Compared to ancient times, we would expect that as humanity advances over time, we become less susceptible to changes in climate mood. However, if anything, these stories confirm our continuous susceptibility to fluctuations in climatic conditions irrespective of how advanced we become.

1 The Rise and Recession of the Romans

1.1 *The Western Roman Empire*

The Roman Empire, centered on the city of Rome, followed the Roman Republic which lasted from 510 to 31 BCE. A period of tumult and turmoil characterized the transition of Rome from a republic to an empire. This period witnessed the surge to dominance of Julius Caesar, who eventually took full power as dictator. The violent end to his eventful life, after his assassination in 44 BCE, prompted a power contest that ultimately ended the Roman Republic leading to the rise of the Roman Empire.

S. Khalifa, *Climate Change, Economic Channels, and Historical Junctures*, https://doi.org/10.1007/978-3-031-91867-4_10

Some scholars posit that climate proxies and written documents indicate that this transition occurred during a period of unusually inclement weather, famine, and disease in the Mediterranean. Historians and scientists have previously speculated that a large volcanic eruption was the most likely cause. To provide evidence for this conjecture, volcanic fallout records in six Arctic ice cores were used to show that one of the largest eruptions of the past 2500 years was the Okmok volcano in Alaska in 43 BCE.[1] This led to drastic changes in climate before the assassination of Julius Caesar, which is argued to be too close to being a mere coincidence. This is also because these[2] "wet and extremely cold conditions during the agriculturally important spring through autumn seasons probably reduced crop yields starting in early 43 BCE and extending at least to early 41 BCE." While it is not usually easy to establish causal linkages, this extreme climate shock[3]—"among the most severe of the past 2,500 y—contributed to reported social unrest and facilitated political change at this important juncture of Western civilization."

After the assassination of Julius Caesar, the triumvirate of Marcus Antonius, Marcus Aemilius Lepidus, and Gaius Octavius assumed power. This arrangement was bound to failure from the beginning. It was not long before Octavius went to war against Antonius in North Africa. After his victory at Actium in 31 BCE, Octavius was crowned Rome's emperor under the name of Augustus. He founded a form of government known as a principate, which combined some elements from the time of the republic with the typical powers of a monarchy. What followed was the Julio-Claudian dynasty that had a sequence of absolutist tyrants such as Tiberius, Caligula, Claudius, and Nero. The end of the dynasty is typically connected to the Great Fire of Rome or the *incendium magnum romae* in 64 CE, when Rome was burned. Afterward, Nero started some reconstruction efforts funded by heavy taxation levied on the provinces. But some of them defied these tax policies, which led to a series of events that culminated in the civil war known as the "Year of the Four Emperors" in turn leading to the end of the dynasty. Thus, Nero brought the dynasty to its end becoming the first emperor to suffer *Damnatio Memoriae*, meaning his era was officially stricken from record by order of the Senate.

Following a war of succession, Vespasian became the first emperor of the Flavian dynasty. Under the new emperor, new taxes were devised to spruce up the empire's financial standing. He was followed by his elder son Titus and then his younger brother Domitian. During that era, foundations were laid for many feats of architecture. The most spectacular of which was the Flavian Amphitheater, known as the Colosseum. This dynasty ended with emperor Domitian who was assassinated in a palace conspiracy by court officials in 96 CE. Domitian was succeeded by an elderly senator, Marcus Cocceius Nerva, who founded the long-lived Nerva-Antonine dynasty. Among those who succeeded him were Trajan, Hadrian, Antoninus Pius, and Marcus Aurelius. These together are known as the Five Good Emperors. Their non-hereditary succession dynasty is considered a golden age, during which considerable expansion and consolidation of the empire took place. Historian Edward Gibbon describes this distinguished era in his *History of the Decline and Fall of the Roman Empire*:[4]

> In the second century of the Christian Era, the empire of Rome comprehended the fairest part of the earth, and the most civilized portion of mankind. The frontiers of that extensive monarchy were guarded by ancient renown and disciplined valor. The gently but powerful influence of laws and manners had gradually cemented the union of the provinces. Their peaceful inhabitants enjoyed and abused the advantages of wealth and luxury. The image of a free constitution was preserved with decent reverence: The Roman senate appeared to possess the sovereign authority and devolved on the emperors all the executive powers of government. During a happy period of more than fourscore year, the public administration was conducted by the virtue and abilities of Nerva, Trajan, Hadrian, and the two Antonines.

Despite all the accomplishments of the era, the attendant evils of excessive centralization prevailed. The concentration of power in the empire at times in the hands of some incompetent and decadent emperors was enough to steer it toward the abyss. Thus, the following century was characterized by turmoil especially as the barbarian invasions weighed heavily on the empire. In addition, usurpations, power contests, political instability, commerce disruptions, harsh taxation, price inflation, and extortion from stationed troops all contributed to economic hardships to the public for decades.

A period of recovery began with Diocletian from 284 to 305 CE, whose broad reforms cemented the cohesion of the imperial administration. His most notable contribution was the introduction of a tetrarchy system to run the empire, which eventually led to a period of tumult with many pretenders to the title of Emperor. This continued until Constantine became the uncontested emperor. Constantine's reign from 312 to

337 CE saw significant and lasting changes to the Roman Empire. In 324 CE, he relocated the capital to Byzantium. His efforts helped reinvigorate the empire for some time. Nevertheless, Constantine's efforts could not save the empire from eventual demise. The last of his line, Theodosius I, was the last emperor to rule over a unified Roman Empire. The Western part of the empire, suffering from incessant invasions and the subsequent flight of peasants into the cities, had grown weaker compared with the Eastern part. When Theodosius I died in 395 CE, the empire split into the Eastern and Western Roman empires.

The West was seriously shaken in 410 CE when the city of Rome was sacked by a nation of Germanic tribes. The final blow fell on Rome in 476 CE, when the German chieftain deposed the last Roman emperor of the western part, Romulus Augustulus. The stronger Eastern part continued as the Byzantine Empire for another millennium.

At its height, the Roman Empire controlled an area including England, the southern half of continental Europe, North Africa, and the Near East. It contained over 20% of the world's population and covered 5 million square kilometers. The Roman Empire was distinguished not only for its military prowess, but also for other notable accomplishments. For instance, Roman roads were without parallel in the ancient world. They were designed and adapted for fast transportation, commercial exchange, mail delivery, pedestrian traffic, and army deployments. Roman city planners achieved unprecedented standards of hygiene with their plumbing, sewage disposal, dams, and aqueducts. Roman architecture was lavishly planned and executed as can be seen in the remaining ruins nowadays. Roman law was a complex body of precedents and principles, which were finally codified as the Codex Justinianus. These laws acted as a frame of reference and a cornerstone for European jurisprudence for a long time. Finally, Latin, which is the language of the Romans, became the medium for a large body of original works in Europe for some time to come.

1.2 Climate in the "Decline and Fall"

The effect of climate on the emergence, decline, and eventual fall of the Western Roman Empire became a hotly debated topic. In this context, it is worth noting that the Roman Warm Period, or the Roman Climatic Optimum, was a period of unusually warm weather in Europe and the North Atlantic which lasted from approximately 250 BCE to 400 CE. A reconstruction of sea surface temperature of the Mediterranean in the last millennium show that[5] "the auspicious climatic conditions of this period, the so-called 'Roman Climatic Optimum', may have contributed to the expansion of the Roman Empire in the various areas of the Mediterranean Sea probably linked to new needs and opportunities." In a similar vein, some climate proxies[6]

> indicate a general warming trend in the late Republican era. Such warming could have shifted the Mediterranean climate to the north. Evidence collected from the Po River Delta, the Adriatic Sea, and the Alps suggests rising temperatures in Italy. These multiple proxies show a detectable warm period, though not one as warm as that produced in the twentieth and twenty-first centuries. This warm period provided favorable conditions for farmers and reinforced other causes for population growth. Social and Cultural shifts interacted with climate to strengthen these trends. During the climate optimum, Roman innovation and adaptation accounted for much of the success in supplying the Empire's population.

However, climate changed after this warm period at a time of vulnerability. Geographer Ellsworth Huntington was one of the first to point our attention to the contribution of climate change as a factor in the fall of Rome.[7] As in many other cases, climate change acted as the last straw after other factors paved the way for an imminent failure. In spite of the empire's resilience,[8] "Roman population growth also made the Empire more vulnerable to more decisive climate disruption. Climate instability during the late Roman era affected agricultural production. Drying in the third century came at the same time that Rome almost collapsed. Good harvests became more infrequent."

These developments led to a dark age which[9] "saw the progressive collapse of civilization-in the sense of town life, literacy, literature, and the arts. But that was not all. The ordinary people who had paid such a price for the glories of Rome paid an even greater price with its demise. Famine and plague racked the lands of the former empire, and it is estimated that the population halved in the late 6th and 7th centuries." Historian Kyle Harper in his description of the causes of the collapse of the Roman Empire in *The Fate of Rome: Climate, Disease and the End of an Empire* also asserts that as the Roman Empire stretched to its limits, the Romans had no idea of the precarious environmental context of what they had established. Eventually[10]

> climate instability pressed on the empire's reserves of strength and intervened dramatically in the course of events. Then, from the later fifth century, we sense the stirrings of a decisive reorganization that culminated in the Late Antique Little Ice Age. A spasm of volcanic activity in the AD 530s and 540s brought the most frigid spell in the entire Late Holocene. Concurrently, the level of energy arriving from the sun slipped to its lowest point in several millennia. As we will see, the deterioration of the physical climate coincided with unprecedented biological catastrophe to overwhelm what was left of the Roman state.

To provide evidence for the effect of climate change on the decline and fall of the empire, we discuss some findings by scholars in this field of study. In this context, some work focus on climate change in the peripheries of the Roman Empire that led to the migration of people from those areas into the Roman territories. This is worth exploring since the decline of the empire occurred in the context of large population shifts in Europe. A wave began with the exodus of Gothic or Germanic tribes due to the Huns incursion into Europe. The Huns, especially under their King Attila, conducted frequent attacks on the Eastern and Western Roman Empires. The Hunnic invasions caused mass displacement of other tribes. Successive waves of migration by the Vandals, Alemani, Franks, Alans, Goths, and others also overwhelmed the empire.

Along these lines, anthropologist Brandon Lee Drake finds four episodes of intense drought which may have persisted for multiple years or even decades in the empire's periphery.[11] These drought conditions not only occurred in the territories that are identified as origins of the tribes which migrated to Roman territories, but also each episode corresponds to one of the four major Germanic migrations. This indicates that these population migrations may have been a strategy to handle adverse agricultural conditions created by a weakened North Atlantic Oscillations. These[12] "shifts to a weakened NAO+ in 376 A.D. and 500 A.D. led to large population migrations across Eurasia that would not only contribute to the collapse of the Western Roman Empire, but also shift linguistic and cultural boundaries for the following centuries."

Besides the peripheries, there is also evidence of climate change within the Roman territories. Evaluating general climatic conditions across the western and eastern parts of the Roman Empire from about 100 BCE to 800 CE, Kyle Harper and other scholars find that the written, archaeological, and scientific proxy evidence indicate that climate conditions changed during the period of the Roman Empire's initial expansion and final contraction.[13] These climatic fluctuations were manifested in changes in precipitation that were not uniform across the western and eastern parts of the empire such that[14]

> [a]round 400 a.d., fluctuation again increased in the western Roman Empire; several indicators point to colder and wetter conditions until precipitation dropped sharply in the first half of the sixth century, at least in northeastern Gaul and in what is now modern Germany. Although radiocarbon dating leaves the exact timing still unclear, sometime between the fourth and the fifth centuries a.d., lake levels show that favorable wet conditions returned to the Levant and persisted for about two centuries. Such regionally advantageous climatic developments might help to explain the success of the eastern Roman Empire as the western Empire dissolved into new polities.

Some scholars present reconstructions of central European summer variability in precipitation and temperature over the past 2500 years.[15] The authors find that increased climate variability from around 250 to 600 CE coincided with the demise of the Western Roman Empire and the turmoil of the migration period such that the exceptional climate variability at the time[16] "coincides with some of the most severe challenges in Europe's political, social, and economic history, during the Migration Period."

It is clear that climate change was not the sole cause of this demise, but it is considered one out of many factors including political problems in the form of internal strife and power contest, economic problems in the form of price inflation and trade disruptions, external pressures in the form of Germanic migrations and barbarian invasions, and health problems in the form of disease outbreaks and spread of plagues. However, the contribution of climate change cannot be denied given the scientific evidence discussed earlier.

1.3 Eastern Roman Empire

The Western Roman Empire was succeeded by the Eastern one, which is sometimes referred to as the Byzantine Empire. Centered in Constantinople, the eastern part of the Roman Empire survived the conditions that caused the demise of the western side and continued to exist until the fall of Constantinople to the Ottomans in 1453 CE. Due to the imperial seat's shift from Rome to Byzantium, the adoption of Christianity, and the predominance of Greek over Latin as lingua franca, historians continue to make a distinction between the earlier Roman Empire and the later Byzantine one.

This empire experienced several cycles of decline and recovery throughout its history. For instance, the early Muslim conquests saw the loss of the empire's wealthiest provinces especially Egypt, the Levant, and Syria. The empire was able to expand once more under the Macedonian dynasty, experiencing a renaissance for about two centuries. The recovery came to an end in 1071 CE with the defeat in the Battle of Manzikert at the hands of the Seljuks. This occurred when an army under the command of the Byzantine emperor was defeated by the Seljuk Sultan, Alp Arslan. Since that time, historians have identified this battle as the first blow that led to the final demise of the Byzantine Empire. The effect[17] "of Manzikert battle which occurred between the Byzantine Empire and the Seljuk State in 1071 A.D. indicates the powers and forces of the Byzantine Empire were destroyed economically and militarily." Thereafter, periods of civil wars and Seljuk incursions led to the loss of most of Asia Minor.

The empire recovered for a while, and Constantinople would continue to be the largest and wealthiest city in Europe until the thirteenth century. However, the empire was dissolved in 1204 CE following the sack of Constantinople by Latin armies at the end of the Fourth Crusade. Despite the eventual recovery of Constantinople in 1261 CE, the reconstituted empire would wield only regional hegemony during its last two centuries of existence. Its remaining territories were gradually annexed by the Ottomans in continuous wars throughout the fourteenth and fifteenth centuries. The fall of Constantinople to the Ottomans in 1453 CE at the hands of Sultan Mehmet II ultimately brought the empire down to its knees. It was this incessant confrontation with multiple Muslim powers that put stress on the empire that caused initially the loss of its wealthiest territories[18] and eventually its final demise.[19]

The early unraveling of the empire began at a time of climate change called the Late Antique Little Ice Age, which was a protracted cooling period in the Northern Hemisphere during the sixth and seventh centuries of the common era. This occurred during the period known as Late Antiquity. That period witnessed three large volcanic eruptions in 535–536, 539–540, and 547 CE. The impact of these eruptions was the phenomenon known as volcanic winter. In the volcanic winter of 536 CE, summer temperatures fell by as much as 2.5 degrees Celsius below normal in Europe. The lingering impact of that volcanic winter was augmented in 539–540 CE, when the second volcanic eruption caused summer temperatures to decline by as much as 2.7 degrees Celsius below normal in Europe. This was one of the most intense and protracted episodes of climate cooling in the Northern Hemisphere.

These volcanic events initiated the Late Antique Little Ice Age, which lasted from 536 to 560 CE. Using wood anatomical thin sections from forest sites and tree species to search for traces of summer cooling between 530 and 550 CE, some scholars find[20] "evidence for the strongest temperature depression between mid-July and early-August 536 CE across North America and Eurasia." Scientists also find that all[21] "16 decades with the most reduced tree growth for our 2,500-year period followed large eruptions. In many cases, such as the coldest decade, from 536 CE to 545 CE, sustained cooling was associated with the combined effect of several successive volcanic eruptions."

Scholars connect these events to social changes during the era. For instance, some scholars show that[22] "[w]hile prolonged warmth during Roman and medieval times roughly coincides with the tendency towards societal prosperity across much of the North Atlantic/European sector and East Asia, major episodes of volcanically forced summer cooling often presaged widespread famines, plague outbreaks and political upheavals." This supports the view that volcanic eruptions leading to changes in climate instigated a series of historical upheavals that could have caused the eventual demise of the empire. In another study, some scholars use tree-ring chronologies from the Russian Altai and European Alps to reconstruct summer temperatures over the past two millennia.[23] The authors find an unprecedented, lasting, and spatially synchronized cooling following a series of large volcanic eruptions in 536, 540, and 547 CE. This cold phase should be[24] "considered as an additional environmental factor contributing to the establishment of the Justinian plague, transformation of the eastern Roman Empire and collapse of the Sasanian Empire, movements out of the Asian steppe and Arabian Peninsula, spread of Slavic-speaking peoples, and political upheavals in China." This cooling period led to increased strain on both the Eastern Roman Empire and the Sassanid Empire, which helped the Muslim conquest of the Levant, Egypt, and Persia. The continual expansion of Muslims over the coming centuries led to the eventual collapse of the Byzantine Empire. This serves as an example of climate change not being the final blow to an empire as in other cases discussed earlier, but rather as a trigger to a downward spiral that led to the eventual demise of that empire.

2 The End of an Era for the Khmer

2.1 Angkor and the Empire Beyond

The Khmer Empire was a powerful state in Southeast Asia which lasted from 802 to 1431 CE. Before its foundation, there were several kingdoms in that part of the world at constant war with each other. A Khmer prince called Jayavarman II led a series of campaigns, subjugating most of these kingdoms and founding a large territorial state.[25] He took the title Chakravartin, or universal ruler, in 802 CE. This date signals the dawn of the empire. Using the city of Angkor as capital, the Khmer empire expanded its territorial base during the subsequent centuries. At its peak, the empire covered a large part of present-day Cambodia, Thailand, Laos, and Vietnam. Throughout the empire's history, the court was involved over and over again in either putting down insurgencies instigated by ambitious nobles or fighting conspiracies against the king. This was particularly the case each time a king dies, when successions were usually contested.

The Khmer built elaborate monumental temples, intricate road networks, bridges, canals, embankments, and water reservoirs.[26] The Khmer also developed agricultural and water distribution systems characterized by state-sponsored hydraulic infrastructure[27] "in an attempt by the state to centralize production." Other scholars also show that after the beginning of the Angkor period[28]

> [o]ver the subsequent 600 years, the city established a number of infrastructure networks including canals, embankments, moats, and reservoirs used to capture, store, and distribute surface water resources. This infrastructural network served several functions, most critically flood regulation and irrigation for agriculture, and developed to become both spatially extensive [covering up to 1200 km2; and internally complex, with many thousands of individual components that were, to a greater or lesser degree, dependent on other components elsewhere in the system. By the end of the 11th century, this network had effectively reached its maximum lateral extent.

The empire's greatest king was Jayavarman VII who forced the Chams away from its territories. As the Khmer empire was on the verge of collapse, Jayavarman VII coalesced an army to confront these invaders who took over Angkor at one point in time. His army achieved a series of victories over the Chams, and after a decisive battle, he saved the empire and expelled the intruders. The scale of his construction achievements was unprecedented. These included temples, monuments, highways, hospitals, and the Angkor Thom complex. Angkor, at its apogee, was the biggest city in the world dwarfing even the great cities of Europe at the time. To show this, some scholars combine Light Detection and Ranging methods, archaeological excavation data, radiocarbon dates, and machine learning algorithms to create maps that model the development of the city of Angkor and its population growth through time and find that[29] "the Greater Angkor Region was home to approximately 700,000 to 900,000 inhabitants at its apogee in the 13th century CE." Jayavarman VII also expanded the empire's territorial control to its zenith.

The empire's decline and final collapse was, however, a gradual rather than a sudden affair. The data[30] "indicate a protracted decline in occupation within the economic and administrative core of the city, rather than an abrupt demographic collapse, suggesting the focus of power began to shift to urban centers outside of the capital during the 14th century." This demise was connected to the great Thai migration of the twelfth to fourteenth centuries of the common era. For some reason, Thai populations started shifting their location southward. They migrated in small groups initially, and then their numbers increased as they established themselves as settlers in marginal areas. Eventually, the Thai created their own small kingdoms. As these kingdoms gained more power, they started to attack and annex Khmer territories. The Thai kingdom of Ayutthaya overtook Angkor in 1431 CE, which constitutes the end of the Khmer empire. The susceptibility of the empire to such a lamentable fate is attributed not only to the strength of its adversaries but also to the weakness that lurked within. The Khmer empire's economy by that time may have deteriorated by increased silting of the extravagant water works that the Khmer core area depended on. This denouement had to do with climate change.

2.2 *Climate Deterioration and Civilizational Demise*

Scientists working on the Greater Angkor Project believe that the Khmer had an elaborate system of water reservoirs and canal networks for the purpose of irrigation for rice. Archaeologists Damian Evans, Roland Fletcher, and other scholars declare that a[31] "survey of the banks, channels and reservoirs at Angkor shows them to have been part of a large-scale water management network instigated in the ninth century AD." In another study, Damian Evans, Roland Fletcher, and other scholars create a comprehensive archaeological map of greater Angkor which[32] "reveals a vast, low-density settlement landscape integrated by an elaborate water management network covering >1,000 km^2, the most extensive urban complex of the preindustrial world."

Some studies provide evidence for the hypothesis that climate change contributed to the demise of the Khmer Empire. For instance, Damian Evans, Roland Fletcher, and other scholars describe the use of airborne laser scanning technology to create high-precision scans of the ground surface beneath the vegetation cover for Angkor where dense forest obscures any traces of this civilization.[33] Their effort confirms that a very large urban population was highly dependent on the delivery of agricultural goods from an extended agro-urban landscape, using a complex system to carry out an unsustainable mode of production. Their data[34] "lend further weight to an emerging consensus that infrastructural complexity, unsustainable modes of subsistence, and climate variation were crucial factors in the decline of the classical Khmer civilization."

As the population grew, there was more strain on this water distribution system. As the system was about to surpass the carrying capacity of the ecosystem, climate change acted as the last straw. During the fourteenth and fifteenth centuries, there were drastic climatic changes. Scholars determined that a period of intense monsoon rains was followed by a severe drought in the Khmer territory. Fluctuating between droughts and flooding was obviously a double-edged sword. Periods of drought led to a decline in agricultural productivity, while violent flooding destroyed the hydraulic infrastructure. The recurrent damage to the water system may have become so severe that any repair was either impossible or too costly to pursue. These events may have caused the inhabitants to drift southward away from the empire's core cities. Along these lines, Damian Evans and other scholars conduct an analysis of tree ring data to show that[35] "the region suffered a series of severe and prolonged droughts, punctuated by episodes of heavy rain, in the mid- to late 14th and early 15th centuries. These would have dealt a double blow to Angkor's hydraulic infrastructure: sustained drought overtaxed the capacity of the baray to act as a 'failsafe', while rapid floods caused critical damage to key components of the hydraulic network and threatened habitation areas."

In a similar vein, archaeologist Roland Fletcher and other scholars examine how the hydraulic city of Angkor experienced decades-long drought interspersed with intense monsoons that contributed to its eventual demise.[36] The authors produce a 759-year hydroclimate reconstruction of the Palmer Drought Severity Index using tree rings from two sites in the highlands of Vietnam's Bidoup Nui Ba National Park. The record shows that Angkor droughts were of duration and severity that would have affected the sprawling city's water supply and agricultural productivity, while the intense monsoon years damaged its water control infrastructure. The authors conclude that[37] "decades of weakened summer monsoon rainfall, punctuated by abrupt and extreme wet episodes that likely brought severe flooding that damaged flood-control infrastructure, must now be considered an additional, important, and significant stressor occurring during a period of decline. Interrelated infrastructural, economic, and geopolitical stresses had made Angkor vulnerable to climate change and limited its capacity to adapt to changing circumstances."

Roland Fletcher and other scholars incorporate archaeological data from the city of Angkor into a model that attempts to quantify the topological damage to Angkor's water distribution network due to climate change.[38] The study shows extensive damage caused by flooding to Angkor's urban water system infrastructure. The systemic vulnerability of the system, when coupled with abrupt climatic change, contributed to the demise of the city. This is because the very large and convoluted water distribution network was prone to cascading failure under the impact of high-amplitude but low-frequency climatic fluctuations which[39] "suggest that the functional breakdown of critical urban infrastructure played a role in the broader demise of Greater Angkor as a viable urban complex in the 14th and 15th centuries CE."

A group of scholars study a sediment core taken from the West Baray, one of the largest reservoirs in the Khmer Empire, to provide evidence on environmental change at Angkor.[40] The authors find that sediment density, composition, and color show that the Baray received greater sediment and water input prior to the fourteenth and fifteenth centuries, and a decreased sediment input and lower water levels in the fourteenth and fifteenth centuries coincident with the megadroughts and contemporaneous collapse of Angkor. Their study[41] "demonstrate[s] that changes in the water management system were associated with the decline of the Angkorian kingdom during that period."

All this evidence asserts that climate change proved to be a source of stress to the empire's economic infrastructure, where the hydraulic water system may not have been capable of coping with changing hydrological conditions of the empire, that could have contributed to its demise. This in addition to the other often cited factors including conflict, conversion to Buddhism, resource exhaustion, changing trade patterns, demographic changes, and others.[42] However, in their effort to list all possible factors contributing to the calamity that befell this empire, Damian Evans, Roland Fletcher, and other scholars conclude,[43] "Although significant gaps remain in our knowledge, the causal linkages between climate variability, societal challenges, and large-scale transformations are particularly well articulated in the Angkorian World and compel us to move beyond merely noting the correlation between events like megadroughts and significant societal change."

3 Climate Inconstancies and Chinese Dynasties

Chinese history is typically divided into various dynastic states. Until the abdication of the last emperor in 1912 CE, Chinese history came to be described in terms of the succession of these dynasties. Some of these dynasties made wonderful achievements and unparalleled accomplishments. Dynasties, however, used to decline and fall due to several factors that became recurrent over time. One of these culprits is climate change which contributed to the collapse of the Han dynasty, the Tang dynasty, the Song dynasty, the Yuan dynasty, and the Ming dynasty. The following sections include their stories.

3.1 The Han Dynasty

The Han dynasty of China lasted from 202 BCE to 220 CE, spanning over five centuries. The dynasty history, however, is split into two periods as it was interrupted from 9 to 25 CE. The first is the Western Han from 202 BCE to 9 CE, followed by the Eastern Han from 25 to 220 CE. The period in between was mostly that of the short-lived Xin dynasty established by a usurper of the throne. The era of the Han dynasty is considered a golden age in China's history with a lasting imprint on Chinese identity. The emperor in this dynasty presided over the government but shared power with both the landed nobility and the appointed ministers who came largely from the gentry. The Han dynasty oversaw periods of economic prosperity and significant advances in science and technology. These include the introduction of paper, the wheelbarrow, the moldboard plow, steering ship rudders, the armillary spheres, the seismometer, and others.

Toward the end, palace eunuchs increasingly interfered in court politics and engaged in violent power struggles. Imperial authority was also seriously threatened by Taoist societies which instigated some insurgencies such as the "Yellow Turban Rebellion" and the "Five Pecks of Rice Rebellion." Besides the disruption caused by the eunuchs and the insurgencies of the Taoists, aspirant army leaders also added to the instability of the time. Following the death of an emperor, palace eunuchs were massacred by some military officers who turned into warlords and divided the empire into spheres of influence.

Some scholars argue that climate change causing a drought was a contributing factor to the social instability leading to the demise of this dynasty. In this context, a study conducted an analysis of the provincial drought and national famine indexes during the Han dynasty to explore the contribution of regional climate change to dynastic instability.[44] The study finds that the[45] "drought disasters and national famines in Henan Province during the Western Han and Eastern Han dynasties were not the most severe of those in each period, but they caused the demise of the dynasty."

3.2 *The Tang Dynasty*

One of the greatest dynasties in Chinese history was the Tang dynasty which lasted from 618 to 907 CE. This was a golden age of reforms which laid the foundation for protocols which are still practiced in China. The period also witnessed achievements in literature, art, architecture, science, and technology including the most impressive scientific inventions in Chinese history such as the gunpowder, the air conditioner, the gas stove, and the woodblock printing.

The dynasty was established when a popular general of the army, the Duke of Tang Li-Yuan, rose in rebellion and assumed power as Emperor Gaozu. The emperor was the one to implement the bureaucratic practices which are still adopted and observed today in China. He also enacted reforms to prevent over-taxation of the peasants and to redistribute land parcels. Emperor Gaozu named his son Li-Jiancheng as heir. This was a decree that his second son Li-Shimin could not concede to, since he expected to be first in the succession line as an award for his efforts in containing some rebellions and protecting the throne. Li-Shimin had fought alongside his father to consolidate the dynasty and, thus, felt he ought to play a prominent role in the future of the empire. Given his grievances, Li-Shimin staged a coup, killed his brothers, and forced his father Gaozu to abdicate to him. Once he became emperor, he took the name Taizong. This second emperor also enacted reforms to the bureaucracy, the military, the social structure, the educational system, and the religious practices.

He was succeeded by Empress Wu Zetian. She is China's only female ruler and one of the most eminent due to her effective leadership, which made China one of the most powerful nations of the time. During her reign, she expanded the empire far beyond its previous territorial limits. The empress also reformed the government, expanded education, amended farming practices, adjusted the tax system, and limited the excesses of the aristocracy. Her reforms laid the foundation for the later success of her successor. Wu Zetian was overthrown in a coup and after a period of chaos, Xuanzong became emperor. Under his reign, the Tang dynasty began its golden age as China became the most prosperous country in the world. Xuanzong, however, fell in love with a woman named Yang Guifei. He started neglecting his duties as emperor for this love affair and agreed to her demands to promote members of her family to crucial positions. All the important reforms that Xuanzong had implemented began to unravel as the members of Yang's family abused their powers for personal benefit. At the end of his reign, Turkish and other foreign peoples invaded China, and some governors ruled autonomously over large parts of Chinese territory. After Xuanzong's death, the dynasty steadily declined and fell apart.

This period of decline was also accompanied by climate change. There was a widespread famine, due to a drought, and the government was doing little to help feed the people. The end of the dynasty was, thus, attributed to changes in climate which led some to conclude that even though[46] "historiographers have ascribed this decline to the influence that eunuchs and slanderous ministers exerted upon weak emperors. However, it seems possible that a change in climate may have played an important role as well. This article uses data provided by Chinese climate historians to suggest that this theory is plausible."

3.3 The Song Dynasty

The Song dynasty ruled China from 960 to 1279 CE. This era is divided into two periods. The first is the Northern Song from 960 to 1125 CE, and the second is the Southern Song from 1125 to 1279 CE. The chaos and political vacuum caused by the collapse of the Tang dynasty led to the division of China into kingdoms. During that time of upheaval, the Song dynasty was founded by an army general. He was endorsed as Emperor Taizu by the army in 960 CE. In the capital city of Kaifeng, he established a strong central command over the empire which marked the beginning of the Northern Song period. He ensured administrative stability by introducing the civil service examination system of drafting state bureaucrats by merit, rather than aristocratic or military pedigrees. He also promoted projects that ensured efficiency in communication throughout the empire. Emperor Taizu was succeeded by his younger brother, Emperor Taizong, who was followed by his son, Emperor Zhenzong.

The stability provided by the long tenure of these emperors, compared to the previous tumultuous periods, gave the Song dynasty the foundations it needed to become one of the most successful in Chinese history. The dynasty was able to govern over a unified China with a booming economy. Kaifeng was one of the most enormous metropolises of the world with a population of more than half a million. As a considerable trade center, Kaifeng was especially famous for its printing, paper, textile, and porcelain industries. Such products were exported along the Silk Road and across the Indian Ocean.

Emperor Zhenzong was followed by Emperor Huizong who neglected his duties to focus on artistic pursuits. He ultimately retired to be succeeded by Emperor Qinzong. Subsequently, a peasant rebellion broke out because of the increasing tax burden, the concentration of landownership, and the oppressive practices of the local authorities. Wars also broke out with the Jurchen from Manchuria who eventually captured the capital city, the retired Emperor Huizong, the acting Emperor Qinzong, and most of the Imperial court. The surviving Song forces under the self-proclaimed Emperor Gaozong withdrew south of the Yangtze to establish a new capital at Lin'an. The Jurchen conquest of northern China and the shift of capital from Kaifeng to Lin'an was the dividing line between the Northern and Southern Song dynasties.

The collapse of the Northern Song dynasty was also brought about to a certain extent by climate change according to some scholars. This came in the form of flooding of the Yellow River that wreaked havoc. Geoarchaeological evidence shows that[47] "[f]rom AD 1048 to 1128, Yellow River flooding killed over a million people, left many more homeless and destitute, and turned parts of the once fertile North China Plain into a silted-up agricultural wasteland. Brought on in part by climate change and the Northern Song dynasty's (AD 960–1127) mismanagement of the environment, the Yellow River floods likely hastened the collapse of the Northern Song dynasty."

The Southern Song dynasty found new ways to bolster its economy. In particular, the government sponsored colossal shipbuilding and harbor improvement projects. They also oversaw the construction of beacons and seaport warehouses to support maritime trade abroad and to sustain China's commerce with the outside world. Technological advancements of the time in navigation included the watertight bulkheads which improved buoyancy, the stern-mounted rudders which enhanced steering, and the sounding lines which determined water depth.

Although the Song dynasty was able to hold back their traditional enemies, a new foe came to power nearby. That was the Mongols assembled under the leadership of Genghis Khan. These nomadic tribes repeatedly attacked and plundered the northern Chinese territories in the first decades of the thirteenth century CE. The Song prepared their armies for an imminent attack. However, there was to be a respite. The Mongols, at the time, were otherwise occupied in expanding their empire into western Asia. It was not until 1268 CE that the Mongol leader Kublai Khan set his eyes on the south of the Yangtze River. The invaders crossed the Yangtze in 1275 CE and proved unstoppable. The Song state paid dearly, for its lack of political unity and its lag in military modernization, and became part of the vast Mongol empire which at the time covered one fifth of the globe.

3.4 The Yuan Dynasty

The Yuan dynasty was founded by the Mongols who ruled China from 1271 to 1368 CE. Their first emperor was Kublai Khan who overthrew the Song dynasty. The stability and peace during that era brought about economic prosperity within China as the emperor and his successors promoted international trade with the wider world. Even though the Mongols made some attempts to appeal to the Chinese, real power and key positions in the newly created provincial administrations of China remained in their hands. Their achievements include patronizing the printing industry, creating an accurate calendar, and developing the maritime Silk Road.

Kublai Khan was succeeded by his grandson Temur Oljeitu as Khan and emperor of China. Continuing with the same institutions and some of the same officials appointed by his predecessor, China enjoyed a peaceful and successful era. Afterward, there was a long line of rulers who reigned for short periods and who struggled to balance the competing factions at all levels of governance. By the fourteenth century CE, the Yuan dynasty had also been beset by a devastating combination of unusually cold winters, flooding of the Yellow River, sweeping famines, spreading plagues, widespread banditry, and peasant uprisings. In this context,[48]

> serious flood damage to the Yangtze delta occurred at a critical moment when this rich granary was badly needed to support other stricken areas. Four-fifths of the Yuan population lived south of the Yangtze, and the area's production of grain, cotton, silk, and salt were all crucial for government revenue and general wealth accumulation. Typhoons and floods here ultimately cost the court far more than its support for hard-pressed Mongolian refugees. These disasters drained increasingly scarce resources from other areas while negatively impacting the dynasty's capacity to support the empire as a whole. In the end, it was the pressure of a major disaster here that sparked the revolt that overthrew the Yuan.

The Mongol rulers also squabbled for power and failed to suppress widespread rebellions. One such insurgency was led by a peasant called Zhu Yuanzhang. Zhu was successful in his attempts to overthrow the emperor. After overtaking Beijing, the last Yuan emperor fled to Mongolia's capital Karakorum. Meanwhile, Zhu declared himself the emperor of China in 1368 CE with the title of Hongwu. Thus, he founded the Ming dynasty.

3.5 The Ming Dynasty

The Ming dynasty was established following the collapse of the Mongol rule in China and lasted from 1368 to 1644 CE. Zhu became the supreme leader of China, declared himself emperor Hongwu, and would continue in office until 1398 CE. His successors continued his efforts to unify China and tighten their grip on power through a strong centralized government. In the early fifteenth century, there were further incursions on

Chinese territories by the Mongols. Emperor Yongle, the second son of Hongwu who had taken the throne after a civil war, opted to relocate the capital from Nanjing to Beijing in 1421 CE to be better placed to deal with any foreign threats. Nanjing, which literally means southern capital, was the primary capital of the Ming until 1420 CE.

Despite challenges from abroad and within, the Ming dynasty witnessed an unprecedented population boom and economic prosperity. These favorable economic conditions would, in turn, create a surge in the arts as a wealthier class developed with a great appetite to show off their appreciation of fine arts. Under this dynasty, China witnessed the blossoming of the production of the blue-and-white porcelains. Other notable architectural achievements of the era included the construction of the Forbidden City, or the imperial residence, in Beijing. The eagerness of the dynasty to expand international ties is captured by China's greatest explorer, Zheng He. The emperor sent Zheng He on seven voyages, involving several hundred ships, between 1405 and 1433 CE. Zheng expeditions led him to sail along routes to the Indian coast, the Persian Gulf, and Eastern Africa.

Despite its initial success, the Ming dynasty began eventually to experience the typical problems that had beset other dynasties in China through the ages. These included intrigues perpetrated by the court eunuchs, abuses of power, a long line of inept rulers who spent more than they should on grandiose projects, factional fighting between ruling families, the ballooning of the civil service apparatus, and peasant rebellions against excessive taxes and the heavy handedness of the landlords. All these factors took their toll on the emperors' hold on power.

In the 1620s, there was also a drop in average temperatures which seriously affected crop yields. Examining the middle and lower reaches of the Yangtze River shows that the[49] "regional mean winter temperature in 1620 was estimated to be 4.4 °C lower than the 1961–1990 mean." This occurred in addition to a wave of floods and droughts that adversely affected the harvest. These climatic events were followed by a widespread famine and peasant uprisings in consequence. In 1644 CE, a rebel army led by Li Zicheng attacked and conquered Beijing. The last Ming emperor hanged himself to avoid being captured. On hearing the news of the capital's fall, the army commander decided to allow a Manchu army into China unimpeded. The Manchus had fought the Ming on several occasions in the past and was then threatening to invade again. The commander did that in the hope they would put down the rebellion. However, the

Manchus took advantage of this situation, killed the leader of the rebel army, and established their own Qing dynasty. China's sunset in the seventeenth century and the contribution of climatic factors was described aptly as follows:[50]

> It was a period of economic growth despite continued poverty among the lower classes. After falling by almost half to around 70 million in the 14th century, the population rose to an estimated 130 million in the late 16th century and to as high as 170 million by the 1650s. Then the empire ran into a devastating crisis similar in many ways to those of the 4th century and the 14th century-as well as to the occurring simultaneously in much of 17th century Europe. There were a succession of epidemics, floods, droughts, and other disasters. Famines devastated whole regions. The population stopped growing and even declined in some regions. Once-flourishing industries shut down. By the 1640s reports from northern Chekiang (the hinterland of Shanghai) spoke of 'mass starvation, hordes of beggars, infanticide and cannibalism.

In this context, a group of scholars identified ways in which climate change contributed to the collapse of the dynasty based on reconstructed climate and historical records on fiscal deterioration, food crises, and the frequencies of popular uprisings and rebellions.[51] The principal ways in which climate change contributed to the collapse of the Ming dynasty include[52]

> [f]irstly, cooling, aridification, and desertification during a cold period destroyed the military farm system, which was the main supply system for the provisioning of government troops on the northern frontiers; these impacts increased the military expenditure from 64 % of total government expenditure in 1548–1569 to 76 % in 1570–1589 and thus aggravated the national fiscal crisis that occurred during the late Ming dynasty. Secondly, climate deterioration (e.g., cooling, aridification, and an increase in the frequencies of frost- and drought-related disasters, etc.) led to a 20–50 % reduction in the per capita production of raw grain in most areas of China, which resulted in widespread food crises and exacerbated the vulnerability of social structures during the last several decades of the Ming dynasty. Thirdly, the severe droughts occurring in 1627–1643 were a key trigger to the peasantry uprising. These droughts also played a significant role to promote the peasantry uprising, especially reviving the peasantry troops by recruitment of famine victims when they nearly perished in 1633 and 1638 and severely

disrupting the food supply for the government troops, resulting in the final defeat of the government troops by the peasantry troops.

Other scholars present new speleothem oxygen isotope records to characterize the "Late Ming Weak Monsoon Periods" during the late sixteenth and early seventeenth centuries.[53] Their analysis suggests that a weak summer monsoon, not seen for nearly 500 years in China, coincided with the late Ming dynasty peasant uprising during the period from 1627 to 1658 CE. This unprecedented[54] "long-lasting aridity/weakening monsoon period was spatiotemporally synchronized with the late Ming peasantry uprising (1627–1658 CE) and the fall of the Ming Dynasty (1644 CE)."

3.6 *Climatic Disturbance and Dynastic Collapse*

As can be seen from all these examples, climate change contributed, along with other factors, to the collapse of one Chinese dynasty after the other. To provide evidence for the effect of climate change on the sequence of dynastic collapse in China, we refer to some studies that examine the statistical association between these climatic events and the occurrences in Chinese history that contributed to the collapse of these dynasties.

To explore the association between climatic change and war in China, some scholars compare paleoclimatic reconstructions with known war incidents in the last millennium.[55] The hypothesis postulated is that long-term climate change caused critical shifts in the land carrying capacity. In favorable climatic phases, the land carrying capacity increased, the incentive for being embroiled in conflict diminished, and the population increased at a fast pace. When climate became unfavorable leading to a decline in the land carrying capacity, the population growth in the previous favorable period could not be sustained. Therefore, armed conflicts over limited resources intensified in more populated areas which consequently would lead to dynastic collapse. Using official records published by governmental entities and historians to determine the times of dynastic changes, the study shows that[56] "climatic change was closely associated with war frequency because the shortage of livelihood resources in cold periods could trigger wars. The outbreak of wars would further weaken state power, eventually leading to dynastic collapse."

Other scholars explore the influence of floods and droughts on internal wars in various agroecological zones in China during the period from

1470 to 1911 CE.[57] Their analysis shows that floods and droughts were significant in driving internal wars in China with provincial variations. The relationship between climate and internal wars is only significant in periods in which population density is increasing or when the upper limit of the land carrying capacity is reached. Along the same vein, some scholars compare paleoclimate reconstructions with a complete record of warfare incidents in eastern China over the past millennium to show that almost all peaks of warfare frequency and dynastic changes occurred in cooling phases.[58] The decline of thermal energy during these phases significantly diminished agricultural yield. Such ecological stress interacted with the increase in population pressures to bring about the high frequencies of warfare over the last millennium.

By comparing historical records with paleoclimatic reconstructions from 10 to 1900 CE, some scholars show that cooling temperatures had a direct positive association with the frequency of external war on Chinese dynasties from the northern pastoral nomadic societies, and an indirect positive association with the frequency of internal war within the Chinese dynasties.[59] The authors conclude that the collapses of the dynasties of the Han, Tang, Song, and Ming are closely associated with low temperature as it is[60] "very probable that cool temperature may be the driving force in causing high frequencies of meteorological, agricultural disasters and then man-made disasters (wars) in ancient China."

To examine the extent to which climate change contributed to Chinese population cycles, historical data and statistical techniques show five major population contractions in China between 1000 and 1911 CE.[61] These events occurred in periods with a cold climate when mortality crises led to population collapses since[62] "population size can also be affected by changes in land carrying capacity, which is contingent upon climate change." To understand how climate change affected population growth dynamics in China from 1000 to 1979 CE, scholars hypothesize that deteriorating climate in agrarian zones caused a drastic shrinkage to the land's carrying capacity which affected food supply per capita.[63] In this context, a protracted cooling period could lead to lower agricultural yields. This is because it would lower the elevation at which crops can be grown, thus decreasing the amount of land available for cultivation, or due to the inability of certain grains to withstand cooler temperatures. In these cases, societies could not deal with the consequences of crop failures when climate deteriorated. This led to more population migration, a lower birth rate, and more disastrous population checks in the form of wars, famines, and epidemics. Such food shortages, thus, led to below-average population growth or even population collapses.

These studies are slightly different from some that we referred to in other contexts. This is because these studies examine the statistical association between climate change and dynastic collapse. This is different than the studies that show a coincidence of a climatic anomaly with a historical incident. In this context, this analysis can check the statistical significance of the effect of climate change on dynastic collapse, the direction of causality from one to the other, and the magnitude of that effect. This does not depend on data collected for one such event, but rather on a collection of observations over time and space. This offers additional reassuring evidence on the association between climate change and societal collapse at least in the context of dynastic China.

Notes

1. Joseph R. McConnell, Michael Sigl, Gill Plunkett, Andrea Burke, Woon Mi Kim, Christoph C. Raible, Andrew I. Wilsong, Joseph G. Manning, Francis Ludlow, Nathan J. Chellman, Helen M. Innes, Zhen Yang, Jessica F. Larsen, Janet R. Schaefer, Sepp Kipfstuhl, Seyedhamidreza Mojtabavi, Frank Wilhelms, Thomas Opel, Hanno Meyer, and Jørgen Peder Steffensen. "Extreme Climate After Massive Eruption of Alaska's Okmok Volcano in 43 BCE and Effects on the Late Roman Republic and Ptolemaic Kingdom." PNAS, 117, 27: 15443–15449, 2020.
2. Ibid.
3. Ibid.
4. Edward Gibbon. History of the Decline and Fall of the Roman Empire. Everyman's Library, 2010. (P. 39).
5. G. Margaritelli, I. Cacho, A. Català, M. Barra, L. G. Bellucci, C. Lubritto, R. Rettori, and F. Lirer. "Persistent Warm Mediterranean Surface Waters During the Roman Period." Nature, Scientific Reports, 10, 10431, 2020.
6. Benjamin Lieberman and Elizabeth Gordon. Climate Change in Human History. Bloomsbury, 2018. (P. 61).
7. Ellsworth Huntington. "Climatic Change and Agricultural Exhaustion as Elements in the Fall of Rome." The Quarterly Journal of Economics, 31, 2: 173–208, 1917.
8. Benjamin Lieberman and Elizabeth Gordon. Climate Change in Human History. Bloomsbury, 2018. (P. 66).
9. Chris Harman. A People's History of the World. Verso, 2008. (P. 104).
10. Kyle Harper in The Fate of Rome: Climate, Disease and the End of An Empire. Princeton University Press, 2017. (PP. 56–58).

11. Brandon Lee Drake. "Changes in North Atlantic Oscillation drove Population Migrations and the Collapse of the Western Roman Empire." Nature, Scientific Reports, 7, 1227, 2017.
12. Ibid.
13. Michael McCormick, Ulf Büntgen, Mark A. Cane, Edward R. Cook, Kyle Harper, Peter Huybers, Thomas Litt, Sturt W. Manning, Paul Andrew Mayewski, Alexander F. M. More, Kurt Nicolussi, Willy Tegel. "Climate Change During and After the Roman Empire: Reconstructing the Past from Scientific and Historical Evidence." Journal of Interdisciplinary History, xliii, 2: 169–220, 2012.
14. Ibid.
15. Ulf Büntgen, Willy Tegel, Kurt Nicolussi, Michael McCormick, David Frank, Valerie Trouet, Jed O. Kaplan, Franz Herzig, Karl-Uwe Heussner, Heinz Wanner, Jürg Luterbacher, and Jan Esper." 2500 Years of European Climate Variability and Human Susceptibility." Science, 331: 578–582, 2011.
16. Ibid.
17. Kamaruzaman Yusoff, Salah Mohammed, Mansoureh Ebrahimi, and Azlizan Mat Enh. "The Battle of Manzikert in 1071 A.D. and Its Consequences to the Byzantine Empire." International Journal of Islamic and Civilizational Studies, 2, 1: 1–7, 2015.
18. Guy Bar-Oz, Lior Weissbrod, Tali Erickson-Gin, Yotam Tepper, Dan Malkinson, Mordechay Benzaquen, Dafna Langgut, Zachary C. Dunseth, Don H. Butler, Ruth Shahack-Gross, Joel Roskin, Daniel Fuks, Ehud Weiss, Nimrod Maroma, Inbar Ktalav, Rachel Blevis, Irit Zohar, Yoav Farhi, Anya Filatova, Yael Gorin-Rosen, Xin Yan, and Elisabetta Boaretto. "Ancient Trash Mounds Unravel Urban Collapse a Century before the end of Byzantine Hegemony in the Southern Levant." PNAS, 116, 17: 8239–8248, 2019.
19. Jacques Malherbe. "The Decline of the Eastern Empire and the Fall of Constantinople: An Omen for Europe?" Athens Journal of History, 10, 2: 87–96, 2024.
20. Ulf Büntgen, Alan Crivellaro, Dominique Arseneault, Mike Baillie, David Barclay, Mauro Bernabei, Jarno Bontadi, Gretel Boswijk, David Brown, Duncan A. Christie, Olga V. Churakova, Edward R. Cook, Rosanne D'Arrigo, Nicole Davi, Jan Esper, Patrick Fonti, Ciara Greaves, Rashit M. Hantemirov, Malcolm K. Hughes, Alexander V. Kirdyanov, Paul J. Krusic, Carlos Le Quesne, Fredrik C. Ljungqvist, Michael McCormick, Vladimir S. Myglan, Kurt Nicolussi, Clive Oppenheimer, Jonathan Palmer, Chun Qin, Frederick Reinig, Matthew Salzer, Markus Stoffel, Max Torbenson, Mirek Trnka, Ricardo Villalba, Nick Wiesenberg, Greg Wiles, Bao Yang, and Alma Piermattei. "Global Wood Anatomical Perspective on

the Onset of the Late Antique Little Ice Age (LALIA) in the mid-6th Century CE." Science Bulletin, 67: 2336–2344, 2022.

21. M. Sigl, M. Winstrup, J. R. McConnell, K. C. Welten, G. Plunkett, F. Ludlow, U. Buntgen, M. Caffee, N. Chellman, D. Dahl-Jensen, H. Fischer, S. Kipfstuhl, C. Kostick, O. J. Maselli, F. Mekhaldi, R. Mulvaney, R. Muscheler, D. R. Pasteris, J. R. Pilcher, M. Salzer, S. Schupbach, J. P. Steffensen, B. M. Vinther, and & T. E. Woodruff. "Timing and Climate Forcing of Volcanic Eruptions for the Past 2,500 Years." Nature, 523: 543–548, 2015.
22. Ulf Büntgen, Dominique Arseneault, ´Etienne Boucher, Olga V. Churakova (Sidorova), Fabio Gennaretti, Alan Crivellaro, Malcolm K. Hughes, Alexander V. Kirdyanov, Lara Klippel, Paul J. Krusic, Hans W. Linderholm, Fredrik C. Ljungqvist, Josef Ludescher, Michael McCormick, Vladimir S. Myglan, Kurt Nicolussi, Alma Piermattei, Clive Oppenheimer, Frederick Reinig, Michael Sigl, Eugene A. Vaganov, and Jan Esper. "Prominent Role of Volcanism in Common Era Climate Variability and Human History." Dendrochronologia, 64, 125757, 2020.
23. Ulf Büntgen, Vladimir S. Myglan, Fredrik Charpentier Ljungqvis, Michael McCormick, Nicola Di Cosmo, Michael Sigl, Johann Jungclaus, Sebastian Wagner, Paul J. Krusic, Jan Esper, Jed O. Kaplan, Michiel A. C. de Vaan, Jürg Luterbacher, Lukas Wacker, Willy Tegel, and Alexander V. Kirdyanov. "Cooling and Societal Change During the Late Antique Little Ice Age from 536 to around 660 AD." Nature Geoscience, 9: 231–236, 2016.
24. Ibid.
25. O. Wolters. "Jayavarman II's Military Power: The Territorial Foundation of the Angkor Empire." Journal of the Royal Asiatic Society of Great Britain and Ireland, 105, 1: 21–30, 1973.
26. Roland Fletcher, Dan Penny, Damián Evans, Christophe Pottier, Mike Barbetti, Matti Kummu, Terry Lustig and the Authority for the Protection and Management of Angkor and the Region of Siem Reap (APSARA) Department of Monuments and Archaeology Team. "The Water Management Network of Angkor, Cambodia." Antiquity, 82: 658–670, 2008.
27. Sarah Klassen and Damián Evans. "Top-down and Bottom-up Water Management: A Diachronic Model of Changing Water Management Strategies at Angkor, Cambodia." Journal of Anthropological Archaeology, 58, 101166, 2020.
28. Daniel Penny, Cameron Zachreson, Roland Fletcher, David Lau, Joseph T. Lizier, Nicholas Fischer, Damian Evans, Christophe Pottier, and Mikhail Prokopenko. "The Demise of Angkor: Systemic Vulnerability of Urban Infrastructure to Climatic Variations." Science Advances, 4, eaau4029, 2018.

29. Sarah Klassen, Alison K. Carter, Damian H. Evans, Scott Ortman, Miriam T. Stark, Alyssa A. Loyless, Martin Polkinghorne, Piphal Heng, Michael Hill, Pelle Wijker, Jonathan Niles-Weed, Gary P. Marriner, Christophe Pottier, and Roland J. Fletcher. "Diachronic Modeling of the Population within the Medieval Greater Angkor Region Settlement Complex." Science Advances, 7, eabf8441, 2021.
30. Dan Penny, Tegan Hall, Damian Evans, and Martin Polkinghorne. "Geoarchaeological Evidence From Angkor, Cambodia, Reveals a Gradual Decline Rather than a Catastrophic 15th-century Collapse." PNAS, 116, 11: 4871–4876, 2019.
31. Roland Fletcher, Dan Penny, Damian Evans, Christophe Pottier, Mike Barbetti, Matti Kummu, Terry Lustig and Authority for the Protection and Management of Angkor and the Region of Siem Reap. "The Water Management Network of Angkor, Cambodia." Antiquity, 82: 658–670, 2008.
32. Damian Evans, Christophe Pottier, Roland Fletcher, Scott Hensley, Ian Tapley, Anthony Milne, and Michael Barbet. "A Comprehensive Archaeological Map of the World's Largest Preindustrial Settlement Complex at Angkor, Cambodia." PNAS, 104: 14277–14282, 2007.
33. Damian H. Evans, Roland J. Fletcher, Christophe Pottier, Jean-Baptiste Chevance, Dominique Soutif, Boun Suy Tan, Sokrithy Im, Darith Ea, Tina Tin, Samnang Kim, Christopher Cromarty, Stéphane De Greef, Kasper Hanus, Pierre Bâty, Robert Kuszinger, Ichita Shimoda, and Glenn Boornazian. "Uncovering Archaeological Landscapes at Angkor Using lidar." PNAS, 110, 31: 12595–12600, 2013.
34. Ibid.
35. Damian Evans, Martin Polkinghorne, Roland Fletcher, David Brotherson, Tegan Hall, Sarah Klassen, and Pelle Wijker. "Perspectives on the Collapse of Angkor and the Khmer Empire." In The Angkorian World. Ed. by Mitch Hendrickson, Miriam T. Stark and Damian Evans. Routledge, 2023.
36. Brendan M. Buckley, Kevin J. Anchukaitis, Daniel Penny, Roland Fletcher, Edward R. Cook, Masaki Sano, Le Canh Nam, Aroonrut Wichienkeeo, Ton That Minh, and Truong Mai Hong. "Climate as a Contributing Factor in the Demise of Angkor, Cambodia." PNAS, 107, 15: 6748–6752, 2010.
37. Ibid.
38. Daniel Penny, Cameron Zachreson, Roland Fletcher, David Lau, Joseph T. Lizier, Nicholas Fischer, Damian Evans, Christophe Pottier, and Mikhail Prokopenko. "The Demise of Angkor: Systemic Vulnerability of Urban Infrastructure to Climatic Variations." Science Advances, 4, eaau4029, 2018.
39. Ibid.

40. Mary Beth Day, David A. Hodell, Mark Brenner, Hazel J. Chapman, Jason H. Curtis, William F. Kenney, Alan L. Kolata, and Larry C. Peterson. "Paleoenvironmental History of the West Baray, Angkor (Cambodia)." PNAS, 109, 4: 1046–1051, 2012.
41. Ibid.
42. Damian Evans, Martin Polkinghorne, Roland Fletcher, David Brotherson, Tegan Hall, Sarah Klassen and Pelle Wijker. "Perspectives on the 'Collapse' of Angkor and the Khmer Empire." In book: The Angkorian World, Edited by Mitch Hendrickson, Miriam T. Stark and Damian Evans, 2023.
43. Ibid.
44. Yanxin Liu and Xiaodong Yan. "Comparison of Regional Droughts Impacts and Social Responses in the Historical China: A Case Study of the Han Dynasty." Physics and Chemistry of the Earth, 117, 102854, 2020.
45. Ibid.
46. Hans van Ess, H. What Role Did Climate Change Play in the Decline of the Tang Dynasty? In: Gehler, M., Rollinger, R., Strobl, P. (eds) The End of Empires. Universal- und kulturhistorische Studien. Studies in Universal and Cultural History. Springer VS, Wiesbaden, 2022.
47. Storozum, M. J., Zhen, Q., Xiaolin, R., Haiming, L., Yifu, C., Kui, F., & Haiwang, L. "The Collapse of the North Song Dynasty and the AD 1048–1128 Yellow River Floods: Geoarchaeological Evidence from Northern Henan Province, China." The Holocene, 28, 11: 1759–1770, 2018.
48. Tana Li. "The Mongol Yuan Dynasty and the Climate 1260–1360." In book: The Crisis of the 14th Century Teleconnections between Environmental and Societal Change? Publisher: Das Mittelalter. Perspektiven mediävistischer Forschung. Beihefte, 2019.
49. Yan Jun-Hui, Liu Hao-Long, Hao Zhi-Xin, Zhang Xue-Zhen, and Zheng Jing-Yun. "Climate Extremes Revealed by Chinese Historical Documents over the Middle and Lower Reaches of the Yangtze River in Winter 1620." Advances in Climate Change Research, 5, 3: 118–122, 2014.
50. Chris Harman. A People's History of the World. Verso, 2008. (P. 222).
51. Jingyun Zheng, Lingbo Xiao, Xiuqi Fang, Zhixin Hao, Quansheng Ge, and Beibei Li. "How Climate Change Impacted the Collapse of the Ming Dynasty." Climatic Change, 127: 169–182, 2014.
52. Ibid.
53. Jingyao Zhao, Hai Cheng, Yan Yang, Wen Liu, Haiwei Zhang, Xianglei Li, Hanying Li, Yassine Ait-Brahim, Carlos Pérez-Mejías, and Xiaoli Qu. "Role of the Summer Monsoon Variability in the Collapse of the Ming Dynasty: Evidence from Speleothem Records." Geophysical Research Letters, 48, e2021GL093071, 2021.
54. Ibid.

55. David Zhang, C. Y. Jim, George Lin, Yuan-Qing He, James J. Wang, and Harry F. Lee. "Climatic Change, Wars, and Dynastic Cycles in China over the Last Millennium." Climatic Change, 76: 459–477, 2006.
56. Ibid.
57. Harry F. Lee, David D. Zhang, Pei Qing, Jia Xin, and Ricci P. H. Yue. "Quantitative Analysis of the Impact of Droughts and Floods on Internal Wars in China over the Last 500 Years." Science China Earth Sciences, 60, 12: 2078–2088, 2017.
58. David D. Zhang, Jane Zhang, Harry F. Lee, and Yuan-qing He. "Climate Change and War Frequency in Eastern China over the Last Millennium." Human Ecology, 35, 4: 403–414, 2007.
59. Zhibin Zhang, Huidong Tian, Bernard Cazelles, Kyrre L. Kausrud, Achim Brauning, Fang Guo and Nils Chr Stenseth. "Periodic Climate Cooling Enhanced Natural Disasters and Wars in China during AD 10–1900." Proceedings of the Royal Society, 2010.
60. Ibid.
61. David Zhang and Harry Lee. "Changes in Climate and Secular Population Cycles in China, 1000 CE to 1911." Climate Research, 42, 3: 235–246, 2010.
62. Ibid.
63. David Zhang, Harry Lee, and Lincoln Fok. "Temperature, Aridity Thresholds, and Population Growth Dynamics in China over the Last Millennium." Climate Research, 39, 2: 131–147, 2009.

CHAPTER 11

One Little Climate Anomaly

From our discussions so far, it became clear that even though climatic conditions can be stable for some time deviations from the usual pattern can occur powerfully and abruptly. Once these changes occur, societies have no alternative but to adapt to the new normal or face drastic consequences. This recurrent story in human history occurred during the Little Ice Age. This chapter is dedicated to the discussion of the causes of this little climatic anomaly and the not-so-little consequences of that event.

1 The Little Ice Age

The Little Ice Age is a climate anomaly that occurred from the early fourteenth century through the mid-nineteenth century. This climatic event followed the Medieval Warm Period that occurred between the ninth and thirteenth centuries. The Medieval Warming occurred when warm conditions prevailed predominantly in the Northern Hemisphere during the Middle Ages.[1] This climatic anomaly also preceded another period of warming that began in the late nineteenth and early twentieth centuries.[2] The Little Ice Age, however, was a period of cooling when mean annual temperatures across the Northern Hemisphere declined relative to that during the millennium between 1000 and 2000 CE. Some even argued that[3] "[t]he Little Ice Age (LIA), which lasted from about 1250 to 1860 AD, was likely the coldest period of the last 8000 years." It is best known

S. Khalifa, *Climate Change, Economic Channels, and Historical Junctures*, https://doi.org/10.1007/978-3-031-91867-4_11

for its profound effect on Europe and the North Atlantic. During that time, these areas witnessed various conflicts, wars, famines, and diseases such that the[4] "cooling and climate variability of the LIA in the late sixteenth and seventeenth centuries came at a time of widespread upheavals and crises in many areas." These events continue to have their indelible mark on our life today.

2 Causes of the Little Ice Age

Scholars attempted to identify the causes of the Little Ice Age including proposals pertaining to changes in orbital cycles, in solar activity, in volcanic activity, in ocean circulation, and in world population. We discuss each one in detail.

2.1 Orbital Cycles

Some scholars propose changes in the orbital cycle of the Earth as a potential cause of the Little Ice Age. This particularly refers to the effect of changes in the Earth's orbital movement on its climate. The Earth's rotations around its axis, and its cycle around the sun, evolve over time due to gravitational interactions with other bodies in the Solar System. Orbital forcing is the effect on climate of these slow changes in the tilt of the Earth's axis and the shape of its orbit around the sun. The Earth's orbit, or its eccentricity, varies between nearly circular and slightly eccentric or elliptic. When it is more elongated, there is more variation in the distance between the Earth and the Sun. This implies alterations in the amount of solar radiation at different times of the year. The tilt of the Earth's axis, or its obliquity, also changes slightly. A greater tilt causes seasons to be more extreme. The Earth's precession, which is a slow wobble of its axis, affects climate by changing the timing of seasons and the amount of solar insolation in different hemispheres throughout the years. By controlling the amount of solar radiation reaching the Earth, these changes affect the temperature on the planet.

To provide evidence for the association between changes in orbital cycles and the Little Ice Age, some scientists present a synthesis of proxy temperatures from the Arctic covering the past 2000 years.[5] Their data indicates a pervasive cooling for the past two millennia which continued through the Middle Ages and into the Little Ice Age. This long-term trend was caused by[6] "the steady orbitally driven reduction in summer insolation." This cooling trend was reversed during the twentieth century.

2.2 *Solar Activity*

Other scientists point our attention to the potential role of changes in solar activity in bringing about the Little Ice Age. In this context, some scientists refer to the "Maunder Minimum" which is a period of a drastic decrease in sunspot activity that occurred between 1645 and 1715 CE.[7] The Maunder minimum coincided with the coldest part of the Little Ice Age. Decreased solar output due to fewer sunspots contributes to cooler temperatures on the planet since the[8] "Sun exhibits centennial-scale activity variations and sometimes encounters grand solar minimum when solar activity becomes extremely weak, and sunspots disappear for several decades. Such an extreme weakening of solar activity could cause severe climate, causing massive reductions in crop yields in some regions."

In this context, some scholars examine peat samples, or partially decomposed plant matter, from northwestern European bogs and show that climatic deteriorations during the Little Ice Age were driven by variations in solar activity.[9] Other scholars report a 1500-year reconstruction of climate and glaciation in the Andes using lake sediments.[10] The authors find four glacial advances between 1250 and 1810 CE which[11] "suggest that solar activity has exerted a strong influence on century-scale tropical climate variability during the late Holocene, modulating both precipitation and temperature. Surface cooling is enhanced at high altitudes by feedbacks involving water vapor, ultimately depressing temperatures in the Venezuelan Andes by -3.2+-1.4°C during the LIA."

2.3 *Volcanic Activity*

Some scholars posit that the abrupt onset of the Little Ice Age was triggered by volcanic activity. When a volcano erupts, its ash spread out into the atmosphere and can cover the entire planet. The ash cloud blocks out some of the incoming solar radiation, which leads to worldwide cooling. In this context, some scholars present records of ice-cap growth from Arctic Canada and Iceland showing that the[12] "onset of the LIA can be linked to an unusual 50-year-long episode with four large sulfur-rich explosive eruptions, each with global sulfate loading >60 Tg." These findings suggest that[13] "repeated explosive volcanism at a time when Earth's orbital configuration resulted in low summer insolation across the NH acted as a climate trigger, allowing Arctic Ocean Sea ice to expand. Increased sea ice export may have engaged self-sustaining sea-ice/ocean feedback unique to the northern North Atlantic region that maintained suppressed summer air temperatures for centuries after volcanic aerosols were removed from the atmosphere."

In addition, a climate model that was developed by climatologist Alan Robock to examine the factors that caused the Little Ice Age shows that[14] "[v]olcanic dust may have been an important cause of climatic fluctuations over the past 400 year." In another contribution, Alan Robock and Melissa Free show that[15] "solar forcings of less than 0.5% are too small to account for the cooling of the Little Ice Age. Volcanic forcings, in contrast, give climate responses comparable in amplitude to the changes of the Little Ice Age."

2.4 *Ocean Circulation*

Some scholars also propose a slowing in the thermohaline ocean circulation as a factor contributing to the Little Ice Age. Thermohaline circulation is a system of deep ocean currents driven by temperature and salinity. These circulations contribute to the distribution of heat in the planet, which impact global climate patterns, by transporting warm water toward the poles and cold water toward the equator. Disruptions to this circulation can cause climatic changes.

Examining the dynamics of the Medieval Climate Anomaly and the Little Ice Age by reconstructing changes in surface ocean circulation show that[16] "surface Atlantic meridional overturning circulation dynamics likely amplified the relatively warm conditions during the Medieval Climate Anomaly and the relatively cool conditions during the Little Ice Age within the North Atlantic sector." Along the same vein, climatologists Francois Lapointe and Raymond Bradley argue that the Little Ice Age was preceded by an exceptional intrusion of warm Atlantic water into the Nordic Seas in the late 1300s.[17] The warmer water[18] "led to the breakup of sea ice and calving of tidewater glaciers; weakening of the blocking anomaly in the late 1300s allowed the large volume of ice that had accumulated to be exported into the North Atlantic. This led to a weakening of the subpolar gyre SPG, setting the stage for the subsequent LIA." In another study, Francois Lapointe, Raymond Bradley, and other scholars present a reconstruction of Atlantic multidecadal variability for the past millennia and show that a reconstruction of[19] "sea ice concentration (SIC) for the coast of southeast Greenland highlights increased values from ~1400–1750 CE. This period coincides with the coldest SST anomalies in the North Atlantic during the LIA."

2.5 *World Population*

In addition to these factors, the decline in the world population was proposed as another factor for the Little Ice Age. In this context, some scientists propose that the human fingerprint on climate began earlier than widely acknowledged. This implies that human activities caused warming trends even before industrialization. Thus, the anthropogenic greenhouse era began much earlier than the industrial revolution which is typically considered the culprit behind the current global warming trend.[20] In this case, population contractions in Eurasia and the Americas decreased that anthropogenic effect and led to the cooling trend of the Little Ice Age. One of these factors that caused a decline in population at the time would be the Black Death, which is estimated to have killed a significant portion of Europeans. The timing[21] "of this 'Black Death' outbreak matches the −10 ppm CO_2 minimum," indicating that[22] "[p]lague-driven CO_2 changes were also a significant causal factor in temperature changes during the Little Ice Age (1300–1900 AD)."

European colonization of the Americas also caused the spread of diseases. Millions of people are estimated to have died due to the so-called Colombian Exchange. This could have contributed to a decrease in population leading to a cooling climate during the Little Ice Age. In this context, we need to discuss indications of the degree of mortality caused by the conquest of the Americas, in addition to evidence from scientific studies that this decline in the world population was a factor in the cooling that occurred during this specific episode of climate change.

To provide evidence for the connection between the decline in the indigenous population of the Americas and climate change, we refer to some studies which focus on the use of fire by these societies. Reconstructions of fire history from soil and sedimentary charcoal records indicate a sustained period of reduced biomass burning from 500 years before present.[23] This suggests that[24] "reduced burning in the Neotropics after 500 cal. yr BP represents part of a pan-American phenomenon associated with massive indigenous mortality, reduced human ignition, and abandonment of previously humanized landscapes. Land-use change in the Americas driven by demographic collapse may also help to explain the large and rapid decline in atmospheric CO_2 concentration during the LIA." Another study also shows a reduction in biomass burning after 500 years before present.[25] This is coincident with the collapse of the indigenous population due to the spread of diseases accompanying the European conquest of the Americas. Along the same vein, some scholars use paleoecological and archaeological evidence to show that the[26] "introduction of Old-World diseases led to recurrent epidemics and resulted in an unprecedented population crash throughout the Neotropics." This indicates that[27] "the post-Columbian carbon sequestration event was a significant forcing mechanism of Little Ice Age cooling."

After referring to these studies showing the connection between the decline in indigenous populations and climate change, we now return to some scholarly work that connects the conquest of the Americas with the high mortality at the time. In this context, the fatalities were ascribed to either the spread of diseases or mass killings of the indigenous populations. According to an estimate from the United Nations,[28] "disease claimed the lives of 80 to 100 million Indians by the first third of the seventeenth century. All these numbers are at best rough approximations, but their implications are clear: the epidemics killed about one out of every five people on earth." Walter Scheidel also discusses the dire consequences of the encounter between the Old and the New Worlds by stating:[29]

> By the end of medieval period, the gradual merging of the Old World's regional disease pools in the wake of commercial and eventually military contacts had ensured maximum coverage, causing many of these killer diseases to become endemic. By contrast, indigenous Americans enjoyed a less severe disease environment and lacked any prior exposure to these Old-World Scourges. Exploration and Conquest opened up what Alfred Crosby called the "Columbian Exchange," transatlantic contacts that swiftly introduced a plethora of infections to the Americas.

The diseases of the Old World were transported by the European invaders to eventually devastate indigenous communities and obliterate societies that flourished in the Americas before Christopher Columbus. For instance, transported diseases such as smallpox are known to have ravaged the Inca empire. In particular,[30] "[s]mallpox radiated throughout the empire like ink spreading through tissue paper. Millions of people simultaneously experienced its symptoms: high fever, vomiting, severe pain, oozing blisters everywhere on the body. Unable to number the losses, the Jesuit Martin de Murúa said that the toll was 'infinite thousands.'" There were epidemic outbreaks of other diseases as well besides smallpox. For instance, the[31] "Tawantinsuyu was invaded by other European pestilences, to which the Indians were equally susceptible. Typhus (probably) in 1546, influenza in 1558 together with smallpox, diphtheria in 1614, measles in 1618—all flensed the remains of the Inka culture. Taken as a whole, Dobyns thought, the epidemics must have killed nine out of ten of the inhabitants of Tawantinsuyu."

These diseases also wrecked the Aztec empire when the Spaniards conquered Mesoamerica. The disease[32] "raced to Tenochtitlan, leading city of the Mexica (Aztecs), where it laid waste to the metropolis and then the rest of the empire." When Hernán Cortés force was attacking Tenochtitlan, the outcome of battle was determined by disease rather than an imbalance of power. This is because[33]

> even this enormous force might not have overcome the empire if while Cortés was building his ships Tenochtitlan had not been swept by smallpox in the same pandemic that later wiped out Tawantinsuyu. Without any apparent volition by Cortés, the great city lost at least a third of its population to the epidemic, including Cuitlahuac. When Cortés and his Indian allies finally attacked, the Mexica resisted so fiercely despite their weakness that the siege has often been described as the costliest battle in history-casualty estimates range up to 100,000. Absent smallpox, it seems likely Cortés would have lost.

To put the effect of this calamity in perspective,[34] "25.2 million people lived in Central Mexico, an area of about 200,000 square miles. After Cortés, the population of the entire region collapsed. By 1620-25, it was 730,000, which is approximately 3 percent of its size at the time that he first landed." Historian William McNeill also posits that[35] "[r]ecent estimates, however, based on sampling of tribute lists, missionary reports and elaborate statistical arguments, have multiplied such earlier estimates tenfold and more, putting Amerindian population on the eve of the conquest at about one hundred million, with twenty-five to thirty million of this assignable to the Mexican and an approximately equal number to the Andean civilizations." Then, he adds:[36]

> Starting from such levels, population decay was catastrophic. By 1568, less than fifty years from the time Cortez inaugurated epidemiological as well as other exchanges between Amerindian and European populations, the population of Central Mexico had shrunk to about three million, i.e., to about one tenth of what had been there when Cortez landed. Decay continued, though at a reduced rate, for another fifty years. Population reached a low point of about 1.6 million by 1620.

Old World Diseases also afflicted the indigenous populations of North America. As an example, Hernando De Soto landed his army near Tampa Bay in Florida in 1539 CE. For four years, his force wandered through what is now Florida, Georgia, North Carolina, South Carolina, Tennessee, Alabama, Mississippi, Arkansas, Texas, and Louisiana. The inhabitants fought back the intruders who were searching for gold, wherever they went. After De Soto expedition left, no Europeans visited this part of the Mississippi for more than a century. In 1682 CE, Europeans appeared once more. They passed through the area where De Soto had encountered settlements, and found it deserted. Historians and anthropologists[37] "believe the culprit was disease."

3 Consequences of the Little Ice Age

The climate anomaly called the Little Ice Age had lots of political, economic, cultural, social, institutional, and other consequences. This event had far-reaching ramifications leading to challenges to the monarchy by landed nobility, challenges to the entire political status quo by common people, challenges to the economic status quo especially the feudal system, challenges to the religious establishment in the form of the Catholic Church, challenges between royal dynasties for dominance, challenges facing empires by subjugated nations seeking independence, and challenges to the minority groups by the dominant majorities. This was particularly the case during the "General Crisis of the Seventeenth Century," which was a period of inclement weather, crop failure, economic hardship, intergroup violence, and immense mortality. Some scholars show that[38] "cooling from A.D. 1560–1660 caused successive agro-ecological, socioeconomic, and demographic catastrophes, leading to the General Crisis of the Seventeenth Century." Some of these events which were global in scope are summarized as follows by historian Geoffrey Parker:[39]

> In the 1640s, Ming China, the most populous state in the world, collapsed; the Polish-Lithuanian Commonwealth, the largest state in Europe, disintegrated; much of the Spanish monarchy, the first global empire in history, seceded; and the entire Stuart monarchy rebelled—Scotland, Ireland, England, and its American colonies. In addition, just in the year 1648, a tide of urban rebellions began in Russia (the largest state in the world), and the Fronde Revolt paralyzed France (the most populous state in Europe); meanwhile, in Istanbul (Europe's largest city), irate subjects strangled Sultan Ibrahim, and in London, King Charles I went on trial for war crimes (the first head of state to do so). In the 1650s, Sweden and Denmark came close to revolution; Scotland and Ireland disappeared as autonomous states; the Dutch Republic radically changed its form of government; and the Mughal Empire, then the richest state in the world, experienced two years of civil war following the arrest, deposition, and imprisonment of its ruler.

These events occurred because cooling dampened agricultural output by shortening plant growing seasons and by shrinking the cultivated land area. The prolonged cooling affected crop growth and livestock survival. Although agricultural production decreased or stagnated in the cold climate, population continued to grow. This led to inflating grain prices and falling real incomes. These changes caused unbearable economic hardship for those from all walks of life, triggering social tensions. Rebellions with demands for political reforms followed, some of which turned into armed conflicts. In addition, the collapse of the infrastructure upon which agricultural production is predicated, because of these wars, left behind substantial damage to the carrying capacity of the land. This created feedback between lower agricultural yield and an endless cycle of violence. This is consistent with the hypothesis that climate change influenced conflict during that time by lowering agricultural productivity:[40]

> During this time, glaciers expanded, and seas froze as far south as present-day Turkey. Temperature declines were accompanied by increased variability in precipitation. Record levels of precipitation, which were preceded and/or followed by droughts, significantly reduced agricultural productivity, which in turn led to famines and conflicts that took various forms, including rebellions, uprisings, and foreign invasions. During the Little Ice Age, there was temporal and spatial variation in the intensity of cooling.

Cooling at the time also contributed to the spread of pathogens and disease vectors.[41] This is because[42] "[s]evere and protracted cold seasons lengthen the period of time spent in close indoor personal contact. Because the living quarters of Europe's working population were small and inadequate, and the standards of personal hygiene marginal, extended cold seasons intensified the risks of louse-borne and respiratory diseases. In addition, extended periods of drought during the warm seasons fostered the diffusion of the bacteria that cause dysentery and other enteric diseases." Chaos, social turbulence, and war pushed people to emigrate. Migration, coupled with individuals' deteriorating health due to poor nutrition, also facilitated the spread of disease epidemics. In addition, when[43] "the harvest failed-or food prices soared for whatever reason-many poor people took to the roads in search of food or charity. They crowded into towns or cities where charitable resources were greater than those in the country; or, if a city closed its gates against the flood of vagrants, they pushed into the overcrowded slums outside the city walls. Diseases that were present in non-epidemic form blossomed into epidemics and were diffused from one locality to another."

When peaks in fatalities occurred, due to conflict, disease, and famine, the annual population growth rate dropped dramatically causing a substantial decline in the agricultural workforce. The effect of this crisis on the huge decline in population in Europe varied from one area to another where[44]

> [i]n the Mediterranean region, famines in the 1590s and plague in 1599, from 1629 to 1631, and from 1647 to 1650 joined other factors in reducing the population of Italy between 1600 and 1650 by about 16 percent, and that of Spain by 14 percent (concentrated in Castile). In Central Europe, the Thirty Years' War created a disorder that intensified every manner of hazard to life. Recent estimates show the lands of the Holy Roman Empire suffering a population decline of 35 to 40 percent. Elsewhere, population growth slowed or stopped but did not decline absolutely; the population of Europe as a whole declined by approximately 5 percent in this period.

The drastic decline in population had a significant adverse effect on city size and urban growth in Europe. Climate change, thus, affected city size through the channels of agricultural productivity, mortality, and migration. This is because cooler temperatures increased mortality, decreased agricultural yields, and motivated migration.[45]

3.1 Challenges to the Religious Status Quo

3.1.1 The Thirty Years' War

Some of the episodes of social instability during the General Crisis developed into armed conflicts. The most important of which is the Thirty Years' War, which was one of the longest and most destructive conflicts in European history lasting from 1618 to 1648 CE. The war is traditionally viewed as a continuation of the conflict within Christendom inflamed by the Protestant Reformation in the sixteenth century, which was the most serious challenge to the Catholic Church. The ensued bloody confrontations between the Catholics and Protestants threatened the delicate balance of power in Europe. The Peace of Augsburg signed in 1555 CE attempted to address these entanglements by allowing the rulers to choose either Lutheranism or Roman Catholicism as the official confession of their state. This landmark settlement tried to preclude the recurrence of conflict by delineating the political boundaries between the two faiths. This arrangement, however, was undermined by the expansion of Protestantism into areas previously designated as Catholic. Another factor was the emergence and growth of other persuasions not acknowledged by the peace settlement, especially Calvinism. This was the trigger of a long chapter of bloodshed in European history.

While differences over faith and imperial authority were critical factors in causing the war, the[46] "war was a religious war in the sense that all parties included faith and church in the common good they sought to defend. However, this general objective had little bearing on decisions for war or peace. The war was not a confessional war. The population did not divide neatly along sectarian lines, nor did faith dictate the choice of allies."

The scope and extent of the war were instead driven by the contest for European dominance between the dynasties in Europe. The outbreak of the war is typically traced to 1618 CE when the Holy Roman Emperor and King of Bohemia, Ferdinand II, attempted to impose Catholicism on his subjects. The Protestant nobles of both Bohemia and Austria rose up in rebellion. Although Ferdinand II and his forces suppressed the insurgency, it drew the involvement of other countries such as Netherlands, Spain, Denmark, Sweden, Poland, and France. The outcome was to turn a local dispute into a broader European drama.

In the heartland of Europe, the different denominations vying for dominance led to a Gordian tangle of alliances as they summoned foreign powers to assist them. Overall, the struggle was between the Holy Roman

Empire, led by the Habsburgs, and a network of Protestant towns and principalities that depended primarily on anti-Catholic powers. However, that was not to be the end of it. Although Holy Roman Emperors were elected, the position had been held by the House of Habsburg since 1440 CE. Thus, a parallel contest involved the rivalry between the Bourbons of France and the Habsburgs of the Holy Roman Empire and the Spanish crown. After 1635 CE, Europe became one wide theater in a struggle between France, supported by Sweden and others, and the Holy Roman Emperor, allied with Spain and others. The number of casualties for the war was in the millions, despite the lack of accurate estimates. This episode is summarized as follows:[47]

> Conflict in the Holy Roman Empire, especially in the Habsburg lands, over religion and over the power of the emperor provoked a civil war in Bohemia in 1618. The Bohemian war both resurrected and created a network of alliances which caused the conflict to continue into the 1620s. The opportunities offered by the disruption in Germany led the Danes to invade in 1625, and the Swedes and French to intervene in the 1630s, which continued the war by bringing in fresh combatants. The result was a conflict that could not be controlled by the Bohemians and the emperor, who had begun it. They were not allowed to extricate themselves until they had completely exhausted themselves and everyone else; as fitting compensation, the Bohemians and the emperor were important losers.

This war was concluded with the Peace of Westphalia in 1648 CE. When the contending powers finally convened in the German province to end the bloodshed, the balance of power in Europe had been decisively altered. Spain lost the Netherlands and its dominant position in western Europe, France became the main Western power, Sweden had control of the Baltic Sea, the United Netherlands was recognized as an independent entity, and the member states of the Holy Roman Empire were granted full sovereignty. The traditional notion of an empire of Europe, headed spiritually by a pope and temporally by an emperor, was permanently abandoned. The essential structure of modern Europe as a community of sovereign states was established as a final outcome of this war.

There are studies that associate this war with changing climatic conditions that[48] "began with a bad winter in 1572-3 and deepened after 1591 into what has been labelled the Little Ice Age lasting in the western hemisphere into the nineteenth century. Previously stable conditions became the exception as winters grew longer and colder, freezing rivers and causing the Alpine glaciers to advance into inhabited regions, in some cases burying entire communities." This affected European people and economies in so many ways such that the[49] "quality as well as the quantity of food production declined, leading to the continent-wide great dearth of 1594-7."

Crop failures caused famine and a drastic decline in consumption. Malnutrition caused a decrease in female fertility and an increase in infant mortality. This dire situation also led to an increase in farmers' default on debt and disruptions to credit arrangements, an increase in the cost of food and in price inflation, a coinage debasement that contributed to hyperinflation, a considerable increase in unemployment and job loss, a decline in overall living standards, and a sharper increase in the discrepancies between classes. The Thirty Years' War[50] "is on such analyses seen as arising from such worsening circumstances. The specific evidence is simply the coincidence of the outbreak of the Bohemian Revolt and the resumption of the Hispano-Dutch war with the peak of the trade, production and currency problems around 1618-21."

3.1.2 The Eighty Years' War

The Thirty Years' War occurred in the wider context of the Eighty Years' War. The Eighty Years' War, or the Dutch Revolt, was primarily an armed conflict between the Dutch rebels and the Spanish Habsburg rule from 1568 to 1648 CE. This was such a long bloody chapter in European history such that[51] "[t]he Dutch Revolt lasted longer than any other uprising in European history-from the iconoclastic fury in August 1566 to the Peace of Munster in January 1648; and it involved more con fighting than any other war of modern times-from April 1572 to April 1607 (with only six months' cease-fire in 1577) and from 1621 to June I647. Its economic, social, and political costs were enormous."

The Habsburg Netherlands was a political entity covering the entirety of the Low Countries comprising present-day Netherlands, Belgium, Luxembourg, and some parts of France. It was held by the Holy Roman Empire House of Habsburg. Their rule began in 1482 CE when the last Valois-Burgundy ruler of the Netherlands died. Upon termination of the Burgundian State, these lands were inherited by the House of Habsburg when Charles V was crowned both King of Spain and Holy Roman Emperor.

Charles V aspired to counter the Protestant Reformation and keep his subjects loyal to the Catholic Church. He was succeeded by his son, Philip II, who continued the anti-heresy and centralization policies of his father. This caused growing indignation among the nobility and commoners of those lands. This exasperation first translated into peaceful protests but later transformed into violent demonstrations by the Calvinists in the summer of 1566 CE. These events are known as the Iconoclastic Fury. The Habsburg Governor feared insurrection and offered some concessions to the Calvinists. But in late 1566 CE and early 1567 CE, the first battles between the insurgents and Habsburg forces took place commencing what would become known as the Eighty Years' War.

King Philip II of Spain deployed his forces and initially regained control over lots of the rebel-held territories. However, there were widespread mutinies in the Spanish army. Under the exiled William of Orange who was the leader of the rebellion, the Catholic and Protestant-dominated provinces sought to establish peace while jointly opposing the King's hegemony. This Pacification of Ghent, signed in 1576 CE, was a declaration by which the northern and southern provinces of the Low Countries decided to put aside their doctrinal differences and called for the expulsion of the Spanish troops from their land, the restoration of provincial prerogatives, and an end to the persecution of Calvinists and others.

But the rebellion failed to sustain itself. Nonetheless, the Union of Utrecht, representing some united provinces in northern Netherlands, continued their resistance. The Union ultimately proclaimed the 1581 Act of Abjuration, which was a declaration of independence by some of these provinces from their allegiance to Philip II. This laid the foundations of the Dutch Republic which received diplomatic recognition from France and England by 1596 CE.

Facing a stalemate, the two sides agreed to a twelve-year truce in 1609 CE. When the truce expired in 1621 CE, war resumed as part of the broader Thirty Years' War. An end to this conflict was attained in 1648 CE with the Peace of Münster, which was part of the Peace of Westphalia. According to this accord, Spain retained the southern part of Netherlands and recognized the northern Dutch Republic as an independent entity.

Such conflict was so complicated in nature that it affected so many parts of the world at the time. The Dutch Revolt[52] "which began among a few thousand refugees in north-western Europe, had spread until it affected the lives of millions of people and brought about the collapse of the greatest world empire seen. In the 1640s there was fighting in Ceylon, Japan, and Indonesia, in southern and western Africa, on the Indian, Pacific and Atlantic Oceans, and of course in Brazil and the Low Countries. It all stemmed from the revolt of the Netherlands. The struggle had become, so to say, the First World War."

3.2 *Challenges to the Political Status Quo*

The General Crisis was also a period of great challenges to incumbent authority and the political status quo. These challenges were undertaken by the nobility in some cases, or by the commoners in others, to protest the absolute authority of the monarchy. Historian Eric Hobsbawm states that[53] "the 17th century was one of social revolt both in Western and Eastern Europe. This clustering of revolutions, has led some historians to see something like a general social-revolutionary crisis in the middle of the century." In this context, it was[54] "a crisis in the relations between society and the state." This section discusses some examples of the challenges that faced the political status quo and others that were able to change it for good. We particularly focus on political developments in France and England only because of their broad and far-reaching implications that ultimately went beyond the borders of these two countries.

3.2.1 The French Fronde

The Fronde was a series of civil wars in France that lasted between 1648 and 1653 CE. The government of King Louis XIV confronted the combined opposition of the princes, the nobility, the provincial appellate courts or Parlements, as well as the commoners. The Parlements were judicial entities consisting of appellate judges, who served as the courts of final appeal of the judicial system. They typically wielded power over a wide array of issues, particularly taxation. Laws and edicts issued by the Crown were not official until the parlements bestowed their consent by publishing them.

The dispute started when the government issued fiscal edicts, most of which were aimed at increasing taxation. The timing of the Fronde directly after the Peace of Westphalia in 1648 CE, which ended the Thirty Years' War, was not a coincidence. The pressure that led to the standoff came in the form of increased taxes as the Crown needed to recuperate from its massive expenditures in that war. The cost of the Thirty Years' War constrained the government from the ability to raise funds by traditional means. The Parlements questioned the constitutionality of the King's actions and sought to check his powers. The insurrection that ensued initially aimed to protect the traditional liberties from royal encroachments and to defend the established powers of the Parlements. These include the prerogative to limit the king's power by rejecting royal decrees on some occasions. Thus, the Fronde began[55]

> when the sovereign judicial courts of the capital led by the Parlement met in joint session to present twenty-seven reform demands to the king and his government. A popular uprising nine months later drove the young king, Louis XIV, and his mother, Anne--of Austria, the queen regent, from the palace of the Louvre in the middle of the night to take refuge at nearby Saint-Germain-en-Laye, where they remained for nearly a year. The judges were left in control of the city. The demands of the Paris high courts and the king's flight triggered revolts in turn by the provincial parlements of Aix, Rouen, and Bordeaux, and these protests became the first stage of the Fronde known as the Judicial Frond.

This conflict broke into an outright war in 1649 CE. The blockade of Paris was not sufficient for the Crown to force the surrender of the Parlement, which was supported by Parisian leaders and some nobility. Faced with the combined turmoil in the provinces and the ongoing war with Spain, the government negotiated the Peace of Rueil which confirmed the concessions to the Parlement. This was considered a tactical success for the King and his allies.

This Judicial Fronde was followed by another one of the nobles. However, the incentives for the nobles in the confrontation were different. The nobles rebelled[56] "because they were dissatisfied with the ministerial governments of Richelieu and Mazarin. They wanted peace with Spain, and they suffered financially from royal tax policies reducing their landed incomes and from the decline in royal patronage accompanying the Habsburg War." This led to the Nobles Fronde.

The armed conflict started when the King's cousin, the Great Condé, who was also a military commander for the government in its war against the Parlement was disappointed in his aspirations for political power. He became rebellious and was arrested in 1650 CE. His friends and allies took up arms in a series of uprisings in the provinces, called the first war of the princes. By the end of 1650 CE, the government was able to deal successfully with these insurgencies. In reaction, the supporters of Condé and the Parisian party, called the Old Fronde, joined forces to bring about the release of Condé and the dismissal of the Chief Minister Cardinal Mazarin. However, the government exploited the divisions among the Frondeurs and issued an order to indict Condé. This was an act that caused Condé to find no alternative but to go to war again, called the second war of the princes which lasted from 1651 to 1653 CE. Even though Condé entered Paris in 1652 CE, his position soon became untenable. He eventually lost the support of the Parisian bourgeoisie and the Parlement. In the face of opposition, Condé fled from Paris to the Spanish Netherlands. The King entered Paris in triumph afterward. With many of the insurgent nobles in exile and a weakened Parlement, the Fronde ended in a clear victory for the court.

There are many factors behind the Fronde which was[57] "a collective protest against a long foreign war (France had been fighting Spain and the Holy Roman Emperor since 1635) and an increasingly heavy burden of taxation. There were secondary, but important, objections to continuing the foreign war in a period of royal minority (the infant Louis XIV succeeded his father as king on May 14, 1643) and the autocratic style of government exercised by Cardinal Mazarin as chief minister and favorite of the queen regent, Anne of Austria." These, in addition to other issues such as[58] "the composition of the ministeriat, the power of the government to levy taxes at will during a royal minority, and the administrative and fiscal consequences of a long war on the French office-holders and tax-payers."

The Fronde represented the final attempt of the French nobility to confront the King. However, these efforts to check the power of the monarchy ended in vain. In the long term, the Fronde served to cement royal control as an absolutist monarchy. In hindsight, this could have paved the way for the final overthrow of the monarchy after the French Revolution. By revealing the inability of either the nobility or the Parlement to offer effective leadership, the people found no alternative but to take matters in their own hands. By showing the potential of rebellion against the monarchy, it displayed the power of defiance as a way, for people, out of their predicament. By strengthening the position of the monarchy, it led the monarchs to exercise absolute power, which caused people to find no other way but to do away with the monarchy altogether. According to some, the French Fronde was the harbinger of the French Revolution.

3.2.2 *The French Revolution*

The French Revolution was a period of upheaval in France that began with the Estates General of 1789 CE and ended with the coup of 18 Brumaire in 1799 CE and the formation of the French Consulate. The revolution was the outcome of several complications that culminated in social, economic, financial, and political crises. The resistance to its proposals by the ruling elite in the *ancien régime*, combined with the indecisive policy of Louis XVI and his cabinet, caused the state to be unable to contain the crisis.

First, there was an economic crisis. Although the eighteenth century was a period of affluence, the benefits were distributed unevenly across social classes. Those whose income derived from agricultural activities, collecting rents and interest, and from trade in goods from France's colonies flourished.[59] On the other hand, the living standards of wage laborers and farmers on rented land fell. Tax data and social tables show that[60] "inequality during the eighteenth century was large but decreased during the revolutionary period (1790-1815)."

Second, there was a financial crisis. As the landed nobility and the church clergy benefited from exemptions, the tax burden fell primarily on the farmers. In this case, taxes were not collected from those who have but were grabbed with gusto from those who have not. Thus, tax collection was not adequate to finance the government excessive spending especially during war years. This is why France funded the Anglo-French War of 1778–1783 CE mostly through loans. Even as the peace resumed, the monarchy continued to borrow heavily. This culminated in a serious debt crisis.[61]

These were followed by a political crisis when a land tax was proposed by the finance minister. The proposal was shunned by the nobility and then by the Parlement. The notables and the Parlement argued that the proposed taxes could only be approved by an Estates General, which was a legislative assembly that represented the three estates of the realm: the clergy, the nobility, and the commoners. The conflict between the crown and the Parlement became a political crisis. Both sides issued a series of public statements declaring their stance and denouncing the position of the other. The government argued that it was combating privilege. The Parlement argued that it was defending the prerogatives of the nation.

In September 1788 CE, the Parlement of Paris ruled that the Estates General should convene in the same form as it last did in 1614 CE. That included the clergy, the nobility, and the commoners or the Third Estate.

This meant that the three Estates would convene and vote separately, and votes would be counted by Estate. In May 1789 CE, the Estates General gathered at Versailles. The Third Estate declared itself to be the National Assembly of the country and that existing taxes were illegal. Shaken by this challenge to his authority, the King conceded to some of their demands. He announced a series of reforms and stated that no new taxes or loans would be implemented without the consent of the Estates General. At the end of the session, the Third Estate declined to leave the hall and declared their intention not to disperse until a constitution had been drafted. The[62] "Third Estate, particularly, the merchants, businessmen, professionals, and artisans, who all had demands for greater power, saw these developments as evidence of their increasing clout."

Confronted with popular protests and mutinies in his armed guards, Louis XVI capitulated on June 7 of that year. On July 14, the mob attacked the Bastille prison. This was viewed as a symbol of the *ancien régime*, where many people had languished behind bars. The Storming of the Bastille led to a series of radical steps by the National Assembly including the abolition of feudalism, the state control over the Catholic Church in France, and a declaration of rights. The following years were dominated by strife for political control, exacerbated by an economic depression. This was also followed by the Revolutionary Wars which were a series of conflicts that lasted from 1792 until 1802 CE that pitted France against Great Britain, Austria, Prussia, Russia, and other countries.

Following the outbreak of the French Revolutionary Wars, armed revolutionaries stormed the Tuileries Palace in an insurrection in August 1792 CE. Afterward, the monarchy was abolished and replaced by the French First Republic. Louis XVI was subsequently executed in January 1793 CE. After another insurrection in June 1793 CE, the constitution was suspended and effective political power passed to the Committee of Public Safety. About 16,000 people were executed, while many thousands more died, in the Reign of Terror which ended in July 1794 CE. Weakened by external threats and internal instability, the Republic was replaced in 1795 CE by the Directorate which sought to restore stability by resurrecting the principles of the rebellion. In 1799 CE, Napoleon Bonaparte seized power in the military coup of 18 Brumaire. This is generally seen as the event that marks the end of the revolutionary period.

Some studies refer to the potential effect of climate in inciting the French Revolution. Around 1770 CE, a period of abrupt cooling took over the Northern Atlantic,[63] "wreaking immediate havoc on shipping, transportation and agriculture." In 1775 CE, severe grain shortages caused by successive years of poor harvest led to a spike in grain prices and the cost of bread. These issues led to riots throughout France because bread was an essential source of food for common people. This was especially problematic considering the population explosion at the time since[64] "There were by the most conservative estimates 5 to 6 million more mouths to feed in 1789 than there had been in 1720." This event was dubbed the Flour War of 1775 CE.

Compounding the worsening climate, the Laki Volcano in Iceland erupted in 1783 CE. Over a few months period, it ejected 120 million tons of sulfur dioxide into the atmosphere. Across northern Europe, the sun could not cut through the persistent haze. Some scholars find that the[65] "1783–1784 CE Laki eruption in Iceland was one of the largest, in terms of the mass of SO_2 emitted, high-latitude eruptions in the last millennium." In addition to the fatalities caused by the foul air, the eruption caused the climate to become extremely volatile in the 1780s. After a long spell of cooling, the summer of 1783 CE was suddenly the hottest on record such that[66] "[w]hile summer cooling is the expected climate response to volcanic eruptions, early instrumental and documentary historical records suggest the summer of 1783 was actually abnormally warm in Europe." The scorching summer gave way to a freezing winter, followed by a warm spring that caused the snow to melt leading to extensive flooding. This pandemonium upended the lives of the French, destroying crops, killing livestock, and creating a vicious cycle of hunger and poverty. All these factors could have driven the population to the brink.

In addition to these events, a severe drought in the spring of 1788 CE caused serious damage to staple crops and an ensuing famine. To examine whether the 1788 CE drought contributed to the outbreak of farmers' rebellions during the French Revolution, climate economist Maria Waldinger constructs a community-level data set with information on local drought severity and peasant uprisings in 1789 CE.[67] The study finds that communities with severe drought conditions more often experienced peasant uprisings against the feudal system. The peasants were[68] "enraged by the fact that they—many close to starvation—owed excessive taxes to their landlords. Their landlords, in contrast, were exempt from all taxation and also enjoyed numerous other political and economic privileges. The peasants attacked their landlords' castles and burned charters enshrining these privileges."

In this context, grain shortages sent prices skyrocketing. With all disposable income going to buy bread, consumer demand for other commodities cratered, driving the shaky economy into a severe downturn. To put the effect of such events in context,[69] "the poorer classes, 95% of whose diet consisted of bread and cereals and which before the drought had to spend about 55% of their earnings on bread, were forced by the famine conditions of the first half of 1789 to spend now 85% and over of their income on this staple food. The severity of the conditions in France will be appreciated if it is borne in mind that the poorer classes constituted nearly 90% of the population."

On July 13, 1789, one of the worst hailstorms in recorded history swept across France. The storm pummeled fields and destroyed orchards and vineyards. In this event,[70] "Torrents of rain fell in cascades and a great barrage of huge hailstones crashed down. Hailstones the size of chicken's eggs and larger pulverized whole fields of wheat and tore through vineyards, trees were stripped of their leaves, whole villages were wrecked with roofs, and windows smashed. Farmworkers ran for what little shelter they could find. Many horses panicked and were killed in the onslaught. The storm is thought to have unleashed 400,000 tonnes of hailstones." This hailstorm[71] "destroyed much of the meagre supplies of grain for Paris and the price of bread rose. It was a dire political and economic situation, and with most of the population facing food shortages it helped to sow the seeds for the French Revolution in 1789."

When the Estates General convened in Versailles in 1789 CE, the population of France had endured long difficult years due to these destructive climatic fluctuations. The traumatized population of France were already on the edge. When rumors of a reactionary conspiracy hit the streets of Paris, the alarmed and angry population leapt to tear down the Bastille, marking the beginning of the revolutionary period.

There is no doubt that the French Revolution was a milestone in human history that left political, economic, social, cultural, institutional, and legal legacies that we are living with till the present day. These include the emergence of national identity and the idea of nation states, the ascent of the middle class, the separation of church and state, the establishment of civil liberties, the end of inherited privileges, institutional reforms, and many more. The ideals of the revolution spread far and away since the[72] "leaders of the French Revolution and, subsequently, Napoleon exported the revolution to these lands, destroying absolutism, ending feudal land relations, abolishing guilds, and imposing equality before the law." In examining the long-lasting consequences of the revolution on Europe, the evidence[73] "points to more rapid economic growth as proxied by urbanization in areas that underwent the radical institutional reforms brought by the French Revolution, especially after 1850. We also presented additional evidence suggesting that the primary channel of influence of French occupation was likely to have been the institutional reforms of the Revolution."

3.2.3 *The English Civil War*

The English Civil War refers to a series of conflicts between Royalists and Parliamentarians from 1642 to 1651 CE. The conflict consisted of the First English Civil War and the Second English Civil War.

The civil war broke out several years after the death of Queen Elizabeth I. The Queen had been succeeded by her cousin, King James VI of Scotland, who was coronated as James I of England in 1603 CE. This created the first union between the Scottish and English thrones. As King of Scots since 1583 CE, James had grown accustomed to Scotland's weak institutional traditions. Upon assuming power in England, the new King was affronted by the constraints the English Parliament had attempted to place on him. By the succession of his son in 1625 CE, Charles I followed his father's dream in hoping to unite England, Scotland, and Ireland into one kingdom. English Parliamentarians were suspicious of such an attempt, fearing that this entity could destroy old traditions that had constrained the English monarchy.

The First English Civil War was fought primarily over the correct balance of power between the Parliament and Charles I. The war started in 1642 CE to assert the parliament's right to participate in the political policy-making process, not to abolish the monarchy. In June of 1642 CE, the English Lords and Commons approved a list of proposals known as the Nineteen Propositions. In these demands, the Parliament sought a larger share in the governance of the kingdom. Before the end of the month, King Charles I refused to make concessions and rebuffed their demands. On the one side, the King and his supporters fought for traditional governance in church and state. On the other, most Parliamentarians initially took up arms to defend what they saw as a traditional balance of power in church and state.

With one defeat after another, and little opportunity to replenish resources, the King sought shelter with a Scottish army in 1646 CE. Charles I was eventually handed over to the English by the Scots and was promptly imprisoned. The war ended with the defeat of the Royalists with the king in custody. This marked the end of the First English Civil War.

Charles I, however, took advantage of the deflection of attention away from him to negotiate a secret treaty with the Scots promising church reforms. Under this agreement, the Scots undertook to invade England on Charles's behalf to restore him to the throne. A Scottish invasion along with a series of Royalist uprisings throughout England ensued. The Parliamentarians under the leadership of Oliver Cromwell engaged the Scots at the Battle of Preston which ended in a victory for the former's troops. This victory marked the end of the Second English Civil War. Royalist defeat in 1648 CE led to the execution of Charles I in 1649 CE. The Parliament of Scotland proclaimed his eldest surviving son, Charles II, King of Scotland in the same year.

Afterward, England entered the period known as the English Interregnum or Commonwealth with a government eventually led by Oliver Cromwell. Cromwell defeated Charles II in the subsequent Anglo-Scottish war in 1651 CE. Both Ireland and Scotland were incorporated into the Commonwealth, and Britain became a unified state. A political crisis occurred after Cromwell's death in 1658 CE. This resulted in the restoration of the monarchy in 1660 CE, and Charles II was invited to come back to Britain from exile to serve as King. These events paved the way for the Glorious Revolution.

3.2.4 The Glorious Revolution

Charles II eventually became the King of England, Scotland, and Ireland from the restoration of the monarchy until his death in 1685 CE. After his death, his younger brother James II sat on the throne. The Glorious Revolution is the sequence of events that led to the deposition of King James II in 1688 CE. Despite his Catholicism, James II became King with widespread backing from the Protestants of England and Scotland, as well as the largely Catholic Ireland. The mostly Protestant gentry in these domains were willing to accept James' personal beliefs so long as he preserved the primacy of the Protestant Church.

Although his subsequent actions eroded this initial backing, it was not until 1688 CE that dissatisfaction turned into a political crisis. When his policies started to thwart the established status quo, he alienated his supporters in England and Scotland and destabilized Ireland. The birth of his son also eliminated his Protestant eldest daughter Mary from the line of succession as heir presumptive. The prospect of a Catholic dynasty undermined James' political clout and pushed a few of his opponents to seek external support in ousting him.

His eldest daughter, Mary, married her Protestant cousin William III of Orange who was the stadtholder of the provinces of the Dutch Republic. Claiming to be responding only to an invitation to protect Protestantism, the Dutch invaded England under the couple's leadership. As William's army advanced upon London, the army of James II disintegrated. The latter was eventually defeated and sent into exile. In 1689 CE, the parliament made William and Mary monarchs of England, Ireland, and Scotland. These events had drastic consequences as[74] "[w]ith a king of undoubted legitimacy squeezed out and a new, albeit related monarch installed and recognized by Parliament, the transaction shook government, nation and church alike."

Scholars argue that the Glorious Revolution had far-reaching ramifications for it allowed the creation of institutions that generated incentives for investment, trade, innovation, and industrialization. These include protection of property, enforcing patents, maintaining the rule of law, removing barriers to economic activities, building infrastructure, and others. Those changes were conducive to the eventual industrialization according to Nobel Laureates Daron Acemoglu and James Robinson who assert that these[75] "foundations decisively changed incentives for people and impelled the engines of prosperity, paving the way for the Industrial Revolution." They also add:[76]

> The Industrial Revolution was manifested in every aspect of the English economy. There were major improvements in transportation, metallurgy, and steam power. But the most significant area of innovation was the mechanization of textile production and the development of factories to produce these manufactured textiles. This dynamic process was unleashed by the institutional changes that flowed from the Glorious Revolution. This was not just about the abolition of domestic monopolies, which had been achieved by 1640, or about different taxes or access to finance. It was about a fundamental reorganization of economic institutions in favor of innovations and entrepreneurs, based on the emergence of more secure and efficient property rights.

They further elaborate that this was the prelude for this radical transformation since[77] "[t]he Industrial Revolution started and made its biggest strides in England because of her uniquely inclusive economic institutions.

These in turn were built on the foundations laid by the inclusive political institutions brought about by the Glorious Revolution. It was the Glorius Revolution that strengthened and rationalized property rights, improved financial markets, undermined state-sanctioned monopolies in foreign trade, and removed barriers to the expansion of industry. It was the Glorious Revolution that made the political system open and responsive to the economic needs and aspirations of society."

3.3 *Challenges to the Economic Status Quo*

Some scholars argue that the General Crisis saw challenges to the economic status quo in the form of the feudal system. Feudalism flourished in Medieval Europe as a way of structuring society by working out the relationship between land holding and labor service. In a feudal system, a peasant known as a vassal was granted a piece of land in return for serving a landlord. Vassals were expected to perform various duties in exchange for their own fiefs, or pieces of land. Some scholars describe this system as follows[78]

> At the turn of the fourteenth century, Europe had a feudal order, an organization of society that first emerged in Western Europe after the collapse of the Roman Empire. It was based on a hierarchical relationship between the king and the lords beneath him, with the peasants at the bottom. The king owned the land, and he granted it to the lords in exchange for military services. The lords then allocated land to peasants, in exchange for which peasants had to perform extensive unpaid labor and were subject to many fines and taxes.

Some argue that the challenges to this economic status quo created an opportune circumstance to drastically change the mode of production in its entirety paving the way for industrialization. For instance, historian Eric Hobsbawm considers that industrialization was potentially an outcome of the events that occurred during the General crisis since the[79] "main result of the 17th century crisis on industrial organization was to eliminate the crafts, and with them the craft-dominated town from large-scale production and to establish the 'putting-out' system, controlled by men with capitalist horizons and operated by easily exploitable rural labour. Signs of more ambitious industrial developments, 'manufactories' and the like, are not lacking, especially in the last third of the century, and in industries like mining, metallurgy and shipbuilding which required a fairly large-scale of operation, but even without these the industrial changes are striking."

This "putting-out system" was a new production system where agents provided raw materials to households who then processed them into finished goods at home. Thus, work in this system is contracted by an agent to subcontractors who complete the project from home. Finished products were returned to the agents for payment by piecework or on a wage basis. This system differed from the handicraft system of home production where the workers purchased materials, produced items, and sold final products themselves.

This newly introduced decentralized domestic system allowed production to expand and to react quickly to market demand. The system was suited to those times because workers were able to avoid commuting from home to work given the decrepit road conditions and the widespread insecurity. This in addition to the fact that these workers also spend a lot of time in their farms or on performing household tasks. Thus, workers had some flexibility to be able to balance farm duties and household chores with the putting-out work. In addition, this system allowed the agents access to a wider workforce in rural areas without having to incur the additional costs of having the workers placed in one location. This changed the economic system to a new one. Chris Harman concludes that this new system was not to be confused with capitalism, even though it seemed to have paved the way for such an economic system eventually:[80]

> The putting out system relied on people who could still regard themselves as their own bosses. But it was step towards fully developed capitalism. The merchant had moved from simply buying and selling goods to worrying about their production, and the direct producers could no longer obtain a livelihood unless a portion of their output went to the merchant as profit. What is more, both the merchant and the producer were increasingly subject to the dictates of markets over which they had no control. Dispersed rural producers lacked the power of the town guilds to limit output and control prices. They had no choice but to keep abreast of new cost-cutting techniques introduced by other producers. The feudal organization of production was giving way to a quite different organization, in which competition led to investment and investment intensified competition. For the moment, this only occurred in a few gaps within the old system. But it was like an acid, eating into and changing the world around it.

These changes are also argued to have been a preamble to wide-scale industrialization and a prelude to the great divergence since this[81] "'industrious revolution' unfolded over an extended period of time, but its *locus classicus* in time and in space was mid-seventeenth-century northwestern Europe. These household structures, urban networks, political institutions, and trading opportunities combined in a historical moment of decentering to bring about a concentration of economic activity and a further differentiation of institutions that soon consolidated into a 'great divergence' that would long endure." The great divergence refers to the divergent economic trajectories of Western Europe and its offshoots from the rest of the world.

3.4 *Challenges to the Social Status Quo*

The economic difficulties of the General Crisis, causing poverty and indescribable hardships, occurred at the same time. Although communities had some contingency plans, they did not always prove effective. Thus, the afflicted often lashed out through waves of violence. Finding a scapegoat in such circumstances is a common way of expressing frustration with unfavorable conditions that are beyond one's control. Evidence from several studies indicates that surges in aggression against marginalized groups, who were accused of being responsible for the Little Ice Age, coincide with years of particularly cold weather. One example of the violent scapegoating during that time was the resurgence of witchcraft trials. Witches were blamed for the change in climate that could not be otherwise explained at the time. This witch-hunt[82] "coincides with a period of lower-than-average temperature known to climatologists as the 'little ice age.'" When the causes behind changes in weather were largely a mystery,[83] "people would have searched for a scapegoat in the face of deadly changes in weather patterns. 'Witches' became target for blame because there was an existing cultural framework that both allowed their persecution and suggested that they could control the weather." Thus, the witch-hunts[84] "took place at the various peaks of the Little Ice Age because a part of society held the witches directly responsible for the high frequency of climatic anomalies and the impacts thereof."

There were also waves of anti-Semitism directed against the Jews in otherwise predominantly Christian societies. Some scholars examine the connection between weather shocks and Jewish persecution in Europe using data from 1100 to 1800 CE.[85] They find that "[a] one standard deviation decrease in average temperature increased the probability of a Jewish community being persecuted from a baseline of 2% every five years to between 2.5% and 3%." In another study on the same subject,[86] "Jews, then, were part of a polemical machine that grafted a wide range of images onto situations that pointed out contemporary moral shortcomings and were used as a call to repentance. As such, Jews were a vehicle and not a particular target. Of course, serving as such a vehicle could only inflame traditional stereotypes and accusations, so the images were not harmless even if they could be somewhat ambiguous."

Others ascribed the cold periods and the subsequent famine, disease, and conflict on divine displeasure. This caused some of them to pressure for a change in certain social behaviors such as gambling, drinking, dancing, clothing, and sexual activities. In addition, the Little Ice Age had an enduring impact on art, literature, fashion, and other components of culture.[87] For example, the only vivid surviving depiction of life during the Little Ice Age can be found in canvases filled with snow-covered landscape paintings of winter scenes done by some of the art masters of the time. The Little Ice Age also inspired some famous writers and poets in their literary pursuits. These include giants such as Charles Dickens, Lord Byron, John Milton, Percy Shelley, and Mary Shelley. In the world of sounds and musical instruments, the wood that is used in making the exceptional Stradivarius violins grew during the Little Ice Age. The unique qualities of this type of wood, caused by cooler temperatures, are thought to have contributed to the violin's intense resonance, superior acoustic properties, and high tonal quality. The effects of this little climate anomaly were not that little after all.

Notes

1. Wallace Broeker. "Was the Medieval Warm Period Global?" Science, 291, 5508: 1497–1499, 2001.
2. Oerlemans, J. "Extracting a Climate Signal from 169 Glacier Records" Science, 308, 5722: 675–677, 2005. Hendy, Erica J.; Gagan, Michael K.; Alibert, Chantal A.; McCulloch, Malcolm T.; Lough, Janice M.; Isdale, Peter J. "Abrupt Decrease in Tropical Pacific Sea Surface Salinity at End of Little Ice Age." Science, 295, 5559: 1511–1514, 2002.
3. Heinz Wanner, Christian Pfister, and Raphael Neukom. "The Variable European Little Ice Age." Quaternary Science Reviews, 287, 107531, 2022.

4. Benjamin Lieberman and Elizabeth Gordon. Climate Change in Human History: Prehistory to the Present. Bloomsbury, 2018. (P. 113).
5. Kaufman, D. S.; Schneider, D. P.; McKay, N. P.; Ammann, C. M.; Bradley, R. S.; Briffa, K. R.; Miller, G. H.; Otto-Bliesner, B. L.; Overpeck, J. T.; Vinther, B. M.; Abbott, M.; Axford, M.; Bird, Y.; Birks, B.; Bjune, H. J. B.; Briner, A. E.; Cook, J.; Chipman, T.; Francus, M.; Gajewski, P.; Geirsdottir, K.; Hu, A.; Kutchko, F. S.; Lamoureux, B.; Loso, S.; MacDonald, M.; Peros, G.; Porinchu, M.; Schiff, D.; Seppa, C.; Seppa, H.; and Arctic Lakes 2k Project Members. "Recent Warming Reverses Long-Term Arctic Cooling." Science, 325, 5945: 1236–1239, 2009.
6. Ibid.
7. John Eddy. "The Maunder Minimum." Science, 192, 4245: 1189–1202, 197.
8. Hiroko Miyahara, Fuyuki Tokanai, Toru Moriya, Mirei Takeyama, Hirohisa Sakurai, Kazuho Horiuchi, and Hideyuki Hotta. "Gradual Onset of the Maunder Minimum Revealed by High-Precision Carbon-14 Analyses." Nature, 11, 5482, 2021.
9. Dmitri Mauquoy, Bas van Geel, Maarten Blaauw, and Johannes van der Plicht. "Evidence from Northwest European Bogs Shows 'Little Ice Age' Climatic Changes Driven by Variations in Solar Activity." The Holocene, 12, 1: 1–6, 2002.
10. P. J. Polissar, M. B. Abbott, A. P. Wolfe, M. Bezada, V. Rull, and R. S. Bradle. "Solar Modulation of Little Ice Age Climate in the Tropical Andes." PNAS, 103, 24: 8937–8942, 2006.
11. Ibid.
12. Gifford H. Miller, Áslaug Geirsdóttir, Yafang Zhong, Darren J. Larsen, Bette L. Otto-Bliesner, Marika M. Holland, David A. Bailey, Kurt A. Refsnider, Scott J. Lehman, John R. Southon, Chance Anderson, Helgi Björnsson, and Thorvaldur Thordarson. "Abrupt Onset of the Little Ice Age Triggered by Volcanism and Sustained by Sea-ice/Ocean Feedbacks." Geophysical Research Letters, 39, L02708, 2012.
13. Ibid.
14. Alan Robock. "The 'Little Ice Age': Northern Hemisphere Average Observations and Model Calculations." Science, 206, 4425: 1402–1404, 1979.
15. Alan Robock and Melissa Free. "Global Warming in the Context of the Little Ice Age." Journal of Geophysical Research, 104, D16: 19057–19070, 1999.
16. Alan D. Wanamaker Jr., Paul G. Butler, James D. Scourse, Jan Heinemeier, Jón Eiríksson, Karen Luise Knudsen, and Christopher A. Richardson. "Surface Changes in the North Atlantic Meridional Overturning

Circulation During the Last Millennium." Nature Communications, 3, 899, 2012.

17. Francis Lapointe and Raymond Bradley. "Little Ice Age Abruptly Triggered by Intrusion of Atlantic Waters into the Nordic Seas." Science Advances, 7, 51, 2021.
18. Ibid.
19. Francois Lapointe, Raymond S. Bradley, Pierre Francus, Nicholas L. Balascio, Mark B. Abbott, Joseph S. Stoner, Guillaume St-Onge, Arnaud De Coninck, and Thibault Labarre. "Annually Resolved Atlantic Sea Surface Temperature Variability Over the Past 2,900 y." PNAS, 117, 44: 27171–27178, 2020.
20. William Ruddiman. "The Anthropogenic Greenhouse Era Began Thousands of Years Ago." Climatic Change, 61: 261–293, 2003.
21. Ibid.
22. Ibid.
23. R.J. Nevle, D.K. Bird, W.F. Ruddiman, and R.A. Dull. "Neotropical Human–Landscape Interactions, Fire, and Atmospheric CO2 during European Conquest." The Holocene, 21, 5: 853–864, 2011.
24. Ibid.
25. Richard Nevle and Dennis Bird. "Effects of Syn-pandemic Fire Reduction and Reforestation in the Tropical Americas on Atmospheric CO_2 during European Conquest." Palaeogeography, Palaeoclimatology, Palaeoecology, 264, 1–2: 25–38, 2008.
26. Dull, Robert A.; Nevle, Richard J.; Woods, William I.; Bird, Dennis K.; Avnery, Shiri; and Denevan, William M. "The Columbian Encounter and the Little Ice Age: Abrupt Land Use Change, Fire, and Greenhouse Forcing." Annals of the Association of American Geographers. 100, 4: 755–771, 2010.
27. Ibid.
28. Charles Mann. 1491. Vintage Books, 2006. (P. 105).
29. Walter Scheidel. The Great Leveler: Violence and the History of Inequality from the Stone Age to the Twenty-First Century. Princeton University Press, 2018. (P. 314).
30. Charles Mann. 1491. Vintage Books, 2006. (P. 96).
31. Ibid. (P. 102).
32. Ibid. (P. 103).
33. Ibid. (P. 143).
34. Ibid. (P. 143).
35. William McNeill. Plagues and Peoples, Anchor Books, 1976. (P. 212).
36. Ibid. (PP. 212–213).
37. Charles Mann. 1491. Vintage Books, 2006. (P. 108).

38. David D. Zhang, Harry F. Lee, Cong Wang, Baosheng Li, Qing Pei, Jane Zhang, and Yulun An. "The Causality Analysis of Climate Change and Large-scale Human Crisis." PNAS, 108, 42: 17296–17301, 2011.
39. Geoffrey Parker. "Crisis and Catastrophe: The Global Crisis of the Seventeenth Century Reconsidered." The American Historical Review, 113, 4: 1053–1079, 2008.
40. Murat Iyigun, Nathan Nunn, and Nancy Qian. "Winter is Coming: The Long Run Effects of Climate Change on Conflict: 1400–1900." National Bureau of Economic Research Working Paper 23033, 2017.
41. John D. Post. "The Mortality Crises of the Early 1770s and European Demographic Trends." The Journal of Interdisciplinary History, 21, 1: 29–62, 1990. John D. Post. "Famine, Mortality, and Epidemic Disease in the Process of Modernization." The Economic History Review, 29, 1: 14–37, 1976.
42. John D. Post. "Climatic Variability and the European Mortality Wave of the Early 1740s." The Journal of Interdisciplinary History, 15, 1: 1–30, 1984.
43. Andrew Appleby. "Epidemics and Famine in the Little Ice Age." The Journal of Interdisciplinary History, 10, 4: 643–663, 1980.
44. Jan de Vries. "The Economic Crisis of the Seventeenth Century after Fifty Years." The Journal of Interdisciplinary History, 40, 2: 151–194, 2009.
45. Maria Waldinger. "The Economic Effects of Long-Term Climate Change: Evidence from the Little Ice Age." Journal of Political Economy, 130, 9: 2275–2314, 2022.
46. Peter Wilson. "Dynasty, Constitution, and Confession: The Role of Religion in the Thirty Years War." The International History Review, 30, 3: 473–514, 2008.
47. Myron P. Gutmann. "The Origins of the Thirty Years' War." The Journal of Interdisciplinary History, 18, 4: 749–770, 1988.
48. Peter Wilson. "The Causes of the Thirty Years War 1618–48." The English Historical Review, 123, 502: 554–586, 2008.
49. Ibid.
50. Ibid.
51. Geoffrey Parker. "Why Did the Dutch Revolt Last Eighty Years?" Transactions of the Royal Historical Society, 26: 53–72, 1976.
52. Geoffrey Parker. "Why Did the Dutch Revolt Last Eighty Years?" Transactions of the Royal Historical Society, 26: 53–72, 1976.
53. Eric Hobsbawm. "The General Crisis of the European Economy in the 17th Century" Past & Present, 5: 33–53, 1954.
54. H. R. Trevor-Roper. "The General Crisis of the 17th Century." Past & Present, 16: 31–64, 1959.

55. Sharon Kettering. “Patronage and Politics during the Fronde.” French Historical Studies, 14, 3: 409–441, 1986.
56. Ibid.
57. Richard Bonney. “Fronde (1648–1653).” The Encyclopedia of War, 2011.
58. Richard Bonney. “Cardinal Mazarin and the Great Nobility during the Fronde.” The English Historical Review, 96, 381: 818–833, 1981.
59. Christian Morrisson and Wayne Snyder. “Les Inégalités de Revenus en France du début du XVIIIe Siècle à 1985.” Revue Economique, 51, 1: 119–154, 2000.
60. Christian Morrisson and Wayne Snyder. “The Income Inequality of France in Historical Perspective.” European Review of Economic History, 4, 1: 59–83, 2000.
61. Eugene Nelson White, “The French Revolution and the Politics of Government Finance, 1770–1815.” Journal of Economic History, 55, 2: 227–255, 1995.
62. Daron Acemoglu and James Robinson. Why Nations Fail: The Origins of Power, Prosperity, and Poverty. Currency, 2012. (P. 287).
63. Mike Duncan. “Climate Chaos Helped Spark the French Revolution—and Holds a Dire Warning for Today.” Time, October 20, 2021.
64. Olwen Hufton. “Social Conflict and the Grain Supply in Eighteenth-Century France.” The Journal of Interdisciplinary History, 14, 2: 303–331, 1983.
65. Julie Edwards, Kevin J. Anchukaitis, Brian Zambri, Laia Andreu-Hayles, Rose Oelkers, Rosanne D’Arrigo, and Georg von Arx. “Intra-Annual Climate Anomalies in Northwestern North America Following the 1783–1784 CE Laki Eruption.” JGR Atmospheres, 126, 3, e2020JD033544, 2021.
66. Ibid.
67. Maria Waldinger. “‘Let Them Eat Cake’: Drought, Peasant Uprisings, and Demand for Institutional Change in the French Revolution.” Journal of Economic Growth, 29: 41–77, 2024.
68. Ibid.
69. J. Neumann. “Great Historical Events That Were Significantly Affected by the Weather: 2, The Year Leading to the Revolution of 1789 in France.” Bulletin of the American Meteorological Society, 58, 2: 163–168, 1977.
70. Paul Simons. “The Hailstorm that Launched a Revolution.” The Sunday Times, July 12, 2019.
71. Ibid.
72. Daron Acemoglu and James Robinson. Why Nations Fail: The Origins of Power, Prosperity, and Poverty. Currency, 2012. (P. 291).

73. Daron Acemoglu, Davide Cantoni, Simon Johnson, and James A. Robinson. "The Consequences of Radical Reform: The French Revolution." American Economic Review, 101, 7: 3286–3307, 2011.
74. James Hertzler. "Who Dubbed It 'The Glorious Revolution?'" Albion, 19, 4: 579–585, 1987.
75. Daron Acemoglu and James Robinson. Why Nations Fail: The Origins of Power, Prosperity, and Poverty. Currency, 2012. (P. 103).
76. Ibid. (P. 197).
77. Ibid. (P. 208).
78. Ibid. (P. 98).
79. Eric Hobsbawm. "The General Crisis of the European Economy in the 17th Century." Past & Present, 5: 33–53, 1954.
80. Chris Harman. A People's History of the World. Verso, 2008. (P. 157).
81. Jan de Vries. "The Economic Crisis of the Seventeenth Century after Fifty Years." The Journal of Interdisciplinary History, 40, 2: 151–194, 2009.
82. Emily Oster. "Witchcraft, Weather and Economic Growth in Renaissance Europe." Journal of Economic Perspectives, 18, 1: 215–228, 2004.
83. Ibid.
84. Wolfgang Behringer. "Climatic Change and Witch-hunting: the Impact of the Little Ice Age on Mentalities." Climatic Change, 43: 335–351, 1999.
85. Robert Warren Anderson, Noel Johnson and Mark Koyama. "Jewish Persecutions and Weather Shocks: 1100–1800." The Economic Journal, 127, 602: 924–958, 2017.
86. Dean Phillip Bell. "The Little Ice Age and the Jews: Environmental History and the Mercurial Nature of Jewish Christian Relations in Early Modern Germany." AJS Review, 32, 1: 1–27, 2008.
87. https://daily.jstor.org/climate-canvasses-of-the-little-ice-age/

CHAPTER 12

Perturbation and Pestilence

1 Plagued by Plagues

Climate change contributed to the spread of diseases in so many instances in human history. These diseases take the lives of many in their wake but also leave others who survive with debilitating conditions that they have to deal with for the remainder of their lives. The history of humanity is inundated with stories of epidemics and pandemics that curtailed the ability of the afflicted communities from leading normal and productive lives. Diseases also burden these societies with the cost of treatment for the sick, the expense of containment efforts, the economic loss caused by absenteeism of those infected from schools and workplaces, and the long-term lingering adverse effects of the disease on the cognitive functions and the psychological impairments of those who endured the illness.

The plague is but one such example. The plague is an infectious disease that affects humans and other mammals, caused by the bacterium *Yersinia pestis*.[1] Humans catch the plague after being bitten by a rodent flea that is carrying the bacterium or by handling an animal infected with the plague. The bacterium[2] "Yersinia pestis is responsible for deadly plague, a zoonotic disease established in stable foci in the Americas, Africa, and Eurasia. Its persistence in the environment relies on the subtle balance between Y. pestis-contaminated soils, burrowing and nonburrowing mammals exhibiting variable degrees of plague susceptibility, and their associated fleas."

S. Khalifa, *Climate Change, Economic Channels, and Historical Junctures*, https://doi.org/10.1007/978-3-031-91867-4_12

To understand the intuition behind the association between climate fluctuations and plague outbreaks, we need to examine the life cycle of pathogens, vectors, and human hosts. A pathogen is an organism causing the disease. Disease vectors are agents that carry an infectious pathogen to another living organism and are mostly blood-sucking insects. The host in this case is the human who gets infected, as the vector injects the disease into its body. The plague system is the outcome of complex interactions between these components, especially in terms of their life cycle, dynamics, and distribution. These factors are influenced by climate parameters.[3]

First, it is widely acknowledged that the abundance of fleas is affected by heat, humidity, and rainfall. These climatic factors have direct effects on the development, the survival, the behavior, and the reproduction of fleas and their populations. Fleas are ectothermic, or cold-blooded animals, who are sensitive to temperature changes. Thus, flea development rates increase with temperature until a critical value. Then, the survival of immature stages decreases if high temperatures are combined with low humidity. In this context, some scholars confirm that[4] "[t]emperature and relative humidity impact flea survival: survival is in fact inversely proportional to air saturation deficit at a constant temperature. Flea larvae are susceptible to desiccation and typically acquire water from adult excreta. Survival of immature stages of fleas in rodent burrows is also affected by soil moisture that is partly controlled by outside precipitation." This implies that the abundance of fleas is climate dependent. Naturally, any perturbation in climatic conditions could cause changes to flea populations.

Second, rodent population dynamics and their survival are also influenced by climate. Precipitation in this case is critical, since rodent reproduction periods often follow wet seasons. Thus, rodent population densities show a clear association with annual rainfall and its seasonal distribution. The effect of temperature is not as clear because rodents are homeothermic, who have a warm body maintained independently of the surrounding environmental temperature. Low temperatures in winter can, nonetheless, affect rodent populations indirectly through lower food availability. Although the life cycle of rodents is short, they are very adaptable and behaviorally adjustable to short-term environmental variations that may affect food supply. However, this mechanism is not capable of coping with ecological stress brought about by long-term climatic deteriorations.

Finally, the effect of climate oscillations for the host could be mediated by conflicts, famines, migrations, and other factors. For instance, climatic deteriorations have a profound effect on agrarian economies. Economic downturn caused by climate change could lead to unaffordable food prices, shortage in food supply, and the worsening of social buffers. This would, in turn, lead to malnutrition, immunodeficiency, and epidemic outbreaks. In situations of economic hardship, public health and hygiene provision is hampered. These also exacerbate disease outbreaks. Climate-induced human evacuations could lead to conditions where people are carrying diseases from one area to another, which increases infectiousness. Climate-induced conflicts could be fertile grounds for the dissemination of disease due to the lack of provision of heath care because of the high level of casualties.

Given these considerations, there has been a series of studies linking climate change to disease epidemics and pandemics. Even though an analysis of the connection between climate change and plagues in Europe found no evidence for the proposed linkage, the evidence[5] "suggests that climate-plague correlation should not be explained by an over-simplified linear model without addressing its non-linearity and complexity over spatio-temporal scaling effect." Taking this caveat into consideration, these same scholars examine the nonlinear and nonstationary influence of climatic change on plague outbreaks in pre-industrial Europe during the period from 1347 to 1760 CE.[6] Plague outbreaks are found to occur after cold waves and dry spells, and that decadal climate variability is essential in driving the cycles of these disease surges during that time. These results[7] "show that both temperature and aridity index are significant in causing plague outbreaks in pre-industrial Europe, with a 5-year time lag."

Along the same lines, ecologist Nils Stenseth and other scholars assert that[8] "[c]limate impacts all components of the plague cycle (host, vector, and pathogen) in various ways and over a wide range of scales (from micro—individual flea life cycle—to macro—a plague area composed of several disjoint foci)." Nils Stenseth and other scholars also find that[9] "high-resolution paleoclimatic indices correlate with plague prevalence and population density in a major plague host species." Nils Stenseth and other scholars also show that climate change affects the type of flea-borne transmission.[10] The first type is biofilm-dependent transmission which takes place when *Yersinia pestis* forms a biofilm in the foregut of the flea that impedes new blood meals. Deprived of food and fluids, the[11] "flea begins to feed more frantically regurgitating infected blood in the process." The second transmission mode is called the early phase transmission. Investigating the dynamics of *Yersinia pestis* within a wildlife plague reservoir located in the Tien Shan mountains in China, the authors conclude that[12] "cold and dry climate negatively affects rodent and flea densities, which in turn favors biofilm-induced plague transmission over early-phase transmission."

We now turn to an exposition of historical outbreaks of epidemics, and a discussion of the studies that show an association between these incidents with climate change. These events include the Antonine Plague, the Cyprian Plague, the First Bubonic Plague, the Second Bubonic Plague, the Third Bubonic Plague, and others.

2 The Antonine Plague

The Antonine Plague, also referred to as the Plague of Galen after the Greek physician who described it, spread in 165 CE.[13] This was at the epitome of the Roman Empire during the reign of the last of the Five Good Emperors, Marcus Aurelius.[14] The first phase of the outbreak lasted until 180 CE affecting the entirety of the Roman Empire, while a second one occurred from 251 to 266 CE. This compounded and exacerbated the effects of the earlier outbreak. It has been proposed that this plague is a useful starting point to mark the beginning of the end of the Roman Empire as it possibly laid the foundations for its ultimate fall.

This plague likely emerged in China, shortly before 165 CE, spreading westward along the Silk Road and through trading ships headed for Rome. Sometime between late 165 and early 166 CE, the Roman army also contracted the disease during the siege of Seleucia on the Tigris. Troops returning from the wars in that side of the world spread the disease to many parts of the empire. This pandemic[15] "ravaged the entire extent of the Roman Empire, from its eastern frontiers in Iraq to its western frontiers on the Rhine River and Gaul, modern France, and western Germany. The disease is identified most often as smallpox, but it may have been anthrax."

At the outbreak of the plague, Rome's army consisted of many highly trained and well-armed legions. The spread of the disease, and the subsequent deaths, caused a shortfall in the recruits for the army especially along the German frontier. This weakened the Romans' ability to defend the empire. At a time of increasing expenses to maintain a far stretched empire, and the essential military forces to ensure the security of the empire's expanse, these events caused income from tax collection to dwindle as well. This also impaired the ability of the empire to spend on its defense from invaders.

The horrific death toll from the disease not only decreased the number of taxpayers, but also candidates for public office, craftsmen and artisans, farmers and herders, and manpower for production. Fewer farmers meant some land was left uncultivated. The scarcity of crops caused steep price increases along with shortages in food supply. Fewer craftsmen implied fewer items being produced which stymied local economies. The lack of merchants, traders, and financiers caused profound interruptions in domestic commerce and international trade. Historian Kyle Harper describes this dire situation by stating,[16] "Signs of the plague, both giant and subtle, are ubiquitous. Building virtually ceased. Mass graves provide chilling testimony and confirm literary reports of unprecedented mortality. Invocations to Apollo, the diverter of plague, appear across the empire. Emergency military conscriptions were levied. The price of goods leapt."

The distribution of income was also affected. These adverse events could serve as an equalizer as it decreases the amount of labor, due to the death toll, which increases the value of labor input in the production process. As there are less laborers to attend to the land, the amount of land available increases and the rent charged by landlords declines:[17]

> The value of rural labor as documented in contracts rose by between a few percent and close to a fifth depending on duration of employment, whereas the real price of donkeys, which also represents labor and which happens to be particularly well documented, went up by half. Conversely the price of non-essential foodstuffs such as oil and, especially, wine dropped relative to that of wheat, enabling workers to purchase more higher-status goods. Expressed in terms of oil and wine, real wages rose considerably more than wheat wages did. The value of land is difficult to compare over time, because we are unable to hold land quality constant: even so, a rough survey produces results that are very similar to the much more securely attested drop in real land rents.

The effects of the plague on the overall conditions of the empire are argued to have led to its eventual demise. This period[18] "characterized by health, social and economic crises, paved the way for the entry into the Empire of neighbouring barbarian tribes and the recruitment of barbarian troops into the Roman army; these events particularly favoured the cultural and political growth of these populations. The Antonine Plague may well have created the conditions for the decline of the Roman Empire and, afterwards, for its fall in the West in the fifth century AD."

Climate change provided the environmental context for the Antonine Plague which was the first of three devastating pandemics that shook the basis of the Roman Empire. By exploring[19] "potential explanations for apparent connections between a changing climate and the Antonine Plague, a link between climatic events and the pandemic's arrival to the Empire emerges." This is because the plague coincided with a cooling period that lasted from 160 to 180 CE. Along these lines, Kyle Harper and other scholars present a temperature and precipitation reconstruction for the period between 200 BCE and 600 CE from a southern Italian marine sediment and conclude that[20]

> the three major pandemic events of Roman antiquity—the Antonine Plague (onset ~165 CE), the Plague of Cyprian (onset ~251 CE), and Plague of Justinian (onset ~541 CE)—are strongly associated with pronounced climate change, although in varying ways. The Antonine Plague occurred during the cold pulse between ~160 and ~180 CE that followed several decades of trends toward cooling and aridity. The Plague of Cyprian coincides with a second phase of severe cooling, with even more arid conditions, after the brief warmer period between ~215 and ~245 CE. Last, the First Plague Pandemic originates at a moment of extreme cooling in the 530s to 540s, and recurrent out-breaks occur in the generally cooler sixth century, notably ~590 CE.

This is not to say that climate change caused the disease, but rather that it created conducive conditions for the spread of such disease that had devastating consequences on the Roman Empire. The concurrence of climate change episodes with these plagues that shattered the empire cannot be a mere coincidence, especially when there is more than one occasion when climatic fluctuations were followed by a plague occurrence.

3 The Cyprian Plague

The plague of Cyprian broke out in Ethiopia about 250 CE and lasted almost two decades. It reached Rome in the following year and eventually spread to other parts of the empire. The plague's name commemorates Saint Cyprian, the Bishop of Carthage, who witnessed and wrote about the plague. This disease episode caused political, economic, and social upheaval. It is estimated to have caused the deaths of approximately 5000 people per day in Rome at its peak. In addition to the thousands of people dying every day in Rome and its vicinity, the outbreak claimed the lives of two emperors, Hostilian in 251 CE and Claudius II Gothicus in 270 CE. The period between the two emperors witnessed political instability with various contenders attempting to claim the throne. The lack of leadership and the depletion of soldiers from the ranks of the Roman legions contributed to a weakening of the empire's ability to fend off external attacks. At that time, the Romans were embroiled in constant warfare on the frontiers of the empire due to a series of incursions by the Germanic tribes.

The spread of disease also caused people in the countryside to flee to the cities. The abandonment of the fields, along with the deaths of farmers who stayed put, caused the collapse of agriculture production. The devastating effects of the disease led to chaos such that[21] "this microbial enemy was just more sinister. In this event, the center could not hold. There is much that must remain uncertain about the Plague of Cyprian, but not this: In its immediate wake, anarchy was loosed on the world."

Even though the plague of Cyprian did not cause the fall of the Roman Empire, it did instigate a crisis[22] "that pushed the imperial system beyond the threshold of resilience. When it struck, the fabric of empire unwound. The Romans had faced challenges before: dynastic conflict, external invasion, class violence, and—yes—famine and plague. Even in the sunniest days of Antonine rule, these adversities were not unfamiliar. But their concurrence and intensity in the ad 250s induced cascading change. Barbarians no longer just menaced the frontier; they pillaged unwalled towns in the imperial interior. The struggle for dynastic legitimacy turned into imperial dissolution."

Kyle Harper and other scholars provide evidence for the contribution of climate change in this crisis that ravaged the Roman Empire, by showing that this plague was coincident with a period of cooling and dry conditions. The accompanied drought devastated parts of the empire. In this context,[23] "[a] second phase of severe cooling with even more arid conditions occurred after the brief warmer period between ~215 and ~245 CE, overlapping the so-called Crisis of the Third Century (~250 to 275), a period of exceptional political turmoil characterized by monetary crisis, imperial fragmentation, and pestilence (the Plague of Cyprian). Our record lends strong support to the inference that climate change was a substantial stressor in Italy during this multifaceted crisis." In another contribution, Kyle Harper refers to the climatic origins of the plague by arguing that the[24] "Cyprian directly refers to the incidence of drought and famine in the period leading up to the outbreak. Dionysius of Alexandria also refers to a time of drought, followed by a flood." Even though the empire was able to withstand the previous Antonine plague, this episode pushed it to its limits since the plague of Cyprian followed its own pattern as[25]

> it was an exogenous shock to a rent-extracting empire, created to maintain legitimacy within and security without, which had been under great stress since at least the second half of the 2nd c. The recovery from the Antonine plague proved the resilience of the system, whereas our plague seems to have presented challenges that were harder to overcome in the short term: the plague of Cyprian pushed the imperial machine beyond a certain threshold, and with the cascading change a new equilibrium had to be found.

4 The First Bubonic Plague

During the reign of the Byzantine emperor Justinian I, from 527 to 565 CE, one of the worst outbreaks of plague occurred claiming the lives of millions of people. The plague of Justinian was a pandemic that has been caused by the bacterium *Yersinia pestis*.[26] This is confirmed by some scholars who show the presence of *Yersinia pestis* DNA in human skeletal remains in a cemetery from the sixth century CE.[27] Another genomic analysis also confirms that the *Yersinia pestis* lineages that caused the plague of Justinian, and the Black Death 800 years later, were independent emergences from rodents into human beings.[28]

The plague of Justinian appears to have originated in Lower Egypt by approximately 541 CE. Then, it spread across the Mediterranean in the ships that transported grain to the core of the Byzantine Empire. Grain was also stored in warehouses which provided a perfect breeding ground for fleas and rats. Some historians also suggested that soldiers, and the supply caravans supporting their military efforts, acted as the means of transmission for rats and fleas carrying the plague. The plague arrived in Constantinople in 542 CE, almost a year after the disease first made its appearance on the outskirts of the empire. The outbreak continued to sweep throughout the circum-Mediterranean until 750 CE.

This plague contributed to the vulnerability of the Byzantine Empire politically and economically. As the disease spread throughout the Mediterranean, the empire's ability to confront its enemies weakened. This was largely attributed to its inability to recruit and train new soldiers due to the spread of illness and loss of life. In the Roman provinces of North Africa and the Near East, the empire was unable to stem the encroachment of Muslim armies. By 568 CE, the Lombards successfully invaded northern Italy and defeated the Byzantines, causing the fracture of the Italian peninsula until its final reunification in the nineteenth century of the Common Era.[29] These are but examples of how the plague conditions weakened the empire along these fronts and others. The decrease in the population affected not only the military forces and the empire's defenses, but also the economic basis of the empire began to tumble as the agricultural sector was shattered. Less people meant fewer farmers who produced less grain causing prices to soar and taxes to decline.

The Justinian Plague affected a significant proportion of the population of Europe. It is not possible to ascertain with certainty the mortality rate during the outbreak. However, estimates vary between 25 and 100 million deaths. The account of an eyewitness, ancient historian Prokopios, asserts that[30] "at first the deaths were a little more than the normal, then the mortality rose still higher, and afterwards the tale of dead reached five thousand each day, and again it even came to ten thousand and still more than that." Historian William McNeill also confirms that the[31] "disease certainly provoked an initial die-off of a large proportion of the urban dwellers in affected regions, and the overall diminution of population took centuries to repair. Precision is, of course, quite impossible; but Procopius reports that at the peak of its first visitation the plague killed 10,000 persons daily in Constantinople, where it raged for four months."

Dead bodies littered the streets of the capital to the extent that the troops were ordered to assist in the disposal of the corpses. Once the graveyards and tombs were filled, burial pits and trenches were dug to dispose of the decomposing bodies. Other bodies were loaded into the towers of the city walls with quicklime poured over them to speed up decomposition, while others were loaded onto ships that were pushed out into the Sea of Marmara and set ablaze.

Some scholars, however, argue that the plague did not have a proportional or comparable effect across the area. For instance, historian Lee Mordechai and Lauren White assert that the[32] "Justinianic Plague would have likely had differential effects across urban areas around the

Mediterranean." Lee Mordechai and Merle Eisenberg attempt to refute the assertions of some scholarly work that has argued that the Justinian Plague killed half the population of the Mediterranean world and led to the end of Antiquity.[33] Instead, they find that the Justinian Plague has led to high mortality only in specific locations. In a similar vein, Lee Mordechai and other scholars conclude that several data including papyri, inscriptions, coins, pollen, and burials lead them to[34] "reject the current scientific and humanistic consensus of the JP (Justinian Plague) as a major driver of demographic change in the 6th century Mediterranean region."

There is also some indication that there were climate fluctuations that preceded the outbreak of the plague. For instance, Procopius wrote,[35] "During these times there was a pestilence, by which the whole human race came near to being annihilated." Then he describes a decade-long cold snap with unusual incidents of snow and frost in the midst of summer, below-average temperatures, and a decrease in sunshine. These colder than usual conditions affected crop harvests, leading to food shortages, that pushed people to move throughout the area. Accompanying these migrants were plague-infected flea-ridden rats, which created the perfect conditions for a pandemic. This change in climate is connected to volcanic eruptions across Europe during that period such that[36]

> [i]n 535 CE, a massive volcanic eruption (perhaps in Rabaul) and its consequent atmospheric shroud caused a rapid global cooling of approximately 3 °C that lasted for a decade. Weather patterns were disrupted, with flooding in Arabia and heavy snowfalls in Mesopotamia. Dramatic crop failures, hunger, and unrest occurred at that same time in central Sweden, Ireland, northern China, and Central Asia's grassland steppes. In Europe this "536 Event" coincided with a background cooling trend. The especially cooler conditions during the late 530s, along with apparent wetter weather, would have created an unusual and brief opportunity for plague-infected rats and fleas to travel north to Pelusium, where grain storage facilities doubtless sustained a thriving rat population. Although infected rats are unlikely to have survived the full journey, infected fleas can survive for long periods in protective materials. It was an easy next step for rats, fleas and bacteria to cross the Mediterranean and infect the citizens of Constantinople.

To provide scientific evidence, some studies examine the climatic fluctuations caused by this volcanic activity at the time. To examine the coincidence of cooling and societal change during the Late Antique Little Ice Age from 536 to 660 CE, some scholars use tree-ring chronologies from the Russian Altai and European Alps to reconstruct summer temperatures over the past two millennia.[37] The study finds an unprecedented long-lasting cooling following a cluster of large volcanic eruptions in 536, 540, and 547 CE. The authors propose this cold phase as an additional environmental factor contributing to the[38] "establishment of the Justinian plague, transformation of the eastern Roman Empire and collapse of the Sasanian Empire, movements out of the Asian steppe and Arabian Peninsula, spread of Slavic-speaking peoples, and political upheavals in China." The authors conclude that this Late Antique Little Ice Age LALIA can be considered[39]

> an additional environmental driver of crop failure, famine and plague, as well as a possible trigger for political, societal and economic turmoil. Outbreak of the Justinian plague between 541 and 543 AD across the Later Roman Empire, as well as its subsequent pandemic development, followed widespread food shortages right after the onset of the LALIA. Spreading apparently from Asia, this persisting disease killed many millions of people and possibly contributed to the reduction of the eastern Roman Empire.

Other scholars also examine climate change during that era and argue that[40] "written sources from the entire Empire document the seriousness of the veiling of solar radiation in 536 and 537, which caused crop failures in different areas. Moreover, many northern European tree rings reveal severe stress during these years, and the solar veiling has been connected with a powerful volcanic eruption." Their findings also confirm that the[41] "quarter-century that included the event of 536 and the outbreak of the Justinianic pandemic of plague was marked by the highest number of famines (eight) recorded for the entire period under review."

5 The Second Bubonic Plague

The Second Bubonic Plague, known as the Black Death, was another pandemic that shattered Medieval Europe from 1347 to 1352 CE. This was the worst plague in human history that took a proportionately higher toll on life than any other known disease up to that point in time. It would take a couple of hundred years for the population of Europe to recover to levels prior to the Black Death. This disease was also caused by *Bacillus* bacterium, *Yersinia pestis*, and is carried by fleas on rodents.[42] The plague originated in Central Asia and was carried to Crimea by Mongol warriors.

It decimated the Tatar army of the Khan Jani Beg who was besieging the Genoese port of Caffa in Crimea in 1347 CE. With his forces collapsing due to the disease, Jani Beg used trebuchets to catapult infested corpses across the walls of the town to infect his enemies.[43] Afterward, Genoese ships carried the epidemic from Caffa to Mediterranean ports from which it spread to the European hinterland.

The death toll from the disease was so high that it had drastic consequences on Medieval Europe. It is estimated that between 30% and 50% of the population of those places affected perished from the plague. According to other accounts, the plague killed one in three wiping out entire villages and towns in Europe.[44] In a similar vein, it is estimated that the plague killed one-third of Europe's population over a period of three years.[45] Others even estimate as much as 60% of Europe's population has perished because of this epidemic.[46] According to yet other estimates, the Black Death killed 75 million people from 1347 to 1352 CE.[47] There were so many dead bodies, where carts filled with corpses became a common sight across Europe. Although it spread unchecked, the Black Death hit some areas more severely than others. Historian Colin McEvedy describes this dire situation as follows:[48]

> In the year 1346 Europe, northern Africa and nearer parts of the Middle East had a total population of approximately 100 million people. In the course of the next few years a fourth of them died, victims of a new and terrifying illness that spread throughout the area, killing most of those unfortunate enough to catch it. The disease put an end to the population rise that had marked the evolution of medieval society: within four years Europe alone suffered a loss of roughly 20 million people. The disease responsible for such grim statistics was the bubonic plague, and this particular outbreak, lasting from 1346 to 1352, was known as the Great Dying or the Great Pestilence. Later it was appropriately referred to as the Black Death, a name that has come down through history.

There were far-reaching ramifications and unprecedented consequences of the plague such that[49] "[h]alf the population was wiped out, vast numbers of villages were abandoned, and millions of hectares of cultivated land went to waste in the great crisis of the 14th century. As Guy Bois tells, 'For more than a century…the greater part of the continent…suffered a massive decline in population and a regression in productive capacity.' In scope and duration, the phenomenon had no known historical precedent."

The disease would come back in less severe outbreaks throughout the medieval period. There were recurrences in 1361–1363 CE, 1369–1371 CE, 1374–1375 CE, 1390 CE, 1400 CE, and 1575–1577 CE. It even spread faster in the seventeenth century than in the fourteenth century according to some accounts.[50] Studies have also proposed that the plague was introduced into Europe multiple times during that period, through trade routes in waves from Central Asia due to climate fluctuations that affected populations of rodents infested with plague-carrying fleas.

In many locations, the prevalent social structure broke down. The shortage of farmers led to demands for an end to serfdom. The institution of serfdom where a laborer stayed in a piece of land and paid rent to a landlord was doomed afterward. The shortage of labor compelled the landlords to substitute their tenants with more mobile workers and more independent workforce. Those who could work were able to demand wages for their labor. Social unrest ensued, and often outright rebellion broke out, when the aristocracy tried to fight these tendencies for change. The general welfare of the peasantry was also enhanced as a diminished population lowered the competition for resources. Some peasants would even increase their landholdings. Land-owning aristocrats, too, were expeditious in claiming the unclaimed lands of those who had perished from the pandemic. These changes brought a new fluidity to the hitherto inflexible social stratification.

Thus, the plague was a turning point in terms of its effect as an income leveler. The Black Death led to a dramatic downturn in population numbers such that[51] "land became more abundant relative to labor. Land rents and interest rates dropped both in absolute terms and relative to wages. Landowners stood to lose, and workers could hope to gain." By changing the trends of land rents and labor wages, the plague unintentionally served as an equalizer since[52] "plagues leveled by changing the ratio of land to labor, lowering the value of the former (as documented by land prices and rents and the price of agricultural products) and raising that of the latter (in the form of higher wages and lower tenancy rents). This served to make landowners and employers less rich, and workers better off, lowering inequality in both income and wealth."

The Black Death did not only influence the income gaps within countries, but some scholars also proclaim a connection between this event and the great wage divergence within Europe by showing that[53] "the wage gap between northwestern Europe and the rest of the continent began to emerge after 1350." Other economists also attribute the divergence between Western and Eastern Europe to the Black Death since it[54] "led to increased bargaining power for labor, the erosion of feudal institutions, and urban growth in Western Europe; in Eastern Europe, it led to new restrictions on the mobility of rural labor and depressed urban development." This initial bifurcation within Europe also paved the way to the eventual great divergence between Western Europe and its offshoots on one hand and the rest of the world on the other.

The feudal system also started to give way to another economic system that paved the way for the rise of market networks:[55]

> Part of the rural population, especially the lords, had become too dependent on the goods produced in the towns for society to revert to a system of production on virtually self-contained estates. As their demand for goods grew, so did their desire for cash, which they could only get by selling a growing production of rural output. Market networks continued to penetrate the countryside, linking each village and household to the traders of the towns. The growth of market networks slowly but surely changed feudal society.

Traditional authority, especially that of the church, was also challenged facing questions on how such a calamity could befall a people. The Church struggled to cope with the plague's damaging consequences. This is due to its lack of ability to justify the occurrence of the disease or to guide their flock in the face of such adversity. In addition, the church lost a lot of its clergy to the plague who had to be promptly replaced by less qualified personnel. This contributed to the decline in the confidence of the Christian laity in the institution of the Church and its leadership. The Catholic Church, thus, lost some of its authority over the salvation of souls as people turned to mysticism in some cases and to excesses in others. This also possibly laid the foundations for the Protestant Reformation as historian William McNeill intimated:[56]

> In the fourteenth century, many priests and monks died; often their successors were less well trained and faced more quizzical if not openly antagonistic flocks. God's justice seemed far to seek in the way plague spared some, killed others; and the regular administration of God's grace through the sacraments (even when consecrated priests remained available) was an entirely inadequate psychological counterpoise to the statistical vagaries of lethal infection and sudden death. Anticlericalism was of course not new in

> Christian Europe; after 1346, however, it became more open and widespread, and provided one of the elements contributing to Luther's later success.

Some researchers propose that a transition from a warm climate to a wetter one in the early fourteenth century created favorable conditions for the plague to propagate. According to this view, the increased precipitation and biomass production in the Eurasian steppes and deserts led to a population explosion of wild rodents which are the typical carriers of the plague bacterium. These rodents then infected domestic rats, which carried the fleas that transmitted the disease to humans. The plague was introduced to Europe also because of climatic conditions in the southern part of the continent. For instance, some argue,[57] "High demand in southern Europe for Black Sea cereals from 1345 onwards was associated with a period of excessive precipitation and cooling negatively affecting cereal supplies in Italy and beyond. Cereal imports from Black Sea coasts resumed once the situation improved in 1347, and by early 1348 Venetian merchants had filled many Italian granaries with Black Sea produce and introduced plague to Europe."

There are several studies that attempt to explore the association between climate change and the Bubonic Plague. To provide evidence that climatic conditions favoring the spread of the plague existed in Central Asia at the onset of the Black Death, Nils Stenseth and other scholars use field data from that area to show that *Yersinia pestis* prevalence in gerbils increases with warmer springs and wetter summers.[58] The desert zones of Central Asia are known to contain natural foci of plague where the great gerbil acts as host. The analysis of tree-ring climate data shows that[59] "conditions during the period of the Black Death (1280–1350) were both warmer and increasingly wet. The same was true during the origin of the Third Pandemic (1855–1870) when the climate was wetter and underwent an increasingly warm trend. Our analyses are in agreement with the hypothesis that the Medieval Black Death and the mid-19th-century plague pandemic might have been triggered by favorable climatic conditions in Central Asia."

To provide evidence that the scale of fatality caused by the Black Death across Europe also depended on climatic conditions, a large group of scholars examine pollen data on landscape change collected from multiple lakes and wetlands in Europe.[60] The study confirms that the plague had a devastating effect in some areas but a negligible or no impact on others.

This is likely because the behavior of *Yersinia pestis* hosts and vectors, and their capacity to transmit the pathogen, is partly constrained by complex interactions with seasonal climate variability and local ecological conditions. In Europe,[61] "different seasons and annually variable climatic conditions may have influenced Y. pestis prevalence and the pandemic's mortality." Thus, the scale of infectiousness in an area depended largely on local ecological and climatic conditions.

Not only was the spread of the plague attributed to these climatic conditions, but the recurrence of the plague was also favored by certain fluctuations in climate. In this context, Nils Stenseth and other scholars examine whether the Black Death was the consequence of a singular introduction of *Yersinia pestis* into Europe, after which the disease established itself in wildlife or urban rodent reservoirs over four centuries and caused recurrent outbreaks.[62] The authors study a dataset of georeferenced bubonic outbreaks and tree-ring records from Europe and Asia. This analysis does not support the hypothesis of a singular introduction but provides evidence, instead, for climate-driven repeated reintroductions of the bacterium into European harbors from reservoirs in Asia. The analysis, thus, supports a scenario where climate fluctuations that positively affect tree-ring growth in the Karakorum mountains can promote plague outbreaks among the rodent populations of Central Asia.

In a related paper, Nils Stenseth and other scholars use a broad spectrum of historical, archaeological, evolutionary, genetic, and ecological evidence to conclude that[63] "there must have existed a reservoir outside of Western Europe [with the Ottoman Empire, Persia, and Central Asia as possible candidates]. Such a reservoir could then feed, with multiple introductions, the second plague pandemic outbreaks in Western Europe along Northern and Southern trade routes. In addition, there might have been continuous recirculation of plague in (Western and Eastern) Europe with the movement of goods, travelers, and troops."

6 The Third Bubonic Plague

The Third Plague is a pandemic that originated in the Yunnan province of China in 1855 CE. The plague started spreading after an influx of Han Chinese relocated to that area to exploit the demand for copper in the nineteenth century CE. By 1850 CE, the population exploded to over 7 million. Increasing transportation throughout the area brought people in contact with plague-infected fleas. People, then, brought the fleas and rats back into expanding urban areas. This episode of bubonic plague eventually spread to other continents.[64] According to some sources, this disease emerged[65]

> from its wild rodent reservoir in the Himalayan borderlands between China and India soon after 1855, and traveling this time not west but east, bubonic plague infected the densely populated provinces of south China before attacking Guangzhou (Canton) and then the British colonial port of Hong Kong in 1894. There it rekindled international fears, especially when it reached Macao and Fuzhou a year later and struck Singapore and Bombay in 1896. Transported rapidly by British steamships throughout the empire and beyond, bubonic plague took only a few years to reach every continent.

Many of the ports infected during the plague were at the time British-held colonies such as those in India, South Africa, and Hong Kong. Thus, the British Empire in these colonies had to act to prevent the spread of the disease. Accordingly, the British often ended up enforcing western hygiene systems, health containment practices, and radical quarantine enforcements in these colonies. Many of these Western sanitary procedures were new to these areas and caused natives' apprehension of the British authorities. For instance, harsh quarantines in India led to resentments by Indians. This is because the Western concepts of hygiene and sanitation[66] "were considered to be the standard and the Indians fell far below that mark which made the ill planned and insanitary native residential sector more susceptible to disease." When the plague broke out in Cape Colony, in South Africa, the colonial government used this event as an excuse to expel a large group of natives into the outskirts of the city worsening segregation. This led to[67] "'the sanitation syndrome', equating black urban settlement, labour and living conditions with threats to public health and security, became fixed in the official mind, buttressed a desire to achieve positive social controls, and confirmed or rationalized white race prejudice with a popular imagery of medical menace." In Hong Kong, the British enforced many locally unfamiliar medical practices, such as floating plague victims out on boats onto the water and cooling plague victims with ice. These practices scared the inhabitants of Hong Kong and led some to migrate back to mainland China, which was then even more badly affected by the plague.[68] The third plague caused the deaths of more than 12 million people in India and China alone, and[69] "Before it petered out around the middle of the twentieth century, the third plague pandemic accounted for something on the order of 15 million deaths, the vast majority among the densely populated lands of India, China, and Indonesia."

To provide evidence for the association between climate change and the third pandemic, we discuss some studies that focused on this issue. For instance, Nils Stenseth and other scholars use cross-spectral and cross-wavelet analyses to explore the connection between the increased rate of plague in China during 1871–2003 CE and some climate elements such as the Southern Oscillation Index, sea surface temperature, and air temperature of the Northern Hemisphere. The authors find[70] "that ENSO-driven climate variation may be important for occurrences of human plague in China."

In another study, Nils Stenseth and other scholars use plague records in China from 1850 to 1964 CE to explore the association between annual disease cases with proxy data on climatic conditions.[71] The analysis shows opposite responses of plague to climate variations in northern and southern China, which are likely related to the different climates and rodent communities in these two parts. In northern China with arid climate, rodents are expected to react positively to high precipitation, whereas in southern China with humid conditions, high precipitation is likely to have a negative effect. Thus,[72] "drier conditions were associated with decreased plague intensity in northern China and with increased plague intensity in southern China. Extreme wetness had, however, opposite short-term effects, leading to a dome-shaped effect of the current-year dryness/wetness index in the north and a U-shaped effect in the south."

Some studies focus on the association between climatic conditions and the spread velocity of the disease. For instance, Nils Stenseth and other scholars use 200 years of plague records and genomic data to examine the factors that influenced the worldwide spread velocity of the third plague.[73] The authors show that precipitation had a positive association with the speed of the spread of disease. On the other hand, temperature exhibited a nonlinear U-shaped association which is likely caused by the different effects that temperature has on the pathogen, vectors, and hosts. In a related paper, Nils Stenseth and other scholars use a dataset that include the date and location of cases for the third plague from 1772 to 1964 CE in China.[74] The study finds that the plague spread velocity was positively associated with wet conditions and not dry ones, because[75] "wet conditions, as measured by flood and drought events, facilitated spatial spread of human plague in China. Wet weather may have increased human contact with plague vectors, for example rodents, and caused the migration of people who had lost their homes in floods. All of these factors may have promoted the spatial transmission of plague."

7 The Spanish Flu

The Spanish Flu of 1918–1919 CE was the worst influenza outbreak of the twentieth century. Influenza is caused by a virus that is transmitted from one person to another through airborne respiratory secretions. An outbreak can occur if a new strain of influenza virus emerges against which the population has no immunity. The pandemic broke out near the end of World War I. This was at a time when wartime censors in the countries embroiled in the conflict suppressed bad news to maintain morale, except in neutral Spain. This created the false impression that the country was the epicenter of the flu.

In terms of the total number of deaths, it was among the most devastating pandemics in human history. The influenza pandemic claimed between 50 and 100 million lives. According to some,[76] "The 'Spanish' influenza pandemic of 1918–1919, which caused approximately 50 million deaths worldwide, remains an ominous warning to public health." Others state that[77] "the 1918 to 1919 H1N1 influenza pandemic is among the most deadly events in recorded human history, having killed an estimated 50 to 100 million persons."

Like other pandemics that we have discussed so far, this outbreak was also associated with climate change. Some scholars present a climatic record from an Alpine ice core showing a significant climate anomaly that affected the continent from 1914 to 1919 CE.[78] According to this study, torrential rain and declining temperatures increased casualties in the battlefields of World War I. This situation set the stage for the spread of the pandemic at the end of the conflict. The coincidence[79] "between increased precipitation and mortality in this pandemic wave in late 1918 highlights the role of environmental conditions in a pandemic's morbidity and mortality." The data also shows that these extreme weather anomalies[80] "brought unusually strong influxes of cold marine air from the North Atlantic, primarily between 1915 and 1919, resulting in unusually strong precipitation events, and that they exacerbated total mortality across Europe, due to the interplay of environmental, ecological, epidemiological, and human factors."

These climatic changes also provided the ideal conditions for the survival of the virus such that prolonged exposure to low temperatures[81] "may also have been a factor in increasing pneumococcal co-infections, which recent studies have found to be more common in the WWI years than previously thought. Retrospective epidemiological studies have now shown that a significant contribution to high mortality during the Spanish Flu pandemic came from pneumococcal co-infections, amounting to as much as one fifth of influenza victims, with a 34% mortality." Like all the other cases discussed in this chapter, this also confirms the contribution of climate change to this particular outbreak.

Notes

1. Rémi Barbieri. "Origin, Transmission, and Evolution of Plague Over 400 y in Europe." PNAS, 118, 39, e2114241118, 2021.
2. R. Barbieri, M. Signoli, D. Chevé, C. Costedoat, S. Tzortzis, G. Aboudharam, D. Raoult, and M. Drancourt. "Yersinia Pestis: The Natural History of Plague." Clinical Microbiology Reviews, 34, 1, e00044-19, 2021.
3. Tamara Ben Ari, Simon Neerinckx, Kenneth L. Gage, Katharina Kreppel, Anne Laudisoit, Herwig Leirs, Nils Chr. Stenseth. "Plague and Climate: Scales Matter." PLOS Pathogens, 7, 9, e1002160, 2011.
4. Ibid.
5. Ricci Yue and Harry Lee. "Climate Change and Plague History in Europe." Science China: Earth Sciences, 61, 2: 163–177, 2018.
6. Ricci Yue and Harry Lee. "Pre-industrial Plague Transmission is Mediated by the Synergistic Effect of Temperature and Aridity Index." BMC Infectious Diseases, 18, 134, 2018.
7. Ibid.
8. Tamara Ben Ari, Simon Neerinckx, Kenneth L. Gage, Katharina Kreppel, Anne Laudisoit, Herwig Leirs, Nils Chr. Stenseth. "Plague and Climate: Scales Matter." PLOS Pathogens, 7, 9, e1002160, 2011.
9. Kyrre Linné Kausrud, Mike Begon, Tamara Ben Ari, Hildegunn Viljugrein, Jan Esper, Ulf Büntgen, Herwig Leirs, Claudia Junge, Bao Yang, Meixue Yang, Lei Xu, and Nils Chr Stenseth. "Modeling the Epidemiological History of Plague in Central Asia: Palaeoclimatic Forcing on a Disease System over the Past Millennium." BMC Biology, 8, 112, 2010.
10. Yujun Cui, Boris V. Schmid, Hanli Cao, Xiang Dai, Zongmin Du, W. Ryan Easterday, Haihong Fang, Chenyi Guo, Shanqian Huang, Wanbing Liu, Zhizhen Qi, Yajun Song, Huaiyu Tian, Min Wang, Yarong Wu, Bing Xu, Chao Yang, Jing Yang, Xianwei Yang, Qingwen Zhang, Kjetill S. Jakobsen, Yujiang Zhang, Nils Chr. Stenseth, and Ruifu Yang. "Evolutionary Selection of Biofilm-Mediated Extended Phenotypes in Yersinia Pestis in

Response to a Fluctuating Environment." Nature Communications, 11, 281, 2020.
11. Ibid.
12. Ibid.
13. R. J. Littman and M. L. Littman. "Galen and the Antonine Plague." The American Journal of Philology, 94, 3: 243–255, 1973.
14. J. F. Gilliam. "The Plague under Marcus Aurelius." The American Journal of Philology, 82, 3: 225–251, 1961.
15. Rufus Fears. "The Plague under Marcus Aurelius and the Decline and Fall of the Roman Empire." Infectious Disease Clinics of North America. 18, 1: 65–77, 2004.
16. Kyle Harper. "The Environmental Fall of the Roman Empire." Daedalus, 145, 2: 101–111, 2016.
17. Walter Scheidel. The Great Leveler: Violence and the History of Inequality from the Stone Age to the Twenty First century. Princeton University Press, 2017. (P. 238).
18. Fiorino Sabbatani. "The Antonine Plague and the Decline of the Roman Empire." Le Infezioni in Medicina, 17, 4: 261–275, 2009.
19. Brandon McDonald. "The Antonine Crisis: Climate Change as a Trigger for Epidemiological and Economic Turmoil." In: Erdkamp, P., Manning, J.G., Verboven, K. (eds) Climate Change and Ancient Societies in Europe and the Near East. Palgrave Studies in Ancient Economies. Palgrave Macmillan, Cham.
20. Karin A. F. Zonneveld, Kyle Harper, Andreas Klügel, Liang Chen, Gert De Lange, and Gerard J. M. Versteegh. "Climate Change, Society, and Pandemic Disease in Roman Italy between 200 BCE and 600 CE." Science Advances, 10, eadk1033, 2024.
21. Kyle Harper. "Solving the Mystery of an Ancient Roman Plague." The Atlantic, November 1, 2017.
22. Kyle Harper. "The Environmental Fall of the Roman Empire." Daedalus, 145, 2: 101–111, 2016.
23. Karin A. F. Zonneveld, Kyle Harper, Andreas Klügel, Liang Chen, Gert De Lange, and Gerard J. M. Versteegh. "Climate Change, Society, and Pandemic Disease in Roman Italy between 200 BCE and 600 CE." Science Advances, 10, eadk1033, 2024.
24. Kyle Harper. "Pandemics and Passages to Late Antiquity: Rethinking the Plague of c.249–270 Described by Cyprian." Journal of Roman Archaeology, 28, 1: 223–260, 2015.
25. Ibid.
26. Feldman M, Harbeck M, Keller M, Spyrou MA, Rott A, Trautmann B, Scholz HC, Päffgen B, Peters J, McCormick M, Bos K, Herbig A, and Krause J. "A High-Coverage Yersinia Pestis Genome from a Sixth-Century

Justinianic Plague Victim." Molecular Biology and Evolution, 33, 11: 2911–2923, 2016. Keller M, Spyrou MA, Scheib CL, Neumann GU, Kröpelin A, Haas-Gebhard B, Päffgen B, Haberstroh J, Ribera I Lacomba A, Raynaud C, Cessford C, Durand R, Stadler P, Nägele K, Bates JS, Trautmann B, Inskip SA, Peters J, Robb JE, Kivisild T, Castex D, McCormick M, Bos KI, Harbeck M, Herbig A, and Krause J. "Ancient Yersinia Pestis Genomes from Across Western Europe Reveal Early Diversification During the First Pandemic (541–750)." PNAS, 116, 25: 12363–12372, 2019.

27. Michaela Harbeck, Lisa Seifert, Stephanie Hansch, David M. Wagner, Dawn Birdsell, Katy L. Parise, Ingrid Wiechmann, Gisela Grupe, Astrid Thomas, Paul Keim, Lothar Zoller, Barbara Bramanti, Julia M. Riehm, Holger C. Scholz. "Yersinia Pestis DNA from Skeletal Remains from the 6th Century AD Reveals Insights into Justinianic Plague." PLOS Pathogens, 9, 5: 1–8, 2013.
28. Wagner DM, Klunk J, Harbeck M, Devault A, Waglechner N, Sahl JW, Enk J, Birdsell DN, Kuch M, Lumibao C, Poinar D, Pearson T, Fourment M, Golding B, Riehm JM, Earn DJ, Dewitte S, Rouillard JM, Grupe G, Wiechmann I, Bliska JB, Keim PS, Scholz HC, Holmes EC, and Poinar H. "Yersinia Pestis and the Plague of Justinian 541–543 AD: a Genomic Analysis." Lancet Infectious Diseases, 14, 4: 319–326, 2014.
29. Erich Anderson. "Welcome Invaders: The Lombards Claim Byzantine Italy." Medieval Warfare, 4, 6, Theme - The Byzantine-Lombard Wars: 6–9, 2014.
30. Lee Mordechai and Lauren White. "Modeling the Justinianic Plague: Comparing Hypothesized Transmission Routes." PLoS ONE, 15, 4, e0231256, 2020.
31. William McNeill. Plagues and Peoples. Anchor Books, 1976. (P. 141).
32. Ibid.
33. Lee Mordechai and Merle Eisenberg. "Rejecting Catastrophe: The Case of the Justinianic Plague." Past & Present, 244, 1: Pages 3–50, 2019.
34. Lee Mordechai, Merle Eisenberg, Timothy P. Newfield, Adam Izdebski, Janet E. Kay, and Hendrik Poinar. "The Justinianic Plague: An Inconsequential Pandemic?" PNAS, 116, 51: 25546–25554, 2019.
35. Michael Rosenwald. "History's Deadliest Pandemics, from Ancient Rome to Modern America." The Washington Post, 2021. https://www.washingtonpost.com/graphics/2020/local/retropolis/coronavirus-deadliest-pandemics/
36. Anthony McMichael. "Insights from Past Millennia into Climatic Impacts on Human Health and Survival." PNAS, 109, 13: 4730–4737, 2012.
37. Ulf Büntgen, Vladimir S. Myglan, Fredrik Charpentier Ljungqvis, Michael McCormick, Nicola Di Cosmo, Michael Sigl, Johann Jungclaus, Sebastian

Wagner, Paul J. Krusic, Jan Esper, Jed O. Kaplan, Michiel A. C. de Vaan, Jürg Luterbacher, LukasWacker, Willy Tegel, and Alexander V. Kirdyanov. "Cooling and Societal Change During the Late Antique Little Ice Age from 536 to around 660 AD." Nature Geoscience, 2016.

38. Ibid.
39. Ibid.
40. Michael McCormick, Ulf Büntgen, Mark A. Cane, Edward R. Cook, Kyle Harper, Peter Huybers, Thomas Litt, Sturt W. Manning, Paul Andrew Mayewski, Alexander F. M. More, Kurt Nicolussi and Willy Tegel. "Climate Change During and After the Roman Empire: Reconstructing the Past from Scientific and Historical Evidence." The Journal of Interdisciplinary History, 43, 2: 169–220, 2012.
41. Ibid.
42. Spyrou MA, Musralina L, Gnecchi Ruscone GA, Kocher A, Borbone PG, Khartanovich VI, Buzhilova A, Djansugurova L, Bos KI, Kühnert D, Haak W, Slavin P, and Krause J. "The source of the Black Death in Fourteenth-century Central Eurasia." Nature, 606, 7915: 718–724, 2022. Spyrou MA, Tukhbatova RI, Feldman M, Drath J, Kacki S, Beltrán de Heredia J, Arnold S, Sitdikov AG, Castex D, Wahl J, Gazimzyanov IR, Nurgaliev DK, Herbig A, Bos KI, and Krause J. "Historical Y. Pestis Genomes Reveal the European Black Death as the Source of Ancient and Modern Plague Pandemics." Cell Host & Microbe, 19, 6: 874–881, 2016. Spyrou MA, Tukhbatova RI, Wang CC, Valtueña AA, Lankapalli AK, Kondrashin VV, Tsybin VA, Khokhlov A, Kühnert D, Herbig A, Bos KI, and Krause J. "Analysis of 3800-year-old Yersinia Pestis Genomes Suggests Bronze Age Origin for Bubonic Plague." Nature Communications, 9, 1, 2234, 2018.
43. Mark Wheelis. "Biological Warfare at the 1346 Siege of Caffa." Emerging Infectious Diseases, 8, 9: 971–975, 2002.
44. Robert Gottfried. The Black Death: Natural and Human Disaster in Medieval Europe. Free Press, 1985.
45. Philip Zeigler. The Black Death. Harper Perennial Modern Classics, 2009.
46. Ole Benedictow. The Complete History of the Black Death. Boydell Press, 2021.
47. John Kelly. The Great Mortality: An Intimate History of the Black Death, the Most Devastating Plague of All Time. Harper, 2005.
48. Colin McEvedy. "The Bubonic Plague." Scientific American, 258, 2: 118–123, 1988.
49. Chris Harman. A People's History of the World. Verso, 2008. (P. 149).
50. David J. D. Earn, Junling Ma, Hendrik Poinar, Jonathan Dushoff, and Benjamin M. Bolker. "Acceleration of Plague Outbreaks in the Second Pandemic." PNAS, 117, 44: 27703–27711, 2020.

51. Walter Scheidel. The Great Leveler: Violence and the History of Inequality from the Stone Age to the Twenty First Century. Princeton University Press, 2017. (P. 298).
52. Ibid. (P. 292).
53. Şevket Pamuk. "The Black Death and the Origins of the 'Great Divergence' Across Europe, 1300–1600." European Review of Economic History, 11, 3: 289–317, 2007.
54. Luis Bosshart and Jeremiah Dittmar. "Pandemic Shock and Economic Divergence: Political Economy Before and After the Black Death." Centre for Economic Performance Paper 1805, 2021.
55. Chris Harman. A People's History of the World. Verso, 2008. (P. 155).
56. William McNeill. Plagues and Peoples. Anchor Books, 1976. (P. 195).
57. A. Izdebski, P. Guzowski, R. Poniat, L. Masci, J. Palli, C. Vignola, M. Bauch, C. Cocozza, R. Fernandes, F. C. Ljungqvist, T. Newfield, A. Seim, D. Abel-Schaad, F. Alba-Sánchez, L. Björkman, A. Brauer, A. Brown, S. Czerwiński, A. Ejarque, M. Fiłoc, A. Florenzano, E. D. Fredh, R. Fyfe, N. Jasiunas, P. Kołaczek, K. Kouli, R. Kozáková, M. Kupryjanowicz, P. Lagerås, M. Lamentowicz, M. Lindbladh, J. A. López-Sáez, R. Luelmo-Lautenschlaeger, K. Marcisz, F. Mazier, S. Mensing, A. M. Mercuri, K. Milecka, Y. Miras, A. M. Noryśkiewicz, E. Novenko, M. Obremska, S. Panajiotidis, M. L. Papadopoulou, A. Pędziszewska, S. Pérez-Díaz, G. Piovesan, A. Pluskowski, P. Pokorny, A. Poska, T. Reitalu, M. Rösch, L. Sadori, C. Sá Ferreira, D. Sebag, M. Słowiński, M. Stančikaitė, N. Stivrins, I. Tunno, S. Veski, A. Wacnik, and A. Masi. "Palaeoecological Data Indicates Land-use Changes Across Europe Linked to Spatial Heterogeneity in Mortality During the Black Death Pandemic." Nature Ecology and Evolution, 6: 297–306, 2022.
58. Nils Chr. Stenseth, Noelle I. Samia, Hildegunn Viljugrein, Kyrre Linne´ Kausrud, Mike Begon, Stephen Davis, Herwig Leirs, V. M. Dubyanskiy, Jan Esper, Vladimir S. Ageyev, Nikolay L. Klassovskiy, Sergey B. Pole, and Kung-Sik Chan. "Plague Dynamics are Driven by Climate Variation." PNAS, 103, 35: 13110–13115, 2006.
59. Ibid.
60. A. Izdebski, P. Guzowski, R. Poniat, L. Masci, J. Palli, C. Vignola, M. Bauch, C. Cocozza, R. Fernandes, F. C. Ljungqvist, T. Newfield, A. Seim, D. Abel-Schaad, F. Alba-Sánchez, L. Björkman, A. Brauer, A. Brown, S. Czerwiński, A. Ejarque, M. Fiłoc, A. Florenzano, E. D. Fredh, R. Fyfe, N. Jasiunas, P. Kołaczek, K. Kouli, R. Kozáková, M. Kupryjanowicz, P. Lagerås, M. Lamentowicz, M. Lindbladh, J. A. López-Sáez, R. Luelmo-Lautenschlaeger, K. Marcisz, F. Mazier, S. Mensing, A. M. Mercuri, K. Milecka, Y. Miras, A. M. Noryśkiewicz, E. Novenko, M. Obremska, S. Panajiotidis, M. L. Papadopoulou, A. Pędziszewska, S. Pérez-Díaz,

G. Piovesan, A. Pluskowski, P. Pokorny, A. Poska, T. Reitalu, M. Rösch, L. Sadori, C. Sá Ferreira, D. Sebag, M. Słowiński, M. Stančikaitė, N. Stivrins, I. Tunno, S. Veski, A. Wacnik, and A. Masi. "Palaeoecological Data Indicates Land-use Changes Across Europe Linked to Spatial Heterogeneity in Mortality During the Black Death Pandemic." Nature Ecology and Evolution, 6: 297–306, 2022. Nils Chr. Stenseth, Noelle I. Samia, Hildegunn Viljugrein, Kyrre Linne´ Kausrud, Mike Begon, Stephen Davis, Herwig Leirs, V. M. Dubyanskiy, Jan Esper, Vladimir S. Ageyev, Nikolay L. Klassovskiy, Sergey B. Pole, and Kung-Sik Chan. "Plague Dynamics are Driven by Climate Variation." PNAS, 103, 35: 13110–13115, 2006.

61. Ibid.
62. Boris V. Schmid, Ulf Büntgen, W. Ryan Easterday, Christian Ginzler, Lars Walløe, Barbara Bramanti, and Nils Chr. Stenseth. "Climate-driven Introduction of the Black Death and Successive Plague Reintroductions into Europe." PNAS, 112, 10: 3020–3025, 2015.
63. Barbara Bramanti, Yarong Wuc, Ruifu Yang, Yujun Cuic, and Nils Chr. Stenseth. "Assessing the Origins of the European Plagues Following the Black Death: A Synthesis of Genomic, Historical, and Ecological Information." PNAS, 118, 36 e2101940118, 2021.
64. Barbara Bramanti, Katharine R. Dean, Lars Walløe, and Nils Chr. Stenseth. "The Third Plague Pandemic in Europe." Proceedings of the Royal Society B, 286, 1901, 20182429, 2019.
65. Myron Echenberg. "Pestis Redux: The Initial Years of the Third Bubonic Plague Pandemic, 1894–1901." Journal of World History, 13, 2: 429–449, 2002.
66. Srilata Chatterjee. "Plague and Politics in Bengal 1896 to 1898." Proceedings of the Indian History Congress, 66: 1194–1201, 2005–2006.
67. Maynard Swanson. "The Sanitation Syndrome: Bubonic Plague and Urban Native Policy in the Cape Colony, 1900–1909." The Journal of African History, 18, 3: 387–410, 1977.
68. Carol Benedict. "Bubonic Plague in Nineteenth-Century China." Modern China, 14, 2: 107–155, 1988.
69. Ibid.
70. Zhibin Zhang, Zhenqing Li, Yi Tao, Min Chen, Xinyu Wen, Lei Xu, Huidong Tian, and Nils Chr. Stenseth. "Relationship Between Increase Rate of Human Plague in China and Global Climate Index as Revealed by Cross-spectral and Cross-wavelet Analyses." Integrative Zoology, 2: 144–153, 2007.
71. Lei Xua, Qiyong Liu, Leif Chr. Stige, Tamara Ben Ari, Xiye Fang, Kung-Sik Chan, Shuchun Wang, Nils Chr. Stenseth, and Zhibin Zhang.

"Nonlinear Effect of Climate on Plague During the Third Pandemic in China." PNAS, 108, 25: 10214–10219, 2011.

72. Ibid.
73. Lei Xu, Leif C. Stige, Herwig Leirse, Simon Neerinck, Kenneth L. Gage, Ruifu Yang, Qiyong Liu, Barbara Bramanti, Katharine R. Dean, Hui Tang, Zhe Sun, Nils Chr. Stenseth, and Zhibin Zhang. "Historical and Genomic Data Reveal the Influencing Factors on Global Transmission Velocity of Plague During the Third Pandemic." PNAS, 116, 24: 11833–11838, 2019.
74. Lei Xu, Leif Chr. Stige, Kyrre Linne´ Kausrud, Tamara Ben Ari, Shuchun Wang, Xiye Fang, Boris V. Schmid, Qiyong Liu, Nils Chr. Stenseth, and Zhibin Zhang. "Wet Climate and Transportation Routes Accelerate Spread of Human Plague." Proceedings of the Royal Society B, 281, 20133159, 2015.
75. Ibid.
76. Jeffery K Taubenberger and David M Morens. "1918 Influenza: the Mother of all Pandemics." Emerging Infectious Diseases, 12, 1: 15–22, 2006.
77. David M Morens, Jeffery K Taubenberger, Hillery A Harvey, and Matthew J Memoli. "The 1918 Influenza Pandemic: Lessons for 2009 and the Future." Critical Care Medicine, 38 (4 Suppl): e10–20, 2010.
78. Alexander F. More, Christopher P. Loveluck, Heather Clifford, Michael J. Handley, Elena V. Korotkikh, Andrei V. Kurbatov, Michael McCormick, and Paul A. Mayewski. "The Impact of a Six-Year Climate Anomaly on the "Spanish Flu" Pandemic and WWI." GeoHealth, 4, e2020GH000277, 2020.
79. Ibid.
80. Ibid.
81. Ibid.

Index[1]

[1] Note: Page numbers followed by 'n' refer to notes.

S. Khalifa, *Climate Change, Economic Channels, and Historical Junctures*, https://doi.org/10.1007/978-3-031-91867-4

B

M

N